Global Justice and International Affairs

Studies in Moral Philosophy

Series Editor

Thom Brooks (Newcastle University)

VOLUME 2

The titles published in this series are listed at brill.nl/simp

Global Justice and International Affairs

Edited by

Thom Brooks

BRILL

LEIDEN • BOSTON
2012

This book is printed on acid-free paper.

Library of Congress Cataloging-in-Publication Data

Global justice and international affairs / edited by Thom Brooks.
p. cm. -- (Studies in moral philosophy, ISSN 2211-2014 ; v. 2)
Includes bibliographical references and index.
ISBN 978-90-04-20343-3 (hardback : alk. paper) 1. International relations--Moral and ethical aspects. 2. Justice (Philosophy) 3. Distributive justice. 4. Globalization--Moral and ethical aspects. 5. Sovereignty--Philosophy. 6. Cosmopolitanism. I. Brooks, Thom. II. Title. III. Series.

JZ1306.G65 2012
320.01'1--dc23

2011034806

ISSN 2211-2014
ISBN 978 90 04 20343 3

CONTENTS

PART IV

WAR AND TERRORISM

NOTES ON PREVIOUS PUBLICATION

Joseph H. Carens, 'The Integration of Immigrants', *Journal of Moral Philosophy* 2(1) (2005): 29–46.

Nicolaus Tideman, 'Secession as a Human Right', *Journal of Moral Philosophy* 1(1) (2004): 9–19.

Michael Green, 'Social Justice, Voluntarism, and Liberal Nationalism', *Journal of Moral Philosophy* 2(3) (2005): 265–83.

Burke Hendrix, 'Authenticity and Cultural Rights', *Journal of Moral Philosophy* 5(2) (2008): 181–203.

Patti Tamara Lenard, 'Motivating Cosmopolitanism? A Skeptical View', *Journal of Moral Philosophy* 7(3) (2010): 346–71.

Igor Primoratz, 'Patriotism and Morality: Mapping the Terrain', *Journal of Moral Philosophy* 5(2) (2008): 204–26.

Gillian Brock, 'The Difference Principle, Equality of Opportunity, and Cosmopolitan Justice', *Journal of Moral Philosophy* 2(3) (2005): 333–51.

Lisa L. Fuller, 'Poverty Relief, Global Institutions, and the Problem of Compliance', *Journal of Moral Philosophy* 2(3) (2005): 285–97.

Tim Hayward, 'Thomas Pogge's Global Resources Dividend: A Critique and an Alternative', *Journal of Moral Philosophy* 2(3) (2005): 317–32.

Gerhard Øverland, 'Poverty and the Moral Significance of Contribution', *Journal of Moral Philosophy* 2(3) (2005): 299–315.

Jonathan Seglow, 'Associative Duties and Global Justice', *Journal of Moral Philosophy* 7(1) (2010): 54–73.

David Lefkowitz, 'Partiality and Weighing Harm to Non-Combatants', *Journal of Moral Philosophy* 6(3) (2009): 298–316.

Gerhard Øverland, 'Conditional Threats', *Journal of Moral Philosophy* 7(3) (2010): 334–45.

Eric Reitan, 'Defining Terrorism for Public Policy Purposes: The Group-Target Definition', *Journal of Moral Philosophy* 7(2) (2010): 253–78.

LIST OF CONTRIBUTORS

Gillian Brock is Associate Professor in Philosophy at the University of Auckland.

Thom Brooks is Reader in Political and Legal Philosophy at Newcastle University. He is editor and founder of the *Journal of Moral Philosophy*.

Joseph H. Carens is Professor of Political Science at the University of Toronto.

Lisa L. Fuller is Assistant Professor of Philosophy at the State University of New York-Albany.

Michael Green is Assistant Professor of Philosophy at Pomona College.

Tim Hayward is Professor of Environmental Political Theory at Edinburgh University.

Burke A. Hendrix is Visiting Assistant Professor of Government at Franklin & Marshall College.

David Lefkowitz is Associate Professor of Philosophy at the University of Richmond.

Patti Tamara Lenard is Assistant Professor in the Graduate School of Public and International Affairs at the University of Ottawa.

Gerhard Øverland is a Project Leader at the Centre for the Study of Mind in Nature at the University of Oslo.

Igor Primoratz is Professorial Fellow in the Centre for Applied Philosophy and Public Ethics at Charles Sturt University and Professor Emeritus of Philosophy at the Hebrew University of Jerusalem.

Eric Reitan is Professor of Philosophy at Oklahoma State University.

Jonathan Seglow is Senior Lecturer in Politics at Royal Holloway, University of London.

Nicolaus Tideman is Professor of Economics at Virginia Tech.

INTRODUCTION

Thom Brooks

Global Justice and International Affairs

Global justice and international affairs is perhaps the hottest topic in political philosophy today. This book brings together some of the most important essays in this area.[1] The essays have all appeared recently in the *Journal of Moral Philosophy*, an internationally recognized leading philosophy journal. This book is divided into four parts: sovereignty and self-determination, cosmopolitanism and nationalism, global poverty and international distributive justice, and war and terrorism. My introduction will give some background to these areas and introduce the essays.

Part I: Sovereignty and Self-Determination

One important issue concerns sovereignty. This issue raises questions about the foundation and content of legitimate political power over citizens. The first chapter by Joseph Carens (2005) examines how we should conceive the integration of legally resident immigrants in contemporary democratic states. Should citizens and immigrants enjoy the same set of rights? If not, then why not and which rights might immigrants possess? This raises further questions about the meaning of citizenship and how immigrants may attain this status. Finally, there are other questions concerning the integration of immigrants. Carens explores a variety of aspects of integration, such as cultural, economic, political, and social integration. He argues that integration is a process of mutual, but asymmetrical adaptation.

The second chapter is Nicolaus Tideman (2004) on whether secession is a human right.[2] His argument is relatively straightforward.

[1] I also recommend Brooks (2008).

[2] I should note that this essay is particularly special: it is the first article the *Journal of Moral Philosophy* published in its first issue. It seems very fitting to include it here and I have been unsurprised by the increasing attention its arguments have received in recent years.

We begin with the idea that people have rights to themselves. If so, then they will have the right to affiliate in a sovereign community with like-minded others. This would require their having a right to secede from any existing sovereign community. If we conceive of rights to territory as belonging equally to all persons and that all persons have rights to themselves, then all persons have a right to secession.

Part II: Cosmopolitanism and Nationalism

A longstanding debate in global justice and international affairs is between cosmopolitans and nationalists (see Brooks 2002). This part brings together four chapters that help shed new light on this debate and related issues. Michael Green (2005) addresses the central issue in the debate: should social justice retain priority over global justice? Liberal nationalists argue that it should because we have special obligations to our co-nationals. Cosmopolitans argues that it should not because nothing short of humanity as a whole should have fundamental significance from a justice-based point of view. Green considers voluntarist and liberal national challenges to cosmopolitans. He argues that neither provides a satisfactory defence of the priority of social justice.[3]

Burke Hendrix (2008) addresses the question of whether states should extend certain customized political protections to minority groups. Hendrix argues that we may be tempted to believe that much may hinge on whether such groups have authentic identities as a collective way of life or political artifacts manipulated by so-called 'ethnic entrepreneurs'. However, the genuine authenticity of such claims is notoriously difficult even in the abstract. Instead, governments should focus more on the claims of small and vulnerable groups and consider the claims of larger groups as political matters.

Patti Tamara Lenard (2010) focuses on a particular challenge for cosmopolitans. It is one thing to claim all persons share equal fundamental moral status, but what motivates us to treat equally those who are far with others who are near? Many of the arguments for motivation appear more favourable for non-cosmopolitan and nationalist

[3] This essay was originally published in a special issue on the topic of 'Global Justice' that appeared in the *Journal of Moral Philosophy* volume two, number three in 2005. Papers included in the issue and this book include Brock (2005), Fuller (2005), Green (2005), Hayward (2005), and Øverland (2005).

accounts. Lenard concludes not that cosmopolitanism cannot offer a satisfactory motivational account, but rather that no such account is yet on offer.

The following chapter by Igor Primoratz (2008) examines the full typology of patriotism: what is it? He begins by distinguishing patriotism from nationalism before considering a range of different ways that patriotism has been understood in a wide ranging and highly valuable discussion. He concludes with a defence of what he calls a distinctly ethical version of patriotism. This understanding of ethical patriotism may even be a moral duty.

Part III: Global Poverty and International Distributive Justice

Perhaps no issue in global justice and international affairs commands greater attention than the problem of global poverty and international distributive justice. This is the largest part in this book with five powerful essays that cover a number of important issues in the area.

In the first chapter, Gillian Brock (2005) asks what kinds of principles of justice should cosmopolitans support? Several have been recommended by others, including the idea of a Global Difference Principle and the idea of a Principle of Global Equality of Opportunity. Brock argues for an alternative principle, namely, the Needs-Based Minimum Floor Princople.

The next chapter concerns the problem of compliance relating to poverty relief. Lisa Fuller (2005) examines proposals for poverty relief by Andrew Kuper and Thomas Pogge. Their proposals rest upon institutional solutions to global poverty. How might these institutional efforts overcome the difficulties of global coordination and enforcement? Fuller argues that the NGO model can be reformed and defended to help better address these problems so long as they are required to be 'accountable for reasonableness'.

Tim Hayward (2005) considers the Global Resources Dividend (GRD) as proposed by Thomas Pogge. Hayward argues that the GRD proposal will in fact be counterproductive and less predictable than Pogge claims, especially when we consider its secondary aim of promoting environmental protection. Hayward argues that a redistributive resource-based tax should not be established along the lines of the GRD, but instead based upon a consideration of a nation's per capita utilization of ecological space.

In the first of his two essays in this book, Gerhard Øverland (2005) argues that our moral responsibility to render assistance is unaffected by whether or not we contributed to a situation by causing harm. This argument focuses upon the moral significance of need. Severe need trumps considerations of contribution. It may then be unnecessary to argue that we should provide assistance as a negative duty for our contributing to global poverty.

The concluding essay in this part examines the conflict between our associative duties and wider obligations of global justice. Jonathan Seglow (2010) addresses three solutions to the so-called 'distribution objection' to civic association duties posed by Samuel Scheffler. While a certain tension may exist now between associative duties and the demands of global justice, they need not exist and may co-exist in more ideal future circumstances.

Part IV: War and Terrorism

The last part focuses on war and terrorism. David Lefkowitz (2009) considers an argument that has been made by both Thomas Hurka and Frances Myrna Kamm: combatants ought to give greater weight to collateral harm to compatriot non-combatants than to enemy non-combatants. Lefkowitz rejects this partiality by use of several illustrative and illuminating analogies.

The second chapter examines the moral status of conditional threats. Gerhard Øverland (2010) queries whether it is morally permissible to use potentially lethal defensive force against threats that are merely conditional. This examination involves a novel understanding of self-defence and how it relates to issues fo risk and moral responsibility.

The final essay is on terrorism and its definition (see Brooks 2010). Eric Reitan (2010) argues that we must have a clear definition of terrorism in order to best evaluate public policy decisions aimed at combatting terrorism. Reitan considers a wide number of popular understandings of what is terrorism in the literature. He proposes an alternative understanding based upon the group-target distinction.

Conclusion

A final comment should be made about how these essays were selected for publication. All chapters originally appeared in recent issues of the

Journal of Moral Philosophy. I founded the journal with Fabian Freyenhagen in 2003 and it launched the following year. The *JMP* has been published quarterly since 2009. All submissions were subjected to rigorous anonymous peer review by our international editorial board and referees. We publish a list of our referees in the final issue of each annual volume. Our standards are high and our acceptance rate is less than 7%. We receive submissions from all over the world with the great majority (about two-thirds) coming from the United States or Great Britain. Furthermore, we have endeavoured to ensure high quality review standards with swift turnarounds and we are normally able to vet about 90% of all submissions in three months with about 85% reviewed in two months or less.

The essays in this volume have satisfied our high standards and all have appeared in recent issues of the *Journal of Moral Philosophy* ensuring their quality and their timeliness. Each was selected for this book because of its real contribution to the general topic. Rather than offer a single narrative, the essays instead may be read in any order and present a number of important perspectives and insights on the topic that should help provide further clarifying illumination on central debates and ideas in the field. Readers interested in learning more about what other essays have been published in the *JMP* should consult this book's bibliography towards the end where the full publication details of all articles is listed. Anyone interested in submitting new work for future issues should submit through our online submission system found on our website.[4]

This book is amongst the first in our new *Studies in Moral Philosophy* book series to be published by Brill, the publishers of the *JMP*. The book series aspires to fulfil the same high standards and quality of its sister journal. We will aim to publish leading work in the areas of moral, political, and legal philosophy. This book helps launch this new series.

I hope you will enjoy reading the essays in this book as much as I have. Many thanks are due to Suzanne Mekking at Brill for her strong support of this book and new book series. My thanks also to Liesbeth Hugenholtz. I am also most grateful to Fabian Freyenhagen for his assistance over the years, as well as to our advisory committee for this

[4] The *Journal of Moral Philosophy* website may be found here: http://www.brill.nl/jmp.

book series. Finally, my most sincere thanks to the authors for choosing the *Journal of Moral Philosophy* for their work. The journal's success is primarily not through any particular effort of its editors, but rather a reflection of the high quality of our author's contributions. We look forward to producing further volumes on other topics.

Bibliography

Brock, Gillian (2005). 'The Difference Principle, Equality of Opportunity, and Cosmopolitan Justice', *Journal of Moral Philosophy* 2(3): 333–51.

Brooks, Thom (2002). 'Cosmopolitanism and Distributing Responsibilities', *Critical Review of International Social and Political Philosophy* 5: 92–97.

Brooks, Thom (ed.) (2008). *The Global Justice Reader*. Oxford: Blackwell.

Brooks, Thom (2010). 'Justifying Terrorism', *Public Affairs Quarterly* 24: 189–95.

Carens, Joseph (2005). 'The Integration of Immigrants', *Journal of Moral Philosophy* 2(1): 29–46.

Fuller, Lisa L. (2005). 'Poverty Relief, Global Institutions, and the Problem of Compliance', *Journal of Moral Philosophy* 2(3): 285–97.

Green, Michael (2005). 'Social Justice, Voluntarism, and Liberal Nationalism', *Journal of Moral Philosophy* 2(3): 265–83.

Hayward, Tim (2005). 'Thomas Pogge's Global Resources Dividend: A Critique and an Alternative', *Journal of Moral Philosophy* 2(3): 317–32.

Hendrix, Burke (2008). 'Authenticity and Cultural Rights', *Journal of Moral Philosophy* 5(2): 181–203.

Lefkowitz, David (2009). 'Partiality and Weighing Harm to Non-Combatants', *Journal of Moral Philosophy* 6(3): 298–316.

Lenard, Patti Tamara (2010). 'Motivating Cosmopolitanism? A Skeptical View', *Journal of Moral Philosophy* 7(3): 346–71.

Øverland, Gerhard (2005). 'Poverty and the Moral Significance of Contribution', *Journal of Moral Philosophy* 2(3): 299–315.

Øverland, Gerhard (2010). 'Conditional Threats', *Journal of Moral Philosophy* 7(3): 334–45.

Primoratz, Igor (2008). 'Patriotism and Morality: Mapping the Terrain', *Journal of Moral Philosophy* 5(2): 204–26.

Reitan, Eric (2010). 'Defining Terrorism for Public Policy Purposes: The Group-Target Definition', *Journal of Moral Philosophy* 7(2): 253–78.

Seglow, Jonathan (2010). 'Associative Duties and Global Justice', *Journal of Moral Philosophy* 7(1): 54–73.

Tideman, Nicolaus (2004). 'Secession as a Human Right', *Journal of Moral Philosophy* 1(1): 9–19.

PART I

SOVEREIGNTY AND SELF-DETERMINATION

THE INTEGRATION OF IMMIGRANTS*

Joseph H. Carens

The challenges posed by immigration vary significantly from one country or region to another, and liberal democratic states vary in the ways they interpret and institutionalize norms of democracy, justice, freedom, and human rights. Nevertheless, it is possible to make some general claims about how liberal democratic states ought to respond to the immigrants in their midst, and that is what this paper will try to do. Let me add that there is a fair amount of convergence in practices as well, so the arguments here are not disconnected from the world as we find it.

Like most academics, I want to begin with some distinctions and clarifications. First, in talking about the integration of immigrants, I will be concerned not only with people who arrive as immigrants themselves but also with their descendants who are born in the new country, the so-called second and third generations. Some of the most important questions about the integration of immigrants concern the fate of these second and third generations (e.g., how does their descent from immigrant parents or grandparents affect their life chances, how do they relate to the society in which they live) even though they are natives and hence not properly classified as immigrants. For the sake of simplicity of exposition, I will often speak only of immigrants, but, unless otherwise specified, I mean this term to include their descendants.

Second, since my focus is on the integration of immigrants, I will not say anything about the process of admissions. I am concerned with those who have in fact arrived. Furthermore, I will focus primarily on immigrants who have legal permission to reside in the receiving society on an ongoing basis. I'll call them residents for short. There are two other important categories of immigrants: those who are present legally

* A version of this article previously appeared in Spanish as 'La integración de los inmigrantes' in Gemma Aubarell and Ricard Zapata (eds.), *Immigración y procesos de cambio: Europa y el Mediterráneo en el contexto global* (Barcelona: Icaria-Institut Europeu de la Mediterrània, 2004), pp. 393–420.

but only with limited terms and conditions (e.g., as students, guest workers, etc.) and those who are residing without formal legal authorization (whether they arrived legally and over-stayed a visa or crossed a border in a clandestine manner or went underground after a refugee claim failed). For the question of the integration of immigrants, the most crucial question about people in these other two categories is whether and how they ought to be moved into the first category, i.e., become people with a legal right to remain on an ongoing basis, but I will not pursue that issue here.

Third, in talking about how states ought to respond to immigrants, I want to distinguish between two ways in which policies may be right or just. On the one hand, we may describe a policy as just in the sense that it is morally required, and on the other hand we may call a policy just in the sense that it is morally permitted, i.e., not prohibited by justice. In the latter case, we may want to try to identify the best practices among those that are morally permissible to the extent that we can generalize across different cases.

Fourth, in thinking about the ways in which states respond to immigrants with regard to integration, I want to distinguish between requirements, expectations, and aspirations. A requirement is something that is formal and explicit. For example, states may specify conditions that must be met before immigrants obtain certain legal rights or before they become citizens through naturalization. An expectation is a norm that is enforced through informal social sanctions rather than legal mechanisms. For example, the public officials or ordinary citizens in the receiving state may have expectations about how immigrants should behave or how they should adapt culturally, and, if these expectations are not met they may be critical of the immigrants even though no formal sanctions follow. Finally, public authorities or citizens may have hopes about the ways in which immigrants will integrate with the receiving society without thinking that these aspirations are enforceable in any sense, even through informal social sanctions. For example, people might think that the process is really going well only if there are high levels of residential and social mixing between immigrants and their descendants on the one hand and the rest of the population on the other without thinking that it would be appropriate to impose particular expectations on people about where they should live and with whom they should socialize. These distinctions matter descriptively because they draw our attention to the range of formal and informal ways in which the receiving society responds to immigrants and they matter normatively because they may affect the moral quality of a policy or practice. For example, a demand that may be morally permissible if expressed as an expectation may be morally impermissible if constructed as a formal legal requirement.

Finally, to avoid misunderstanding, let me distinguish at the outset between the question of who has the right to make a decision and the question of whether or not a decision is morally right. The mere fact that we assign responsibility for making decisions on some matter to an individual or a collective does not mean that we have no independent basis for critically evaluating those decisions. This is abundantly evident in the case of individuals. We have good reason to construct legal regimes that leave individuals great discretion in deciding how to live their lives, but that does not mean that we can never have a basis for moral criticism of the choices they make. Not everything that is legally permissible is morally justifiable. So, too, with states. The fact that states are sovereign and that the ideal of democracy entails a deep commitment to collective self-determination does not mean that we cannot criticize the choices that democratic states make.

I will divide the rest of my discussion into three main parts. The first will be concerned with the legal rights that immigrants should have. The second will focus on access to citizenship. The third will consider questions about the policies and practices that can promote the integration of immigrants once they have the appropriate bundles of legal rights (including access to citizenship).

Legal Rights of Immigrants

In modern liberal democratic societies legal rights are fundamental. It is true, of course, that formal legal equality is not sufficient. Legal equality may coexist with great substantive inequality among citizens. Nevertheless, any conception of equal citizenship has to start from the idea of legal equality.[1]

What about immigrants who are not citizens? What legal rights should they have? Is that even a question that we can answer in a

[1] Of course, some forms of differentiated legal rights (e.g., affirmative action rights) may be designed to realize rather than deny the ideal of civic equality. Whatever one's view of the merits of such contested arrangements, it is clear that they are not intended to enforce subordination and inequality in contrast to, say, feudal legal distinctions between the nobility and the peasantry.

general way? To begin, we should notice that states routinely grant many legal rights not only to citizens and immigrants but to anyone who is on their territory and subject to their jurisdiction (like tourists or other temporary visitors). Everyone is entitled to protection of their person and property, for example, and, in principle, the quality of protection is not supposed to depend in any way on one's citizenship status. Anyone accused of a crime is entitled to a fair trial, regardless of one's national origin or citizenship status. Of course there are differences between states in the way these legal rights are constructed and interpreted, so that, for example, the rules of evidence or of criminal procedure may vary from one state to another so that evidence that would be considered in one jurisdiction may be excluded in another. But the treatment of individuals within the same jurisdiction is not supposed to vary. For example, states cannot legitimately have one set of rules regarding what counts as evidence in a criminal trial for citizens and a different set of rules (presumably less favourable to the accused) for non-citizens or even non-residents.[2] In principle at least, these sorts of fundamental rights apply even to those who are present without authorization, although, in practice, their rights are much less secure because they are afraid to appeal to the authorities for protection.

While everyone who is subject to the state's jurisdiction, even if only temporarily, enjoys some legal rights, citizens possess legal rights that temporary visitors or unauthorized residents normally do not. The right to vote in elections, the right to participate in the labour market, and the right to receive social services are some obvious examples. Again, we may note that the precise bundle of rights citizens enjoy varies from one state to another because different states have different institutions and policies (e.g. with respect to income support and health care). In another context one might want to evaluate these arrangements critically, but here we want to keep the focus on the integration of immigrants. For those purposes, therefore, we can simply take whatever bundle of rights citizens have in a given state as the standard

---

[2] It may seem that I am belabouring the obvious here but recent statements and actions by the Bush administration in response to the terrorist attacks of September 11 2001 make it necessary to emphasize the point since they explicitly envisage the idea of using different standards for citizens and non-citizens in prosecuting those accused of terrorism.

against which to compare the rights of immigrants and ask how they should resemble or differ from one another.

My central claim is that, with the exception of the right to participate in national elections or hold high public office and with a few other minor qualifications involving the passage of time, immigrants should enjoy the same legal rights as citizens. Furthermore, I contend that this equivalence of the rights of citizens and the rights of residents is not simply the best practice but rather that it is something that justice requires.

My argument rests upon an understanding of the nature and purpose of political authority in liberal democratic states. Liberal democratic principles may be interpreted in various ways, but, however interpreted, they entail a deep commitment to treat those subject to the state's authority fairly and equally. So, the first principle is that differential treatment requires justification. That is why it is not morally permissible to have two sets of procedures in legal proceedings, one for citizens and another for non-citizens.

Now, differential treatment may often be justified. Those (like tourists) who are subject to the state's authority only on a genuinely temporary basis may legitimately be denied the legal right to work or to benefit from social programmes because they are visitors, not members of society.[3] But what about immigrants who have a right of ongoing residence? They are in a very different category. Living in a society on an ongoing basis makes one a member of that society. The longer one stays, the stronger one's connections and social attachments. For the same reason, the longer one stays the stronger one's claim to be treated as a full member. At some point a threshold is reached, after which one simply is a member of society, *tout court*, and one should be granted all the legal rights that other full members enjoy.

The norm I am defending here is not very far from existing practice in Europe and North America. One of the striking developments in the area of immigration during the late twentieth century was the extent to which the legal distinctions between citizens and resident non-citizens

[3] I am implicitly assuming here, for the purposes of this essay, the right of the state to control immigration, at least for the most part. In another context, one might want to challenge that presupposition, and I have done so in Joseph H. Carens, 'Aliens and Citizens: The Case for Open Borders', *Review of Politics* 49.2 (Spring 1987), pp. 251–73 and *idem*, 'Reconsidering Open Borders', *International Migration Review* 33.4 (Winter 1999), pp. 1076–91.

were reduced.[4] Scholars disagree about the source of these developments. Some emphasize the pattern of convergence on a new status for immigrants and attribute this to the emergence of new international human rights norms.[5] Others insist that attention to the details of particular cases will show that the changes were due to local causes, the political and legal factors at play within particular national traditions.[6] Whatever explanatory account one accepts—in my view, those emphasizing domestic factors have provided convincing evidence that the changes were not an explicit or even conscious response to emerging international norms but they offer no explanation for the convergence—the facts of the matter are not in dispute. A pattern of systematic and widespread legal differentiation between immigrants and citizens has been replaced by a pattern in which immigrants generally enjoy the same civil, social and economic rights as citizens (and in which people who are initially admitted on a temporary basis acquire stronger rights of ongoing residence the longer they stay). Many of these changes were brought about by courts acting in the name of legal norms that reflected deep liberal democratic principles. In other words, they were seen not merely as prudent changes in policy but rather as transformations required by justice.

There are two important caveats to this broad picture. First, while security of residence and access to employment of immigrants have greatly improved, there remain some significant gaps between the rights of immigrants and the rights of citizens in these areas. Second, the trend towards equality of rights between citizens and immigrants is not inevitable or irreversible. In the late 1990s the United States restricted the access of legal immigrants, even long-settled ones, to a variety of social programmes. To the best of my knowledge, this sort of policy change has not yet been introduced in Europe, but it has been

[4] Tomas Hammar, *Democracy and the Nation State: Aliens, Denizens and Citizens in a World of International Migration* (Aldershot, UK: Avebury, 1990); James F. Hollifield, *Immigrants, Markets, and States: The Political Economy of Postwar Europe* (Cambridge, MA: Harvard University Press, 1992); David Jacobson, *Rights Across Borders: Immigration and the Decline of Citizenship* (Baltimore: Johns Hopkins University Press, 1996); Christian Joppke, *Immigration and the Nation-State: The United States, Germany, and Great Britain* (Oxford: Oxford University Press, 1999); Peter Schuck, *Citizens, Strangers and In-Betweens: Essays on Immigration and Citizenship* (Boulder, CO: Westview Press, 1998); Yasemin Nuhoglu Soysal, *Limits of Citizenship: Migrants and Postnational Membership in Europe* (Chicago: University of Chicago Press, 1994).

[5] Soysal, *Limits of Citizenship*; Jacobson, *Rights Across Borders.*

[6] Joppke, *Immigration and the Nation-State.*

advocated by some. In Europe, moreover, the development of the European Union has led to the creation of important new rights for citizens of member states, including mobility rights and rights of access to employment. Most of these rights have not been accorded to people who are permanent residents in an EU state but who hold citizenship only in a state outside the EU (so-called third country nationals). So, the gap between the bundle of legal rights enjoyed by citizens and the bundle enjoyed by residents has widened.

Both justice and wise policy require the consolidation of this general movement in the direction of reducing differences between citizens and residents.[7] EU rules have done that for citizens of other EU countries, effectively sweeping away many of the past objections about feasibility. For example, the EU rules on access to public employment in member countries have opened up this important sector of the labour market (at least in terms of legal principle) to non-citizens from other EU countries. As a result, none of the objections to restricting the access of immigrants from outside the EU carry much persuasive weight. It becomes a transparent device for favouring citizens over residents, i.e., for discriminating against people who are permanent members of society but do not yet have the status of citizen. (The same discrimination occurs at the federal level, though not at the state or provincial level, in the United States and Canada.) There is no plausible moral justification and no persuasive policy reason for not granting third country nationals who are established residents in one EU country the same bundle of legal rights with respect to other EU member states that EU citizens enjoy.[8]

Access to Citizenship

If immigrants have most of the same rights as citizens, why does formal citizenship still matter? There are three reasons. First, the key political

---

[7] Joseph H. Carens, 'Citizenship and Civil Society: What Rights for Residents', in Randall Hansen and Patrick Weil (eds.), *Dual Nationality, Social Rights and Federal Citizenship in the US and Europe: The Reinvention of Citizenship* (Oxford: Berghahn Books, 2002).

[8] Ricard Zapata-Barrero, 'State-based Logic versus EU-based Logic towards Immigrants: Institutional Evidences and Normative Dilemmas (or EU's State Fundamentalism towards Immigrants)', paper presented at 29th Joint Sessions of Workshops, European Consortium for Political Research, 6–11 April 2001, Grenoble, France.

rights of voting in national elections and holding high public office remain attached to citizenship. This is an arrangement that seems to me likely to persist for the foreseeable future and also one that is morally permissible (though I do not think it would be unjust for a state to extend these rights to non-citizens) so long as immigrants have appropriate access to citizenship itself. (I will say what counts as appropriate access below.) Second, the political and legal reality is that the rights of citizens are generally more secure than the rights of non-citizens. The developments in the US and the EU that I cited above that have increased the relative value of citizenship rights illustrate the point, and the US case shows that even established legal rights may be taken away. Moreover, other legal rights, such as rights of residence and re-entry from abroad, are likely to remain more extensive and certainly more deeply entrenched institutionally for citizens than for residents. These advantages of citizenship may not be defensible on the basis of moral principle but they are real. Third, citizenship has great symbolic importance as a mark of full membership.

Who is a citizen and who is not is obviously a fundamental element of political life. It involves the construction of the political community itself. Therefore, it might be thought that something of this sort ought to be regarded as beyond the purview of external critics, something to be decided only by current citizens on the basis of their understanding of the community. As I noted at the outset, however, there is a crucial difference between saying someone has a right to decide some issue and saying that whatever they decide is right. Obviously, states must decide for themselves what their laws regarding access to citizenship (by birth or naturalization) will be. This does not mean, however, that their laws cannot be subject to critical scrutiny from the outside. For example, it is not morally permissible for states to exclude people from citizenship on the basis of race or religion as the United States, Germany, and South Africa have done at times in their past.

What does justice require and what does it permit with regard to access to citizenship for immigrants and their descendants? Let's look first at the claims of the descendants and then work our way back towards the immigrants themselves. And to see what is owed to the recent descendants of immigrants, let us consider the claims of people whose immediate ancestors are not immigrants. In other words, I want to look first at what justice requires with regard to access to citizenship for the children of citizens in order to investigate the question of what justice may require regarding access to citizenship for the children of those who are not (yet) citizens.

One of the puzzles about asking what justice requires with regard to access to citizenship is that citizenship is a status that is usually acquired at birth. (At least this is true of the first citizenship[s] one acquires.) How can anyone deserve anything at birth? Of course, no one can deserve citizenship at birth in the sense of having done something personally that merits it, but one can deserve it in the sense that denying citizenship to someone situated in a particular way at birth would be wrong. Consider what one might call the 'normal' case: a child born within the territory of a state in which his or her parents are already citizens. Every state grants citizenship automatically to such children at birth. This is more than an administrative corollary of an international system in which the world is divided into states, however. It would be morally wrong to deny citizenship to such children. Why? Citizenship is the status that establishes one's position as a full member of a political community (even though many of the rights of membership cannot be exercised until the children mature). Children of citizens born in a state in which their parents are citizens are morally entitled to that status because of the social ties between them and the wider society created by and foreseeable from the circumstances of their birth. It is reasonable to expect that these children will grow up in the society in which they have been born, receive their social formation there, and acquire a fundamental interest in being able to participate as full members of the political community. That is why they deserve citizenship. Of course, these expectations may not be fulfilled. The child's parents may take her to another country at an early age. She may choose herself to leave as an adult. But these possibilities are not enough to make the transmission of citizenship contingent, dependent on how things go in the child's life. She is a citizen at birth and she remains one unless she deliberately does something to renounce that citizenship as an adult or her parents do that on her behalf while she is still a minor.

Consider now the children of citizens who live outside their country of citizenship. So far as I have been able to determine, if the citizen parents once lived inside their country of citizenship for some period of time, every country in Europe and North America also grants their children citizenship at birth, although in some cases if the child also has another citizenship this transmission of parental citizenship is made contingent upon the child spending some years living in the country of parental origin before a certain age. Even if the transmission to the first generation born abroad is not contingent, the transmission to the next is likely to be. I am not aware of any country in Europe or North America today that provides citizenship on the basis of descent no matter how remote, so long as there is some citizen ancestor.

What should we make of this pattern from a moral perspective? I think these rules are generally defensible and that they reflect the same normative logic that informs the automatic granting of citizenship to the children of resident citizens, namely that moral claims to citizenship depend on one's social ties and on the likelihood that one will actually live in the community. For the first generation born abroad the parents' connections to the community of origin are sufficiently strong to create a powerful interest for the children to have a right to 'return' and settle there whether with their parents or as an independent life choice. It would be wrong to deny these children some effective access to citizenship. But the ties are much weaker in the succeeding generation and of vanishing significance in the one after that.[9] It would be wrong to regard citizenship in a liberal democracy as a sort of feudal title or property right that could be passed on from one generation to the next regardless of where the heirs actually lived their lives. As the proximity to an ancestor who lived in the country decreases, so too does the plausibility of any justification for automatically granting citizenship.

What does this suggest about access to citizenship for the descendants of immigrants? It suggests that what matters normatively are the strength of one's social ties and the likelihood that one will spend one's life in the community. Justice requires that the descendants of immigrants be granted citizenship automatically, as the children of citizens are, when they grow up in a country and receive their social formation there. We have every reason to believe that such children will live their lives in the society and they have a right to be treated as full members of the political community. Since the state has considerable

[9] In all this I am assuming that there are no special circumstances such as forced exile by the parents and effective impossibility of return by the children for a couple of generations or persecution of the descendants of the expatriates because of their identification with the country of origin. These sorts of factors (which reflect actual histories) would complicate the analysis and would perhaps justify exceptions to the generalizations in the text.

power to shape their social formation (through systems of compulsory education and by other means), these children cannot rightly be subjected to any tests of acculturation or adaptation as a condition for acquiring citizenship (just as the children of citizens are not subject to such tests). I would go further and insist (although I do not have the space to spell out the argument here) that it would not be sufficient merely to give them a right to citizenship, leaving it optional as to whether they take up that right or not. Citizenship is not optional for the children of citizens, and it would be wrong to make it so. For the same reasons, it is wrong to make it optional for those descendants of immigrants who grow up in a country. It should be conferred automatically at birth if the child is born in the country and the parents are permanent residents or automatically at some later stage (say, after a certain number of years of schooling) if the child arrives in the new country at a young age. (Of course, I do not mean to deny here the right of expatriation and abandonment of one's citizenship, but that is a basic human right that everyone enjoys, not something distinctive to the descendants of immigrants. Moreover, one normally cannot exercise the right of renouncing one's nationality while one is still a resident. One must leave, thus severing the key social ties that undergird citizenship.)

If we look at practice, we can see that reforms in citizenship and naturalization laws in a number of European countries in the past few decades have produced dramatic changes in access to citizenship for the descendants of immigrants that fit with the normative logic I have outlined here, even if they do not always go as far as I think they should. These reforms have been introduced in the face of deeply entrenched conceptions of citizenship and political community that many people thought would make such changes impossible. In general terms, and with occasional exceptions, the pattern is this. There is widespread acceptance of the view that excluding the descendants of immigrants from citizenship generation after generation is incompatible with any plausible account of liberal democratic principles. Countries with traditions of *ius sanguinis*—transmission of citizenship on the basis of descent from citizen parent(s)—have supplemented those rules with provisions for the acquisition of citizenship on the basis of *ius soli*—transmission of citizenship on the basis of birth in the country—for children born to parents who are permanent residents. Almost every European country now has a law providing for the automatic acquisition of citizenship by the third generation and for automatic or at least optional acquisition of citizenship by the second generation.[10]

In North America both Canada and the United States have followed the common law tradition of *ius soli* which made anyone born on the soil of the country a citizen. North American smugness on this point ('we have no problem of the second generation') should be slightly tempered by recognition of the fact that the use of this rule is largely a historical accident of a legal inheritance from Britain where the rule reflected the attempt by British kings to consolidate their sovereign power not any deliberate effort to integrate immigrants. From a normative perspective a *ius soli* rule that grants citizenship to everyone born on the territory is considerably broader than justice requires, and the reforms by other common law jurisdictions such as the UK, Ireland, and Australia to limit *ius soli* to the children of citizens and permanent residents is morally permissible in my view.[11] Moreover, complacency about the integrative effects of a *ius soli* rule has led North Americans to ignore the claims of those in the second generation who are born abroad (and so do not acquire citizenship at birth) but come at a very young age. Access to citizenship for these members of the second generation is sometimes better protected in European legislation than it is in North America.

Finally, what about the first generation? It follows from the logic of the arguments sketched out above, with regard to the attribution of citizenship at birth, that the immigrants themselves should have access to citizenship once they have firmly established themselves as members of society. The issue here cannot be whether they still have ties to another society or whether they might return there someday but rather the fact that they have made a life for themselves in the society they have entered and have a right to continue living there. In these

[10] Patrick Weil, 'Access to Citizenship: A Comparison of Twenty-Five Nationality Laws', in T. Alexander Aleinikoff and Douglas Klusmeyer (eds.), *Citizenship Today: Global Perspectives and Practices* (Washington, DC: Carnegie Endowment for International Peace, 2001).

[11] I would add two provisos to this, however. First, if children are raised in a society, they should automatically acquire citizenship regardless of the legal status of their parents for the sorts of reasons laid out in the text. (British law recognizes this.) Second, it would be morally wrong for the United States to modify its *ius soli* provisions for historical and symbolic reasons that are contextually specific, and it would be a bad practice for Canada to do so in large part because this practice has become so firmly associated in Canadian public discourse with a welcoming stance towards immigrants.

circumstances it is wrong to deny them the status of full political membership with a right to participate in the self-determining processes of the community.

What may be required as conditions for the acquisition of citizenship? The key difference between the immigrants themselves and the second and third generations is not that they might leave. After all, people from the second and third generations and indeed citizens who are not the descendants of immigrants emigrate as well. The key difference is that society has not had the opportunity to shape their social formation as children. Does this mean that it is morally permissible to require proof of adaptation from them? I think not (though I should acknowledge immediately that my contention here departs much further from practice and even from current trends than my earlier claims). All that may be required in the end is that immigrants live in the country long enough.

I offer two arguments in support of the view that a long-established residency should be a sufficient basis for the acquisition of citizenship, one from the interests of the individual and the other from the nature of democracy. First, the longer one lives in a society, the stronger one's interest in living there, and, at some point, a threshold is passed that should entitle a person to the full protections of citizenship itself. Second, sane, competent adult members of a democratic community should be able to participate in the community's process of self-determination, and the fact that one lives on an ongoing basis within the boundaries of the community should be sufficient to establish that one is a member of the community. If the political authorities or even a democratic majority were morally entitled to exclude people from citizenship on the basis of their views about what one should know or how one should behave in order to be a citizen, that would undermine the very idea of democracy as an inclusive form of political community. Everyone recognizes this with regard to the children of citizens and they have begun to see it with regard to the descendants of immigrants, but it also applies to the immigrants themselves.

In thinking about the acquisition of citizenship by immigrants, we should keep in mind the distinction that I introduced at the outset between requirements, expectations, and aspirations. There may well be forms of adaptation that it is reasonable to *expect* of immigrants without constructing those expectations as requirements for citizenship. Similarly one may hope for and even encourage certain forms of integration without using these as standards for granting or withholding citizenship.

If we look at practice, we can see that most states are a long way from the position I have argued is required by justice. Nevertheless, what is most striking about policy developments in recent years is the tendency within Europe to ease the requirements for naturalization and to shift from a discretionary system where public officials assess applicants for citizenship in light of vague criteria and with some conception of the interests of the state in view to an entitlement system where the applicant has a right to citizenship if certain relatively clear criteria are met. Both of these developments reflect movement in the direction I am advocating.

All states have residency requirements for naturalization. Some residency requirement is clearly permissible under my analysis. The real question is when does the residency requirement become too demanding. There is no way to answer this question with any precision. I can note that in European countries there seems to be an emerging norm of requiring about five years as a permanent resident before one becomes eligible for naturalization. That does not seem unreasonable to me so long as provision is made to give substantial credit for any time spent living legally in the country even if the immigrant had a more provisional sort of residency permit at first. States often require some competence in an official language and sometimes require proof of economic self-sufficiency, some knowledge of the history and institutions of the country, and the absence of any serious criminal convictions. I would criticize all of these requirements for the reasons given above, although I would also concede that none of them pose major obstacles to most immigrants seeking naturalization so long as they are set at modest levels and applied reasonably.

The biggest formal obstacle to voluntary naturalization is the requirement that some states impose that applicants for citizenship renounce any previous citizenship when the new one is granted. Many states do not require this and even more do not enforce the requirement. Nevertheless, there is probably no more important formal (and feasible) step that could be taken to promote the naturalization of immigrants and thus their full legal integration than to abolish even the symbolic opposition to dual citizenship. I cannot review here all the arguments on this issue which has now generated a significant scholarly discussion.[12] I will simply note that there has been an

[12] Hammar, *Democracy and the Nation State*; Rainer Baubock, 'Citizenship and National Identities in the European Union,' Working Paper Series No. 4 (Harvard Law

increasing incidence of dual and multiple citizenships, even in countries that require renunciation of prior citizenships in naturalization. This results in part from the elimination of gender bias in the transmission of citizenship so that a child whose parents have different citizenships almost invariably inherits both. Many of the practical problems that opponents of dual citizenship feared have simply not arisen, making the opposition to it now largely one of (dubious) principle.

Finally, I will note that all states treat the acquisition of citizenship as something that ought to be left to the choice of immigrants rather than conferred upon them automatically. This was my own view in the past as well, but I have to say that I have been persuaded by Ruth Rubio-Marin's argument in a recent book that this is wrong.[13] Once the immigrants are full members they should in principle become citizens. We do not treat the acquisition of citizenship as an optional matter for people who acquire it at birth, even when they have a second or third citizenship, and we are mistaken in treating it as entirely optional for immigrants. At some point when people have lived in a country long enough, they should simply become citizens automatically.[14]

Beyond Legal Integration

Equal legal rights and the acquisition of citizenship are necessary and important means for the integration of immigrants and their descendants, but they are not sufficient. Everyone knows that formal equality may often mask great substantive inequalities, and that legal rights may mean different things depending upon how public officials and even ordinary citizens treat the holders of those rights.

School, Jean Monnet Chair, 1997); Peter Spiro, 'Dual Nationality and the Meaning of Citizenship', *Emory Law Journal* 46 (1997), p. 1411; Schuck, *Citizens, Strangers and In-Betweens*; David Martin, 'New Rules on Dual Nationality for a Democratizing Globe: Between Rejection and Embrace', *Georgetown Immigration Law Journal* 14 (1999), p. 1; T. Alexander Aleinikoff and Douglas Klusmeyer, 'Plural Nationality: Facing the Future in a Migratory World', in T. Alexander Aleinikoff and Douglas Klusmeyer (eds.), *Citizenship Today: Global Perspectives and Practices* (Washington, DC: Carnegie Endowment for International Peace, 2001).

[13] Ruth Rubio-Marin, *Immigration as a Democratic Challenge: Citizenship and Inclusion in Germany and the United States* (Cambridge: Cambridge University Press, 2000).

[14] It might be appropriate to modify this general principle, however, when the laws of the country of origin would impose negative consequences on any of their citizens who acquire a new citizenship, even involuntarily.

What does justice require and permit with regard to the integration of immigrants and their descendants beyond granting them equal legal rights and access to citizenship? What may immigrants reasonably expect of the receiving society and what may the receiving society reasonably expect of them? What policies should states adopt with regard to housing, education, employment, language, religion, and political participation in order to promote the integration of immigrants? How should people (officials, established citizens, immigrants and their descendants) behave and what should be done if people do not behave as they should?

It is much more difficult to answer these sorts of questions with precision than the earlier questions about whether immigrants should have the same legal rights as citizens and should have access to citizenship. One key problem is that institutions, public cultures, and policy environments vary significantly from one state to another for reasons and in ways that have nothing to do with immigrants. One state may have a highly regulated labour market and another decentralized, unregulated one. One state may have extensive public housing and another very little. The ways in which public services are delivered, the culture of the civil service, and the patterns of politics may vary considerably from one state to another. Any policies designed to promote the integration of immigrants must inevitably be inserted into and interact with these pre-existing contexts. So a policy that works well in one environment may be a complete failure in another.

Even that statement may be problematic because it assumes that we can distinguish a successful policy from a failure. But what presupposition lies behind that? Should we assume that successful integration of immigrants means that their descendants will be indistinguishable from the rest of the population: spacially intermixed in their homes and workplaces, socially inter-twined through marriages and friendships, culturally alike in their beliefs, behaviours, and ways of life, and comparably placed in the kinds of work they do and in the patterns of their educational and economic achievement? There is certainly considerable attraction to this vision, because it enables us to extend the idea of equality that we used earlier for legal rights to other spheres and other dimensions of social life. It enables us to distinguish general problems in a society (say, an inequality of life chances due to inadequacies of education or economic policy) from problems connected specifically to immigration. It establishes a critical standard.

On the other hand, the standard may be too critical or not critical enough, precisely because it implicitly takes as a standard whatever the non-immigrant population has and does. It is, at least potentially, an assimilationist standard.

What is wrong with assimilation as a standard? For one thing, it is incompatible with the kinds of liberal legal rights the enjoyment of which we are assuming here has been assured and with the norms about free choice and privacy that undergird many of those rights. In a liberal state, the government cannot tell people where to live or whom to marry or what people to have as friends or what jobs to take, or what to wear or how to live, so long as they are not harming others. Indeed, if one accepts Mill's argument in *On Liberty*, as I do, it is not morally permissible to use the informal sanctions of public opinion to determine these matters for individuals or to impose expectations based on the majority's way of doing things. Moreover, if one adds to this rather individualistic account of why liberalism must be open to pluralism, some recognition of the ways in which cultural traditions and identities can be collective goods, one broadens the basis for challenging any ideal of assimilation. Here we can pay attention to the interests that people may have in associating with people with whom they share a particular cultural identity, in having that identity reflected in the public sphere and accommodated in public life, and in passing that identity on to their children. Therefore, we cannot simply take as unproblematic the notion that we can measure the success of the integration of immigrants against the standard of proportional sharing in whatever the majority has and does.

Does this mean that we cannot say anything after all about the integration of immigrants beyond the sphere of equal legal rights? No, but the first point about the variation in public institutions and cultures means that in making claims that apply to a wide range of liberal democratic states we may have to be content with general principles about outcomes, attitudes, and approaches and their implications in various areas rather than specific policy prescriptions. The latter require a much more fine-grained contextual analysis. And the second point about cultural pluralism means that we will have to try to distinguish the differences between immigrants and the rest of the population that flow from the cultural commitments of the immigrants from the ones that are the product of obstacles placed in their way by the receiving society.

Let me sketch briefly the sorts of things I think can be said from a normative perspective, given these limits—first with regard to the general principles that we can use to evaluate outcomes, approaches, and attitudes, and second with regard to the application of these principles to a couple of concrete areas: housing and language. This sketch will be illustrative rather than exhaustive.

First, the standard of proportional equality does provide a good first measure of integration. If immigrants and their descendants are not receiving a share of the social goods that a society produces proportional to their share of the population, that requires an explanation and a justification if it is to escape condemnation. Any appeal to the immigrants' own culture or preferences as the explanation and justification should be scrutinized with care. This is especially true as one moves from the immigrants themselves to the second and third generation. Those who migrate to advanced industrial societies often do so because they value the economic opportunities that these societies offer. In these respects at least, they want what most of the rest of the population wants. It may be inevitable that new arrivals fare somewhat less well on average, other things being equal, than those already there, because new arrivals have less of the informal knowledge and other forms of social capital that one acquires from growing up in a society and that enable people to navigate a social order successfully (although the fact that immigrants who are not refugees have been willing to move from a familiar social context may suggest that they are particularly willing to sacrifice and work hard to achieve their material goals). In any event, the second and third generations, by definition, have grown up in the society. If they lack social capital, it is society that has failed to provide it.

With regard to approaches, the first principle should be that of evenhandedness rather than either strict equality or complete indifference.[15] Immigrants bring change with them. That is inevitable, and it is not grounds for constructing the immigrants as a threat or a problem. What is required is the recognition of the need for some sort of mutual adaptation between immigrants and those in the receiving society. This mutual adaptation cannot be mechanically equal, however. The people in the receiving society have a legitimate interest in

[15] Joseph H. Carens, *Culture, Citizenship, and Community: A Contextual Exploration of Justice as Evenhandedness* (Oxford: Oxford University Press, 2000).

maintaining most of their institutions and practices. Formal and informal norms are pervasive in any complex modern society. They are often an important kind of collective good, making it possible for people to coordinate their activities without direct supervision or instruction. To a considerable extent, it is reasonable to expect that immigrants will learn how things work in the receiving society and will conform to these formal and informal norms. At the same time, however, it is not reasonable to insist that nothing can change, that the distinctive experiences, values, and concerns of the immigrants can never be relevant to an evaluation of the formal and informal norms. The way things are done may reflect unconscious and unnecessary elements that come to light only when they are confronted by people who object to them. If immigrants have reasons for wanting things to be done differently, they deserve a hearing and their interests must be considered. Sometimes practices can be changed without any real loss to anyone else beyond the adjustment to the change. Sometimes it may be appropriate to leave existing rules in place and provide exemptions for immigrants. What is required, in short, is a sensitive balancing of considerations that takes the interests of the immigrants seriously.

Third, with respect to attitudes, what justice requires is a certain kind of public culture, one that recognizes the immigrants as legitimate members of society and treats them with respect. One might think this is already established with the granting of equal rights, but what is at issue here is the way people behave, especially public officials but also ordinary citizens. The value of formal equality is greatly reduced if the representatives of the state and the rest of the citizenry treat you as outsiders who do not really belong and who have somehow acquired a status that is really undeserved.

This claim that justice requires certain attitudes towards immigrants may seem at odds with my earlier embrace of Millian liberalism which emphasizes the rights of individuals to think and act as they choose without being subject to the sanctions of public opinion. There is a tension here but it is one that is internal to this kind of liberalism. *On Liberty* itself, which is famous for its critique of the coercive force of public opinion, is, at the same time, an attempt to change public opinion. Mill is trying to persuade people that certain kinds of behaviour are wrong and unjust. If the project is successful, a new social norm emerges, one that brings the sanction of public opinion down upon those who act as though they are entitled to criticize the self-regarding actions of others.[16]

Let me try to indicate briefly how these general guidelines might be applied to a couple of particular areas of public policy affecting the integration of immigrants. Take housing first. On the one hand, where people choose to live must be regarded as a matter of individual choice, and, in a capitalist economy, of their ability to pay. But even among people who have comparable levels of income, some may choose to spend more on their housing than others (because of differences in their preferences). For these reasons, it might seem difficult to say whether a particular housing pattern for immigrants is objectionable.

On the other hand, it is helpful to remember that the defenders of racial segregation in the American South (which had as one of its many consequences that African Americans lived in wretched housing conditions, even by the standards of the times) always used to say that African Americans[17] preferred to live with their own kind and under those conditions. It is one thing if people from a similar ethnic background choose to live in the same area because they want the comforts and opportunities that come from living in a place where there are people who speak one's native tongue, where the shops and restaurants provide familiar and desired products, and where there are other people at hand who can help one navigate the unfamiliar byways of the wider society. It is quite another matter if people have no real alternative because they are shut out of housing opportunities elsewhere by formal or informal mechanisms.

For some new immigrants the quality of housing is a relatively low priority compared with the desire to save money to enable their family to join them, but this is a transitional phase. No one really chooses to live in a shanty town or a *bidonville*.

These arguments, like many of the others, apply with even more force to the second and third generations. By that stage, any patterns of ethnic housing concentration should be examined closely to ensure that they actually reflect the choices of those who are concentrated, not their exclusion from other alternatives.

---

[16] I don't know how far this norm has become entrenched in Barcelona, but I can attest that it is very well established in the Toronto classrooms where I teach. There students are very reluctant to pass judgment on anything about the way people live except the tendency to pass judgment.

[17] This was not the term they used, of course.

Now consider the issue of language. A shared language or a small set of shared languages is an important, arguably essential, collective good in a modern society. It is reasonable, for the most part, for those in the receiving society to expect that immigrants will adapt to them in this area, at least over time, but for the same reason it is obligatory for the receiving society to facilitate that adaptation for the first generation and to secure it for the second and third in a way that enhances their life chances. This means that those responsible for public education have to pay attention to the difficulties that arise when the language of the school is not the language of the home and have to think about ways to prevent immigrant children's capacities from being underdeveloped and undervalued. (The precise form such policies should take will depend on local factors but it would not be right simply to assume that things will work out without any policy at all.)

At the same time it is desirable, though I would not claim it is morally required, to provide public support for the languages of the immigrants (e.g., through supplementary heritage language programmes or other means). These languages are a potential resource for the receiving society and often an important source of cultural identity for the immigrants.

One cannot reasonably expect the languages of immigrants to become new official languages in most circumstances (though there may be exceptions in particular cases) nor can one expect that most public employees will learn the language of the immigrants. In some rare cases (as when one is accused of a crime), an immigrant may have a fundamental right to a translator. In most others, translation services are not required as a matter of justice, but they are not purely discretionary either. If the number of immigrants who speak a particular language is at all significant, then they may reasonably expect that some public employees will try to learn their language and also that native speakers of their language (who also speak the dominant language) will be hired into the public service and will be able to serve as linguistic (and cultural) mediators. Immigrants are members of the public, and so their needs should be taken into account in the delivery of public services. This is true not just of social service agencies with the primary task of dealing with immigrants, but also of core public services such as the police and fire protection agencies, bureaucracies charged with routine administrative tasks, and so on. Thus even in the area of language, where the need for immigrants to adapt to the receiving society is perhaps the greatest, there is an obligation for the receiving society also to adapt to the immigrants in some respects.

Conclusion

In sum, liberal democratic states that receive immigrants must take a number of steps to see that the immigrants are not left on the margins of society. First, they must provide the immigrants with a bundle of legal rights that is basically the same as the rights accorded citizens, except for the right to vote or to run for high public office. Second, they must provide citizenship automatically to any of the descendants of immigrants who receive a substantial part of their social formation in the new country, and they must provide relatively easy access to citizenship to the first generation of immigrants, even to the point of conferring citizenship automatically upon them too, once they have been in the country for many years. Finally, they must devise a range of substantive policies that take into account the desires that most immigrants have for economic and social opportunities similar to those enjoyed by the existing population so that the receiving society is not placing obstacles in the way of immigrants who seek to pursue these opportunities. At the same time the receiving societies have to respect the cultural identities and commitments that the immigrants want to maintain. What this requires in any particular case can be determined only by a sensitive contextual analysis.

SECESSION AS A HUMAN RIGHT

Nicolaus Tideman

Human rights provide a defense against governmental power. The broadest claim that people can make against the power of a government is that the government has no legitimate power over them. One way to defend this claim is by asserting that people have a human right to secede and wish to exercise that right. If a right to secede is recognized, then the harm that governments can cause to people is limited to the costs of severing the ties of common citizenship between those who wish to secede and the rest of the society represented by that government. While these costs can be considerable, they are often far less than the costs that abusive governments impose on their citizens. This paper explores the logic of the argument that people have a right to secede.

My argument for a right to secede is based on two premises:

1. Every person has a right to himself or herself.
2. All persons have equal rights to natural opportunities.[1]

These are the premises of a philosophical tradition called 'left-libertarianism'. Vallentyne and Steiner trace the roots of left-libertarianism to Grotius and Pufendorf in the seventeenth century.[2] Thomas Paine's *Agrarian Justice* and Henry George's *Progress and Poverty* contributed strongly to the left-libertarian tradition. A number of modern writers work in a left-libertarian framework, but they differ widely among themselves as to how the basic premises of the framework are to be understood.[3] Therefore, while recognizing my debt to the left-libertarian tradition, I ask that my argument be evaluated on its own terms.

---

[1] A natural opportunity is a scarce resource that is provided by nature, such as land, water, ocean fish, minerals, virgin forests, the frequency spectrum and geosynchronous orbits. While I present the argument in terms of equal shares, the argument would not be changed in any essential way if equal shares were replaced by specified unequal shares.

[2] Peter Vallentyne and Hillel Steiner, *The Origins of Left-Libertarianism* (New York: Palgrave, 2000).

[3] Peter Vallentyne and Hillel Steiner, *Left-Libertarianism and its Critics* (New York: Palgrave, 2000).

My argument for secession, in brief, is as follows. A right to oneself includes the right to do a variety of things that others might disapprove of. But the rights of the individuals to themselves include the right to form nations that prohibit actions to which individuals have rights, by virtue of their rights to themselves. The conflict between the rights of individuals to themselves on the one hand, and the rights of individuals to form nations that impose standards of conduct on the other hand, can be resolved if, and only if, those who wish to reject the standards desired by those who choose to live in nations have the right to form their own sovereign nations.

1. *The Right to Oneself*

At the level of logical argument, the right to oneself is an axiom, not susceptible to examination. Yet there is evidence that can be adduced to support the idea that a 'right to oneself' is an important foundation of our shared ideas of personhood. There are the words of the US Declaration of Independence:

> We hold these truths to be self-evident, that all men are created equal, that they are endowed by their Creator with certain inalienable Rights, that among these are Life, Liberty, and the pursuit of Happiness.

This is one version of a right to oneself.

During the Cold War, one of the characteristics of Russia that made it clearest that that nation did not accord its citizens the rights they ought to have was its refusal to allow all who wished to emigrate to do so. The same characteristic colors our views of Cuba and North Korea today. Whatever else it may be, a right to oneself is a right to cease associating with fellow citizens who insist on a form of society that one rejects, particularly when there is some other nation that will permit the objectors to join them.

The record of the US in this regard is not perfect. During the Vietnam war, there was a half-hearted effort to prevent draft-age American men from moving to Canada. But the tension between this action and the nation's basic beliefs was strong enough that the US could not bring itself to worry much about preventing men from sneaking out.

A military draft itself is a denial of a person's right to himself. The greatly diminished role that the draft plays in American life today is to some extent a consequence of the conflict between a draft and the American understanding of a person's right to himself.

One view of a right to oneself can be constructed from the various rights enumerated in the Bill of Rights in the US Constitution and similar documents: freedom of association, freedom of speech, freedom of religion, freedom of the press, and so on. But this is more like a list of domains where tension has arisen in the past and has been resolved in favor of freedom. The most fundamental aspect of a right to oneself is the right to decide, moment by moment, what we will do with our lives.

2. *The Limit on the Right to Oneself*

There is a standard limit on the right to oneself. We are not allowed to interfere with one another. My right to extend my hand is limited by the proximity of your face. While this may seem obvious, the generalization is not always clear. If I view the sound of a power lawnmower as an assault on my eardrums, can I prevent my neighbor from ever using one? The impossibility of a world in which no one has any effect on anyone else makes it necessary to establish conventions regarding the effects on one another that will and will not count as assaults. And because most of the effects that people have on one another are attenuated by distance, most such conventions need not be global. If local conventions suffice, then they can vary from place to place. There can be places where the sound of a lawnmower on a Sunday morning is an assault on one's neighbors, and other places where it is not; places where nudity is expected in public, places where it is tolerated, and places where it is prohibited. Each person's right to him or herself is limited by the established conventions, applying to all persons, that protect the rights of others to themselves.

3. *What Beings have Rights to Themselves?*

The beings with rights to themselves, with which this article is concerned, are competent human adults. Children, often enough, are inclined to make choices that, they later realize, have consequences that are adverse to their true interests. This suggests that it is reasonable to restrict to some extent the exercise of what would otherwise be their rights to themselves. The extent of appropriate restrictions on children is a complex question that is outside the scope of this article. The article also does not address the issue of mentally incompetent adults.

One might ask whether non-human sentient beings have rights to themselves. My answer is that they may well have rights, but it will not work to treat them as having the same kind of rights that humans have, because we cannot converse with them. We cannot explain to them what is expected to protect the rights that others have to themselves. If humans ever establish a level of communication with one or more non-human species that permits confirmation that other species accept the rights of others and seek equal rights for themselves, and if such species give no evidence of making choices that are adverse to their true interests, then I know of no basis on which they might be denied equal rights.[4]

4. *Equal Rights to Natural Opportunities*

Most claims of exclusive access to land or other natural opportunities originate in conquest of peoples who previously conquered other peoples. To regard such actions as generating respectable claims is to condemn ourselves to a world of continual war, as people seek to become the latest, and perhaps the last, conquerors. Sometimes the claim is 'we were here first'. This too is an inadequate justification for excluding others. Apart from the fact that virtually no one anywhere in the world can demonstrate that there were no violently dispossessed prior claimants to 'their' territory, there is no universal writ establishing that those who come first have rights to whatever they can grab.

The proper form of a nation's claim to territory is, 'We need to live somewhere, we have been living here lately, and what we claim is no more than our share'. If a nation does claim more than its share, then it owes compensation to those who thereby have less than their share.

When territorial claims are made in this way, those who wish to secede can properly say, 'The claim that justifies excluding others from the territory that we jointly occupy is the combination of your claim and ours. Some of us, being dissatisfied with the prospect of a future as your fellow citizens, desire to separate our claim to territory from yours. Give us exclusive control over our share of what has been jointly yours and ours'.

---

[4] This discussion is informed by the ideas developed by Bruce Ackerman in *Social Justice in the Liberal State* (New Haven: Yale University Press, 1980), pp. 69–74.

5. *The Argument for a Right to Secede*

The fundamental argument for permitting secession is that individuals may find it impossible to agree on standards of conduct for being citizens of the same nation, and there is no basis for identifying who is right in such disagreements.

We have often succeeded in resolving disagreements that might have led to secession. We have agreed not to object to one another's religions. We have agreed not to object to what one another say and print. We have agreed to confine nudity to specified places. All of this agreement is wonderful. There is probably widespread agreement that we have a better world when people can find a basis for get ting along and tolerating the differences that they have with one another.

Nevertheless, a right to oneself entails both a right to extreme liberty and a right to intolerance of that liberty in one's fellow citizens. There is no magic formula for determining what must be tolerated and what may be prohibited.

Consider some examples. We have laws against polygamy. I can understand how people might want to have polygamous relationships as an expression of their rights to themselves. I can understand how people might want to live in nations that have outlawed polygamy. The argument for a right to secession is that those who wish to live in polygamous relationships do not have a right to insist that their fellow citizens tolerate such behavior. Nor do those who wish to prohibit polygamy have a right to prohibit it throughout the world. Those who wish to prohibit polygamy do have a right, when they are politically dominant, to say, 'Not in our nation. If you want to do such a thing, form your own nation'. But they must then permit the polygamists to actually form their own nation.

We have laws against consuming marijuana. I can understand how people might want to consume marijuana as an expression of their rights to themselves. I can understand how people might want to live in nations that have outlawed consuming marijuana. If the two groups cannot reach an accommodation, then those who do and do not wish to live in a nation where marijuana is consumed should have the opportunity to satisfy their wishes.

We have laws against driving while drunk. I can understand how people might want to drive while drunk as an expression of their rights to themselves. I can understand how people might want to outlaw drunk driving by their fellow citizens. If you think it is obvious that drunk driving can justifiably be prohibited, how would you answer the drunk who says, 'Everyone takes some risk of harming his fellow citizens when he drives. I only want to drive a mile home drunk from the bar at two a.m. However more likely it is per mile that I will harm someone, I will compensate by driving fewer total miles, so that I am less likely than the average driver to harm others'. If we had an obligation to do everything we could to reduce accidents, we would need to reduce the speed of cars to fifteen miles an hour, at most.

The next example is for those readers who had no difficulty justifying liberty in all of the previous examples. Suppose that someone wants to raise money for his family by charging admission to watch him commit suicide. Could you understand how, if there were such a person, he might claim only to be seeking to exercise his right to himself, while his fellow citizens might insist that they wanted a nation that did not permit such a thing? The AIDS epidemic induced even San Francisco to prohibit unsafe sex in commercial bathhouses, over the objections of some who said that such a prohibition was an unjustifiable infringement on individual liberty.[5]

I find it understandable that people would want to raise armies with which to defend their nations; I also find it understandable that people might believe that a good nation is one that eschews an army.

The argument for a right to secession is that there is no recipe for determining what behavior is properly prohibited and what must be tolerated. A right to oneself includes both the right to individual liberty and the right not to be 'assaulted' by the liberty of one's fellow citizens. It is to be hoped that people can work through their differences and find accommodations that all can accept. But when irreconcilable differences arise, protection of the rights of all requires the possibility of secession. To avoid this claim, one would need to assert that for every conflict about rules that might arise, there is a group that is wrong, and it is possible to know which group it is. There is no basis for such an assertion.

---

[5] Randy Shilts, *And the Band Played On* (New York: St Martin's Press, 1987), pp. 489–91.

6. *Why Democratic Process is Not an Answer*

We usually resolve disagreements about rules through democratic process. Through democratic process we determine what we will permit. But democratic process cannot establish what we should permit. The fact that a majority wants a particular outcome does not make that outcome right. If this proposition is not self-evident, then the possibility of cycles in majority-rule voting should clarify it. When there are three options, *A*, *B*, and *C*, among which a choice must be made democratically, it is possible that those who must make the choice will find that a majority favor *A* over *B*, another majority favors *B* over *C*, and a third majority favors *C* over *A*. This happens, for example, when there are three voters whose preference rankings are *ABC*, *BCA*, and *CAB* respectively. This possible intransitivity of majority rule establishes that 'a majority prefers *X* to *Y*' cannot imply that '*X* is better than *Y*', since the latter relationship must be transitive. '*X* is better than *Y*', and '*Y* is better than *Z*', implies that '*X* is better than *Z*', but 'a majority prefers *X* to *Y*' and 'a majority prefers *Y* to *Z*' can be consistent with the falseness of 'a majority prefers *X* to *Z*'.

Democratic process is a wonderful device for making group decisions. Although we are often able to use this device with great success, it does not establish infallibly what is best. As a matter of logic, one cannot claim, 'Because we have decided democratically, we now know the right way to resolve this disagreement. Those of you who lost must accept that course you favor is wrong'. We need to say to the losers, 'We have heard your arguments, and we have not been convinced. We have decided to do things our way. If you want to do things differently, form your own nation'. And then we must ensure that it is possible for them to do so.

7. *Why Local Option is Not Sufficient*

It might seem that secession is overkill. Why isn't local option enough? Some US states have at times permitted their counties to decide individually whether to permit the sale of alcoholic beverages. This, it might be argued, should be the model for dealing with disagreements about what behaviors should be permitted.

Sometimes local option works well enough. It works for activities such as noise and nudity, where the harm that people feel is attenuated by distance. It doesn't work when people are offended by the thought of being a fellow citizen of someone who wants to express his/her right to him/herself in a particular way, offended by the possibility that their nation could permit such a thing to occur. The behaviors most likely to provoke such reactions seem to be associated primarily with sex, violence, religion and intoxication, although there may be some associated with the accumulation of wealth and its transmission to children as well.

While we can urge people to be tolerant and accept local option within a nation, I can find no basis for insisting that they have an obligation to accept local option in all cases. If a majority insists that a particular behavior is utterly unacceptable in their fellow citizens, and the minority insists that they must have the opportunity to express their rights to themselves, then the two groups need to become citizens of different nations.

8. *Why the Possibility of Emigration is Not Sufficient*

One traditional way of accommodating differences is to have the dis-satisfied minority emigrate. Several American colonies were established by groups whose religious practices were not tolerated in Britain. In the 1950s, Americans would say to their communist fellow citizens, 'If you don't like it, move to Russia'. Today, a person who wants to be free to smoke marijuana can be told to move to Amsterdam or Copenhagen; one who wishes to have multiple wives can be told that he needs to become a citizen of an Islamic nation.

While the possibility of emigration limits the hardship of those who wish to express their rights to themselves in ways to which majorities object, it is not sufficient. A man may want more than the four wives to which Islam limits him. Or he may want an occasional glass of beer along with three wives. A person may find the necessity of learning a new language an insuperable barrier. Or she may find that, while there are nations that would be acceptable to her, they are not willing to allow her to immigrate. There is no basis for saying to people, 'The world already has enough nations. Make do with one of those that will accept you'.

The right of people to themselves requires that there be a place where they can express that right without needing to be concerned about the objections of their fellow citizens. The only way to accomplish this is to provide that if they and their fellow citizens come to an impasse, then they have the right to form their own nation.

9. *Some Mechanics of Secession*

A minority who wish to secede have a right to a share of territorial resources with a value that is proportional to their number. They do not have a right to fragment their nation in whatever way they choose. The majority has an obligation to provide the minority who wish to secede with territory of appropriate value. They satisfy this obligation when they provide territory with value proportionate to the number of persons who wish to secede, in whatever place is convenient for the majority. While it might seem that it is unfair to those who wish to secede to give them no choice in what territory they receive, it is not possible to guarantee the satisfaction of both the majority and the minority, so one might as well leave the decision with the more numerous group, subject to the requirement that territory of proportionate market value be provided. Other things being equal, the majority will have an incentive to part with the territory that has the least value to themselves, relative to the market, and this is likely to be the territory to which the minority are particularly attached.

There is no minimum or maximum size for a group that has a right to secede. A single person has a right to secede. A nation has a right to secede from a person. One would hope that such an action would not be taken lightly, but it might be appropriate in cases such as those of habitual child molesters who cannot be trusted not to reoffend.

10. *Bargaining Consequent to Recognition of a Right to Secede*

If a right to secede were recognized, it would not be exercised nearly as often as it would be used to negotiate different outcomes of conflicts over rights. Consider the issue of marijuana use. If the millions of Americans who want to make the use of marijuana a regular part of their lives had a recognized right to secede with their share of territory, I expect that some of them would begin to organize a secession, if that were necessary to secure the opportunity to use marijuana without the threat of jail. While I could be wrong, I expect that the majority who oppose the use of marijuana would decide that they would rather permit the use of marijuana in some places under local option than allow the nation to split up over such an issue. People who want to use marijuana could then move to such places, and the jail population could be greatly reduced.

Consider the case of a child molester who cannot be trusted not to reoffend. If we threaten to secede from him, he might volunteer to live under restrictions that would prevent him from reoffending.

Support for poor persons is another issue where bargaining under the possibility of secession could be expected to yield a different result. If the landless poor were accorded the right to secede with a proportionate share of land, then they could be expected to seek to exercise that right unless their continued citizenship provided support or public services equal in value to the rent of their share of land.

Highly talented people could not necessarily expect to strike the same deal. If people are generally offended by great wealth, then they can say to those who become rich because they are highly talented, 'Yes, you have a right to leave with your share of land if you want, but we might not mind. Unless you are willing to share a significant part of what your great talent produces, we are not interested in having you as fellow citizens'. This provides the possibility of an alternative ending to Robert Nozick's story of Wilt Chamberlain, who becomes rich through his talent in a society that starts with equality.[6]

The abortion issue is one where it is not clear that any bargaining solution is possible. It would not surprise me if both sides of that issue feel so strongly about their positions that any proposed resolution would lead one side or the other to seek secession if that were allowed. But if that is true, then the two sides deserve the chance to live in separate nations.

11. *Issues that Secession Does Not Resolve*

Some issues are not resolved by the possibility of secession. Abortion may be one of them. Any action that is seen as attack upon beings that ought to be accorded rights may so enrage the powerful persons in a powerful nation that the nation may try to stop the action by force, even if the actors are citizens of another country. The bombing of Yugoslavia by the US to stop genocide and ethnic cleansing of Albanians

[6] Robert Nozick, *Anarchy State and Utopia* (New York: Basic Books, 1974), pp. 160–64.

from Kosovo is a recent example. Protests by the Yugoslavian government that what they were doing was an internal matter did not answer the American concern. (It might be noted that if the world shared a commitment to the idea that a nation's claim to territory must be proportionate to be respectable, then Serbs would not have been able to get more resources per capita for themselves by driving out and killing the Albanians.)

In a similar way, I can imagine opponents of abortion arguing that it would not be sufficient to eliminate abortion from their nation; they had an obligation to eliminate it from the world. In this event, secession would be of no use to them and possibly counterproductive.

The effort by the confederate states to secede from the US lacked respectability because its central purpose was to perpetuate slavery. If a group sought to secede so that they might abuse their children without interference, the group from whom they sought to secede could reasonably refuse to accede to their request. If the citizens of Rhode Island sought to secede in order to re-establish whaling in defiance of an emerging international consensus that whales are to be protected, the US could reasonably refuse their request. If Alaskans sought to secede, the US might reasonably require reliable guarantees that the oil wealth of that state would be shared with others.

If we are to resolve the conflicts that arise because some people believe that others are trampling the rights of third parties, it will need to be by reaching a consensus on what beings have what rights. The possibility of secession does not resolve such conflicts.

12. *Conclusion*

People have rights to themselves. A reasonable conception of a right to oneself includes both the right to do things that others find offensive (while not infringing on the rights of others) and the right to confine one's affiliation to others who do not offend. These apparently conflicting rights can be resolved if, and only if, people have a right to secede.

PART II

COSMOPOLITANISM AND NATIONALISM

SOCIAL JUSTICE, VOLUNTARISM, AND LIBERAL NATIONALISM

Michael Green

Societies occupy a central, yet problematic, place in our thinking about justice. Contemporary political philosophy in the broadly liberal tradition primarily concerns social justice: the distribution of benefits and burdens among the members of a society. On the face of it, however, global justice, the distribution of benefits and burdens among all people, is of far greater significance. It is also a more fundamental theoretical topic since we have to know what resources societies legitimately control before we can sensibly discuss how they should distribute resources among their members. I will consider two attempts to defend the centrality of social justice on the ground that the members of a society have special obligations to one another. I will argue that the difficulties faced by these attempts suggest there are deep problems with our understanding of social justice.

There are many ways in which social justice may be said to be central to our thinking about justice. Social justice is the topic for most theories of justice insofar as they address questions about how the institutions of an individual society could be justified or what a just society would be like. Questions about what a just world would be like, by contrast, are rarely addressed. Methodologically, most of these theories assume that the justification of a society's institutions is to be addressed exclusively to its members; the justice of a society's institutions is thought to depend on whether they serve the interests of, or are acceptable to, its members, whereas the interests or opinions of non-members are not thought to be relevant. Substantively, the principles of justice put forward by these theories largely concern the internal organization of societies.[1] I will address a substantive point that I will call the *priority of social justice*. By the priority of social justice, I mean to refer to two

[1] One could accept the methodological point and reject the substantive one. If the members of a society accept what I will characterize as a cosmopolitan conception of justice, the method of addressing justifications to them may yield cosmopolitan substantive principles of justice.

propositions. The first is that there is an asymmetry between global and social justice such that principles of social justice take priority over similar principles of global justice in this sense: the basic principles of social justice either do not apply to the world at all or they are significantly less demanding when applied globally. For example, many believe that a society could be just only if its members have equal opportunities to earn material wealth; by contrast, few believe justice requires that all people in the world have equal opportunities. According to the second proposition of the priority of social justice, social justice takes priority over the demands of other groups: the members of a society must comply with the demands of social justice, even if they have good reason to believe they are required to act on behalf of other social groups instead. For example, if opportunities are to be equal across a society, there will be limits to what I can do to enhance the prospects for children in my family, neighborhood, race, or religion: I must abide by these limits even if I identify more strongly as a member of these groups than as a member of the society I inhabit. I believe that most of us more or less explicitly accept the priority of social justice and that it is entailed by most theories of social justice, although there are different views about how demanding social justice is. In any event, it is what I will discuss.

By a society I will mean a population or group of people; a society is thus distinct from a state, which is a political institution. Social justice, as I understand it, is concerned, at least in part, with the relationships among the members of a society and not merely with the behavior of a state. The population that makes up a society is large, mostly anonymous to one another, governed by a single state, and occupies all of a territory such as those demarcated as colored blocks on a political map. A society's population is at least potentially diverse with respect to age, ethnicity, gender, kinship, ideology, race, region, religion, and, perhaps, with respect to language and desires for continued political unity. The members of societies are thought to share common economic, political, and social systems, such that one might consider one society's systems apart from those of other societies. Commonly accepted examples of societies in the tradition that I am targeting are those that inhabit the prosperous liberal countries of North America, Europe, and the South Pacific such as the United States, France, and New Zealand.

Despite its familiarity, the priority of social justice is open to at least two criticisms. *Cosmopolitan critics* hold that justice is fundamentally global in scope and deny that there are significant differences between principles of justice for societies and principles of justice for the world as a whole. Cosmopolitans have a good *prima facie* case for regarding the world as unjust since the global gaps in living standards, freedom, and opportunities are extreme and cannot plausibly be attributed to individual choices or preferences. How, for example, could it be fair that those born in the United States expect to live twice as long as those born in Sierra Leone? If there were a trade agreement that would marginally reduce equal opportunities among Americans but greatly improve the standard of living in Sierra Leone, our principles of social justice appear to require that Americans refuse to accept it. Cosmopolitans ask how this could be a requirement of justice. They attack the priority of social justice by trying to show that our conception of social justice is implicitly global in scope and that arguments for liberal, egalitarian principles of justice on the social level also support liberal, egalitarian principles of justice for the world. If they are right, there is no fundamental distinction between principles of social justice and principles of global justice and thus no reason why the former would take priority over the latter.

While cosmopolitans argue for treating the world more like we treat societies, others believe we should treat societies more like we treat the world. *Particularist critics* of the priority of social justice believe that it gives too much weight to membership in societies and underestimates the moral and political significance of other groups, such as those based on class, culture, ethnicity, kinship, region, or religion. I will refer to all such groups as sub-groups since they do not include all of the members of a society. I do not thereby mean that they are perfect subsets of societies; on the contrary, many of these groups cross social and international boundaries. Many people identify more strongly with a sub-group than with a society and they may care significantly more about fellow members of a sub-group than they care about distant, anonymous members of their society. When the achievement of social justice conflicts with the demands of a sub-group, particularist critics ask why obligations to the society should take precedence. Why is it unjust to favor one's responsibilities to a sub-group over one's social obligations but not unjust to favor social obligations over global ones? If our ties to one particular group, the society, limit our obligations to the world, why are our obligations to that group not limited in turn by ties to other, apparently more significant groups?

In other words, particularist critics ask why one particular kind of social group among others should have fundamental significance as far as justice is concerned. Cosmopolitan critics ask why any social unit short of humanity as a whole should have fundamental significance as far as justice is concerned. The two criticisms are familiar, but are rarely discussed in tandem. Nonetheless, those who wish to defend the priority of social justice must respond to both critics. One of this paper's themes is that this is very difficult to do.

One way of trying to meet this challenge is to show that the members of societies have special obligations to one another. We are familiar with the thought that we have obligations to particular people by virtue of having a relationship or some kind of interaction with them: for example, I am thought to owe restitution to those I harm, the performance of my promises to those to whom they were made, and special consideration to my friends or family members. In commonsense moral thinking some relationships generate not just discrete obligations to others but alter the priorities that we put on other duties and obligations. Parents, for example, are thought to be required to give priority to their children's interests even over significantly needier children whom they would, but for their own child's needs, be required to help.[2] If the relationship among the members of a society could be shown to generate special obligations such as these, that might provide a rationale for the priority claims and answer the two critics.

There are other ways of defending the centrality of social justice, of course. For example, one might think that it stems from moral requirements on political institutions as opposed to obligations among the members of a society: social justice, one might think, is something that a modern state must secure and understanding why this is so will reveal the rationale for its centrality even if individuals do not bear any distinctive duties towards the members of their societies. I cannot consider the merits of such a view here, but I will explain why the appeals to special obligations strike me as worth considering. First, many of us believe we have special obligations to the members of our society and

[2] For discussion of how special obligations are thought to affect the weight given to different moral requirements, see Samuel Scheffler, *Families, Nations, and Strangers: The Lindley Lecture* (Lawrence, KS: Department of Philosophy, University of Kansas, 1994), pp. 4–6, reprinted in Samuel Scheffler, *Boundaries and Allegiances: Problems of Justice and Responsibility in Liberal Thought* (New York: Oxford University Press, 2001), pp. 51–53. I should note that my project is different from Scheffler's. He is concerned with a class of obligations; I am concerned with their application to the specific case of social justice. Thus, my cosmopolitan critics do not call the justification of all special obligations into question, whereas that is the point of Scheffler's distributive objection.

we have good reason to want to know more about this belief's content and justification. Second, the existence of special obligations among the members of a society would give the political institutions of the modern state a kind of moral basis that an institutional argument would not. It would show that there are reasons for having and preserving political institutions committed to social justice. On the face of it, by contrast, institutional arguments would not show that we should have political institutions dedicated to social justice but only that this is a requirement on those that exist. The argument from special obligations would thus give us greater guidance than an-institutional argument concerning the nature and powers of sovereign states. Insofar as the ongoing processes of globalization present us with choices about the future of the sovereign state, this is a matter of genuine political significance.

I will examine two attempts to vindicate the belief that we have special obligations to the members of our societies. According to one, special obligations among the members of a society have a voluntary basis: they are created by the voluntary behavior of those who bear them, much like promises. According to the other, the relevant obligations are associative: they are based on membership in a society, even if such membership cannot be characterized in voluntaristic terms.[3] I will argue that both proposals face significant difficulties, largely due to the fact that their strongest replies to the cosmopolitan critic require significant concessions to the particularist critic.

Voluntarism

I will begin with attempts to show that social obligations are voluntary obligations. There are several voluntarist positions in political philosophy. Some propose a necessary condition for social obligations: individuals have obligations to a society only if they have voluntarily accepted those obligations.[4] Others claim that voluntarily accepting

[3] The term 'associative obligations' comes from Ronald Dworkin, *Law's Empire* (Cambridge, MA: Harvard University Press, 1986), pp. 195–216. See also Scheffler's remarks (Scheffler, *Families, Nations, and Strangers*, p. 20 n. 2).

[4] Such voluntarists need not oppose all principles of social justice even if the members of a society have not voluntarily accepted social obligations. For example, according to one sophisticated version, the commonsense requirements of social justice can be analyzed as belonging to one of two technically defined categories: they may be understood as obligations, which must be voluntarily assumed and may be owed

social obligations is sufficient to generate such obligations; someone who believes this may, or may not, hold that it is also a necessary condition. Finally, one might hold that the members of at least some societies actually have valid, voluntarily assumed obligations to one another. I will discuss this last position under the name *social voluntarism.*

Since there are no literal social contracts in any society, the most pressing problem for social voluntarism is to locate the relevant voluntary ties. Several ways of meeting this challenge have been proposed. The members of a society may be thought to have tacitly agreed to bear social obligations by living without protest among one another. Their obligations may be based on their having received or pursued cooperatively produced benefits. One might even think that the fact that the members of a society would agree to accept social obligations, if they were presented with a choice between that and a realistic alternative, shows that social obligations have a voluntary basis.

One might doubt whether any of these stories could ever show that social obligations have been voluntarily assumed but I will not pursue this kind of objection. For even if we grant that any of these ties might be sufficient to generate voluntary obligations there would be a problem in appealing to social voluntarism to defend the priority of social justice against the particularist critic. Since sub-groups have a better claim to voluntary obligations than societies do, it will not be plausible to say that the members of sub-groups have voluntarily accepted social demands that come at the expense of sub-group demands. The relationships among the members of many sub-groups are much more a matter of choice than are those among the members of a society. I do not mean that becoming a member of a sub-group is always a matter of voluntary choice. Rather, my point is that the members of sub-groups often voluntarily interact with one another to a far greater extent than they interact with the members of the society as a whole. Insofar as identification with a group can be said to reflect one's will in being consistent with what one wants or believes, sub-groups often have a better claim to their members' voluntary identification as well. Voluntary ties among the members of a society are secured by finding some sort of

exclusively to a particular society, or they may be understood as natural duties, which might, in theory, extend to any sufficiently just society. See A. John Simmons, *Moral Principles and Political Obligations* (Princeton, NJ: Princeton University Press, 1979), pp. 191–201. Though it would be revisionary, the denial that there are obligations of social justice, so understood, is thus not necessarily the same as denying that the commonsense moral requirements of social justice have any support at all.

behavior that is similar to explicit voluntary assumptions of obligations. But even if one granted that such ties could ground obligations, why would ersatz voluntary ties such as these give social obligations a stronger voluntaristic basis than obligations to groups that have the genuine voluntary support of their members? Thus, when the two kinds of demand conflict, the particularist will argue that it is implausible to assert that the members of sub-groups will have voluntarily agreed to prefer the social demand over that of the sub-group.

The social voluntarist's reply to the cosmopolitan critic appears at first glance to be even weaker. The case for cosmopolitanism is compelling on its face. Given that, why should people be allowed voluntarily to opt out of what appear to be their duties of justice to the world? Even if there were a written social contract, signed by every member of a wealthy society, why would that make their indifference to global inequality any more just? It does not help to appeal to the interests of the beneficiaries of the social contract. The cosmopolitan critic objects that the gap between the wealthy and poor countries of the world is unjust and that the priority of social justice magnifies this by requiring the members of wealthy countries to serve one another even at the expense of the poor. Adding that the members of wealthy countries have voluntarily established this practice hardly addresses the cosmopolitan's point. If anything, it makes the priority given to social justice seem even less fair.

The social voluntarist may reply that the cosmopolitan critic underestimates the importance of being able to generate obligations through voluntary commitments that can weigh against competing demands. There is little doubt about the importance of being able to exercise voluntary control over obligations. In addition to giving us control over our moral lives it enables us to form relationships that require others to trust us more than they otherwise might.[5] This interest would be poorly served if voluntary obligations could not stand against other moral claims or the promisor's own interests. A social voluntarist may argue that this interest in having voluntary obligations is sufficiently strong that, so long as they are undertaken for innocent

[5] Joseph Raz emphasizes the general interest in forming personal relationships as a basis for promissory obligations; see Joseph Raz, 'Promises and Obligations', in P.M.S. Hacker and Joseph Raz (eds.), *Law, Morality, and Society* (Oxford: Oxford University Press, 1977) and Joseph Raz, *The Morality of Freedom* (Oxford: Oxford University Press, 1986), pp. 173–76.

purposes, and not, for example, merely to avoid other obligations, any plausible account of morality must recognize them as genuine obligations and give them substantial weight against even the claims of global justice.

This is an appealing rationale for voluntary obligations among individuals, but it is less persuasive as an account of why voluntary obligations to a society might have the weight attributed to them. This is so because voluntary obligations do not play the same role in the social cases as they do in individual cases. The members of societies cannot rely on voluntary commitments because they are anonymous to one another: you are unlikely to know whether I have voluntarily committed myself to obey social rules and *vice versa*. Societies rely on their members' voluntary compliance with rules, but not on their voluntary commitment to do so. Voluntary obligations are used to alter one's duties beyond what would otherwise be expected. But social obligations are not thought of as adding anything; they are what we expect of others as a matter of course and are not thought to depend on special voluntary behavior. Even when voluntary commitments are made, as with citizenship oaths required of immigrants, other members of a society do not rely on them; they rely instead on the incentives and rules that bolster compliance and trust among the overwhelming majority of citizens who take no such oaths. So the general case for giving weight to voluntary obligations does not apply to societies since voluntary obligations in large groups do not serve important interests and enable valuable relationships.

Nor will this argument about the importance of voluntary obligations fully dismiss the cosmopolitan critic's objection. The cosmopolitan may grant that we have important interests in being able voluntarily to generate and to resist obligations. But, this critic will say, these interests must be balanced fairly against everyone else's interests. Since the cosmopolitan critic maintains that the priority of social justice fails to adjudicate among everyone's interests in a fair way, citing additional interests in pursuing voluntary obligations does not much advance the case.

The cosmopolitan may admit that the social voluntarist has pointed out an important constraint on what positive claims a cosmopolitan conception of justice might make. For example, a cosmopolitan may concede that there are reasons to avoid involuntary or unwanted political or social relationships and that this consideration could conceivably favor arrangements that are less than fully optimal at promoting global justice. But what the cosmopolitan will reject is the suggestion that the interest in being bound to a voluntary social obligation is strong enough to rationalize a significant asymmetry between social and global concerns. What is at issue is whether there is a difference between social and global justice, such that voluntary commitments could justify resisting the latter but not the former. However, if the interest in making voluntary commitments and relationships is strong enough to rationalize resisting the claims of the poor and oppressed in the world, it would be strong enough to do the same within a society. If my voluntary commitments to my society oblige me to pursue social rather than global justice, why shouldn't my voluntary commitments to a sub-group require me to devote myself to the sub-group at the expense of social justice? Responding to the cosmopolitan critic in this way would thus leave the priority of social justice open to attack from the particularist critic.

Liberal Nationalism

The failures of social voluntarism may strike some as beside the point. While many people believe that they have special obligations to the members of their society, few think that these obligations have been voluntarily assumed. On the contrary, it is commonly believed that social obligations have an associative basis: they are thought to be based simply on belonging to a society, even if that cannot be construed in voluntary terms. Liberal nationalists take this commonsense belief seriously and seek to explain it. I will argue that there are gaps in the accounts of these obligations given by some prominent liberal nationalists and will present what I regard as the most compelling case for the position.

Some reject the liberal nationalist project out of hand on the grounds that nationalism is necessarily ethnocentric, reactionary, and violent. Of course, many nationalists have these flaws but liberal nationalists are only committed to defending nationalism insofar as it conforms with liberal morality, even if there are no actual instantiations of it. In any event, the historical record does not support this objection to the liberal nationalist project. Nationalism is an implicitly egalitarian view insofar as national identity is the socially significant relationship that is thought to cross other social divisions; all members of the nation are equally members, regardless of sex, religion, race, and so on. Historical studies of nationalism treat the liberal democratic revolutions in the Americas and Europe as the first instances of politically successful nationalism and show how nationalism was intimately connected with the development of popular democracy.[6] Nor are nationalists committed to the thought that some nations should dominate others. Nations are typically conceived of as inherently limited and existing alongside one another; unlike Christian churches, nations are not conceivably universal and not even the most fanatical nationalists believe there could be such a thing as the one, true nation. A nationalist could thus hold that all nations have equal rights to exist. Finally, while there is certainly room for debate about the future relationship between nationalism and broadly progressive ideals, at present the members of many liberal societies think of themselves as belonging to nation-states without obviously having racist beliefs or violent dispositions. Insofar as there are nations whose nationalism is not obviously objectionable, liberal nationalism is worth consideration.[7]

Suppose, then, that liberal nationalism is not a simple contradiction in terms. What are nations, the social entities that nationalists champion? Like societies, nations are thought of as groups of people and not political institutions. National populations typically are large, anonymous, and diverse in many respects. Their members are thought to share some combination of objective features—such as a shared culture, a common language, political institutions such as a state, or a common history—and subjective ones—such as their recognition of one another as members of a common group, feelings of mutual obligation, beliefs that the group is a community, and beliefs that the group ought to be politically sovereign. Liberal nationalists, along with many historians and social scientists, tend to emphasize subjective features.

---

[6] These are among the themes of Benedict Anderson and Eric Hobsbawm's celebrated books on nationalism, though both are deeply sceptical of the future relationship between nationalism and progressive liberal politics. See Benedict Anderson, *Imagined Communities* (London: Verso, rev. and exp. edn, 1991) and Eric J. Hobsbawm, *Nations and Nationalism since 1780* (Cambridge: Cambridge University Press, 2nd edn, 1992).

[7] David Hollinger makes a case for the moral acceptability of the way national identity is understood and used in the United States and it is plausible to suppose that a similar case could be made for most contemporary liberal societies. See David A. Hollinger, 'National Solidarity at the End of the Twentieth Century: Reflections on the United States and Liberal Nationalism', *Journal of American History* (Sept. 1997), pp. 559–69.

For example, David Miller holds that nations are groups whose members share certain beliefs, desires, and commitments: they 'recognize one another as compatriots' and have 'a shared wish to continue their life in common'.[8] My belief that I belong to a particular nation is mistaken if the other members do not 'share my beliefs and reciprocate my commitments'.[9] By contrast, our nation's existence is not called into question if we hold objectively false beliefs about its history; on the contrary, sharing a myth may well be one of the things that unites us as a nation.[10] Yael Tamir also holds that a combination of shared beliefs and commitments are essential to the constitution of national groups. She maintains that both 'the existence of national consciousness' and 'feelings of belonging and connectedness' are necessary for a group to constitute a nation.[11] Those concerned with giving informative definitions of 'nation' will want to add some objective features as well: people have commitments to groups other than nations and adding that the members of a nation must have national consciousness or view one another as compatriots does not do much to elucidate the term 'nation'. Miller and Tamir accept this, but doubt that any particular objective features are necessary.[12] It is not important for my purposes to press the definitional point any further. I am looking for a rationale for the priority of social justice and so wish to consider the kind of argument liberal nationalists make for special obligations among the members of a nation. I do not believe their arguments obviously turn on any feature that might distinguish nations from societies and so do not have much at stake in pursuing what, exactly, they take nations to be.

Liberal nationalists do not, typically, argue from the objective features of nations to conclusions about moral obligations: their position

---

[8] David Miller, *On Nationality* (Oxford: Oxford University Press, 1995), p. 22.

[9] Miller, *On Nationality*, p. 23.

[10] Ernest Renan, for example, famously argued that forgetting and historical error are essential for nations, in 'Qu'est-ce qu'une Nation?', in E. Buré (ed.), *Ernest Renan et l'Allemagne* (New York: Brentano's, 1945 [1882]), p. 174. For discussion of Renan's disarmingly subtle point, see Anderson, *Imagined Communities*, pp. 199–203. For Miller's view, see Miller, *On Nationality*, pp. 34–42.

[11] Yael Tamir, *Liberal Nationalism* (Princeton: Princeton University Press, 1993), pp. 65, 110.

[12] Miller believes that nations are typically historically continuous groups that can be described as making decisions, and that they possess both a geographical homeland and a common public culture. See Miller, *On Nationality*, pp. 23–25. Tamir maintains that the members of a nation must have some undefined combination of objective features in common, such as a language, history, or territory. See Tamir, *Liberal Nationalism*, pp. 65–69.

is not that there is something about sharing a history, language, homeland, or culture that binds the members of a nation to one another. They do not argue that those who refuse to identify with or recognize obligations to their nation are making some sort of mistake. Instead, their moral arguments appeal to the shared subjective features of belief and felt commitment. They urge their fellow liberals to take beliefs about national obligations seriously, but their positive arguments for these beliefs, especially in the light of the kinds of arguments advanced by the two critics, are not as clear as one might hope.

Miller concentrates largely on a point of moral theory. He distinguishes between two 'accounts of the structure of ethical thought' that he calls ethical universalism and ethical particularism.[13] The difference between these two views is that ethical particularism allows relationships among persons to generate moral requirements as a matter of fundamental moral principle and ethical universalism insists that only general features of human beings, such as rationality or sentience, are of fundamental moral concern.[14] The point that Miller is concerned to make is that special obligations among the members of a nation can have genuine, fundamental, moral priority over duties to non-members only if one accepts ethical particularism and that, so understood, the content of such obligations would be determined by the nation's public culture.[15] The project, in other words, involves finding a place for commonsense feelings of national obligation in a philosophical scheme rather than offering a direct defense of them.

It is true that, in illustrating his claim about the relationship between ethical universalism and ethical particularism, Miller presents what he calls a 'justifying account' of an ethical particularist's version of national obligations.[16] Two kinds of argument are involved in this account. First, the goals of people who identify with a nation tend to coincide with national obligations so as to reduce conflict between national obligations and personal projects.[17] Second, ethical particularist accounts of national obligations can better support some of the practices of liberal societies than ethical universalist accounts do: for example, an ethical particularist version of nationalism is more congenial to widely accepted views about the importance of national self-determination

[13] Miller, *On Nationality*, p. 49.
[14] Miller, *On Nationality*, p. 50.
[15] Miller, *On Nationality*, pp. 49–80.
[16] Miller, *On Nationality*, p. 79.
[17] Miller, *On Nationality*, pp. 66–68.

than cosmopolitan views of justice are.[18] But neither kind of argument establishes the existence of special national obligations. The point about the congruence of self-interest and national obligation shows, at most, that the objection that national obligations are too burdensome on individuals is less pressing than it might otherwise be. It does not ground such obligations by itself. The second kind of point assumes that the current practices of liberal societies are basically correct and thus does not advance the case against the critics, each of whom questions those practices.

Sometimes, liberal nationalists write as if commonsense beliefs about national obligations should be accepted at face value, as if they established the existence of national obligations on their own.[19] But while one might agree that the existence of strong beliefs or feelings of obligation serves as evidence for the existence of such obligations, it is another thing to say that they ground or explain them. There is a difference between feeling obligated and actually being obligated since one's feelings of obligation can fail to match the obligations that one actually has: I may feel obligated when, in fact, I am not or I may fail to appreciate obligations that I actually have. Moreover, simply citing feelings of obligation will not do the explanatory work needed to address the particularist and cosmopolitan critics. Someone who had feelings of obligation towards her fellow nationals but wanted to explain or justify them, especially in the light of doubts or questions about them, would not find it helpful to be reminded that she has feelings of obligation. That is something she already knows.

Even when national feelings are not taken directly to support special national obligations, they are generally taken as necessary conditions of national obligations: if feelings of commitment and obligation are understood as necessary conditions of belonging to a nation, then they

[18] Miller, *On Nationality*, pp. 76–79, 103–108. This point applies to a particular ethical universalist view with a very expansive understanding of global obligations. Miller charges that ethical universalists who believe there are global obligations to protect basic rights are committed to displacing local governments. He also considers a less expansive ethical universalist view: that considerations of reciprocity provide a rationale for social welfare programs. Against this view, he argues that an ethical particularist account which emphasizes membership in a society can better explain why those whose health problems preclude net social contributions are eligible for benefits. Miller, *On Nationality*, pp. 71–72.

[19] See, for example, Tamir's claim that, obligations to obey the laws of a particular state 'are not grounded on consent, reciprocity, or gratitude, but on a feeling of belonging and connectedness' raises the same problem (Tamir, *Liberal Nationalism*, p. 135). See also Tamir, *Liberal Nationalism*, p. 121.

are necessary conditions of bearing obligations to other members of one's nation. The difficulty here is that the threat from the particularist critic will be greatest when feelings of obligation to the nation are weak or in conflict with feelings of obligation to sub-groups. The particularist criticism poses a genuine alternative to the priority of social justice when the members of a sub-group have strong feelings of obligation to one another that are in tension with their feelings of obligation to the nation. Nationalists who allow too much to rest on the depth of feeling associated with national identification would have nothing to say in such a case: if feelings were to shift, so would one's obligations.[20] Nationalists may say that this is impossible since to believe one belongs to a nation is, by definition, to believe one has obligations to other members. But this does not ring true: the members of actual nations sometimes bitterly hate one another, fight civil wars, or simply feel indifferent towards one another. Furthermore, granting that nations are, by definition, united by feelings of obligation would not answer the particularist challenge. Why should anyone remain a member of a nation, so defined, rather than abandoning it for some other particular group?

Another way of putting the point is this: if liberal nationalism's answer to the critics were to depend on feelings of national obligation, then it would not offer significantly greater support for the priority of social justice than social voluntarism does. Liberal nationalists sometimes construe their project as defending the legitimacy of feelings of national obligation that people already have; they do not seek to impose national obligations on those who do not identify with a particular nation but merely wish to defend the beliefs and feelings of those who do. In taking feelings of national obligation for granted, however, liberal nationalism amounts to a defense of one possible motivation for accepting social obligations. As such, it is hard to see what it would gain over a view that makes no discrimination at all concerning one's motivations for accepting obligations, provided one does so voluntarily. Under either social voluntarism or liberal nationalism, individuals would have considerable latitude in determining whether social

---

[20] Miller, for example, distinguishes national obligations from those owed to 'lesser communities' on the grounds that 'the potency of nationality as a source of personal identity means that its obligations are strongly felt and may extend very far' (Miller, *On Nationality*, p. 70). This sort of argument for the priority of national obligations is, obviously, vulnerable to shifting feelings.

obligations have the crucial feature that is thought to answer the critics: on the voluntarist account, this depends on an individual's will while on the nationalist account, it depends on feelings. That is a difference but it is not enough to show that liberal nationalism's defense of the priority of social justice is significantly more robust than that given by social voluntarism.

A second way of taking commonsense beliefs about national obligation seriously would be to accept commonsense ways of explaining or conceptualizing national obligations. These explanations often rest on analogies with other intimate social groups that are widely accepted as sources of special obligations. For example, nations are sometimes thought of as a kind of kinship group; after all, their members are said to share a fatherland, a mother tongue, and bonds of fraternity. Some scholars claim that nations are simply the largest group whose members believe they have a common ancestry.[21] Nations are also conceived of as analogous to sacred communities, friendships, and other relationships based on a shared interpersonal history or project.[22] A nationalist may say that the similarities between nations and these other groups explain national obligations by showing that national obligations have the same basis as other, less controversial, obligations such as those among family members or friends. So understood, national obligations need not depend on feelings or beliefs insofar as it is widely believed that one can fail to have appropriate feelings of obligation towards one's friends or family while still actually bearing those obligations.

These analogies are all contentious, but even if one grants that they are meaningful it is hard to see how they could be used to fend off the

[21] This is the theme of Walker Connor's work on nationalism (*Ethnonationalism: The Quest for Understanding* [Princeton: Princeton University Press, 1994]). The American cases pose problems for Connor's thesis, insofar as American nationalists think of their nation as composed of people with different ancestral backgrounds. This is a familiar feature of nationalism in the United States. For South American cases, see Anderson's discussion of nationalism's 'creole pioneers' (Anderson, *Imagined Communities*, ch. 4). A more plausible suggestion is that the members of a nation think of one another as possible family members, either because of past or possible future kinship ties. This is the idea behind Michael Lind's claim that a truly unified American nation depends on interracial marriage. As Lind observes, 'if people discriminate on the basis of physical race when it comes to the most fundamental matters—sex, reproduction—they can hardly be expected to overlook physical race in a thousand lesser areas of life' (Michael Lind, *The Next American Nation* [New York: The Free Press, 1995], p. 290).

[22] For an interesting account along the last two lines, see Thomas Hurka, 'The Justification of National Partiality', in Robert McKim and Jeff McMahan (eds.), *The Morality of Nationalism* (Oxford: Oxford University Press, 1997).

critics. For every way in which a nation might be like a more intimate group, the particularist critic is likely to find a sub-group that bears an even stronger resemblance. Arguments based on analogies between nations and other groups can thus offer support for national obligations that is, at best, only as strong as that given to obligations among the members of the other groups. Suppose, for example, that nations are said to be like kinship groups. How could national obligations based on such an analogy possibly take precedence over obligations to real kinship groups? As with social voluntarism, it is hard to see how obligations based on an ersatz relationship could have a more compelling basis than those based on the real thing. On the other hand, the cosmopolitan critic may ask how these analogies could support the asymmetry between social and global justice. Principles of social justice are expected to put limits on what people can do for the sake of their friends and families in the name of fairness to other members of the society. By the same token, a cosmopolitan may say, principles of global justice should put similar limits on what people can do for the sake of their societies in the name of fairness to everyone else. Since, by hypothesis, the relationships to be constrained by the respective principles of justice are the same in kind, there is no obvious reason why the constraints of justice should be weaker on the global level than they are on the social level. Thus, this way of taking commonsense nationalist beliefs seriously seems unpromising.

There is a third way of taking commonsense beliefs about national obligations seriously. One might adapt Samuel Scheffler's general strategy for defending associating duties to the specific case of national duties.[23] Specifically, one may say that the commonsense beliefs are not just about obligations but are also beliefs about the value of belonging to a nation and that this thought about the value of national membership may help to explain special, national obligations. Nationalists may seek to show, first, that the members of a nation have good, non-instrumental, reasons for valuing their national membership and, second, that these reasons for valuing national membership are also reasons for giving priority to other members of the nation. By 'non-instrumental' reasons, I mean reasons for valuing national membership for its own sake and not merely because it is a means to achieving some other aim. As an illustration of this strategy, consider a parallel

[23] Samuel Scheffler, 'Relationships and Responsibilities', *Philosophy & Public Affairs* 26.3 (1997), reprinted in Scheffler, *Boundaries and Allegiances*, pp. 97–100.

argument concerning friendship. Most of us think we have good, non-instrumental, reasons for valuing our friendships. We have instrumental reasons for valuing friendship too, of course, but they would not explain why we have reason to care especially about the particular people who are our friends or what is distinctively valuable about friendships as opposed to, say, a business partnership or other relationship that is of merely instrumental value. Recognizing and acting on these non-instrumental reasons for valuing friendship, however, necessarily involves giving special priority to one's friends since to be a friend is, in part, to give special consideration to the needs and interests of one's friends. Someone who did not think there was any reason to care more about the interests of her friends than those of a stranger would fail to understand her reasons for valuing her friendship and fail to be a good friend. A nationalist may try to show that something similar is true of nations, namely, that my reasons for valuing my national identity are also reasons for giving special consideration to the needs and interests of other members of the nation. In response to the particularist critic, the nationalist may reply that those who do not feel obligated to their nations are mistaken, much like those who fail to appreciate their reasons for valuing their friendships. In response to the cosmopolitan critic, the nationalist may say that the reasons for valuing national membership, like our reasons for valuing other commonly accepted sources of special obligations, are deeply important to our lives, such that no plausible account of morality could dismiss them. Respecting these reasons and values, however, involves giving priority to the members of one's nation over the world as a whole.

The first question to ask about such a strategy is whether national identity really is valuable in relevant ways. Many of the ways that nations are thought to be valuable seem irrelevant to this account of national obligations. For example, in many circumstances, nations provide their members with protection against threats from other groups.[24] But to value a nation for the protection it provides is to value it in an instrumental way and, by hypothesis, special obligations to a nation are to be explained by appeals to the nation's non-instrumental value.

[24] In many cases, unfortunately, the immediate protection gained from identifying with a nation or ethnic group produces greater insecurity in the long run as it leads others to identify with an opposing group. For an account of national and ethnic identification that emphasizes these factors, see Russell Hardin, *One for All: The Logic of Group Conflict* (Princeton: Princeton University Press, 1995).

It is also the case that many people value participation in their nation's culture.[25] But their reasons for valuing participation in a national culture are not reasons for giving special weight to the interests of the members of their nation. We would have just as much reason to participate in our national cultures, use the language, follow the customs, and value the traditions, as we do now even if we disclaimed all national obligations. Barring outside interference, national cultures survive if their members value them; they do not depend on and probably could not be sustained by a sense of obligation. In this respect, nations are more like scholarly communities than they are like friendships. Scholarly communities are valuable to the extent that their members follow norms of open academic inquiry and exchange. They will retain their value even if scholars do not regard one another as having any special moral claims compared with non-scholars.

These points notwithstanding, nationalists may still have a case. Many people find non-instrumental value in belonging to large, anonymous groups such as nations. Modern social life involves countless seen and unseen interactions and relationships with anonymous strangers. The value of these anonymous relationships varies considerably with the prevailing social environment. For example, the assumptions held by strangers can make walking down the street harrowing, depressing, unremarkable, or rather pleasant. More abstractly, the members of a society with broad support for a social welfare system may be less likely to think of their social position with feelings of resentment or shame than the members of societies without such a social *ethos*. Many of us value relations, even with anonymous others, that are open, generous, and free of suspicion and resentment. We desire to have such relationships even if they are not useful for achieving other goals. Some societies are fortunate to have established customs of social solidarity, that is, customs of decency, respect, and caring; these customs produce a social environment in which anonymous interactions have the valuable qualities I have described.

[25] Most philosophers who are sympathetic to nationalism emphasize the cultural value of nations, mostly for the purpose of establishing that nations or cultures have certain rights. See, for example, Will Kymlicka, *Multicultural Citizenship* (Oxford: Oxford University Press, 1995); Avishai Margalit and Joseph Raz, 'National Self-Determination', *Journal of Philosophy* 87 (1990), pp. 439–61. For an argument that the value of cultures is overstated, see Jeremy Waldron, 'Minority Cultures and the Cosmopolitan Alternative', *University of Michigan Journal of Law Reform* 25 (1992), pp. 751–93.

When this is so, the members of these societies can, by following these customs, share such valuable relationships even with anonymous fellow members. Those who live in such a society may thus have reasons for giving special consideration to their fellow members since valuing social solidarity, much like valuing friendship, involves giving special priority to the members of one's society. In this way, and perhaps others, a nationalist may say that national relationships are valuable in ways that explain the priority of social justice.[26]

While there is much more to say about the value of anonymous social relations, I would like instead to ask how the argument I have sketched could be used to defend the priority of social justice. Success against the particularist critic depends on showing that national membership is valuable to all the members of a society or nation, especially when compared with the value of membership in a sub-group. Sometimes, it might be. But what has to be shown is that there are stronger reasons for valuing one's participation in the society as a whole than there are for valuing one's membership in a sub-group, especially when the two are at odds. How often will that be true? The relationships among the members of sub-groups can also be valuable; why think that my relationships with members of the more remote social entity will generally be more valuable? For example, how valuable is social solidarity to the wealthy? If I live in an insulated neighborhood or town, how much interaction with the broader society will I have? In addition, different people may value different things about their membership in a national group. I may take pride in our nation's military successes and cherish its tradition of rugged individualism while others look to its progressive social movements and value its egalitarian ideals. It seems evident that the ways we value our national membership will have different implications for social justice. The nationalist may reply that those who deny the value of engaging in relationships of social solidarity are mistaken and that they really do have strong

[26] One may object that there is nothing distinctively nationalistic about this sort of argument since it turns on the value of relationships among the anonymous members of a society and not only on the value of relationships among the members of a nation. I suspect that this is correct but do not wish to pursue the point. For my purposes, the basic argument is still relevant even if it leads away from nationalism *per se*. The task is to explain the priority of social justice; the philosophical view behind liberal nationalism is of interest to me insofar as it seems to expose something significant about societies.

reasons for recognizing the value of such relationships, even if, in fact, they do not. But it is not easy to see how successful this strategy will be. Again, the particularist critic poses the greatest threat when there are genuine social alternatives that are in tension with one's ties to the wider society. The assumption that there will generally be better reasons for valuing relationships at the social level that are fairly uniform within a diverse population is a very strong one that, it seems to me, is unlikely to be true.

Nor will the appeals to the value of social relationships directly answer the cosmopolitan's concerns about the fairness of the global distribution of benefits and burdens. Pointing out the value of national relationships to those who participate in them does not alleviate this concern and may in fact exacerbate it by adding yet another benefit to the side of those who already seem to have an unfair share. Still, a cosmopolitan may acknowledge that the value of social relationships constrains a cosmopolitan conception of justice. If people have compelling, apparently legitimate, reasons to value the maintenance of social solidarity where it exists, and these can stand in tension with their reasons for making the world more just, then there may be limits on what cosmopolitans can expect people to do in the name of justice.

What the cosmopolitan critic will insist on is that the constraints that national obligations put on cosmopolitan conceptions of justice should not be different from the constraints that other associative obligations put on social justice. Defenders of the priority of social justice do not concede that associative obligations among sub-groups of a society could support inequalities and other apparent injustices within a society on nearly the scale that exist in the world today. Cosmopolitans press those defending the priority of social justice to explain the asymmetry of the relationship between associative obligations and justice on the social and global levels: why should they undermine global justice to a greater extent than they undermine social justice? Conversely, if associative obligations can rationalize the gaps and inequalities on the global level, then the particularist critic will insist that they should be able to rationalize similar gaps and inequalities on the social level. In other words, if the interest in preserving valuable social relationships is strong enough to rationalize the enormous gap between the wealthy and the poor in the world, it should be strong enough to allow the wealthy to withdraw from their obligations to the society.

Conclusions

Neither social voluntarism nor liberal nationalism provide a satisfactory defense of the priority of social justice. Moreover, the two views make quite similar argumentative moves in combating the particularist and cosmopolitan critics. If social obligations depend on an individual's will or feelings of obligation, then they are vulnerable to shifts in individual feelings away from the society and towards other, particularist, groups. For this reason, both views have similar weaknesses with respect to particularist critics. On the other hand, the fact that individuals would prefer to or would benefit from bearing social obligations that limit their obligations to the world does not directly address the cosmopolitan's complaint about global fairness and justice. On the contrary, the fact that individuals benefit from their social ties amplifies the cosmopolitan's concerns. The cosmopolitan holds that, according to plausible measures of distributive justice, the world is unjust. The additional benefits that the members of wealthy societies receive from their ties to one another seem, if anything, to make the situation worse. In this way, both views have similar weaknesses with respect to cosmopolitan critics.

Furthermore, the two views share an interesting problem: their strongest position against the cosmopolitan critic involves significant concessions to the particularist critic. Both social voluntarists and liberal nationalists argue that the interests protected by their respective special obligations are compelling enough to resist the cosmopolitan critic. But if that is so, then the particularist critic will seek to make a similar point in opposition to social obligations: similar interests among the members of sub-groups should justify their withdrawal from social obligations. In other words, if there is an interest compelling enough to justify inequality and apparent unfairness on the global level, that interest will be compelling enough to justify the same on the social level. If that is so, however, then the priority of social justice, which holds that there is a great asymmetry between global and social justice, is false.

I believe that the difficulty of answering both critics at the same time runs in the other direction as well: the strongest reply to the particularist involves concessions to the cosmopolitan critic. For example, a straightforward way of answering the particularist critic would be to say that the requirements of social justice are needed to ensure that everyone is treated fairly. Such appeals to fairness and the need to protect everyone's interests would present a powerful reply to a variety of particularist criticisms of social justice. However, this sort of argument runs the risk of abandoning the field to the cosmopolitan critic since the cosmopolitan's point is that the priority of social justice is insufficiently responsive to considerations of fairness and equality among all the people in the world. The possibility that concerns me is that, were we to consider alternative rationales for the priority of social justice, we would find this pattern being repeated, such that the strongest replies to particularist critics involve significant concessions to the cosmopolitans. That, coupled with the results from this paper, suggests that defenses of social justice face a dilemma: they can respond effectively to one critic or the other, but not both.

At this point, I have only considered two, very closely related, defenses of the priority of social justice and so I cannot claim to have proven that all defenses of social justice must face this dilemma. But it strikes me as a challenge that ought to be met. Societies occupy an important place in our moral thinking, but I do not believe that we have an adequate understanding of why or whether they should do so. The relationship among the members of a society shares some of the features of interpersonal relationships and some of the features of whatever relationship unites humanity as a whole: my society is a particular group to which I belong and feel attached, but its members are anonymous strangers to me. Our commonsense moral code has principles governing intimate personal relationships and principles governing our interaction with strangers. When we try to explain our beliefs concerning the moral status of societies, we often do so in terms of the principles familiar from these other cases. I suspect that we will always find these accounts strained and unsatisfying and, if we cannot replace them, that we will find the priority of social justice unsatisfying as well.[27]

[27] I would like to thank the following people for reading and commenting on this paper: Sara Austin, Rachel Barney, Christopher Kutz, Jeff McMahan, Martha Nussbaum, Debra Satz, Henry Shue, and Samuel Scheffler.

AUTHENTICITY AND CULTURAL RIGHTS*

Burke A. Hendrix

Introduction

Do 'minority nations' or 'minority cultures' deserve customized political protections? Part of the answer may depend on what we believe the character of the claimants to be. Are the identities at stake merely political artifacts, created by 'ethnic entrepreneurs'[1] seeking wealth and political power, or are they 'authentic' expressions of an ongoing collective life? This essay will argue that the real character of groups is generally difficult to recognize, and that 'authenticity' is a problematic notion even in the abstract. Given these uncertainties, I will argue that states will generally fare best if they treat only the claims of small and vulnerable groups as moral issues, while treating the claims of larger groups as political challenges to be worked out through the bargaining and competition of democratic politics. I will suggest that states should generally allow small minorities to self-identify, and should customize legal protections to fit their desires in many circumstances. This solution provides opportunities for exploitation of state laws, however, and I will close by considering how such problems might be defused in practice, with particular attention to the criteria for recognizing Indian tribes in the United States.

Consent and Equality

Claims for self-government rights and other customized political protections by minority groups often rely on the combination (or conflation) of two very different arguments, one invoking collective self-determination and the other cultural difference. The first relies on

* The author would like to thank Jason Frank, Paul Schumaker, conference audiences in Los Angeles and Chicago, and an anonymous reviewer for the *Journal of Moral Philosophy*.

[1] The term 'ethnic entrepreneurs' is borrowed from Brian Barry, *Culture and Equality* (Cambridge, MA: Harvard University Press, 2001), e.g. p. 197.

some notion of *collective consent*, while the second invokes some notion of *equal treatment*.

Self-determination arguments make strong claims for a 'group' to be self-governing. In the form of 'national self-determination', this principle emerged most strongly in the wake of World War II as colonized territories asserted rights to choose their own political future, but the intellectual roots of such claims are much deeper.[2] The objection to colonialism was not merely one of misrule, but one of rule without agreement – an argument with obvious resonance against European states claiming to rule their own citizens with 'consent of the governed'. While the importance of collective consent might be defended in many ways, much of self-determination's appeal relies on an implicit (and sometimes explicit) analogy between individuals and groups: when ruled by force, both have rights to resist and to struggle for lost independence. For obvious reasons, this analogy is imperfect at best, but its grip is nonetheless difficult to escape fully – isn't the alternative simply to allow the triumph of unjustified coercion?

Arguments for cultural rights, on the other hand, are more often based in some notion of equal treatment, understood as treating diverse people equally well.[3] Such arguments claim that different cultural groups live according to different rules, which are equally valuable,[4] or at least equally entrenched in viable societies. To treat all persons with equal respect, this argument holds, these differences must be reflected in policies and institutions.[5] The analogies with individuals here are clear as well, even if they likely have less historical resonance. To ignore barriers faced by the physically handicapped would fail to take them

---

[2] In considering the roots of 'self-determination' as an idea, *see*, for example, the discussion in Bernard Yack, 'Popular Sovereignty and Nationalism', *Political Theory* 29 (2001), pp. 517–36. For a concise discussion of international law on self-determination, *see* S. James Anaya, *Indigenous Peoples in International Law* (New York: Oxford University Press, 2000).

[3] Cf. Ronald Dworkin, *Taking Rights Seriously* Cambridge: Harvard University Press, 1977), p. 227.

[4] This need not imply any commitment to moral relativism. Most kinds of cultural practices have both costs and benefits, and the practices of different cultures can be, on balance, equally valuable even if both are in need of pervasive reforms in various ways.

[5] Will Kymlicka's *Multicultural Citizenship* (New York: Oxford University Press, 1995) is perhaps the best-known argument for cultural rights, but there are many others as well. A particularly interesting alternative formulation is that in Joseph Carens, *Culture, Citizenship, and Community* (New York: Oxford University Press, 2000). *See also* Michael Walzer, *Thick and Thin* (Notre Dame: University of Notre Dame Press, 1994) and Michael Walzer, *On Toleration* (New Haven: Yale University Press, 1997).

seriously as persons, for example, and a failure to make provisions for the collective lives of groups sharing different cultural beliefs may involve a similar lack of respect. To treat all persons equally well, this justification suggests, we must be sensitive to our real differences.

Whatever their historical connections, arguments for self-determination and cultural protection need not go together in all instances. We can imagine a set of persons calling themselves a 'nation' while entirely sharing cultural beliefs with another 'group' (e.g. Scotland and England), and can also imagine a set of persons sharing a culture who do not regard themselves as members of a political collective with a right to choose its own separate future. Most actors claiming special protections for 'their group' do invoke both principles, however, even if they have to valorize petty differences or imagine non-existing political unity to do so. Indeed, such arguments sometimes slide into circularity. If we ask why a set of people form a 'group' fit for self-determination, we may be referred to a shared culture – and if we ask why a set of individuals are entitled to specialized cultural protections, we may be told that this is necessary for them to exercise self-determination.

Yet the moral cogency of such claims derives far more from cultural difference than from 'self-determination' in its raw form. Although all governments should presumably strive to receive the consent of the governed, in practice this simply cannot be achieved.[6] No one will ever be entirely satisfied with the regime in which they live, and some are so dissatisfied that they do not even find the existing order minimally tolerable. We clearly cannot allow individuals within contemporary societies to exempt themselves from political authority simply because they find that authority personally repugnant (although this is no excuse for creating repugnant systems of authority). We will inevitably want *reasons* when individuals reject existing arrangements: if they are mere malcontents who have no coherent justifications for their rejection, their lack of consent should presumably count far less to us. While consent should be a goal of states, then, its absence does not automatically dissolve authority relations.

Treating people equally well, on the other hand, seems to have a more foundational status. Indeed, the primary reason to value consent

---

[6] *See* A. John Simmons, *Moral Principles and Political Obligations* (Princeton: Princeton University Press, 1979); A. John Simmons, *On the Edge of Anarchy* (Princeton: Princeton University Press, 1993).

in the first place is because it takes everyone's opinions to be equally important. If treating persons from different cultures exactly the same often shows unequal respect, then we have an obvious case for contextualizing legal protections more carefully. (Imagine that you addressed everyone in English or Swahili, regardless of their background or fluency. Is this equal treatment? Only in a trivial sense. Now imagine that you have coercive power over them.) Arguments for cultural rights seem based on clear reasons, and have a clear appeal: if people are relevantly different, treat them that way. People in wheelchairs should not be forced to climb stairs; likewise, people from one culture should not be governed by rules appropriate for another.

If the case for cultural rights is more plausible, however, it is far from sealed. Worries about identical treatment constituting actual inequality are clearest when the gaps between cultures seem truly wide. Consider this example from anthropologist Fred Myers, of Pintupi Aborigines in Australia dealing with the pickup truck of someone recently deceased:

> Personal property of a deceased is always destroyed or given away to that person's 'mother's brothers' from far away, because a person's effects are identified with him or her and make close relatives sad. The Alumbra community planned initially to swap vehicles with another community in order to remove the truck from sight because it reminded them of the dead man. They eventually thought better of this, realizing that they would still have to see this truck since it would be in the area. In the end they decided to burn it and thus efface its associations with sad memories.[7]

Most of us, I suspect, will find this behavior strikingly strange. Wouldn't it be far more profitable simply to sell the vehicle, or to continue to use it despite the associations? Apparently this community did not see either option as appropriate.[8] In light of such cultural dissonance, do we really believe we could (or would) draft legislation appropriate for the Pintupi over the long term, particularly since this is merely an example of many interconnected practices?[9]

---

[7] Fred Myers, 'Burning the Truck and Holding the Country: Pintupi Forms of Property and Identity', in Edwin N. Wilmsen (ed.), *We Are Here* (Berkeley: University of California Press, 1989), p. 26.

[8] For an account of the reasoning underlying this choice, *see* Fred R. Myers, *Pintupi Country, Pintupi Self* (Berkeley: University of California Press, 1986), p. 117.

[9] For an evocative first-hand account of the repeated failure of Australian policies, *see* Ralph Folds, *Crossed Purposes: The Pintupi and Australia's Indigenous Policy* (Sydney: University of New South Wales Press, 2001).

We could, of course, think of examples even more clear. Imagine that a stone-age tribe is discovered on an unexplored island tomorrow. Would we hope that some state would immediately rush in to rule them? Presumably not. Even if we believed that some sort of idealized Lawgiver from outside the community could legislate perfectly, there are no such perfect persons in our world, and many reasons to believe that self-rule would be entirely appropriate, even if this newfound group was engaging in actions that we found troubling or even repulsive. (There are probably limits, but given the widespread anomie and despair that usually follows such interventions, the practices involved would have to be truly horrific.) In practice, many poor and ineffective states allow tribal groups within their midst to rule themselves through either intentional or unavoidable neglect, but this often results in predation by profit-seeking private parties, and so is a very imperfect cure. Ideally, we would want states to both provide protections for such groups against outsiders and to leave groups largely to run their own affairs – i.e., we would want some workable system of local self-government and other cultural rights.

The problem, however, is that the stable, effective democracies with the most capacity to administer carefully-designed systems of cultural rights rarely have such clear-cut examples of cultural difference within their borders. They have more often groups for whom 'cultural identity' is more fluid, more ambiguous, and more colored by past and present government policies. In such cases, states face a harder task in deciding when to offer specialized protections and how to construct them appropriately. In these circumstances, it is tempting to look for objective standards of group 'authenticity'. While such standards cannot be abandoned altogether, however, I will argue that we should seek to minimize such considerations whenever we can.

Identity and Change

The problem for supporters of cultural rights is that particular cultural practices change over time, and (more importantly) that people often perceive themselves to be much more different than they actually are. The forces that drive cultural change are familiar: new technologies, new forms of governance, new demographic trends, new patterns of geographical interaction, and all kinds of other changes can reshape the way that people interact and the kinds of values that they hold.

Cultures can also change for what we might call 'internal' reasons – some ideas go out of fashion as misguided or outdated, some are overturned as vicious and oppressive to particular people, and others just fade away through a kind of cultural drift. Still, we shouldn't mistake cultural change for cultural *convergence*, or convergence on particular technological products with convergence all the way down – recall the Pintupi community, which chose to burn a pickup truck rather than sell it or continue to use it.

The more severe difficulty for regimes of cultural rights is that actual cultural distance and particular cultural identities do not always match up – many groups believe themselves to be different when they really are not. Nor is there any way to ensure that identities will *ever* reliably match up with objective reality. To have an identity is to tell a story about who one is and how one got that way, and these stories are always incomplete in all sorts of ways. Simply condensing the entire story of one's life down into something comprehensible requires substantial simplification, and the reinterpretation of many events to make them consistent with the central narrative. This incompleteness allows for considerable flexibility in identities over time, as different elements take on a changed salience with new circumstances, but identities nonetheless have strongly path-dependent effects – what I think about myself now will shape how I behave in the future, and how I will interpret events that happen to me. Moreover, identities tend to call attention to whatever makes a person different from most others (with close friends and family often excepted), which naturally minimizes the apparent importance of whatever similarities may exist.

Although cultural identities only form a part of individual identities, they are collective in ways that individual identities need not be, and for that reason are highly responsive to expectations about what others believe and desire. If I identify myself as a member of a group, but hold an opinion about that group's character that is much different from that of most others, I find myself in a bind – either I must no longer see myself as a group member, or I must reshape my opinion of the group's character. In such cases, some people will simply abandon their feelings of group membership, particularly if another group of the relevant type is readily at hand.[10] But in other cases, perhaps many more, individuals

[10] For example, many academics who regard themselves as extremely cosmopolitan have just transferred their loyalty to some vision of the international professorate, which is hardly coterminous with humankind as a whole.

will find ways to reshape their understanding of the group's character so they can continue to fit in. Thus identities can often have powerful feedback effects on cultural practices themselves – individuals will behave in particular ways because this seems appropriate for 'someone like them', even if they have no additional reasons to behave in this way. Indeed, it is very hard to be sure why people engage in many kinds of practices that are purportedly typical of their cultural group – do they do so for independent reasons (e.g. because they believe it is most conducive to happiness), or simply because they feel they must do so to remain a group member? Substantial parts of cultural life are probably play-acting in this way – but how much, and in regard to what things?

If cultures are always changing, and identities always incomplete and yet nonetheless action-guiding, it is easy to see how cultural identities could over time become seriously out of touch with actual cultural differences between groups. Groups can believe fundamental differences to exist where none actually do, and can see unities where they do not exist. Indeed, it seems likely that most of us frequently imagine our purported forebears in ways they would not have seen themselves, imputing to them values and beliefs that are ours rather than theirs. These changes happen even if we try to hold carefully to their historical legacies. In fact, this kind of disjunction may be *most* acute in such circumstances – can we really maintain continuity with historical figures who lived with very different kinds of worlds? What simplifications are necessary to even try?[11] Most of us would like to 'really' be whatever it is that we identify ourselves as – but what can that possibly mean, and how would we ever know if we have achieved our goal?

Moreover, the kinds of identities that people have are never negotiated by all those involved from a position of relatively equal influence. Those with ready access to print, radio, and television have far more opportunity to reshape identities than do those who lack such resources.[12] When an ordinary person tries to change a collective identity, he or she has to proceed in a care-ful and eclectic fashion, testing these ideas out on others to see how they react. Those with access to mass media, on the other hand, can propose self-conceptions to many

[11] For a serious attempt to do exactly this that probably does not succeed in its goals, *see* Taiaiake Alfred, *Peace, Power, Righteousness* (New York: Oxford University Press, 1999).

[12] *See*, for example, Benedict Anderson, *Imagined Communities* (New York: Verso, 1991).

people at once, and while they cannot force others to accept them, they are nonetheless very hard to argue and negotiate with. (We need not assume that such people are generally motivated to take advantage of others, of course – their outsized influence remains whatever their motivations may be.) Perhaps most strangely, the one-sided nature of mass media means that collective identities can change even if very few people are persuaded that these changes are beneficial. Those who hear an argument often enough in public may come to believe that others accept it, and simply play along to avoid personal conflict – expectations of consensus can become *de facto* consensus. There are limits, of course – cultural identities can rarely be fully reversed or inverted – but there is nonetheless substantial room for change over time even if no one ever actually intended this or foresaw what the change might consist in.

Recognition and Authenticity

Given the myriad vicissitudes of cultural identity, one can legitimately ask, as many critics of cultural rights do: why are particular self-understandings deserving of political protection? After all, designing customized legal protections is never a simple matter. It usually involves economic costs and unstable political bargains, while introducing fractures and passions into political life that many would prefer to avoid (particularly when their own group is not involved). Moreover, it may be very hard to construct specialized protections that really satisfy the aspirations of those who demand them, since these aspirations may be unrealistic, excessively open-ended, or inconsistent with treating others fairly. If cultural practices are always changing and identities often do not reflect real differences anyway, wouldn't we be better off simply ignoring claims for specialized political protections in favor of one law for everyone, while focusing our energy on guaranteeing everyone an equal chance to shape that law?[13]

Perhaps more worrisomely, any regime of cultural rights we choose will *itself* change the kinds of cultural practices and identities that exist in the world. As I noted above, those with public stature or access to

[13] *See*, for example, Jeremy Waldron, 'Minority Cultures and the Cosmopolitan Alternative', in Will Kymlicka (ed.), *The Rights of Minority Cultures* (New York: Oxford University Press, 1995).

mass media have powerful levers through which to influence identities, and this becomes particularly troubling if these people have motivations to reshape identities in particular directions – it is surely no accident that many identities take more strident forms when the potential for profit is involved.[14] Specialized protections themselves can offer substantial prizes for individuals who can brand themselves as strong leaders of the group – new regional legislatures or bureaucracies create jobs and attention for hopeful politicians, and new sources of funding or new control over old sources. Offering these sorts of opportunities thus provides substantial dangers of reshaping identities in problematic (and potentially explosive) directions.

Nor do the difficulties with a regime of cultural rights stop there. Even when group leaders are not motivated by self-interest, and even when groups really do start off from a position of strong cultural difference, it is inevitable that any political protections offered will change the group's character over time. In some cases, such protections can foster a kind of artificial cultural stasis.[15] All groups change all the time in complicated ways, but specialized cultural protections can sometimes freeze certain aspects of these processes. While no set of specialized protections can prevent change altogether, it can sharply limit the *directions* available for potential change, particularly if it requires groups to maintain continuity with past traditions if they are to retain their status.[16] If groups have traditionally held land collectively, for example, states may create particularized legal frameworks for such collective ownership, which will then freeze the group into this way of life until the law can be changed. And demanding a change in the law would be dangerous for obvious reasons – if the 'group' is changing fundamentally in its beliefs, won't it lose its claims to cultural distinctiveness, and therefore to any specialized protections whatsoever?

---

[14] This need not be conceptualized as simple and intentional greed. Most of us are very adept at convincing ourselves that we are pursuing morally admirable goals when our self-interest is deeply tied up in a particular decision. (I do not mean to suggest that all cultural identities and moral judgments are dictated by self-interest, only that this is a recurrent tendency in all of us.)

[15] *See*, for example, the worries raised in Russell Hardin, 'Group Boundaries, Individual Barriers', in David Miller and Sohail H. Hashmi (eds.), *Boundaries and Justice: Diverse Ethical Perspectives* (Princeton: Princeton University Press, 2001).

[16] *See*, for example, Elizabeth A. Povinelli, *The Cunning of Recognition* (Durham: Duke University Press, 2002).

Indeed, most arguments for cultural rights seem to proceed as if the cultural distance between groups were more or less fixed.[17] (Particular cultural practices need not remain fixed – it seems to be relative distance that matters.) If the Pintupi cease to burn the vehicles of dead persons and begin to sell them like other Australians, and begin to converge with the mainstream in many other regards as well, at some point specialized protections no longer seem appropriate. There are thus motivations for the Pintupi to play up their degree of difference so that these protections are not lost, and to ensure that new members of the community see the value of being different from others. In such communities, changes to meet altered circumstances may be especially difficult – not only must the community decide how to reconcile new beliefs with old, but they must also be careful to keep sufficiently distant from the mainstream to maintain any sort of separate status. Insofar as groups really are different, the tendency of protections based on culture may be to keep them that way, but sometimes at a very high cost.

Seeking to construct protections that are appropriate for a group's 'real' character, then, can easily slide into questions about cultural 'authenticity' for which there are rarely clear answers. Are the Pintupi still 'authentically' different if state laws help to keep them that way? In fact, the example outlined above is more ambiguous than I suggested when presenting it. The pickup truck in question had not, strictly speaking, been the property of the recently deceased, although it was burned as if it were. The truck had actually been provided by the Australian government, to help the re-establishment of Aboriginal communities in traditional locations (the 'outstation' policy). According to Myers,

> For historical reasons, Pintupi men associate the founding of past outstation communities with the granting of four-wheel drive Toyotas by the Department of Aboriginal Affairs or the Aboriginal Benefits Trust Fund. As a result of this association, it appears, they believe that a community's autonomy will be recognized in the granting of such a vehicle. Men often say that they are the 'boss' of an outstation at such and such a place, but they are waiting to go there because the government has not yet given them their Toyota. Possibly, the attraction of gaining control over such a vehicle is the very reason that people have been eager to establish outstations.[18]

---

[17] *See*, for example, the critiques in Waldron, 'Minority Cultures'.
[18] Myers, 'Burning the Truck', p. 25.

How should we react to these new facts? Remember that the Pintupi community actually did burn the truck in question, which few of us would even consider. This government policy does not automatically make them culturally identical to other Australians. But does it render them in some sense less 'authentic', and their cultural practices therefore less worthy of protection? Or is this policy simply an appropriate way of aiding Pintupi communities to achieve goals that they hold for independent reasons, a policy of particular importance given the historical mistreatment most Aboriginal groups have received from the Australian state?

It seems wildly presumptuous to say that *all* claims of cultural difference are necessarily unjustified and inaccurate. But it is also clear that evaluating particular cases accurately is very difficult, especially given our own cultural identities and interests, which undoubtedly provide us with dubious reasons for judging one way or the other. Theories of self-determination purport to provide an answer to the question of who should make such judgments – the group itself – but these theories seem less than overwhelming when there are reasons to distrust virtually all sides of the debate. Who is well placed to decide whether groups are actually different in the right kind of ways? This is far from clear. In these circumstances of ambiguity, what should states ultimately do about cultural rights?

Dealing with Ambiguity

The obvious default solution is to do away with specialized protections for minority cultures altogether. Thus one might argue that states are better off to 'get out of the culture business', and to let changes in culture and identity take their course without political interference.[19] We should not take this as a cynical or bigoted view – it may be simply a well-intentioned response to the problems noted above. If most 'groups' demanding particularized rights are likely to be less than 'authentic', we may be likely to get it right more often if we simply do nothing, particularly if specialized protections will often turn out to be badly constructed and therefore ineffective or counterproductive. This might be regarded as a principle of 'do no harm': if cultural

[19] Waldron, 'Minority Cultures'; cf. Barry, *Culture and Equality*.

protections are very difficult to get right, it may be best for states to simply stay out entirely.

The problem, of course, is that entirely ignoring real cultural difference where it exists can have harsh consequences.[20] When cultural practices really are different, applying laws tailored for different beliefs and preferences is not really a form of 'staying out' – it is a form of intervention, and often a very coercive one. As Will Kymlicka notes, state laws are never merely neutral.[21] In practice, they are always shaped by particularistic cultural expectations, and in many cases these create real disjunctions with the values of other cultures. (See, for example, Myers's discussion of Pintupi views on land ownership, which are radically complex. Inheritance for the Pintupi has traditionally depended upon *where* one was born, rather than to whom, and is unfamiliar in a variety of other ways as well).[22] While it may ultimately prove necessary on balance for states to avoid specialized cultural protections, some benign statement that states should 'get out of the culture business' probably cannot describe reality. Creating perfectly neutral policies for everyone within a state that includes minority cultures is never a real option in our world. If we ultimately believe that states should never offer customized protections for minority groups, we should not pretend to be thereby exercising perfect neutrality – we should admit that we are making a set of tradeoffs with uncertain costs and benefits.

Throughout the remainder of this essay, I want to outline an alternative way for states to offer customized cultural protections, one that substantially reduces the centrality of questions about authenticity. This alternative is for states to adopt a rule of thumb that treats the claims of relatively large minority groups merely as matters of political expediency, while treating the claims of small groups as matters of justice. Large, politically organized groups (e.g. Quebecois nationalists) will virtually always demand specialized protections – indeed, we would not recognize them as 'groups' if they did not – and such groups must generally be pacified if democratic governance is to continue. On the rule I am proposing, state leaders should regard this continuance of stable democratic governance as their primary concern where large minorities are concerned – they need not feel morally bound to honor their

[20] *See* e.g. Folds, *Crossed Purposes*.
[21] Kymlicka, *Multicultural Citizenship*.
[22] Myers, 'Burning the Truck', pp. 26-35; Myers, *Pintupi Country*, ch. 5.

claims, but should treat them like any other powerful interest group: negotiating, bribing, threatening, and seeking their assistance whenever appropriate. Only for small groups should they feel morally bound to behave otherwise.

Large groups such as the Quebecois may, in fact, be as 'authentic' as much smaller groups; the difficulties of recognizing the real cultural difference remain in either case. But large groups have far more opportunity to protect themselves in democratic political life, and their members are far less vulnerable to attacks on their individual self-respect. If members of a large group occasionally have their identities dismissed as a mere political construction, they have many others from whom to find solace. Larger cultures are less vulnerable to political mistreatment for similar reasons. Even if Quebecois were (counterfactually) unable to use French in public business or to teach it to their children in schools, French would have little danger of immediate disappearance. Those who value French would continue to use it in many circumstances, including publishing books and newspapers in the language. (Indeed, they would have a deep well of cultural materials from France itself always available for ready consumption, even if neither the idioms nor values are quite the same.) Relatively large minority identities, then, are generally much less immediately endangered than those of much smaller groups. There is thus less need for states to think carefully about what sort of protections they deserve – in general, they will succeed in getting what they need, and it will often be no immediate moral crisis if they do not.

For very small cultural minorities, on the other hand, the absence of customized political protections can have destructive effects far more quickly. If one shares a set of cultural practices with 5 million people, these practices are on substantially firmer footing than they may be if one shares these practices with 50,000, 5,000, or 500.[23] Such groups remain difficult to recognize as authentic, of course, but it nonetheless seems more important for states, state leaders, and democratic citizens to have greater moral concern in such cases. Very small groups of this type generally have relatively few resources for protecting themselves in

[23] How should we judge smallness? Since the relevant concern here is the ability to defend oneself in democratic politics, smallness seems to depend in part on the total population of the country involved, but absolute numbers also seem to make a difference for things like the production of cultural artifacts or the maintenance of a language.

democratic politics (unless they are unusually wealthy), and will often have sharp difficulties in creating and maintaining cultural artifacts. In the absence of some system of cultural rights, groups like the Pintupi can easily be squeezed into extreme poverty and despair by a political system that is mostly deaf to their needs. Not all of the small groups that receive protections will really deserve them, of course – but some will, and seem unlikely to receive them otherwise.

My recommended strategy, then, is for states to minimize questions of authenticity whenever possible, and to focus instead on the relative *size* and *vulnerability* of groups that self-identify as potential candidates for specialized protections.[24] (Perhaps the best measure of vulnerability is relative poverty.) States should behave as if small, relatively defenseless groups generally deserve specialized political protections, while assuming larger groups deserve such protections only if they are able to secure them through democratic politics.[25] The losses entailed in this strategy are easy to recognize: large groups will have to take their democratic chances, even if they are authentically different, while many small groups that are not authentically different will have increased opportunities for exploitation of state laws. The gains are also clear: small groups that actually are authentically different will have better chances of receiving the kinds of protections they need.

Of course, part of our judgment about the relative costs and benefits of this strategy depends on what sort of protections are to be offered. I want to argue that states should generally try to provide small groups with the kinds of protections they claim to need, at least within limits. If small cultural groups claim to need rights to self-government, states should take their claims seriously and seek to design an appropriate local regime. If they claim to need exemptions from certain types of laws, states should seek ways to balance these needs against other public goals. If they claim a need to teach their own language in public schools, states should help them to do so, while ensuring that their children will also be tolerably competent in the language of the majority culture and the basic facts of human life and skills necessary to survive outside of the group. (Groups should not be allowed to fully disable

[24] In trying to largely circumvent questions of authenticity, the argument I am making here has some affinities with that in Jacob T. Levy, *The Multiculturalism of Fear* (New York: Oxford University Press, 2000).

[25] Allowing such protections may also be necessary for groups seeking them through violence, but this involves a radically different set of considerations than can be addressed here.

their young members from leaving, but must balance their own survival against the possible future choices of their children.)[26] Some of the demands of such groups seem certain to make us uncomfortable, since they will seem either excessive or undemocratic, but states will probably receive the best overall results if they are prepared to put up with at least some discomfort in tolerating cultural practices.[27]

The obvious objection is that this policy allows far too much room for mischief, for far too little gain. If the minority cultures involved are very small, opponents of cultural rights would argue, they are not likely to survive anyway, and so we should simply help them to integrate into the mainstream despite their wishes.[28] Moreover, they might object that this policy naturally invites abuse, since ethnic entrepreneurs may find it easier to recruit a small group to their cause than a large one – indeed, they may find it possible to invent such groups more or less from scratch. A broad spectrum of opportunists, the objection goes, will fool the state into funding their own petty little fiefdom, and political leaders will soft-headedly go about accepting whatever concocted identity each provides.[29] Even if a few culturally different groups actually end up in the mix, it will not have been worth the costs and trouble once all things are considered.

None of these are trivial concerns, and some opponents of cultural rights would doubtless take them as decisive. Yet I think it is easy to overstate the potential for mischief by cultural entrepreneurs, especially where small groups are concerned. At one level, it is less easy for opportunists to create cultural identities out of nothing than opponents of cultural rights sometimes pretend – the path-dependent character of identities means that existing identities can rarely be entirely reshaped by a few choice words. Few of us are really eager to identify ourselves as part of an endangered minority if we do not already have at least some reasons for doing so. Moreover, many forms of customized cultural rights are not terribly attractive as opportunities to exercise power or gain wealth. Consider an American

---

[26] Hardin, 'Group Boundaries'.

[27] *See*, for example, the kinds of considerations outlined in Levy, *Multiculturalism of Fear*, pp. 51-62.

[28] Hardin, 'Group Boundaries'; Allen Buchanan, *Secession* (Boulder: Westview Press, 1991), pp. 54-55.

[29] Brian Barry characterizes Iris Marion Young's arguments for cultural recognition with the words of the Dodo from *Alice in Wonderland*: 'Everybody has won, and *all* must have prizes.' Barry, *Culture and Equality*, p. 95.

Indian reservation in the United States before the growth of legalized gambling. Most reservations are quite small, usually with less than 10,000 residents and often with far fewer.[30] There is not really a great deal of glory associated with governing such a territory. One could easily get the same experience running for office in a small municipality, without all the fuss of trying to create new identities first. Or consider education in one's 'ancestral language' – why would anyone want such a thing, if they did not already identify that language as somehow important to them? (Will one become wealthy or powerful or famous by doing this?) Not all minority groups are this small, of course, but the most vulnerable are, and those are the ones I have argued we should worry most about protecting. Do we really expect profit- or glory-seeking individuals to be suddenly drawn into a burgeoning field of minority-identification, if this is all they have to gain? Certainly, the Pintupi were receiving a new Toyota pickup truck from the Australian government for opening an outstation – but how many Australians would actually identify themselves as Aboriginal and move into the deep outback merely for this reason? I suspect very few.

In general, then, fears of materialistic and political motives can be easily overstated where small groups are involved, so long as the protections involved do not confer drastic economic advantages. (This is less true as groups become progressively larger, because opportunities for power and profiteering increase as well.) Worries about the widespread misuse of cultural rights are thus most relevant when recognition as a minority group carries with it immediate and tangible economic benefits that are excluded to most citizens. The most decisive solution is simply not to include within the package of cultural rights any legal protections that might confer such advantages – yet these advantages may sometimes be very helpful in protecting cultures, particularly if those involved are already relatively poor, as the most vulnerable usually are. Extra resources mean extra opportunities to get out of poverty, extra chances to create cultural artifacts, extra economic chances for individuals to find a job within their 'home' culture, and so on. Perhaps, then, we should be willing to

---

[30] For a somewhat dated but very accessible overview, *see* Klaus Frantz, *Indian Reservations in the United States* (Chicago: University of Chicago Press, 1999). The primary Navajo reservation is the obvious exception here, with over 175,000 Indian residents.

tolerate somewhat higher dangers of exploitation by such groups – but how much?

Something like these kinds of unusual advantages currently characterizes the situation of American Indian tribes in the United States. In the remainder of this essay, I want to look briefly at the standards governing Indian rights to operate gambling facilities, and to outline the legal standards used in considering which groups are eligible for recognition as Indian tribes in the first place. As will be seen, existing law does raise some worries about opportunism, but these may be worth the costs, and at any rate could be removed without destroying most existing protections. The more troubling questions arise when we begin to consider the question of why Indians should have these kinds of rights while other potential cultural groups do not. As will be seen, the kind of balances that have been made remain imperfect ones, and depend in many ways on the particular history of the United States.

Gaming, Recognition, and Self-Determination

United States law since the 1980s[31] has allowed Federally-recognized Indian tribes to operate profit-oriented gambling facilities on their reservation lands[32] if gambling is permitted for any purposes by the particular state in which they live.[33] All states but two (Utah and Hawaii) permit at least some form of gambling,[34] often for limited purposes such as charitable fund-raisers, and Indian tribes have the right to offer to Indians and non-Indians alike whatever classes of games are permitted by the state in this way.[35] In many cases, tribes have negotiated pacts

[31] The current legal framework went into effect in 1988, with the passage of the Indian Gaming Regulatory Act (IGRA), but many tribes had opened bingo halls under permissive judicial rulings over the preceding decade. The IGRA itself was sparked by a Supreme Court decision in favor of tribal gaming rights, *California v. Cabazon Band of Mission Indians*, 480 U.S. 202 (1987).

[32] Tribes can operate gambling facilities on reservations or other lands held in trust by the Federal government, or on other lands with the agreement of the state itself.

[33] 25 U.S.C. § 2701-2721, in Robert N. Clinton, Carole E. Greenberg and Rebecca Tsosie, *American Indian Law* (Newark: LexisNexis, 2004), pp. 422-51.

[34] Sixteen of the states that allow gambling do not have Federally-recognized Indian tribes within their borders, however, so the distribution of Indian gambling is more restricted than this indicates.

[35] Importantly, the stakes for charitable and other forms of gambling allowed to most state citizens are often sharply limited; Indian tribes are under no legal obligation to limit their games to similarly small dollar amounts, once the game has been allowed at all.

with states (under Federal legislation) allowing for so-called 'Class III' gambling facilities so that they can operate casino-style games including slot machines and blackjack.[36] Indian reservations thus have a substantial competitive advantage in this regard: they have rights to operate games that the surrounding state generally allows non-Indians to operate only on a sharply limited basis, and for that reason are able to draw non-Indians from surrounding areas into their gaming facilities.

Many tribes (about 200, of 562 total) have attempted to take advantage of this opportunity, with uneven effects.[37] Those tribes with territories closest to urban areas or otherwise easily accessible to large populations have been able to profit most effectively, while those that are far from urban areas have been less able to take advantage. (Many tribes have not even tried to open casinos because of their isolated location.[38] Others, including the populous Navajo Nation, are opposed to gambling on moral grounds.) Perhaps unsurprisingly, those tribes that are closest to urban areas often seem to have an ambiguous cultural character from being surrounded by non-Indians, while more rural tribes tend to be poorer and often appear more in touch with historical ways of life. This has sometimes led to objections that gambling does nothing to help 'real' Indians, while providing unjustified opportunities to those groups that are no longer authentically different from other Americans.[39]

While there is much more that could be said about specific aspects of the law governing Indian gambling, I want to call attention instead to the recent legal *reconstitution* of several tribes, and the standards used by the Bureau of Indian Affairs (BIA) in this process. In fact, two of the country's most successful tribal casinos are operated by groups that were not Federally recognized until recently, one until the 1980s and the other since the early 1990s.[40] Several other groups have received

---

[36] For an overview of the history of gaming law, *see* Dale W. Mason, *Indian Gaming* (Norman: University of Oklahoma Press, 2000).

[37] Charles Wilkinson, *Blood Struggle* (New York: W. W. Norton, 2005), p. 336.

[38] Wilkinson, *Blood Struggle*, p. 337. Indeed, about 230 Federally-recognized tribal groups (of 560) are in Alaska, where isolation makes commercial gambling an option for very few, and some others within the lower 48 states are similarly isolated.

[39] *See*, for example, the examples in Renee Ann Cramer, *Cash, Color, and Colonialism* (Norman: University of Oklahoma Press, 2005).

[40] The Mashuntucket Pequots were recognized in 1983, while the Mohegan Tribe of Connecticut was Federally recognized in 1994. Both tribes have become quite successful, the Pequots strikingly so; *see*, for example, the description of their gaming

Federal recognition in the same period, and a far larger number (over 250) have either submitted petitions for future recognition or have voiced a desire to do so.[41] Since petitions for recognition generally take a substantial time to assemble, present, and be approved or rejected, it is probably a mistake to accuse past petitioners of merely seeking gambling profits,[42] but the potential for these profits may nonetheless have troublesome effects on both ongoing and future bids for Federal recognition.

According to BIA regulations, tribes seeking recognition must meet seven criteria.[43] Four of them are relevant here. (The remainder are limited technical issues).[44] First, tribes must demonstrate that they have been identified by non-members (e.g. state governments, anthropologists, newspapers) as an 'Indian tribe' on a 'substantially continuous' basis over the past century. Second, they must show that they are in fact a 'distinct community' by demonstrating a collective character using other types of evidence (e.g. rates of intermarriage, ways of holding property). Third, the group must demonstrate that it now has and has traditionally had at least some internal organizing structures (e.g. it has acknowledged leaders or can coordinate reliable collective action).

---

facilities in Cramer, *Cash*, pp. 75-77. The Pequots actually did not go through the process outlined here. They were instead recognized by an act of Congress, but the standards governing Congressional recognition are far more amorphous than the bureaucratic standards outlined by the Bureau of Indian Affairs (BIA), and for that reason I have not raised this complicating issue within the body of the essay. Indeed, the Pequots were recognized despite the opposition of the BIA, which did not believe the tribe could meet its standards for recognition; *see* Cramer, *Cash*, pp. 44-45.

[41] Cramer, *Cash*, pp. xii, 40-43.

[42] Cramer (*Cash*, pp. 78-81) notes that the Mashuntucket Pequots were trying to build tribal enterprises and seeking Federal recognition considerably before gambling had even emerged as an option, although their tribal chairman Skip Hayward became an immediate advocate once he learned that another tribe had successfully set up bingo facilities. Although the Mohegans received Federal recognition only in 1994, they began the process in the late 1970s, and have generally had far fewer questions raised about their motivations in this regard. Cramer (*Cash*, p. 103) notes that 'None of the tribes that have been recognized since 1978 were post-[IGRA] petitioners'.

[43] 25 C.F.R. § 83.8, in Clinton, Greenberg and Tsosie, *American Indian Law*, pp. 816-33. I have rearranged the original (a) through (g) listing of the criteria here for reasons of exposition, although I fear this will be exasperating to anyone who already knows the relevant law.

[44] The remaining three criteria are that: (a) the group must provide evidence of its membership criteria and governing system; (b) most of the group's members must not be already enrolled in some other tribe; and (c) the tribe must not have been historically 'terminated' as a legal entity by the Federal government, as many tribes were in the 1950s.

Fourth, its members must demonstrate genealogical descent from a recognizably Indian population.

What should we think of these standards? The first three seem relatively easy to defend as plausible criteria for deciding which groups are entitled to self-government rights. The first of them, substantial identification by non-members, raises some concerns because it renders recognition of the group subject to judgments about its character by outsiders, but a broad variety of sources are accepted as evidence here, including newspapers, anthropologists, and (perhaps most importantly) recognition by other Indian tribes. It would be hard to imagine a substantial cultural identity that outsiders had never noticed, so this criterion is probably unobjectionable despite its initial appearance. The second requirement, that tribes demonstrate that they are a 'distinctive community' using other sorts of evidence, seems to pass muster with even less concern, particularly since a broad variety of evidence is acceptable here, including information about rates of marriage within the group or with other Indian groups, shared labor or economic activities, shared religious activities, unique cultural patterns, and (perhaps surprisingly) evidence of discrimination by non-Indians. It is hard to imagine a set of people considering themselves a group who could not provide evidence for at least some intensive interactions in this way. The third requirement, that tribes demonstrate evidence of internal organizing structures, is probably also necessary and defensible – could we imagine a system of cultural rights for a group that did not see itself as politically united for any purposes whatsoever?

The basic intent of all three standards is to ensure that only groups with a long history as collectives are able to receive recognition, but notice that none of the three focus centrally on any substantive notion of cultural authenticity. Evidence of cultural difference is relevant for both external and internal judgments about 'groupness', but other kinds of information (e.g. collective activities) are accepted as well, and there is no real requirement that tribes continue to behave in traditional ways or that they outline the full range of ways in which they believe themselves to be culturally different. Groups that can show historical continuity over time are *prima facie* regarded as sufficiently authentic for legal purposes, regardless of what may have really held them together. What matters is not the character of the group today so

[45] *See*, for example, the concerns raised in Cramer, *Cash*, pp. 61-62.

much as its history *as* a group. These kinds of historical connections seem particularly important when recognition may potentially bring with it rights to set up gambling operations in the future – at a minimum, the kind of evidence required prevents groups from simply being invented on the spot. While a very close look at these standards would undoubtedly reveal areas for improvement,[45] these first three standards seem a plausible way of limiting the potential for abuse while keeping debates about contemporary cultural authenticity mostly minimized.

The final criterion listed above, however, is far more problematic – this is that tribes must demonstrate biological descent from a population historically recognized as Indian. To put the matter bluntly, it is hard to see why mere genealogy should count. Would the group's character be less authentic if, over the span of a hundred years, they had adopted a majority of members with no biological relationship but who accepted the group's values entirely? It is hard to see how mere biological descent can either destroy or create cultural difference. The obvious reason for the inclusion of this criterion is that Indian tribes are virtually the only group in the United States allowed an extensive set of cultural rights, and because 'Indian' remains a substantially racial category.[46] But there is no obvious moral reason why 'groupness' and cultural protection should be regarded as inherited in this way, and such a focus on race is troubling on many grounds.

There are two likely justifications for limiting the groups eligible for cultural rights in this way, which work best in tandem. The first is that American Indians have often been mistreated specifically because of their race, so that 'extra' protections in this instance are a form of reparative justice, to remediate insofar as possible the continuing effects of this history. The second, and more clearly important for this essay, is that cultural rights must have *some* sort of limits to prevent an explosion of groups seeking to profiteer, and that recognizing those eligible by descent is one legally determinate way of doing this. Combined, these two justifications seem relatively strong: cultural protections must be limited somehow, so why not limit them to

[46] Cramer (*Cash*), who carefully outlines the kind of racialized discourses surrounding the process of recognition in the states of Alabama and Connecticut, is herself remarkably evasive about who an 'Indian' might be. She seems to believe that Indian is neither a racial nor cultural category, but it is hard to determine what she might put in the place of these.

groups whose members can point to the continuing effects of past mistreatment?

Yet despite appearances, these two justifications cannot limit special protections to American Indians alone. Presumably the same criterion of past mistreatment would apply to African-Americans, and it does not seem implausible to suggest that unique cultural groupings have emerged among African-American communities in some areas – why wouldn't these groups be entitled similar rights? One might suggest, of course, that American Indians have unique inheritance rights to cultural protections stemming from their first occupancy in what is now the United States, but it is hard to see why these rights might trump those of African-Americans, whose ancestors were brought here against their will. Even if (following Will Kymlicka) we believe that distinctive groups created by recent immigrants should not be eligible for an extensive set of group rights,[47] this kind of argument clearly will not work for most black communities, nor will it work for those Latino communities in the American Southwest whose tenure predates the authority of the United States.[48] Indeed, if what really matters is cultural difference, then there are may be reasons to allow customized rights even to groups historically formed through voluntary immigration, so long as these groups are relatively small, have an extended history in the United States, and can meet the same kind of criteria that Indian tribes must meet (substantial evidence of 'groupness' over an extended period of time, such as the last century). The most likely candidates in this regard would probably be communities that initially formed for religious reasons and communities that have long been either geographically, economically, or socially isolated.[49]

But wouldn't permitting cultural rights to non-Indians simply open the floodgates to innumerable groups that will use cultural difference as a mask for profiteering, particularly in the era of legalized gambling? Not necessarily. The surest way to avoid this problem would be simply to sever cultural protection from concerns about poverty – we could,

---

[47] Kymlicka, *Multicultural Citizenship*.

[48] Considerations of population size, however, may be sufficient to disqualify some of these claimants, depending on how inclusive they attempted to be.

[49] Ongoing religious communities like those of the Amish make religious rather than cultural claims for the rights they pursue, and for that reason raise additional complexities that cannot be addressed here.

for example, allow customized profit-making activities like gambling only to groups that can demonstrate relative poverty, or perhaps even allow them to the poor in general, regardless of whether they have cultural claims or not. Thus, for example, we might allow poor communities anywhere to construct gambling operations, and remove the gaming rights of Indian tribes that become relatively wealthy. It would obviously take substantial development to decide exactly how this should be done with the fewest dangers to all involved, but the basic outlines of such a change seem plausible enough.

With this motivation removed, it seems very unlikely that particularized cultural rights would be so profitable as to bring out an unmanageable number of claimants. We could also construct the procedures for cultural recognition for non-Indian groups to be somewhat more challenging, on the theory that Indian groups are more likely to have *started out* from a more extreme position of cultural difference, even if this need not have carried over until the present day. We could make the applications for recognition both more imposing and more useful, for example, by requiring non-Indian groups to outline in great detail the kind of rights they were seeking and the kinds of costs and benefits these might have, both for themselves and nonmembers. In many cases, trying to specify these clearly would reveal to the group that it shared less than it believed, or that a customized regime of cultural rights was not really the appropriate goal for them, and this would be the end of the story. Doubtless a few groups would pursue this option and succeed in being recognized. As with Indian tribes, some would be 'authentically' different, while others would not, but so long as the groups recognized in this way were relatively small (as I have suggested, this matters a great deal), the dangers posed when the wrong kinds of group receive recognition would seem limited.

Context and History

There is, I suspect, something very strange about the idea of non-Indian groups within the United States receiving these kind of cultural rights, and this strangeness is telling in important ways. Throughout this essay, I have tried to outline a strategy by which states can maximize the chance that small and vulnerable cultural minorities will get the protections they need and deserve, while minimizing the dangers and disruptions. It does not follow, however, that the abstract rule of thumb

I have proposed should be simply transferred into state policy without regard to context and history, nor that supporters of cultural rights should focus their energy on lobbying for such changes. History and context always matter, even if we know what goals we would ultimately prefer to achieve.

In the present day, Indian tribes are virtually the only groups in the United States allowed an extensive set of cultural rights, and these rights are entrenched in a broad array of laws up to and including the Constitutional level.[50] Defending cultural rights for Indian nations is thus a defense of existing law, while any expansion of such rights to other groups would require a substantial revision to the status quo, and both state leaders and supporters of cultural rights should take this into account when deciding how to proceed. For states, maintaining a manageable and coherent regime of law is always important, and any changes would need to be carefully fitted to whatever legal structures already exist, including alternative kinds of protections that many other minorities already have. Particular legal regimes can provide different types of incentives toward action or inaction, and all of these have to be weighed up in all their specificity before important changes are made, even if leaders know perfectly well what goals they want to achieve. It may ultimately be that opening up cultural rights to non-Indian groups would require revisions to existing law so massive and untested that the costs and dangers would not be worth the benefits, but this kind of judgment remains very much to be made.

Advocates of cultural rights, on the other hand, will have to be conscious of their relative opportunities for success in such circumstances. This is particularly true since other kinds of groups that might seek recognition have fewer resources to draw on within the cultural identity of the majority. For many non-Indians, quasi-independent Indian nations are seen as somehow necessary to their understanding of the United States, as a kind of continuing link to their mythologized view of American history. The continuing existence of Indian nations is seen as a kind of echo of the Wild West that confirms their view of (white) Americans as people who were boldly able to conquer an immense continent against the resistance of a worthy if savage foe. This kind of

[50] Indian nations are mentioned twice in the Constitution. The first is in regard to taxation (Art. I, sec. 2, cl. 3), and the second is the so-called 'Indian Commerce Clause' (Art. 1, sec. 8, cl. 3): '[The Congress shall have Power] To regulate Commerce with foreign Nations, and among the several States, and with the Indian Tribes.'

mythologizing of Indian nations is an extremely double-edged sword, but it nonetheless opens up a space for cultural rights that might not exist for other groups (such as African-American communities) that might claim to be culturally different.[51] Supporters of cultural rights thus have reasons to fear that advocating such rights for additional groups might undermine the protections Indian tribes now have rather than opening up similar opportunities for others, and for that reason should proceed with care and attention to the cultural identities of those on all sides of these questions.

Each country is different in the kind of resources that groups may have to draw upon in pursuing cultural rights, and there is probably no way around that. The Pintupi community in Australia, discussed earlier in this essay, faces a different set of challenges in gaining and maintaining cultural rights than do indigenous groups in New Zealand, or Canada, or Brazil, and different strategies will have different kinds of dangers and benefits in each country. The rule of thumb I have tried to outline here suggests that state policies will generally fare best if they treat the claims of small, vulnerable groups as matters of justice, while treating those of larger groups as matters of political expediency, but it does not tell us how best to ensure that states follow this principle, nor how it should be instantiated within the particular political context of each country. As with any important political or moral question, much work remains to be done in specific contexts in order to determine how best to achieve these broad goals. I hope I have shown here that we can at least reduce this work somewhat by bracketing questions about authenticity for which there are rarely clear answers.

[51] This does not mean that Americans should not be confronted with the unpleasant historical facts of how the United States has treated Indians, but does suggest that Indians probably have a different set of resources in this regard than do other groups whose history is also misremembered. See *also* Burke A. Hendrix, 'Memory in Native American Land Claims', *Political Theory* 33 (2005), pp. 763–85.

MOTIVATING COSMOPOLITANISM? A SKEPTICAL VIEW*

Patti Tamara Lenard

We are clearly not cosmopolitans, if by 'cosmopolitan' we mean that we are willing to prioritize equally the needs of those near us and those far from us. It may be that – as survey research sometimes tells us – a certain subset of the educated elite believe they owe duties across national borders, and quite stringent duties at that. As a matter of fact, however, most of us regularly prioritize the needs of our friends and family, of our neighbors, of our co-nationals, and many others besides, in our daily lives. As Thomas Pogge observes in frustration, we seem to be 'quite tolerant of the persistence of massive and severe poverty abroad even though it would not cost us much to reduce such poverty dramatically'.[1] It is not clear that this is a moral failing, however; rather, there may be good, moral reasons to prefer and protect (rather than to repeal and rescind) our tendency towards moral partiality, or so I shall argue.

I would not, however, like to deny that cosmopolitanism is a tremendously attractive ideal: it puts forward a political and ethical perspective that emphasizes the obligations we have to individuals qua individuals, and argues for ignoring national boundaries in determining just behavior towards others. But it should, it seems to me, worry us that cosmopolitanism remains far from finding itself widely accepted (from a moral perspective) or implemented (from an institutional perspective); instead, there are many philosophers and social theorists who remain deeply skeptical about the plausibility, feasibility, and, indeed, the moral status of cosmopolitan premises and institutional proposals. In my view, the main struggle that cosmopolitanism has yet to face squarely has to do with *motivation*, and this is the subject of

* I owe thanks to many people for their helpful comments and suggestions, including: Garrett Wallace Brown, Michael Frazer, Jacob J. Krich, Seth P. Lazar, David Miller, Joseph Schwartz, Will Smith, Zofia Stemplowska, Daniel Weinstock, Lea Ypi, the Nuffield Political Theory Workshop, my co-panelists and the friendly audience at the panel 'Global Justice', American Political Science Association Annual Conference 2007, and an anonymous reviewer for this journal.

[1] Thomas Pogge, 'Moral Universalism and Global Economic Justice', *Politics, Philosophy and Economics* 1.1 (2002), p. 30.

this paper. Why, in other words, should we be motivated to carry out the category of duties we might call 'cosmopolitan'? How will we sustain an ongoing, moral commitment to the global institutions that will be charged with carrying out these duties? Cosmopolitanism, I argue, has yet to wrestle with the motivational challenges it faces: any good moral theory must be one that well-meaning people can and will be motivated to adopt, and cosmopolitanism has yet to fashion an account of itself to which individuals can and will commit. I argue, further, that cosmopolitan efforts to motivate the duties we have towards others rely, often implicitly, on insights best captured by the liberal nationalist thesis, that is, the thesis that national communities are the best vehicles, morally speaking, through which individuals can carry out their obligations to others.

The paper is organized as follows. In the first section of the paper, I outline in brief and broad strokes the main tenets of nationalism and cosmopolitanism, as well as the tensions between them. In the course of this discussion, I illustrate a recent trend in cosmopolitan writings that proffers evidence of my claim that cosmopolitanism relies on the motivational resources generated by nationalism. I then turn to an evaluation of the way that cosmopolitanism attempts to generate moral motivation. Some cosmopolitans suggest that the principles of cosmopolitanism are themselves sufficient to motivate compliance with them. I suggest that this argument is flawed, for precisely the reasons that motivate this paper (i.e., we are cosmopolitan neither in our attitudes nor our behaviors towards others). Other cosmopolitans suggest that the solidarity we share as humans is thick enough to generate a commitment to carrying out duties towards *all* others. This argument relies, I shall suggest, on insights derived from – and presently best theorized from within – nationalist theory. I then consider and reject two objections to the view I outline: that I confuse cosmopolitan's plausibility as a moral position with its feasibility and that I am failing to heed an emergent cosmopolitanism evident in the global environment today. I conclude by observing that, until such time as cosmopolitans are able to offer a genuinely persuasive account of moral motivation, an account that will induce commitment by ordinary people, the nationalist thesis remains compelling from the motivational perspective.

Tensions between Cosmopolitanism and Nationalism

For nationalists or particularists, nations are ethical communities. Co-nationals value their membership in nationally bounded communities, and the moral significance of these boundaries – in particular that co-nationals *value* the relationships they share – generates obligations among co-nationals that they do not owe to other human beings as such.[2] The partiality that nationalists demonstrate towards co-members is both legitimate and morally valuable, and therefore to be encouraged and sustained over time (I elaborate this view in the next section). The ethical ties that derive from our membership in a shared community motivate a loose reciprocity based on relations of trust – the willingness to aid fellow members now, since we trust that, at some point in the future, the aid will be returned. In general terms, co-nationals are willing to make sacrifices on each other's behalf; they are willing to put aside their own interests in the present, in the expectation that others will do the same for them in the future. Of central importance to this argument is the sense that individuals themselves are motivated by the bonds of solidarity they share with co-nationals, bonds that generate special obligations among them. In the nationalist's account, the source of obligations and the motivation for carrying them out overlap: the special obligations to co-nationals, as well as the motivation to carry out these obligations, both derive from the valued relationships among them.

Cosmopolitans, on other hand, reject the claim that national partiality is legitimate and valuable, at least from the perspective of carrying out duties of justice. Rather, they display skepticism towards the central nationalist argument, namely, that nations are ethical communities among which special obligations apply. Instead, cosmopolitan theorists focus on the individual as 'the ultimate unit of moral concern', and therefore focus their attention on the nature and content of obligations that individuals – independently of national or local boundaries and particularities – have to each other as members of a shared humanity, obligations that derive from a concern with protecting the equal rights of *all* individuals.[3]

As I have described it above, cosmopolitans share a moral position centered on a commitment to the equality of individuals. Yet, there is tremendous debate among cosmopolitans concerning the kind of

[2] David Miller, *On Nationality* (Oxford: Oxford University Press, 1995), p. 49; Margaret Moore, 'Cosmopolitanism and Political Communities', *Social Theory and Practice* 32.4 (2006), p. 26; Samuel Scheffler, *Boundaries and Allegiances: Problems of Justice and Responsibility in Liberal Thought* (Oxford: Oxford University Press, 2001).

[3] Kok-Chor Tan, *Justice without Borders: Cosmopolitanism, Nationalism and Patriotism* (Cambridge: Cambridge University Press, 2004), p. 1.

equality that matters, as well as the mechanisms by which we might well carry out this cosmopolitan project. One group of cosmopolitans worries in the main about global distributive inequality, and offers arguments for why this inequality is morally objectionable (i.e., a violation of our commitment to the individual as the primary unit of moral thinking), as well as how we might go about implementing global redistribution of a kind that will meet the demands of justice. For some cosmopolitans, it is our complicity in fostering and sustaining global poverty that generates the moral requirement that we work towards alleviating it.[4] For others, there is no good moral reason to limit our commitment to equality of opportunity – one popular interpretation of the equality that liberal egalitarians defend – to the domestic realm. Rather, we ought to focus on implementing something like global equality of opportunity – in particular, through economic redistribution from wealthy to poor countries – on a global scale.[5] Even among cosmopolitans who are concerned with distributive justice on a global scale, moreover, there is considerable difference among them with respect to their appreciation for national boundaries.[6] However, none believes that national boundaries (or any other less-than-global, group-defined boundary, for that matter) generate special moral requirements of the kind that might legitimately *trump* the obligations that we owe to all of humanity (to be clear, cosmopolitans do not reject the view that some relationships, like family relations, may well entail special obligations). However the argument in favor of protecting equality on a global scale is framed, then, it is clear that one common element among cosmopolitan theorizing is the refusal to allow national boundaries to constrain the considerations in a significant way.

At this point, it is worth observing an objection that cosmopolitans sometimes launch at nationalist accounts, and which goes to the issue of moral motivation at the heart of this paper. This objection is that, in justifying special duties towards co-nationals, nationalists

[4] G.A. Cohen, *If You're an Egalitarian, How Come You're So Rich?* (Oxford: Oxford University Press, 2000); Pogge, 'Moral Universalism and Global Economic Justice'.

[5] Gillian Brock, 'Global Poverty and Desert', *Politics* 26.3 (2006), pp. 168–175; Simon Caney, *Justice Beyond Borders: A Global Political Theory* (Oxford: Oxford University Press, 2005).

[6] For sympathetic accounts of the value of nations within cosmopolitanism, see Kwame Anthony Appiah, *Ethics of Identity* (Princeton, NJ: Princeton University Press, 2005); Tan, *Justice without Borders*. For a less sympathetic view, see Thomas Pogge, *World Poverty and Human Rights* (Cambridge: Cambridge University Press, 2002).

simultaneously deny the existence of any duties at all to those beyond national borders. David Miller describes this objection to his own view, among others: 'cosmopolitans who deny the intrinsic value of nationality may be motivated by the worry that if they recognize special duties to compatriots, these will obliterate duties to humanity at large. If so, their worries are groundless'.[7] Nationalists can and do quite consistently argue for *special* duties towards co-nationals alongside quite stringent *general* duties towards non-nationals.[8] Miller himself suggests that partiality towards co-nationals is limited by the requirement that certain basic rights are protected worldwide.[9] Equally, Samuel Scheffler is clear, even as he defends the special duties that pertain among co-nationals, that 'considerations of distributive fairness [at the global level] serve to limit both the strength and the content of people's special duties'.[10]

The objection, however, captures an important distinction between what is at stake between cosmopolitanism and nationalism. It is worth distinguishing, if only roughly, between thin and thick duties – where thin duties are those that are loosely associated with non-harm and thick duties are the more demanding duties connected to protecting egalitarianism and robust democratic participation. Thin and thick duties are bundled together in most accounts of cosmopolitanism – i.e., cosmopolitans believe that whatever it is that motivates us to abide by the harm principle should equally motivate us to participate in rigorous, global redistributive projects and robust democracy.[11] Nationalists, on the other hand, believe that we should be motivated to abide by the (rather thin) harm principle as a result of our common humanity, but that more rigorous duties – pertaining to egalitarianism and democracy – will require a thicker account of motivation (an account of motivation that they provide, from within their defense of associative

[7] Miller, *On Nationality*, p. 69.

[8] This is not to downplay the distinction between the views, however, since nationalists will demand that in cases of conflict, individuals prioritize the needs of compatriots, whereas cosmopolitans will view this prioritizing as illegitimate and therefore unjust. David Miller warns against the dangers of attempting to reconcile nationalist and cosmopolitan positions in David Miller, 'Debate: Caney's International Distributive Justice: A Response', *Political Studies* 50 (2002), pp. 974–977.

[9] David Miller, *National Responsibility and Global Justice* (Oxford: Oxford University Press, 2007). See chapter 9 especially.

[10] Scheffler, *Boundaries and Allegiances*, p. 109.

[11] This distinction is made in a variety of ways in the literature, most commonly, as the distinction between the duty to aid (i.e., the *thin* duty to aid) and the duty of justice (i.e., the *thick* duty of justice).

duties). They are skeptical, in other words, of the claim that the carrying out of thick duties – especially those connected to distributive justice – can be carried out at the global level without the provision of additional moral, motivational, resources.[12]

In summary, then, cosmopolitans and liberal nationalists are incompatible moral positions along three dimensions: (1) whereas nationalists defend the legitimate moral status of national boundaries, cosmopolitans reject the moral status of boundaries, at least insofar as the redistribution of resources is concerned;[13] (2) cosmopolitans believe that we have obligations of distributive justice to humanity as a whole, whereas nationalists believe these obligations hold only among co-nationals (although this commitment is generally constrained by a view that basic rights must be secured globally before preference to co-nationals is morally legitimate); and (3) cosmopolitans believe that duty to others in and of itself should be sufficient to motivate democratic participation and loose reciprocity, whereas nationalists argue that it is the relations we have with co-nationals that serve to motivate us to carry out our democratic and redistributive duties. It is the third dimension which occupies the remainder of this paper, though I will have some observations to make about the second along the way.

Motivating Cosmopolitanism?

Although there are principled differences between cosmopolitanism and nationalism, we have seen that their concerns are in at least one important way overlapping: both bodies of thought worry about material inequalities – whereas nationalists tends to focus their concern on the inequalities that pertain within national boundaries, cosmopolitans display greater concern for inequalities that pertain among individuals on a global scale.[14] At issue, however, is the precise mechanism

[12] Christian Joppke suggests, for example, that the movement towards post-national membership is necessarily connected to the 'hollowing-out of the content of citizenship, particularly its redistributive side'. Christian Joppke, 'Citizenship between De- and Re-Ethnicization', *European Journal of Sociology* 44.3 (2003), p. 456.

[13] The contrast is phrased in this way because there are cosmopolitans who observe the inherent value of nations in other areas.

[14] Additionally, both nationalists and cosmopolitans recognize the importance of democratic self-rule and collective decision-making procedures – whereas nationalists often argue that democratic values are best instantiated at the nation-state level, cosmopolitans emphasize the extent to which individuals are excluded from decisions

by which individuals can be motivated to redistribute resources to the needy. For the nationalist, the ethical ties that bind co-nationals do the motivational work necessary to establish and sustain the loose reciprocity that is essential to an ongoing commitment to redistributive schemes. The connection is not a *necessary* one, at least not in the sense that the claim is that the only way to motivate loose reciprocity is through the ties of nationalism;[15] rather, their claim is a more modest one, namely, that national ties are tremendously effective in doing so, so effective, in fact, that no equivalent replacement has been found. In other words, if the objective is to secure a commitment to the duties that sustain loose reciprocity, we need *some kind* of motivation, and national ties provide one. For nationalists, cosmopolitanism fails to provide a persuasive account of moral motivation of this kind.

Cosmopolitans have two related responses to this claim, pertaining to the motivational resources on which they draw (or fail to draw). Both responses challenge nationalism's claim that the source of duties and the motivation to carry them out derive from the same source, namely, the value that co-nationals place on the relationships they share. The first response denies that obligations derive from relationships in the first place, and then ties the motivation to carry out obligations towards others *solely* to the recognition that such duties exist. This response objects to nationalism's apparent (but not real, as I will argue) emphasis on *feeling* as a source of obligation towards others. The second response rejects the nationalist claim with respect to the source of duties, while recognizing the importance of finding additional motivational resources, in addition to the sheer motivational force of the

taken in global or international institutions, but which nevertheless have tremendous impact on their lives. Cosmopolitans often argue that individuals should be involved in any decision that affects them, regardless of whether these decisions are made outside of national boundaries. Nationalists will not (of course) deny that individuals should be involved in the decisions that affect them, nor even that individuals should have the opportunity to participate in global institutions; rather, their claim is that democratic participation, and the goods that flow from it, continue to be best secured at the domestic level.

[15] Andrew Mason accuses David Miller of arguing that the connection is necessary. I have argued elsewhere, however, that Mason misreads Miller (but also that Miller does overstate the case). What is, of course, necessary according to Miller is the view that special obligations are defined in part by the obligations that attend them. I will have more to say about this, below. Andrew Mason, *Community, Solidarity, and Belonging: Levels of Community and their Normative Significance* (Cambridge: Cambridge University Press, 2000).

duties themselves, to press actors into carrying them out. Let me turn to these and explain why we should find them wanting.

Response 1: External Principles Motivate? (Or Not)[16]

Some cosmopolitan thinkers reject the view that we need to feel any kind of solidarity with others in order to carry out our duties to them in the first place. On this view, we carry out our obligations towards others simply because it is our duty to do so – that we have no sense of connection with others, that we do not feel that we share much in common is, effectively, irrelevant. Cosmopolitans often justify a commitment to general duties by invoking a commitment to the individual – not only do they begin with a stated commitment to the equal moral worth of all individuals, in other words, they display this commitment by invoking liberty, or equality, or human flourishing. For these cosmopolitans, then, we owe general duties to individuals as such, and solidaristic associations do not have the capacity to generate special duties that take priority over general ones (even if they do contribute in some sense to liberty, or human flourishing, or equality etc.).[17] Duties of distributive justice are obligatory 'quite independently of whether we and the starving are united by a communal bond or committed to sharing resources with one another'; moreover, they derive from a commitment to the equality of all individuals as such.[18]

On this view, then, duties ought to be independently motivating; we should be motivated to carry out duties of justice simply because we are the kinds of creatures who carry out these duties. That nationalists reject this sort of claim is one complaint that cosmopolitans raise against

[16] The debate reported in this section and, indeed, throughout the paper is clearly one version of the ongoing, long-standing debate in moral theory between Kantian and Humean accounts of moral motivation. Cosmopolitans – at least Pogge and Caney – are clearly relying on the persuasiveness of the Kantian view, and I am responding (along with the nationalists I invoke here) with a modified Humean view. For more on this debate see Vittorio Bufacchi, 'Motivating Justice', *Contemporary Political Theory* 4 (2005), pp. 25–41; Laurence Thomas, 'Moral Motivation: Kantians versus Humeans (and Evolution)', *Midwest Studies in Philosophy* 13 (1988), pp. 367–383. Both of these accounts are broadly sympathetic to the Humean tradition.

[17] Of course, cosmopolitans do not deny the existence of special duties *per se*; they are perfectly happy with the suggestion that special duties can emerge from *voluntary* agreements of various kinds. They object to the idea that special duties derive from *non-voluntary* agreements. For a discussion, and a refutation, of the view that special obligations can emerge only from voluntary agreements, see chapter 6 of Scheffler, *Boundaries and Allegiances*.

[18] Pogge, *World Poverty and Human Rights*, p. 176.

them. For example, Simon Caney argues that the liberal nationalist claim – which justifies national partiality – 'relies on an impoverished moral psychology, assuming that people are motivated solely by loyalties and attachments to members of their community'.[19] This nationalist commitment underestimates our capacity to be moved to act dutifully on the basis of our commitment to moral principles: it 'underestimates peoples' ability to be motivated by their moral values'.[20] For Caney, that an action is just or moral is sufficient to demand that we carry it out – that action X is moral is reason in and of itself to carry it out. But this sort of account of the status of moral dictates makes it difficult to answer the question that motivates this paper, namely, why aren't people cosmopolitan, in the sense that Caney demands? In response, Caney might offer a variety of answers. Perhaps, he might say, people are committed to principles of justice, but believe that the current global economic order is just. This, for example, is an element of Thomas Pogge's explanation for the failure of cosmopolitan principles of distributive justice to take hold: 'my impression is that most people in the rich countries think of our global economic order as basically just'.[21] Or, he might say, they *are* committed to justice, but can't find a way to act according to the demands of justice – there are no plausible institutions of global reach that can serve to coordinate their just actions. It is, he might continue, 'excessively burdensome' to demand that individuals act justly if others around them are not doing so.[22] Or perhaps they have no real motivation to act according to the dictates of justice (they prefer to keep what they have to themselves), even while recognizing that the principles of justice ought to demand their allegiance. This latter explanation is consistent with Caney's displeasure at nationalism's commitment to the view that moral demands are in part evaluated with respect to whether they have purchase from within the moral psychology of ordinary individuals.

In whatever way he explains the failure of individuals to be cosmopolitan in the sense that he demands, however, he is committed to the view that individuals – insofar as they fail to act according to the

[19] Caney, *Justice Beyond Borders*, p. 133.
[20] Caney, *Justice Beyond Borders*, p. 132.
[21] Pogge, 'Moral Universalism and Global Economic Justice', p. 33.
[22] This discussion is influenced by my reading of the final chapter of Cohen's *If You're an Egalitarian, How Come You're So Rich?*, in which he is responding to a variety of claims made by Thomas Nagel with respect to the challenges associated with having individuals live up to their stated moral ideals.

demands of justice as he sets them out – are derelict in their moral duties. In other words, in explaining the gap between principle and practice – in explaining why it is that individuals do not behave in a way that is consistent with justice – Caney and others have three possible explanations: (1) institutional explanations (the institutions necessary for me to act justly do not exist); (2) moral failure explanations (individuals do not act justly, in spite of their *knowing* that they should do – they suffer, perhaps though not necessarily, a weakness of moral will); and (3) intellectual failure explanations (individuals *would be* cosmopolitan if only we could persuade them that the global economic order is unjust).[23]

However, Caney can make only limited use of a response that focuses on individuals' failure to act justly *in the face* of their recognizing what constitutes just action on their part. If, that is, he wishes to suggest that one decisive objection against nationalists is that they under-estimate individuals' capacity to act according to moral principles, he cannot then make recourse to a 'weakness of will' sort of argument in explaining why it is that so few people are proper, distributional cosmopolitans. In other words, he must commit himself either to the view that individuals are ignorant and uninformed with respect to the demands placed on them by duties of justice, or to some form of institutional explanation, i.e., that individuals would be cosmopolitan in their behavior (since they are already cosmopolitans in principle), if institutions existed to coordinate their activities in a fair and equitable manner. The latter explanation still fails to account for our being unmotivated to bring about the institutions that could coordinate the redistribution that is consistent with cosmopolitan accounts of distributive justice.

Caney's objection that nationalists cannot accommodate the reality that individuals are motivated by their principles is connected to his objection to the apparently nationalist emphasis on *feeling* to motivate the carrying out of duties. In Caney's interpretation of nationalism, nationalists rely heavily on whether individuals feel the pull of their duties – according to nationalists, he writes, individuals have obligations only so long as they 'follow our sentiments and inclinations and these are local in character'.[24] This argument fails, suggests Caney, because it

[23] For an interesting account of why gaps might exist between moral theory and moral practice, see chapter 10, 'Political Philosophy and Personal Behavior', of Cohen, *If You're an Egalitarian, How Come You're So Rich?*

[24] Caney, *Justice Beyond Borders*, p. 131.

relies on the tremendously implausible claim that obligations are mandatory only for those who feel themselves motivated to carry them out – on this view, then, duties are voluntary rather than obligatory, and we are left with a rather spineless conception of duty.[25] This suggestion, moreover, is a 'highly dubious assumption', which implies that it is possible to be absolved of one's obligations simply by feeling no motivation to fulfil them. This surely, as Caney observes, cannot be correct. He observes that, so often, critics of unjust practices and communities rely on a universal principle of justice of some kind, and that this universal principle may not motivate those criticized to alter their behaviors. Those who criticized South Africa's apartheid, for example, were right to do so – from the perspective of morality – even though those perpetuating it were in no way motivated to alter their behaviors in response to this criticism (and even though some among those who perpetuated it rejected the objection that it was unjust).[26] It cannot be true that those who engage in slavery or apartheid or other heinous actions are not obligated to halt them *immediately* simply because they have no inclination or desire to do so – the obligation to refrain from slavery or to recognize the equality of all individuals are obligations *independently* of whether individuals *feel* motivated to carry them out. In other words, nationalism's mistake is that it 'assumes that one (conceptual) property of a valid moral scheme is its ability to induce people to comply with it'.[27] Rather, Caney seems to be suggesting, a reason that fails to motivate may still be a good reason.[28]

[25] Caney is not alone in making this observation. Margaret Moore, for example, observes that the nationalist account 'leaves unclear the precise nature of the obligations, whether voluntary or not'. Margaret Moore, *The Ethics of Nationalism* (Oxford: Oxford University Press, 2001), p. 36. Caney is therefore rejecting the Humean claim that a desire to carry it out is an essential feature of any genuine moral duty.

[26] Caney deploys this argument against Michael Walzer's persuasive argument in *The Company of Critics: Social Criticism and Political Commitment in the Twentieth Century (New York: Basic Books, 2002).* There, Walzer argues that the best, and most effective, critics are those who operate from within a society – the connected critic – rather than those who operate from outside of it. Critics who operate from outside a community are likely to be viewed with suspicion, and to be rejected on the grounds that they don't understand the nature of the community they are criticizing or that they don't have its best interests at heart, in offering their criticism. In other words, Caney's objection that South Africa's external critics were right in objecting to apartheid, even when the South Africans didn't agree, supports Walzer's claim that insiders are more likely to be effective in extending criticism that is likely to have purchase.

[27] Caney, *Justice Beyond Borders*, p. 42.

[28] Of course, this objection is connected to the ways in which this debate maps on to the ongoing debate, since at least Bernard Williams's essay 'Internal and External

It is a mistake, however, to equate the nationalist concern with offering an account of how principles can motivate – indeed, how they must motivate in order to find adequate support – with feeling, an equation that Caney relies on in order to reject nationalism's moral status. David Miller, for example, writes of nationality that it is 'something [which is] for the most part unchosen and unreflectively acquired'.[29] Even though these shared identities are strongly felt they nevertheless are unchosen; it therefore makes sense to think of the commitments that arise from them likewise as unchosen and effectively unreflectively acquired. As Dworkin suggests, obligations that derive from membership in an association are not adequately described as 'a psychological property', since they emerge from a 'group's practices of asserting and acknowledging responsibilities', that is, from how the group acknowledges and defines itself and the responsibilities that emerge from these definitions.[30] In other words, morally valuable associations – including nations – are in large part defined by the obligations that members agree they have and are committed to carrying out; consequently, it is possible for any one member to be wrong about the nature of the obligations she holds. In his objections, therefore, Caney appears to muddle the nationalist's account of the source of obligations with her account of its motivating power. Caney interprets the nationalist position as though it were saying that it is the motivating power that generates the obligations themselves (hence his claim that feeling is responsible for generating obligations); rather, the nationalist position is that valued relations among co-nationals play two *independent though connected* roles, that of providing the source of obligations and that of providing the motivation to carry them out. It is therefore not the case that obligations among co-nationals are voluntary in the sense that Caney suggests; they may nevertheless be strongly felt, and this strength of feeling can be harnessed to motivate the carrying out of these duties.[31]

Reasons' between internal and external reasons. Bernard Williams, *Moral Luck* (Cambridge: Cambridge University Press, 1982), pp. 100–113.

[29] Miller, *On Nationality*, p. 43.

[30] Ronald Dworkin, *Law's Empire* (Cambridge, MA: Belknap Press, 1986), p. 201.

[31] Nationalists also offer what Caney calls a *societal* argument for the claim that a plausible account of distributive justice depends on a motivational story of some kind. On this view, he says, nationalists argue that individuals must identify in some sense with the institutional scheme in which they participate. It is, he says, a 'sociological claim about the feasibility of schemes of justice' in the presence or absence of shared bonds among citizens. This argument, says Caney, fails in part because it relies on the

The discussion above illustrates a larger problem in cosmopolitan theorizing more generally – namely, its account of moral motivation is deeply wanting. In arguing that moral principles might well motivate in the absence of feeling, Caney fails to offer an account of what it means to motivate in the first place. How do individuals come to be motivated to act according to their principles? How do moral principles motivate individuals to carry them out? It seems clear enough that any story about how it is that individuals become motivated to act according to moral principles requires that individuals *internalize* them in some sense – it is insufficient to suggest that they ought to motivate, when in many instances they fail to do so. In other words, in order to motivate individuals moral principles must have some purchase with normal, human psychology.[32]

On the other hand, nationalists offer a compelling story of moral motivation, one that seems to capture the true moral psychology of modern individuals – it is from within the special relations that co-nationals share that their obligations to each other emerge. This way of interpreting the *special* obligations that characterize the relations among co-nationals (as distinct from the *general* obligations that all individuals owe to all other individuals) is typically defended from within a theory of associative duties. Associative duties are defined as those that 'provide positive benefits for one's associations, duties that go beyond whatever positive duties we may have toward people in general'.[33] These duties hold among 'members of significant social groups' which are characterized by 'socially salient characteristics', and their source is the relationships themselves.[34] For defenders of associative

necessity of shared national sentiments, whereas it seems clear that many multi-national states successfully sustain various kinds of distributive policies. Further, the sociology that grounds the claim is faulty since it offers no good reason to think that cosmopolitan obligations cannot provide the motivational resources nationalists demand. Caney, *Justice Beyond Borders*, p. 131.

[32] In other words, there is no conceptual incoherence in Caney's view that because X is a moral is reason in and of itself to carry X out. But Caney fails to ask the additional question – are we the kinds of moral beings who behave in this way? As political philosophers, one of our roles is to offer a set of principles that people *as they are* are willing and able to accept – Caney's view is too demanding in this sense. As Kwame Anthony Appiah has asked in his recent book on the psychology of moral action: 'What would be the point of norms that human beings were psychologically incapable of obeying?' Kwame Anthony Appiah, *Experiments in Ethics* (Cambridge, MA: Harvard University Press, 2008), p. 22.

[33] Scheffler, *Boundaries and Allegiances*, p. 51.

[34] Scheffler, *Boundaries and Allegiances*, pp. 49, 102.

duties, that certain kinds of relationships give near-immediate rise to moral obligations is a matter of common-sense morality.[35] In other words, the obligations we have to others derive from the relationships we have with them: 'we account for special responsibilities...by citing the nature of our relationships to that person. We have special duties, we may say, because she is our sister, or our friend, or our neighbour'.[36] Obligations are inherent in the notion of familial relation, of friendship, of neighborliness: even if we cannot definitively list which specific obligations are incumbent on us as members of any of these relations, it is clear that to be a member of any one of them means, in large part, to be willing to carry out the obligations to which they give rise.[37] As David Miller writes, 'the duties in question must be integral to the relationship, in the sense that the relationship could not exist in the form that it does unless the duties were generally acknowledged'.[38]

It may seem clear enough that we have special obligations towards those who are close to us – our friends, family members and so forth. In these kinds of cases, it seems straightforward to claim that our personal relations generate obligations that we need to take seriously in order for the relationship to continue as that kind of relationship. But what may seem less clear is whether special obligations attend relationships that are not as clearly personal.[39] Nationalists, however, argue that nations are sufficiently like these other forms of relations that they too generate special obligations among members. Nations are, crucially, communities that their members value, and the special obligations that pertain among co-nationals derive in large part from the value that the

[35] In other words, the obligations emerge from the relationships themselves *as opposed to* a specific interaction or set of interactions. Dworkin, *Law's Empire*, p. 196; Scheffler, *Boundaries and Allegiances*, p. 64.

[36] Scheffler, *Boundaries and Allegiances*, p. 97.

[37] Defenders of associated duties acknowledge the open-endedness of the duties that are entailed by any given special relationship. The precise content of the duties entailed by any one relationship 'may vary depending on the nature of the relationship giving rise to the duty...the duties of the participants are often difficult to delineate with precision'. Critics often express skepticism of associative duties on the grounds of its open-endedness, however. Scheffler, *Boundaries and Allegiances*, p. 53.

[38] David Miller, 'Reasonable Partiality Towards Compatriots', *Ethical Theory and Moral Practice* 8 (2005), p. 65.

[39] Dworkin identifies four features of an obligation-generating-community, and that these obligations be felt as 'personal', in the sense of 'run[ning] directly from each member to each other member, not just to the group as a whole in some collective sense' is one of them. The others are that the obligations be special rather than general, as described above, and that they flow from an (1) *equal* (2) *concern* for all members of the group. Dworkin, *Law's Empire*, pp. 199–201.

members see in their relations to each other. The nation – in order to define itself, and in part to account for the worry that the family/friend–nation analogy fails to justify, on its face, the special duties that obtain among co-nationals – relies heavily on what David Miller terms a 'shared public culture', i.e., a shared ethos that manifests itself in overlapping values, norms and expectations among members of a community.[40] In other words, national boundaries identify a group of people who, based on the existence of a shared public culture, have ethical duties towards each other that take priority over those they have towards others more generally.

In sum, and to repeat, for nationalists a bounded community provides (a) a tremendously important *source* of obligations towards others, and (b) the *motivation* necessary to carry these obligations out. Since these obligations derive from the bounded community itself, they do not extend – as a matter of principle as well as a matter of fact – towards humanity in general. A bounded community thus is well-equipped to provide the motivation needed for citizens to act to sustain or protect a series of benefits that it values – in particular, redistribution (founded on loose reciprocity) and democracy. These are in an important sense connected claims – the obligations to co-nationals and the motivation to carry them out derive from the same source.

Response 2: Cosmopolitan Solidarity?

Not all cosmopolitans, however, agree that the source of moral motivation emerges solely from a commitment to moral principles, even if they do acknowledge the motivational challenges that cosmopolitanism faces.

Martha Nussbaum, for example, concedes that there are difficulties associated with generating the requisite motivating solidarity at the global level by appealing to 'humanity'. She writes of cosmopolitanism that it 'offers only reason and the love of humanity, which may seem at times less colorful than other sources of belonging'.[41] A commitment to humanity at large may appear to have trouble in motivating us to act on

---

[40] I've written about the concept of a shared public culture, elsewhere. See Patti Tamara Lenard, 'Shared Public Culture: A Reliable Source of Trust', *Contemporary Political Theory* 6.4 (2007), pp. 385–404.

[41] Martha Nussbaum, 'Patriotism and Cosmopolitanism', in Josh Cohen (ed.), *For Love of Country: Debating the Limits of Patriotism* (Boston, MA: Beacon Press, 1996), p. 15.

its behalf. Indeed, Nussbaum is not alone in observing that a commitment to something like global solidarity may appear abstract or empty. Carol Gould likewise worries that a commitment to something like a 'universal solidarity', understood as a 'feeling of fraternity among all human beings worldwide…would be quite empty'.[42] Although, in principle, an ideal world would be one in which the aims and objectives, and pain and suffering, of each and every individual is of deep concern to us, scholars of global justice do concede – at the very least – a kind of challenge that the notion of an abstract humanity has in serving to motivate ordinary people to carry out their apparent duties towards all others. As Andrew Dobson writes:

> [T]he most common answer to the question 'why be cosmopolitan?' is 'because we are all members of a common humanity'… [A]t the level of principle, the answer is an effective one…at the level of motivation, however, the answer runs out of steam: the cerebral recognition that we are all members of a common humanity seems not to be enough to get us to 'do' cosmopolitanism.[43]

Not all cosmopolitans are prepared to concede or accept this conclusion, however. Indeed, some cosmopolitans suggest that it may very well be a mistake to paint cosmopolitanism as relying on a commitment to an abstract humanity or an empty solidarity. There are two linked strategies pursued by cosmopolitans who suggest that something like cosmopolitan 'solidarity' can be rich enough to motivate the carrying out of thick duties towards others. One strategy emphasizes the extent to which we do have relations with others, both near and far. For example, Catherine Lu suggests that the 'moral allegiance' that cosmopolitanism induces should be derived from a commitment to humanity understood as the 'humanity in all those with whom we associate who can claim to be human, friend, stranger, or foe'.[44] It is our interactions with *individuals*, in other words, that lead us to a greater understanding of the plight of humanity worldwide. In interacting with the particular lives and challenges of those around us, we can move outwards to an understanding of the human condition more generally. Dobson agrees, suggesting that cosmopolitan's historical reliance on an abstract

[42] Carol Gould, 'Self-Determination Beyond Sovereignty: Relating Transnational Democracy to Local Autonomy', *Journal of Social Philosophy* 37.1 (2006), p. 57.

[43] Andrew Dobson, 'Thick Cosmopolitanism', *Political Studies* 54 (2006), p. 182.

[44] Catherine Lu, 'The One and Many Faces of Cosmopolitanism', *Journal of Political Philosophy* 8.2 (2000), p. 265.

humanity suffers for failing to recognize the extent to which 'nearness' 'has a bearing on our motivation to respond to the prompts of motivation'. He continues, 'what cosmopolitanism requires is a "nearness" to vulnerable, suffering, disadvantaged others'.[45] In other words, it is our interactions and interconnections with *specific* others in ever-wider 'networks of interconnections between people, associations, and political associations' that define ongoing global integration, that generates something Gould contrasts with the empty, universal solidarity she disparages: 'transnational solidarity'.[46]

The second and related strategy employed by cosmopolitan advocates of a thicker solidarity – say, transnational solidarity, or its equivalent[47] – is to emphasize not merely the fact of interconnections but the emotional resources that allow for these connections and the emotional responses that emerge from them. Lu, for example, suggests that we can develop a thick solidarity through our shared understanding of the evils of cruelty; individuals can understand the wrong of cruelty wherever it is inflicted, and it is through this shared understanding that we can enlarge our sense of what we owe to others. Or, as Carol Gould suggests, we can aim at a transnational solidarity that emphasizes a 'sort of social empathy with people in other communities'.[48] We can be *empathetic* towards the struggles that other face, and this empathy can serve as the foundation for larger transnational solidarities. For these cosmopolitans, then, the aim is to show that

---

[45] Dobson suggests that nearness is important in his response to Thomas Pogge. Dobson says, of Pogge, that his explanation for the failure of cosmopolitan duties of justice to motivate recognizes the extent to which individuals in the affluent world are divorced and isolated from the suffering and poverty in the developing world. I'm not sure Pogge is indeed vulnerable to this objection, since Pogge's strategy is *precisely* to persuade members of affluent countries that they are causally implicated in sustaining poverty in developing countries. But, says Dobson, Pogge offers 'no suggestion as to how we might turn strangers into friends and neighbours (as it were)', and this may be true. Dobson, 'Thick Cosmopolitanism', p. 171.

[46] Gould, 'Self-Determination Beyond Sovereignty', p. 46.

[47] I say, here, 'or its equivalent', because of late there are several examples of attempts to theorize a thicker conception of cosmopolitan solidarity: Stuart White suggests a 'mediated universalism'; Andrew Dobson offers a 'thick cosmopolitanism'; Toni Erskine an 'embedded cosmopolitanism'; Dobson, 'Thick Cosmopolitanism'; Toni Erksine, 'Embedded Cosmopolitanism and the Case of War: Restraint, Discrimination, and Overlapping Communities', *Global Society* 14.4 (2000), pp. 569–590; Stuart White, 'Republicanism, Patriotism and Global Justice', in Daniel Bell and Avner de-Shalit (eds.), *Forms of Justice* (Lanham, MD: Rowman and Littlefield, 2003).

[48] Gould, 'Self-Determination Beyond Sovereignty', p. 58.

'universal emotions...can become the grounds on which a stronger sense of moral obligation to the human race...can be established'.[49]

What these cosmopolitans observe is that – although it would be nice if, as Caney suggests, people were 'motivated [solely] by their moral values' – in practice, individuals are motivated by their connections with others. In other words, they concede an element of the basic associativist claim, that relationships are very often felt as the real source of duties, as well as the motivation for carrying them out. Lu, Gould and other cosmopolitans believe the global arena might in some sense be a community of shared identity or solidarity, in which interconnections with others generate a motivation to carry out duties towards them. But, in these accounts of the cosmopolitan position, it is no longer presumed that the abstract conception of 'humanity' can provide the requisite motivating work. Rather, these scholars suggest, it is through something like the felt connections with specific others with whom they share values or norms that individuals are able to reach out to others on a more global scale. It is through interactions and, importantly, *interconnections* with others that we come to feel a wider transnational solidarity.

It is worth recalling, here, the difference in how special and general duties are conceived by nationalists and cosmopolitans, respectively. Nationalists argue that nations generate duties among co-nationals; duties among co-nationals are thus one category of 'special duties', i.e., 'duties that we have only to those particular people with whom we have had certain significant sorts of interactions or to whom we stand in certain significant sorts of relations'.[50] The commitments we have towards others as a result of these relationships, or associations, are the '*actual source* of people's associative duties'.[51] Cosmopolitans are generally committed either to the view that there are no legitimate special duties towards others or to the (less radical) view that special duties towards others are sometimes legitimate but may never trump the duties we have towards others in general.

But, in the accounts of cosmopolitanism reported above, there is a reliance on a version of associative duties. Rather than justifying

[49] Andrew Linklater, 'Cosmopolitanism', in A. Dobson and R. Eckersley (eds.), *Political Theory and the Ecological Challenge* (Cambridge: Cambridge University Press, 2006), p. 114.

[50] Scheffler, *Boundaries and Allegiances*, p. 49.

[51] Scheffler, *Boundaries and Allegiances*, p. 49. Emphasis added.

cosmopolitanism in strictly individualist terms, in other words, they suggest that we owe duties to humanity as a whole based on a *thick* solidarity that binds us all. On this interpretation of cosmopolitanism, the objection to special duties is not that relationships or associations cannot generate duties, but that there is no legitimate reason to think that national boundaries are specially placed to generate duties; instead, the only association that matters is the association of humanity, and it is in some sense our relationships or associations with humanity from which our duties are derived. The significance of the transition from a commitment to individuals qua individuals (as demonstrated in Caney's cosmopolitanism) and individuals as members of a common association is significant; it relies on the motivational resources provided by integration into a common humanity. They argue, as do nationalists, that *associations* generate duties or that all general duties are special duties; the objection to nationalism is to partiality rather than associationism.

However, these cosmopolitan views are subject to an important objection. It is not clear that the integration provided by the thicker solidarity they envision will be able to motivate the carrying out of thick redistributive duties towards others. Indeed, none of these cosmopolitans follows up their arguments with an account of what they entail with respect to thick redistributive duties. While nationalism has been successful at integrating (sometimes violently, it must be admitted) individuals into an association that generates duties, among them redistributive duties, to which members feel committed, cosmopolitanism has been less successful (thus far) at generating a real sense of integration or membership. And without genuine integration, whatever solidarity they claim that their cosmopolitanism might generate may well fail to sustain commitment to the loose reciprocity that is essential to the extensive resource redistribution that will be necessary to generate something like Caney's global equality of opportunity.

The problem for these accounts of cosmopolitanism is one of emotional range. Individuals as a matter of course feel obligations to those who are near to them. Nation-states have been successful in part because they are able to capture the imagination of its members, who believe that although they may never encounter most of their co-nationals, they do have obligations to them that emerge from a sense of shared nationality. Importantly, the obligations that we sustain as a result of national ties are a long time in the making: 'the moral understanding on which the community is founded takes shape over a long period of time'.[52] As a matter of fact, then, it is not impossible that over time the global community envisioned by cosmopolitans could take shape in such a way as to generate felt-obligations among its members (even if 'the prospect of realizing any form of world government in the foreseeable future is quite dim'.[53])

It seems to me that cosmopolitans who argue for a global society in which the interconnections among its members generate felt-obligations fail to take seriously – as a matter of human moral psychology – the possibility of a limit to the power of any emotion to generate a rigorous sense of interconnections. It may be that at some point the community is simply *too big* to be able to capture the moral imagination in the way that the nation-state has done so successfully. So, if cosmopolitans are envious of the power of interconnections at the domestic level, and if they wish to harness their power to develop a view defending the power of interconnections at the global level, they will need to ask whether cosmopolitanism will eventually – as a motivating source – fall victim to the limits of emotional range. Indeed, Carol Gould acknowledges this in her account of global (transnational) solidarity. She writes:

> [W]e can first of all put aside the idea that a norm of transnational solidarity would require that one feel and act supportively toward all individual human beings worldwide, or even toward all those who need help in fulfilling their human rights. A norm that required people to feel, express, or stand in solidarity with every other human being would be impossible to apply, if not also utterly vague.[54]

Another account of the process of developing 'global ties' of the kind described in this section suggests that 'the place of historically evolved, deep-seated solidarities is taken by abstractly constructed, less deeply rooted but more comprehensive solidarity relationships'.[55] In other words, it is a mistake to think that cosmopolitan solidarity – even if it extends to people beyond the nation-state, and even if it can be

[52] Michael Walzer, 'The Moral Standing of States: A Response to Four Critics', *Philosophy and Public Affairs* 9.3 (1980), p. 211.

[53] Moore, 'Cosmopolitanism and Political Communities', p. 628.

[54] Carol Gould, 'Transnational Solidarities', *Journal of Social Philosophy* 38.1 (2007), p. 155.

[55] Robert Munch, 'The Transformation of Citizenship in the Global Age: From National to European and Global Ties', in Hanspeter Kriesi, et al. (eds.), *Nation and National Identity: The European Experience in Perspective* (Ohio: Purdue University Press, 1999), p. 115.

thickened in some sense – will be able to sustain the commitments we may have to the loose reciprocity that underpins redistributive duties (goods that are effectively provided at the nation-state level).[56] At some point, it may just be that the story we're told about our connections to others will fail to motivate us to act on their behalf and in their interests. If, in other words, we interpret the moral status of national boundaries as emerging from the importance of the relations co-nationals have with each other, which is an instantiation of a general principle of associationism (rather than as an exclusive claim about the moral status of nation-states), cosmopolitans may legitimately employ associationist insights to their advantage. They must, however, deal with the very real limits – from the perspective of ordinary human moral psychology – of associationism.

Objections to the Skeptical View

There are at least two objections to the skepticism I've expressed about the possibility of motivating a commitment to thick cosmopolitan duties. One objection is that I'm guilty of a 'time-line' fallacy. A second and related objection is that we are in the midst of witnessing an 'emergent' cosmopolitanism, which I fail to heed.[57]

[56] Indeed, this is just the argument that Munch is making, although he doesn't lament the change. His analysis owes much to Emile Durkheim's *Division of Labour*, and the transition Durkheim describes from mechanical to organic solidarity. It appears to be Munch's view that we are now to take a third step, and move from the organic solidarity that describes nation-states to a kind of weaker, but nevertheless global solidarity that will emerge from a global rather than a national division of labour. It may also be that this kind of cosmopolitan solidarity is not solidarity at all. Shlomi Segall suggests that solidarity consists in four features: integration, commitment to a common good, empathy and trust. Lu, Gould and others do seem to be arguing that cosmopolitan solidarity consists in empathy and integration, but they have not yet shown evidence that it can provide for a commitment to the common good or trust. Richard Rorty, moreover, suggests that the project of a cosmopolitan solidarity is impossible. He writes, we ought to 'get rid of the notion of universal moral obligations created by membership in the species, and substitute the idea of building a community of trust between ourselves and others'. Emile Durkheim, *The Division of Labor in Society* (New York: Free Press, 1984); Richard Rorty, 'Justice as a Larger Loyalty', in P. Cheah and B. Robbins (eds.), *Cosmopolitics: Thinking and Feeling Beyond the Nation* (Minneapolis, MN: University of Minnesota Press, 1998), p. 56; Shlomi Segall, 'Political Participation as an Engine of Social Solidarity: A Skeptical View', *Political Studies* 53 (2005): p. 362.

[57] I thank Garrett Wallace Brown for pressing me with respect to both of these objections.

Objection 1: Time-line Fallacy (or the Feasibility Objection)

According to the first objection, I am responding to a vision for the future – we ought to be cosmopolitans – with a mere empirical claim about the present – we are not cosmopolitans now. I am, as a result, guilty of arguing that because cosmopolitanism hasn't come to pass, it will never do so. That cosmopolitanism hasn't come to pass, the objection continues, is not evidence that it will not do so, and in suggesting otherwise, I am committing myself to the view that human moral psychology is invariant and inflexible over time. That cosmopolitanism is not *feasible* in the present does not mean that it will be forever unfeasible; its unfeasibility in the present, moreover, has little to do with its moral plausibility.[58] That we are not cosmopolitans now is a moral failing that we ought to work towards ameliorating; in suggesting a focus on the nation-state, as the source of thick duties towards others, I am merely holding things up. I am, moreover, ignoring the lessons that history offers us: nationalism's motivating power, at least historically, has often derived from its roots in religious traditions defined by a commitment to concern for a wider humanity. In the past, cosmopolitanism and nationalism were less clearly distinct traditions than they were two (non-exclusive) responses to the conditions of modernity.[59] Consequently, there is no reason to think that cosmopolitans require an entirely distinctive account of moral motivation.

However, I should not be taken as denying the *possibility* of generating a sufficiently rigorous, or thick, association among the world's people, in such a way that the relations among us generate both thick

[58] There is considerable confusion in the debates between cosmopolitans and their critics about the distinction between the feasibility of cosmopolitanism in the short or long term and the plausibility of cosmopolitanism. It is of course possible that cosmopolitanism is the most plausible of moral views, even if it remains forever unfeasible for a variety of reasons, moral, institutional and so on. My objective in this paper is to distinguish plausibility from feasibility, and to focus some attention on the moral feasibility of cosmopolitanism.

[59] I thank an anonymous reviewer for the journal for pointing this out to me. As the reviewer also notes, the attempt to qualify nationalism by the term 'liberal', as some thinkers do, is an attempt to harness the universalizing impulses that are central to cosmopolitan thinking. See, for example, Yael Tamir, *Liberal Nationalism* (Princeton, NJ: Princeton University Press, 1993). For an argument that observes the connections between the emergence of nationalism and (enlightenment) cosmopolitanism, see Pheng Cheah, 'The Cosmopolitical – Today', in Pheng Cheah and Bruce Robbins (eds.), *Cosmopolitics: Thinking and Feeling Beyond the Nation* (Minneapolis, MN: University of Minnesota Press, 1998).

obligations towards each other and the motivation to carry them out. It is perhaps worth pointing here to Robert Dahl's account of the transition from direct to representative democracy over the course of several hundred years. Dahl observes that by the 1700s, the size of modern democracies was such that it was widely acknowledged that direct democracy was no longer a possibility. Although it seems obvious to us that a concept of representation was required in order to sustain democracy within ever-widening constituencies, 'until the eighteenth century, the standard view was that democratic or republican government meant rule by the people...democracy would have to be town meeting democracy; representative democracy was a contradiction in terms'.[60] The concept and practice of representation emerged and was modified, over time, as a way to sustain a version of democracy in the face of increasing numbers of people living in one constituency. The move from direct to representative democracy represented a sea change in the practice and theorizing of democratic politics; it may be that cosmopolitan practice and theorizing requires a sea change of this kind.

In other words, I should not – and this is in part why I invoked Robert Dahl's observations concerning the transition from the rejection of representative institutions as consistent with democracy to the view that they are essential to democracy – be taken to be claiming that a cosmopolitan world cannot emerge as a matter of logical or moral necessity. It may be that the institutional structures that could sustain (or generate) a real cosmopolitanism have not yet been constructed. Indeed, I think this is how cosmopolitans might well answer the challenge I'm posing to them in this paper: they might say, cosmopolitanism is a vision for the future, and our job in the present is to generate the institutions that will create cosmopolitans.[61] We are responsible, the futurist cosmopolitan might say, for developing the desire among individuals to carry out cosmopolitan duties, for generating a moral system – and the institutions necessary to fulfil the demands that this system places on us – that will motivate individuals to comply with

[60] Robert Dahl, *On Democracy* (New Haven, CT: Yale University Press, 1998), p. 94.

[61] And, indeed, following G.A. Cohen, I agree that institutions in large part serve to structure motivations. See chapter 8 of *If You're an Egalitarian, How Come You're So Rich?* For an argument that highlights the role of institutions in securing the fulfilling of moral duties, for non-moral reasons, see Robert E. Goodin, *Motivating Political Morality* (Oxford: Blackwell, 1992).

them. In the short term, we may employ coercive mechanisms to ensure that cosmopolitan duties are carried out (indeed, we may be morally obligated to do so); in the long term, however, we will need a certain kind of moral motivation to take hold in order to ensure that these duties are stably and ongoingly met.

In responding as such, cosmopolitans first concede too much and, second, change radically the tenor of their position. In accepting cosmopolitanism as a future-oriented project, they deny a fundamental tenet of cosmopolitanism as it is now constructed, as a view that we have duties of justice *in the present* that must be carried out, and that we have moral reasons *in the present* to do so. In conceding that individuals do not yet have the motivation to carry out their thick cosmopolitan obligations, they concede the capacity to motivate is essential to a plausible moral system (and as I showed, above, Caney for one is reluctant to concede such a thing). In other words, it is consistent with my own view to accept the possibility of a future-oriented cosmopolitanism that focuses on developing and molding cosmopolitans out of present-day nationalists – it may very well be, moreover, that the motivational power of cosmopolitanism simply grows from the motivational power that nationalists rely on at present – but it is not consistent with cosmopolitan theory as it is presently expressed.

Objection 2: Denial of Emergent Cosmopolitanism

According to the second objection, I am belittling the very real emergent cosmopolitan moves that have been made of late. The moves to which these critics point are at least twofold: (1) international cooperation with respect to the environment, health concerns, and other issues of apparently global concern, and (2) the adoption of cosmopolitan-type duties as elements of a nationally shared public culture.

With respect to international cooperation, I should not forget, as my argument may seem to, the very real cooperation we witness as countries work together, for example, to limit the spread of the avian flu or environmental disasters, in particular as demonstrated by the emergence of regional, transnational and global institutions. This sort of cooperation, to combat issues that concern us globally, may be the harbinger of a more cosmopolitan attitude – they may, in other words, indicate the beginning of a normative shift from mainly nationally-oriented perspectives to cosmopolitan perspectives, which may well continue over time. At the very least, we might say that these institutions, which facilitate greater-than-national-level cooperation, fill the motivation gap that I have identified in this essay.[62]

These examples are unpersuasive, however, since they reflect merely individual states' self-interests in – in the case of avian flu – preventing the disease from penetrating their borders. As far as I can tell, there is little evidence of a normative shift, and plenty of evidence that states are willing – as they have always been – to cooperate in such moments as their self-interest demands it. Again, moreover, this worry seems to me to do an injustice to cosmopolitanism as it is traditionally expressed, as a view about the duties we have to bring about justice *in the present* rather than a view about whether cosmopolitans can be created in the future. That said, I cannot deny the possibility that institutions may serve to build a kind of solidarity which, in turn, will motivate individuals, and individual states, towards more extensive concern for outsiders.[63]

Even if I reject international cooperation as evidence of an emergent cosmopolitanism, perhaps I should take more heed of national cultures that are sometimes described by a commitment to outsiders. For example, Canadians frequently report, in surveys, the view that part of what it means to be Canadian is a commitment to 'peace-keeping' in conflict-prone areas (though this commitment is being tested with respect to its participation in NATO's Afghanistan mission).[64] What this indicates to me, however, is not an emergent cosmopolitanism – rather, it seems to indicate that communities that are characterized by thick duties are among the most willing (and most able) to carry out quite stringent duties to outsiders.

Earlier, I suggested that cosmopolitans are wrong to object that nationalists claim that in prioritizing the needs of co-nationals, they are immune from obligations to outsiders. There is, instead, considerable positive evidence that a commitment to domestic justice does not preclude support for outsiders. Indeed, it may serve to enhance

[62] I thank an anonymous reviewer for pressing me to think about the role that institutions play in resolving the 'motivation gap' I have identified; the expression 'motivation gap' is the reviewer's and not mine.

[63] For more about building cosmopolitan institutions, see Daniele Archibugi, David Held and Martin Kohler (eds.), *Reimagining Political Community: Studies in Cosmopolitan Democracy* (Cambridge: Polity Press, 1998); Andrew Kuper, *Democracy Beyond Borders: Justice and Representation in Global Institutions* (Oxford: Oxford University Press, 2004).

[64] Don Munton and Tom Keating, 'Internationalism and the Canadian Public', *Canadian Journal of Political Science* 34.3 (2001), pp. 517–549.

support for outsiders: countries that do best at internal redistribution – Sweden and Norway, for example – are consistently among those that contribute the most to foreign aid.[65] As, for example, Joseph Schwartz suggests, it may well be that our 'aspirations for greater international solidarity must be grounded in transnational movements that have sufficient presence in particular states to compel these polities to adopt... policies that enhance global labor, environmental, and human rights conditions'.[66] In other words, I think the evidence at least as we have seen it thus far points us towards a commitment to nationalism that is able to sustain a commitment to redistributive policies and democratic participation domestically, alongside a solid commitment to meeting (at least some of) the needs of the poor, globally.

Conclusions

The argument in this paper is simple: as it has been articulated thus far, cosmopolitanism has not proven up to the task of generating motivations for carrying out duties to others, internally. In order to motivate individuals to carry out duties, I've argued, cosmopolitans have had to rely on the insights best generated from within theories of associative duties.

I've tried to make this argument by following this path. I began by outlining the nationalist position as well as the main tenets of cosmopolitanism, and I indicated the key areas of tension between cosmopolitanism and nationalism. I suggested that, whereas nationalists believe that the source of obligations is the relations among co-nationals, and that these relations equally generate a motivation to carry out these obligations, cosmopolitans reject these claims. From here, I considered cosmopolitan attempts to generate motivation and elaborated why they fail: either they do not take seriously the issue of motivation (since they expect that cosmopolitan duties are enough on

[65] See OECD, Development Co-operation Directorate, at http://www.oecd.org/countrylist/0,3349,en_2649_34447_1783495_1_1_1_1,00.html (statistics from 2004–2005).

[66] It is worth noting that Schwartz does not offer an account for *why* it would be that domestic solidarity appears to be a precondition for global solidarity. In discussions with him at the American Political Science Association (APSA), he agrees that this is a pressing question, for which we as of yet have no clear answer. Joseph Schwartz, 'From Domestic to Global Solidarity: The Dialectic of the Particular and Universal in the Building of Social Solidarity', *Journal of Social Philosophy* 38.1 (2007), p. 132.

their own to generate motivation) or they attempt to forge an 'association' of humanity that can take advantage of the resources provided by associative theories of obligation. I argued that this latter strategy is vulnerable to the limits of sympathy – it may be that individuals, as we know them, simply cannot extend their concern far enough to motivate a robust cosmopolitan solidarity that will, in turn, sustain a commitment to thick obligations on a global scale. I then rejected two objections to my own skepticism – that I'm guilty of a time-line fallacy and that I'm guilty of paying insufficient attention to recent normative shifts towards a cosmopolitan ethos.

I should say, at this point, that there is nothing objectionable (for me) in the observation that cosmopolitanism may not have motivational resources of its own. It may very well be that cosmopolitanism is a theory that extends egalitarianism to the global level, and that the rejection of national boundaries as morally relevant will cease to form a key element in future articulations of cosmopolitanism. It may be that cosmopolitan theory has accomplished its goal, in other words, in persuading us that the fact of existing tremendous global inequalities are objectionable to the extent that wealthy nations are morally required to do much (much!) more than they are presently doing to ameliorate them (in particular, because they are in large part responsible for generating them in the first place).[67]

My argument in this paper is manifestly not that cosmopolitanism is unable to provide motivational resources from within itself, nor even that it is objectionable to rely on the motivational resources generated and elaborated elsewhere (in this case, within the domain of nationalist theorizing). My argument is rather that thus far cosmopolitanism has not provided a compelling account of motivation that divorces itself adequately – and so does not fall back on – the motivational insights that are central to nationalist principles.

[67] It seems to me, in fact, that this view would be quite Kantian in tenor. It might be, as Kant's account suggested, that it is wrong to think of cosmopolitanism as a complete moral philosophy – a complete moral philosophy, among other things, would need an adequate account of human psychology. Rather, as Kant suggested – and as I think some cosmopolitans forget – it may be best to argue for a kind of 'cosmopolitan right' as part of a broader ethical and political theory. I thank Will Smith for pointing this out.

PATRIOTISM AND MORALITY: MAPPING THE TERRAIN

Igor Primoratz

No one (except, of course, an advocate of 'realism' in politics) would deny that patriotism is a proper subject of discussion in moral philosophy: a position or attitude that needs to be subjected to moral judgment. Beyond this point, moral philosophers tend to disagree. Some see patriotism as a virtue, or a moral requirement, or even as *the* moral requirement, the fount and bedrock of all morality. Others consider it a non-moral attachment in need of moral scrutiny. The latter differ among themselves about the upshot of such scrutiny. On one view, patriotism ought to be constrained, but not necessarily eradicated. Others reach a much harsher conclusion: from a moral point of view, the balance sheet of patriotism is clearly negative, and we should work for its demise.

Given such a wide range of views on the morality of patriotism, it might be useful to provide a map of the terrain: a critical account of the main positions on the issue. That is one of the tasks of this paper. The other is to present and argue for my own view. The two tasks are complementary: much of what I have to say in support of the view I hold emerges from the criticism of other views.

What is Patriotism?

Before addressing the question of its morality, I need to say something about what patriotism is and how it relates to nationalism. As this paper focuses on patriotism as a subject in its own right—related to, yet distinct from, nationalism—the tendency to conflate the two must be overcome and a reasonably clear distinction made.

Neither common usage nor the way the two terms are used in scholarly discourse are of much help. In both, the question of the relation between patriotism and nationalism is disposed of much too quickly. This is sometimes done by reducing patriotism to a mere emotional underpinning of nationalism, which is understood as a political ideology or philosophical theory.[1] Some scholars have succumbed to the popular tendency of presenting 'our' stance as patriotism, taken to mean a reasonable, natural and wholesome loyalty to one's country and compatriots, while portraying 'their' attitude as nationalism, understood as irrational, invidious and aggressive.[2] Debates about nationalism itself have often proceeded at cross-purposes due to the ambiguity of the term (political or civic vs. ethnic or cultural nationalism) and to a wide range of competing definitions and conceptions of 'nationalism' and 'nation' advanced at different levels of discourse.

There is, however, a way of distinguishing between patriotism and nationalism I find helpful, and will assume throughout this paper. One of its virtues is that it is simple; another, that it begs no moral questions. First we need to put to one side the political sense of 'nation' that makes it identical with 'country', 'state' or 'polity', and the political or civic type of nationalism related to it. In this context, we need concern ourselves only with the other, ethnic or cultural sense of 'nation', and focus on ethnic or cultural nationalism. We can do so without attempting to spell out the relevant understanding of 'nation'; it is enough to characterize it in terms of common ancestry, history, and a set of cultural traits. Both patriotism and nationalism involve love of, identification with, and special concern for a certain entity. In the case of patriotism, that entity is one's *patria*, one's country; in the case of nationalism, that entity is one's *natio*, one's nation (in the ethnic/cultural sense of the term). Thus patriotism and nationalism are understood as the same type of a set of beliefs and attitudes, and distinguished in terms of their objects, rather than the strength of those beliefs and attitudes, or in terms of theory vs. its emotional underpinnings.

Patriotism, then, is love of one's country, identification with it, and special concern for its well-being and that of compatriots. This calls for a few brief comments. First, this is only a definition. A full account of patriotism would include the patriot's beliefs about the merits and achievements of the *patria*, his need to belong to a collectivity and be a part of a wider narrative, to be related to a past and a future that transcend the narrow confines of an individual's life and its mundane concerns, as well as social and political conditions that affect the ebb and

[1] *See* Elie Kedourie, *Nationalism*, 4th edn (Oxford: Blackwell, 1993).

[2] *See* Michael Billig, *Banal Nationalism* (London: SAGE Publications, 1995), pp. 55–59.

flow of patriotism, its political and cultural influence, and more. But for the purposes of this paper, a mere definition—a statement of the necessary and sufficient conditions for the application of the term—should suffice. Second, at least in modern usage, the patriot's love of his country is not restricted to the land and those living in it, but also encompasses the state and its citizens. *Patria* is not merely a geographic, but also a political term. Third, there is, obviously, considerable overlap between country and nation, and therefore between patriotism and nationalism: much that applies to one will also apply to the other. But when a country and polity is not ethnically homogeneous, the two may part ways.

'The Last Refuge of the Scoundrel'

'Patriotism is the last refuge of the scoundrel': this is the best known quotation about patriotism, and one of the most popular political quotations of all time. Yet it is not helpful here. Our source for it is Boswell's *Life of Johnson*. Having reported it, Boswell hastens to add that Johnson 'did not mean a real and generous love of our country, but that pretended patriotism which so many, in all ages and countries, have made a cloak of self-interest'.[3] Indeed, in a book entitled *The History of English Patriotism* we learn that 'there has never been a man more intensely and narrowly patriotic than he, who said, half seriously, that all foreigners were fools, and who could hardly be brought to look upon a Scot as a man and a brother', and also that 'on one occasion, without the least provocation, he burst out … "I am willing to love all mankind, *except an American*"'.[4]

We also have Johnson's thoughts on genuine patriotism, spelled out in a pamphlet written on the eve of the elections of 1774, where we are told that 'a Patriot is he whose public conduct is regulated by one single motive, the love of his country', and that 'no man can deserve a seat in parliament who is not a PATRIOT'.[5] The famous aphorism is about fake patriotism: not about patriotism, but about those who fake it in order

[3] *Boswell's Life of Johnson*, ed. G.B. Hill (Oxford: Clarendon Press, 1887), vol. 2, p. 348.

[4] E. Wingfield-Stratford, *The History of English Patriotism* (London: John Lane, The Bodley Head, 1913), vol. 1, pp. 503, 567.

[5] S. Johnson, 'The Patriot', in J.P. Hardy (ed.), *The Political Writings of Dr. Johnson: A Selection* (London: Routledge & Kegan Paul, 1968), p. 91.

to promote their own private or factional interests—that is, about political scoundrels.

'Our Country, Right or Wrong'

There is a different type of scoundrel: one who is both a true patriot *and* a scoundrel. In the summer of 1860, Count Cavour, Prime Minister of Piedmont, who played a central role in the unification of Italy, was ostensibly negotiating with the government of the Kingdom of Naples with a view of forming an alliance, while at the same time arming volunteers to invade it and sending agents to stir up an uprising in Naples. Talking about that to friends, he said: 'If we had done for ourselves the things which we are doing for Italy, we should be great rascals'.[6]

This remark could be taken in more than one way. I suggest it is best construed as showing Cavour as a disciple of Machiavelli, who had argued that, in view of human nature and the nature of politics, a prince had 'to learn how not to be good, and to use this knowledge or not use it according to necessity'.[7] A prince needs to learn how to break his promises, to dissemble and deceive, and to use force, sometimes in a cruel way and on a large scale, whenever that is required in order to maintain, strengthen and extend his power. A prince is assumed to be concerned primarily, if not solely, with his own power and glory, rather than with the good of his subjects. Thus Machiavelli's advice is not obviously relevant to the issue of patriotism and morality. We might make it relevant by reading it in the light of the concluding chapter of *The Prince* and its impassioned plea for a leader to rise up, liberate Italy from foreign yoke, and turn it into a single, unified polity. But we need not go into that; for Machiavelli offers the same advice to politicians and common citizens of a republic: 'When the safety of one's country wholly depends on the decision to be taken, no attention should be paid either to justice or injustice, to kindness or cruelty, or to its being praiseworthy or ignominious'.[8] Whatever the paramount political concern is—the power and glory of a prince, or the safety of a republic—if it requires

[6] G.M. Trevelyan, *Garibaldi and the Making of Italy: June-November, 1860* (London: Longmans, Green & Co., 1928), p. 23.

[7] N. Machiavelli, *The Prince*, ed. P. Bondanella, trans. P. Bondanella and M. Musa (Oxford: Oxford University Press, 1984), p. 52.

[8] N. Machiavelli, *The Discourses*, ed. B. Crick, trans. L.J. Walker (Harmondsworth: Penguin Books, 1998), p. 515.

setting aside moral considerations, including even those most weighty, that is what a true prince, and a true citizen, should do. If he succeeds in establishing and preserving a principality (as Cavour did, albeit not as a prince), or in safeguarding a republic, all this injustice, cruelty and ignominy will be soon forgotten. 'Our country, right or wrong.'[9]

Of course, 'our country, right *or wrong*' cannot be *right*, at least from the moral point of view. The saying encapsulates a stance that is quite widespread, but amounts to a rejection of morality, whenever the safeguarding of important interests of our country calls for acting as great rascals do. Therefore those who hold moral beliefs, adhere to moral rules, espouse moral values cannot but reject this type of extreme patriotism outright. For those who appreciate them, moral considerations are overriding: they trump non-moral considerations with which they come into conflict. To be sure, there are two types of cases where moral considerations might be thought not to override non-moral ones: when the price of doing the right thing is prohibitive, and in cases of 'supreme emergency', where acting in accordance with a moral rule will have literally disastrous consequences for a large number of people. But these are only apparent exceptions. Moral requirements have a built-in provision that compliance will not be bound up with paying a prohibitive price. And in cases of 'supreme emergency', the necessity of avoiding a disaster by going against a weighty moral rule is itself a moral consideration; what is to be avoided is not a disaster *simpliciter*, but a *moral* disaster. To reject the supremacy of morality, then, is to reject morality itself.

A Central Moral Virtue

The next understanding of patriotism along this spectrum is that termed 'true' or 'robust' patriotism by its advocates, and 'extreme' by its critics. Its advocate among contemporary philosophers is Alasdair MacIntyre. In his lecture 'Is Patriotism a Virtue?' this kind of patriotism is contrasted with liberalism as a philosophy committed to certain universal values and principles. The two are presented as alternatives, each with its attractions and hazards, rather than as the correct and

9 The source of this widely popular saying is a toast given by Stephen Decatour, US naval officer (1779–1820), in Norfolk, Virginia, in April 1816: 'Our country! In her intercourse with foreign nations, may she always be in the right; but our country, right or wrong!'

incorrect view of the self, community, and morality, respectively. Yet anyone familiar with MacIntyre's book *After Virtue* will take this profession of neutrality with a grain of salt, and will interpret the argument of the lecture as a defence of patriotism.

In *After Virtue*, MacIntyre insists that human beings and their actions must be understood and judged from the point of view of the community they belong to, in terms of the identity and the roles this community provides them with.

> I am never able to seek for the good or exercise the virtues only qua individual… It is not just that different individuals live in different social circumstances; it is also that we all approach our own circumstances as bearers of a particular social identity. I am someone's son or daughter, someone else's cousin or uncle; I am a citizen of this or that city, a member of this or that guild or profession; I belong to this clan, that tribe, this nation. Hence what is good for me has to be the good for one who inhabits these roles. As such, I inherit from the past of my family, my city, my tribe, my nation, a variety of debts, inheritances, rightful expectations and obligations. These constitute the given of my life, my moral starting point. This is in part what gives my life its own moral particularity.[10]

While this argument highlights the importance of community as such for the moral life and applies this claim to a range of communities to which an individual might belong, in the lecture on patriotism it is one particular community, one's country and polity, that comes to the fore. On the liberal understanding of morality, where and from whom I learn the principles and precepts of morality is as irrelevant to their contents and to my commitment to them, as where and from whom I learn the principles and precepts of mathematics is irrelevant to their contents and my adherence to them. For MacIntyre, where and from whom I learn my morality is of decisive importance both for my commitment to it and to its very contents. There is no way of understanding and adopting morality as such; it always comes in a particular version, as the morality of this or that community, and the individual can come to understand moral rules and make them his own only 'in and through the way of life of [his] community'.[11] To be sure, moral rules are justified in terms of certain goods they express and safeguard; but these

[10] A. MacIntyre, *After Virtue*, 2nd edn (Notre Dame: University Press of Notre Dame, 1984), p. 220.

[11] A. MacIntyre, 'Is Patriotism a Virtue?', in I. Primoratz (ed.), *Patriotism* (Amherst, NY: Humanity Books, 2002) (henceforth: *Patriotism*), p. 48.

goods, too, are always given as part and parcel of the way of life of a particular community.

The individual becomes a moral agent only when informed as such by his community. He also remains a moral agent, lives and flourishes as one, because he is sustained in his moral life by his community:

> To obey the rules of morality is characteristically and generally a hard task… *I* can only be a moral agent because *we* are moral agents… I need those around me to reinforce my moral strength and assist in remedying my moral weaknesses. It is in general only within a community that individuals become capable of morality [and] are sustained in their morality… Detached from my community, I will be apt to lose my hold upon all genuine standards of judgment.[12]

This might be termed the argument from moral education, growth and sustenance. Its second step suggests a further argument, that of identity. If I can live and flourish as a moral agent only in my community, as its member, while playing the role this membership involves, that means that my very identity is inseparably bound up with that of my community, its history, traditions, institutions and aspirations. Accordingly,

> if I do not understand the enacted narrative of my own individual life as embedded in the history of my country… I will not understand what I owe to others or what others owe to me, for what crimes of my nation I am bound to make reparation, for what benefits to my nation I am bound to feel gratitude. Understanding what is owed to and by me and understanding the history of the communities of which I am a part is… one and the same thing.[13]

If so, patriotism cannot be contrasted with morality. It is rather a central moral virtue, and indeed the core and bedrock of morality. It provides strong motivation for acting morally. The competing, liberal understanding of morality fails to provide such motivation when it is most needed, in cases where there can be no appeal to mutual interest.

The object of patriotic loyalty is one's country and polity; but this does not mean that a patriot will uncritically support any government that holds power in her country, or any form of government that might be in place there. On this point MacIntyre's conception of patriotism

12 MacIntyre, 'Is Patriotism a Virtue?', pp. 49–50.
13 MacIntyre, 'Is Patriotism a Virtue?', p. 55.

differs from the type of extreme patriotism that has been widespread throughout history and seems to be quite popular today. The patriot's allegiance, he says, is not to the *status quo* of power, but rather to 'the nation conceived *as a project*'. One can oppose one's country's government, or the system of government, in the name of the true character, history and aspirations of the *patria*. To that extent, this type of patriotism is critical and rational. But this must have a limit: for a patriot, at least some practices and projects of her country, some of its 'large interests', will be beyond questioning and critical scrutiny. To that extent, MacIntyre grants that patriotism, as he understands it, is 'a fundamentally irrational attitude'.[14] But he also contends that a more rational and therefore more constrained loyalty would fall short of true patriotism, and might be considered at best its 'emasculated' variety.

This view of patriotism is exposed to an array of objections. Some challenge its philosophical foundations, MacIntyre's communitarianism; others question the step from communitarianism to patriotism; still others seek to rebut his arguments from moral education, growth and sustenance, and from identity. I will take a critical look at these two arguments in the section 'A Morally Indifferent Partiality', below. Here I want to focus on what I think is the central issue for an overall assessment of this type of patriotism. MacIntyre writes that 'on occasion patriotism might require me to support and work for the success of some enterprise of my nation as crucial to its overall project…when the success of that enterprise would not be in the best interest of mankind'.[15] One might argue that this is enough to discredit his defence of patriotism, but that would beg the question at issue. Still, MacIntyre's admission raises the decisive question: can one embrace this type of patriotism, without thereby renouncing such basic moral notions as universal justice and common human solidarity?

This is one of the issues emphasized in Tolstoy's classic critique of patriotism. Tolstoy argued that patriotism is utterly incompatible with these notions, that it is merely egoism writ large, an exclusive and ultimately aggressive concern for one's own country, and a major cause of international misunderstanding, tension and war.[16] The root of war, he wrote, 'is the exclusive desire for the well-being of one's own people;

[14] MacIntyre, 'Is Patriotism a Virtue?', p. 52.
[15] MacIntyre, 'Is Patriotism a Virtue?', p. 53.
[16] *See* L. Tolstoy, 'On Patriotism' and 'Patriotism, or Peace?', in *Writings on Civil Disobedience and Non-violence* (Philadelphia: New Society Publishers, 1987).

it is patriotism. Therefore, to destroy war, destroy patriotism.'[17] MacIntyre might retort that *special* concern for one's country's well-being—a defining trait of patriotism—is not the same as, and need not evolve into, an *exclusive*, let alone *aggressive*, concern for it. This is true, and should count as a point in defence of patriotism—but not the type of patriotism advanced by MacIntyre. MacIntyre's patriot may promote his country's interests in a critical, and therefore non-exclusive way, over a range of issues. However, when it comes to those 'large interests' of his country that are beyond criticism and must be supported in an irrational way, his concern will inevitably become exclusive, and eventually aggressive too. At this point, Tolstoy's critique of patriotism applies with full force. If we think of justice in universal, rather than parochial terms, if we acknowledge common human solidarity as a weighty moral consideration, and if we consider peace of paramount importance and will countenance war only if it is just, we must reject the kind of patriotism advocated in MacIntyre's lecture.

'If Right, to be Kept Right; and if Wrong, to be Set Right'

Tolstoy and MacIntyre are poles apart. One emphasizes the basic moral notions of universal, impartial justice and common human solidarity, and rejects all patriotism as incompatible with them and responsible for much enmity and strife among countries. The other rejects cosmopolitan impartialism as false to the way we become, remain and flourish as moral beings, and incapable of providing motivation for acting morally; he then offers a version of extreme patriotism instead. Yet both present us with the same stark choice: we must adopt either a sweeping universalism that leaves no room for love of and loyalty to one's country and polity, or a patriotism that sets aside fundamental moral considerations of justice and humanity whenever 'large interests' of the *patria* are at stake, and ultimately grounds all morality in local attachment. MacIntyre is aware that some might hope for a compromise, but denies that there is room for it: anything that falls short of his robust version of patriotism would no longer be patriotism, but merely an empty slogan that serves as a cover for an essentially universalist view. The nature and strength of patriotism is revealed most clearly in situations of conflict. In a conflict that concerns one's country's survival or

[17] Tolstoy, 'Patriotism, or Peace?', p. 140.

other 'large interests', whether generated by scarcity of resources or by incompatible ways of life, true patriotism would require loyalty to the *patria*, including the willingness to kill and die for it, even though that meant going against the considerations enjoined by universal morality. 'Restricted' patriotism, on the other hand, would have those considerations override love of and loyalty to one's country. That might lead either to neutrality between one's own country and the enemy, or to actually supporting the enemy, whose cause is found just, against one's own country.

In response to MacIntyre's defence of a robust type of patriotism, some philosophers have nevertheless searched for a middle way. Thus Marcia Baron proposes a version of patriotism that is compatible with liberal morality.[18] She argues that the conflict between impartiality and partiality is not as deep as MacIntyre makes out: morality allows for both types of considerations, but at different levels. At one level, one is often justified in taking into account one's particular attachments and commitments, including those to one's country and compatriots. At another level, one can and should reflect on such attachments and commitments from a universal, impartial point of view, and determine their proper scope and weight, allowing, for example, 'that with respect to certain matters and within limits, it is *good* for an American to judge as an American, and to put American interests first'.[19] In such cases, partiality is seen as legitimate and indeed valuable from a universal, impartial point of view. This is how we think of our preferences for, and moral obligations to, our family, friends or local community: the partiality involved is appropriate, not only for us, but for anyone, provided, of course, that it is kept within certain limits.

Stephen Nathanson, too, argues that impartiality required by universal morality allows for particular attachments and special obligations, including those to one's country and compatriots. The Ten Commandments, for instance, are mostly impartial, but they also include 'Honor *your* father and *your* mother.' Nathanson spells out his version of patriotism, claiming that it is immune both to Tolstoy's critique of patriotism and to MacIntyre's strictures against anything that falls short of his own, extreme version of patriotism.[20] Nathanson's central claim is that

---

[18] Baron, 'Patriotism and "Liberal" Morality', in *Patriotism*.

[19] Baron, 'Patriotism and "Liberal" Morality', p. 64.

[20] S. Nathanson, 'In Defense of "Moderate Patriotism"', in *Patriotism*, and *Patriotism, Morality, and Peace* (Lanham, MD: Rowman & Littlefield, 1993).

patriotism involves a special concern for one's country, but that this concern need not be unconstrained, nor exclusive and aggressive.

Like other special attachments and commitments, those to one's country can and should be constrained by moral rules that apply universally. This 'moderate patriotism' encourages people to promote the interests of their country and compatriots only in ways permitted by moral rules. For instance, while it may require the patriot to fight for his country, it will do so only if the war is, and remains, just. An extreme patriot will not flinch from fighting for his country whether its cause be just or not, and often in whatever way it takes to ensure its victory.

Moderate patriotism is not exclusive. Its adherent shows special concern for her country and compatriots, but that does not prevent her from having a measure of concern for other countries and their inhabitants. Moreover, it allows for the possibility that the concern for human beings in general will sometimes override the concern for one's country and compatriots. Extreme patriotism, by contrast, gives greater weight to the (large) interests of one's country and compatriots than to those of other countries and their inhabitants whenever the two come into conflict.

Finally, moderate patriotism is not uncritical and automatic. For its adherent, it is not enough that the country is *her* country. She also expects it to live up to certain moral and other standards and thereby deserve her support, devotion and special concern for its welfare. When it fails to do so, she will submit it to sustained moral criticism and seek to get it to mend its ways. This approach is captured in a saying about patriotism that adds a twist to the popular 'Our country, right or wrong': 'My country, right or wrong; if right, to be kept right; and if wrong, to be set right!'[21] On the other hand, an extreme patriot of the more popular sort loves his country uncritically, stands by it whatever it does, and tends to see any serious criticism of it as inappropriate, if not as outright treason. An extreme patriot of the more philosophical sort, invoked by MacIntyre, does the same, as long as his country's 'large interests' are at issue.

Nathanson also rebuts MacIntyre's attempt to collapse moderate patriotism into universalism. In some cases, it will indeed be right to refuse support to practices or policies of one's own country, if they are

[21] Carl Schurz, German-American politician (1829–1906), in a speech in the US Senate, 29 February 1872.

unjust or inhumane. But a moderate patriot will not be neutral in each and every case of conflict of her country's rights and interests and those of another. In particular, in a struggle concerning the very survival of her own and another community, in which no just accommodation is possible, universal morality will not require that she remain neutral. She will be justified in joining her own country's efforts. The fact that she will do so with a sense of deep regret, rather than with a jingoistic attitude all too typical of extreme patriots, only shows the moral superiority of her position.

Baron and Nathanson have succeeded in constructing a middle-of-the-road position that avoids both sweeping universalism that leaves no room for patriotic attachment and loyalty, and extreme patriotism that acknowledges no universal moral considerations. They have convincingly rebutted MacIntyre's attempt to collapse moderate patriotism into cosmopolitanism, and shown that this type of patriotism is morally unobjectionable.[22]

A Morally Indifferent Partiality

To say that moderate patriotism is morally unobjectionable, however, is not to say that it is morally valuable or even required. Both Baron and Nathanson fail to distinguish between these three positions clearly and consistently enough.[23] Yet neither the second nor the third thesis

[22] More recently, Kok-Chor Tan has been advancing the same position, presenting it as a version of cosmopolitanism ('Patriotic Obligations', *The Monist* 86 [2003]; *Justice without Borders: Cosmopolitanism, Nationalism and Patriotism* [Cambridge: Cambridge University Press, 2004]; 'The Demands of Justice and National Allegiances', in G. Brock and H. Brighouse (eds.), *The Political Philosophy of Cosmopolitanism* [Cambridge: Cambridge University Press, 2005]). Strangely, he nowhere makes any reference to the work of M. Baron or S. Nathanson.

[23] Baron first appears to be arguing that moderate patriotism is good ('Patriotism and "Liberal" Morality', p. 64) or 'deserves to be regarded as a virtue' (p. 70), but later says that the claim she is defending is more modest: patriotism is only 'a plausible candidate for being a virtue' (p. 75). As she explains, her aim 'is not the lofty one of showing that properly understood, patriotism is a virtue, but only that there is, for someone who accepts the "morality of liberalism", at least one conception of patriotism which it is plausible for her to hold to be a virtue' (p. 85, n. 28). But we are not told just why one might hold that moderate patriotism is indeed a virtue; and what Baron's arguments show is only that such patriotism is morally permissible. (Baron's paper was originally published in 1989. In her 2001 postscript, she tones down her claims for patriotism even further; see pp. 81–82.) Nathanson, too, vacillates between different claims for moderate patriotism. Sometimes he seems to be defending such patriotism as but a morally permissible preference for one's own country (*Patriotism, Morality, and Peace*,

follows from the first; if we are to accept either the claim that moderate patriotism is a duty, or the claim that it is morally valuable, its proponents need to provide further argument.

One might expect such argument to be couched in communitarian terms. When discussing Alasdair MacIntyre's defence of patriotism, I canvassed—but did not assess—two such arguments: from moral education, growth, and sustenance, and from identity. MacIntyre means these arguments to ground his own, extreme version of patriotism; but they could equally be marshalled in support of moderate patriotism.

The first argument could be construed in two different ways. MacIntyre could be taken as saying that, as moral beings, we have no choice but to be patriots. Given the facts of moral education, moral development, moral life, if I were to discard my allegiance to my country, I would thereby be opting out of morality. For there is no morality as such, over and above the moralities of particular communities, nations, polities. And there is no morality *for me* but the morality of *my* community, *my* country. Alternatively, he might be taken as saying that, as a matter of fact, I *can* set myself free of allegiance to my community and its moral norms and values, but *ought not* to do so.

On the first interpretation, the argument greatly exaggerates the repercussions of the fact that the individual owes his moral education and growth, his moral norms and values, his very capacity of moral deliberation and action, to his community. The individual *sets out* as a moral agent who identifies morally with the community, subscribes to its norms and shares its values. But he need not *remain* this way: he is not condemned to lifelong loyalty to the particular morality his community imparted in him. He can evolve in more than one direction. He can deploy the very capacity for moral judgment his community helped him develop to submit the norms and values of that community to critical scrutiny, and argue for all manner of change. I do not mean mere tinkering with the community's morality, for MacIntyre's position allows for that. I am talking about radical moral critique of one's country, one's polity, of the sort that challenges its basic beliefs and

p. 169); sometimes he portrays it as a special duty, analogous to the duty one has to one's family (pp. 42–44, 65–66, 71); at other times, he seems to be suggesting that moderate patriotism is a virtue (p. 113); at other times still, he presents it as a moral ideal (pp. 48, 199, 209). But, again, there is no explicit argument for any of the positive claims for moderate patriotism; what Nathanson's arguments actually establish is only that this type of patriotism is morally allowed.

commitments. That, too, is a possibility; indeed, all major change in moral belief and practice takes place in the wake of such challenge.

On another reading of MacIntyre's argument, he is saying that the option of morally parting ways with one's community does obtain, but one should not take it. Why not? Perhaps the reason for sticking with the community and its morality is that if I do not, I am 'apt to lose my hold upon all genuine standards of judgment'. But surely this hazard, too, is greatly exaggerated. Every case of radical *and* serious, i.e. intellectually and morally respectable, critique of one's community's morality is evidence to the contrary: in every such case a community's morality is judged, and found wanting, by applying some 'genuine standards of judgment'. Is the objection, then, one of ingratitude? But if my community provided me with moral education, rather than indoctrination, it will have endowed me not only with certain moral norms and values by which to live and judge myself and others, but also with the wherewithal for engaging in moral thinking on my own. If so, surely I should make use of it and follow its logic wherever it might lead, rather than adhere complacently to the norms and values of my community. Indeed, that might be thought the most appropriate type of gratitude, rather than lack of it.

The other communitarian argument for moderate patriotism as a duty is that of identity. It is already suggested by the preceding one: if an individual can live and flourish as a moral agent only as a member of a community, by playing the role involved in this membership, then her very identity is bound up with that of her community. The fact that she belongs to a community, a country, a polity, rather like the fact that she is a member of a family, has great importance for her sense of self, her very identity: it is a fact she will cite when telling us who and what she is. Her country is something she identifies with, and also something others identify her with. One's relation to one's country and compatriots is thus quite unlike one's relation to other countries and their inhabitants. It is a special relation: one *belongs* to one's country; on the other hand, this sense of belonging to one's country is *part of one's very identity*. This relation involves special concern of the sort one could not have for other countries and for human beings in general. Without such concern, what sense can the expression 'my country' have?

This argument, too, fails; whatever plausibility it may have trades on the ambiguity of 'identity'. The term can be intelligibly used either in a factual, morally neutral sense, or in a sense that involves certain moral obligations. An individual may reside continuously in a country since his birth, be registered as a citizen, and possess all the usual documents. He may speak the country's language and fully participate in its social and cultural life. He may participate in its political life (perhaps only with a view to promoting the interests of his class or region). He may obey the country's laws and authorities (perhaps without ever giving much thought to the reasons for doing so, or because he reckons that disobedience does not pay). When asked who he is, what he is, his reply may include a reference to the country he lives in, the polity whose citizen he is, as an important item without which the reply would be significantly incomplete. In view of all this, he may refer to the country as *his* country.

Then again, he may also believe that he has a moral duty to show special concern for the welfare of his country and compatriots. In replying to the question who and what he is, he may mention this specifically moral belief, holding that otherwise the reply would remain significantly incomplete.

These are two different (partial) accounts of identity. The second, morally loaded account may, but need not, accompany the first, morally uninvolved account. If someone, in telling us who and what she is, offers the first, but at the same time rejects the second, the answer will not be inconsistent. It will not be reason enough to suspect that her identity is incomplete, or that her talk of 'her country' is an indication of misunderstanding or hypocrisy. In other words, not everyone who intelligibly and sincerely speaks of 'her country' is necessarily a patriot. A person who is not a patriot is not necessarily someone who fails to perform a moral duty—a failure to be explained in terms of her flawed identity.

While the view that patriotism is morally mandatory is obviously at home in communitarian philosophy, it could also be supported by arguments that do not presuppose a communitarian view of self and community. There are at least three such arguments: from gratitude, from fairness, and from the common good.

When asked to explain why they think they owe special concern to their country and compatriots, many patriots talk of gratitude they feel towards, and believe they owe to, their country. So does Maurizio Viroli: 'We have a moral obligation toward our country because we are indebted to it. We owe our country our life, our education, our language, and, in the most fortunate cases, our liberty. If we want to be moral persons, we must return what we have received, at least in part, by serving the common good'.[24]

Viroli is exaggerating the benefits we have received from our country; any gratitude owed for being born or brought up is normally owed to parents, rather than *patria*. But there are some important benefits we have received from our country. Are we not bound to show gratitude for them, and is not the obvious way to do so to show special concern for the country and compatriots?

I think not; for the standard arguments against the gratitude theory of political obligation apply with equal force to the argument from gratitude in the present context.[25]

We usually talk of gratitude in interpersonal relations. We also speak of gratitude to large and impersonal entities: one's school, university, profession, even one's country. But on closer inspection this often turns out to be an abbreviated way of referring to gratitude to certain specific persons who have acted within and on behalf of these large entities. That is so because the debt of gratitude is not incurred by *any* benefit received. If a benefit was conferred inadvertently, or advisedly but for the wrong reason—say, to improve the benefactor's public image—gratitude will be misplaced. We owe a moral debt of gratitude (rather than mere 'Thank you!' required by good manners) only to those who confer benefits on us deliberately and for the right reason: out of concern for our own good. And we cannot talk with confidence about the reasons a large and complex group or institution has for its actions.

If we put these worries aside, we can consider our compatriots as a mere aggregate of individuals. Do we owe them a debt of gratitude for the benefits our life in their midst has conferred on us? Again, we must ask about the reason for their law-abiding behaviour and social cooperation in general. Yet there is no single reason, common to all or even most of them. Some do their bit without giving much thought to the reasons for doing so. Some believe that doing so is, in the long run, the most prudent policy. Some act out of altruistic motives. Only the last group—surely a tiny minority—would be a proper object of our gratitude.

Moreover, gratitude is appropriate only for a benefit conferred freely, as a gift, and not for something that has been paid for. But most of the benefits one receives from one's country or polity are of the latter sort:

---

[24] M. Viroli, *For Love of Country: An Essay on Patriotism and Nationalism* (Oxford: Oxford University Press, 1995), p. 9.

[25] *See* A.J. Simmons, *Moral Principles and Political Obligations* (Princeton: Princeton University Press, 1979), chapter 7.

benefits paid for by law-abiding behaviour in general, and through taxation in particular.

The benefits the individual has received from her country might be thought to ground the duty of patriotism in a different way. One's country is not merely a patch of land inhabited by strangers to whom one owes nothing beyond what one owes to any other human being. It is rather a common enterprise that produces and distributes all manner of benefits, many of them of great importance to the individual. These benefits are made possible through the cooperation of those who live in the country, participate in the enterprise, owe and render allegiance to the polity. But for their cooperation, there would be none of these benefits to distribute and enjoy. The rules that provide the unity of purpose and the concert of action and determine the distribution of burdens and benefits enjoin, among other things, special concern for the welfare of compatriots which is not due to outsiders. Such concern is one of the basic prerequisites of the whole venture. But if so, then showing special concern for one's compatriots is a matter of fair play: it is only fair that one should do one's part, just as they do. To fail to reciprocate would be to take part in the distribution of something one did not help produce, to take advantage of one's compatriots.[26]

Unfortunately, this account leaves out a small, but highly significant group: those who make virtually no contribution to the common enterprise, but not because they choose to be free riders, nor because they object to the way the enterprise is organized and operated or, more radically, to the very idea of the moral, rather than merely pragmatic, division of humanity into countries, nations, polities. I have in mind those who would do their part if they could, but cannot because of some serious, lasting, incurable handicap for which they bear no responsibility. Since they contribute nothing, there is nothing to reciprocate for. Fair play does not require that we show special concern for them.[27]

This implication becomes even more problematic when we recall that it is just those people who are most in need of such concern, and present a particularly telling test of one's patriotism: concern for them would testify to the disinterested nature of the patriotic stance, and thus to its authenticity. A patriot accords considerable intrinsic value to the *patria*, and understands her concern for its welfare and that of her

---

[26] *See* R. Dagger, 'Rights, Boundaries, and the Bonds of Community: A Qualified Defense of Moral Parochialism', *American Political Science Review* 79 (1985).

[27] *See* R.E. Goodin, 'What is So Special about Our Fellow Countrymen?', in *Patriotism*, pp. 150–52.

compatriots as highly significant in itself, rather than a matter of give and take.

It might be argued that the rule enjoining special concern for our country and compatriots, just like other rules concerning special attachments, is justified by the good consequences of its adoption. Duties of this type mediate our fundamental, general duties and make possible their most effective discharge. They do so by establishing a division of moral labour, necessary because our capacity of doing good is limited by our circumstances. Each of us can normally be of greater assistance to those who are in some way close to us than to those who are not.

The trouble with this defence of patriotism is that patriots themselves will be reluctant to embrace it, for two different, but related reasons. They will find it much too weak, and alien to what they feel patriotism is all about. The duty of patriotism, just like all other special duties when construed in rule-consequentialist terms, will prove too weak: it will give way to the duty of general beneficence whenever the two come into conflict and acting on the latter is going to have better consequences than acting on the former. For any patriot worth his salt, this will surely be much too often.[28]

Moreover, this defence of patriotism presents the duty of special concern for one's country and compatriots as a pragmatic device for assigning to individuals some of their universal duties. Accordingly, it owes its moral force to the moral force of those universal duties. But if so, then, as one proponent of this understanding of patriotism concedes, 'it turns out that "our fellow countrymen" are not so very special after all'.[29] They merely happen to be the beneficiaries of the most effective way of putting into practice our concern for human beings in general. The special relationship between the patriot and the *patria* and compatriots—the relationship of love and identification—has been dissolved.

If so, we have no reason to think of patriotism as a moral duty, at least until some novel, more convincing argument for that claim is produced. Does that mean that there is nothing to be said for patriotism from a moral point of view?

---

[28] This is an instance of a more general, structural problem in rule-consequentialism. I discuss it in some detail in *Justifying Legal Punishment*, rev. edn (Atlantic Highlands, NJ: Humanities Press, 1997), pp. 118–28.

[29] Goodin, 'What is So Special about Our Fellow Countrymen?', p. 153.

Not necessarily. One might concede that special concern for one's country and compatriots is not a duty, but go on to argue that it is morally valuable, if one as a matter of fact shows such concern. Patriotism might be thought a moral virtue.

Some moral virtues might be considered obligatory. But that is not the case with all moral virtues: some are not mandatory, but it is good if we possess them. An example of the latter type is the sort of concern for those in extreme need shown by the late Mother Theresa, or for people in great danger and distress exhibited by members of humanitarian organizations such as Doctors Without Borders. A person showing concern for others well beyond the degree of concern for others required of us all is thought to be a morally better person than the rest of us (other things equal). On the other hand, when we fail to follow the example set by such persons, that is no reason for moral condemnation. For what they are doing is beyond the call of duty. Patriotism is a *special* concern for the welfare of one's country and compatriots, a concern beyond what we owe other people and communities; is it not, then, a supererogatory virtue?

To ask this is to ask: Is a patriot a *morally* better person than a person who is not a patriot (other things equal)? Is the special concern for one's country and compatriots that defines patriotism *morally* valuable? If it is, just why?

If we ask the analogous question about the kind of concern for other human beings shown by Mother Theresa or by Doctors Without Borders, the answer would seem to be that such concern is morally valuable for the same reason that makes a more modest degree of concern for others a duty falling on each one of us. The same moral value, sympathy for and assistance to people in need of it, grounds a certain degree of concern for others as a general moral duty and explains why a significantly higher degree of such concern is a moral ideal.

This explanation, however, does not apply in the case of patriotism. Patriotism is not but another extension of the duty of concern for others; it is a special concern for *my* country *because* it is *my* country, for *my* compatriots *because* they are *my* compatriots. Unlike Mother Theresa, who showed concern for every destitute, sick, dying person she could reach, and Doctors Without Borders, the concern of the patriot is by definition selective; and the selection is performed by the word 'my'. But the word 'my' cannot, *by itself*, play the critical role in an argument showing that a certain line of action is *morally* valuable. If it had the magic required for the task, one might deploy the same type of argument to show that other kinds of partialism, such as tribalism, racism or sexism, are *morally* valuable too.

If my argument in this section is convincing, patriotism is neither a moral duty nor a supererogatory virtue. That means that, morally speaking, there is nothing to be said *for* it. We have all manner of preferences for places and people, tend to identify with many groups, large and small, to think of them as in some sense ours, and to show special concern for their members. But however important in other respects these preferences, identifications and concerns might be, they lack positive moral significance. They are morally permissible as long as they are kept within certain bounds, but morally indifferent in themselves. So is patriotism.

'A Lively Sense of Collective Responsibility'

In Richard Aldington's novel *The Colonel's Daughter*, a character claims to be a patriot, and insists that patriotism and nationalism are entirely different attitudes. 'Patriotism is a lively sense of collective responsibility. Nationalism is a silly cock crowing on its own dunghill and calling for larger spurs and brighter beaks'.[30] This is a throwback to a way of distinguishing patriotism and nationalism I rejected at the outset; but I would like to explore, briefly, the understanding of patriotism offered by Aldington's hero.

As discussed so far, both extreme and moderate patriotism aim at defending and promoting the worldly—political, economic and cultural—interests of one's country and compatriots. Thus they fit the characterization of nationalism in the quotation: they are after larger spurs and brighter beaks. The difference between them is the length to which these will be pursued: both Machiavelli's and MacIntyre's extreme patriots will ultimately go to any length, when the 'large interests' of the *patria* are at stake, whereas the moderate patriot portrayed by Baron and Nathanson will acknowledge that universal justice and common human solidarity set limits to what may be done in this pursuit. Baron also calls for an expanded understanding of patriotism as a special concern for the flourishing of one's own country, including its 'moral flourishing'. The concern for the moral flourishing of one's country, she suggests, should be seen as an additional

[30] R. Aldington, *The Colonel's Daughter* (London: Chatto and Windus, 1931), p. 53.

manifestation of patriotism, and one that should make it even more acceptable to adherents of universal, liberal morality.[31]

Baron's position is thus half-way between the usual, worldly type of patriotism, and what I propose to term its distinctively ethical type. The latter would put aside objectives such as the country's political power, riches or cultural vibrancy—things that constitute the country's well-being in a mundane, non-moral sense. It would be concerned instead with the country's distinctively moral well-being, its moral identity and integrity. A patriot of this sort would not express her love for the *patria* by seeking to husband her country's resources and preserve its natural beauty and its historical heritage, or make it rich, powerful, culturally preeminent, or influential on the world scene. Instead, she would want to see her country live up to moral requirements and promote moral values, both at home and internationally. She would work for a just and humane society at home, and seek to make sure that her country acts justly beyond its borders, and shows common human solidarity towards those in need, however distant and unfamiliar.

In addition to these concerns for the moral integrity of her country at present, she would also be concerned for its past moral record and its implications for the present. She would support, and perhaps initiate, attempts at exploring the dark chapters of the country's history, acknowledging the wrongs perpetrated in decades or centuries past, and responding to that past in appropriate ways, whether by offering apologies or making amends, and by making sure such wrongs are not perpetrated yet again.

To be sure, a patriot of this, distinctively ethical type, would want to see justice done, rights respected, human solidarity at work at any time and in any place. But her patriotism would be given expression in her special concern that *her* country be guided by these moral principles and values, a concern more sustained and more deeply felt than her concern that these principles and values should be put into effect generally. She would feel that her own moral identity is inextricably interwoven with that of her country, that the moral record of the *patria* is hers too. Unlike a patriot of the more mundane type, she might not feel great pride in her country's worldly merits and achievements. However, she would be proud of the country's moral record, when it inspires pride. But her patriotism would be expressed, above all, in a critical

31 Baron, 'Patriotism and "Liberal" Morality', pp. 75–77.

approach to her country and compatriots. She would not deny, justify, excuse or belittle her country's unjust or inhumane practices, laws or policies, whether at home or abroad, as a patriot of the more popular type is much too prone to do. On the contrary, she would feel entitled, and indeed called, to submit them to critical moral scrutiny, and to speak out and act so that they may be identified, acknowledged and dismantled. She would not shirk her part in collective moral responsibility for wrongs present or past, but would rather willingly shoulder it. Thus her patriotism is accurately characterized as, essentially, 'a lively sense of collective responsibility'.

This characterization also suggest that, while we have no moral reason to adopt moderate patriotism of the more usual, mundane sort, we do have moral reason to show special concern for our own country's moral well-being.

Normally, when someone is wronged, someone else benefits from that wrong. When a society maintains an unjust or inhumane practice, or when a polity enacts and enforces an unjust or inhumane law, or lays down and implements such a policy, at least some, and sometimes many, of its members reap benefits from it. Sometimes such a practice, legislation or policy affects people beyond the country's borders; in such cases, the whole society or polity may benefit.

In all these cases, the responsibility for the injustice or lack of basic human solidarity lies, in the first instance, with those who make the decisions and those who implement them. It also lies, in the second instance, with those who give support to such decisions and their implementation. But some responsibility in this connection also accrues to those who have no part in the making of the decisions or in their implementation, nor proffer their support, but accept, rather than merely receive, the benefits such a practice, law or policy generates.[32] These are fairly straightforward types of collective moral responsibility.

Such responsibility may also accrue to those who have no part in designing or putting into effect immoral practices, laws or policies, do not support them or benefit from them, but do benefit in various ways from being members of the society or citizens of the polity at issue. One may derive considerable psychological benefit merely from membership in and identification with a society or polity: from the sense of belonging, support and security such membership and identification

[32] On the distinction between accepting and receiving benefits *see* Simmons, *Moral Principles and Political Obligations*, pp. 125–32.

afford. It seems to me that, if people accept, rather than merely receive, such benefits, while knowing about the immoral practices, laws or policies of their society or polity, or having no excuse for not knowing about them, that, too, generates collective moral responsibility.

It may be thought unduly harsh to talk of collective responsibility in relation to some wrongdoing accruing to individuals who make no causal contribution to that wrongdoing and have no control over its course. But I am not suggesting that they are responsible in the same way and to the same degree as those who make the decisions, those who implement them, or those whose support makes the decisions and their implementation possible, and that they are as blameworthy as those others. I am only saying that, in accepting benefits from those wrongs, or from their association with the wrongdoers, they underwrite those wrongs. In doing so, they accrue a degree of moral responsibility and join the class of those properly blamed. Their share of responsibility relating to the wrongs at issue is lesser and the blame to be laid at their door is lesser too—but they still bear *some* moral responsibility and deserve *some* moral blame on that account. They cannot say in good faith, 'Those wrongs have nothing to do with us! We are in no way implicated in them!'

Furthermore, it might be argued that, independently of any benefits, sheer solidarity with one's society or polity is enough to relate the individual to its immoral acts or practices about which she knows, or has no excuse for not knowing, even though she is otherwise not implicated in those acts or practices. The kind of solidarity I have in mind involves a community of interest, a common lot, and bonds of sentiment, and is usually indicated by vicarious pride and shame. To be sure, here the term 'responsibility' might be thought too strong; if so, we can talk of moral taint instead. Although one is in no way causally connected to the wrongdoing of which one's society or polity is guilty, nor even implicated in it through the acceptance of some benefits, one may still be considered morally tainted by one's solidarity with those who are.[33]

Thus I have a moral reason to develop and exercise a special concern for the moral record, the moral identity and integrity of my country and compatriots. I ought to be concerned about immoral practices of my society, immoral laws and policies of my polity, since they tend

[33] *See* J. Feinberg, 'Collective Responsibility', H. McGary, 'Morality and Collective Respon-sibility', and L. May, 'Metaphysical Guilt and Moral Taint', in L. May and S. Hoffman (eds.), *Collective Responsibility* (Savage, MD: Rowman & Littlefield, 1991).

to impose collective moral responsibility which I, too, have to shoulder, or to taint the moral record of many members or citizens, including myself. I ought to be concerned that such practices, laws and policies be identified, acknowledged and done away with, and that their harmful effects be redressed. By doing so, I will also be concerned for an important aspect of my own moral identity and integrity.[34]

Summing Up

In this paper, I approach patriotism as a topic in moral philosophy. Patriotism is first distinguished from nationalism in terms of the objects of these attitudes. The kind of patriotism that provides the last refuge to the scoundrel is put aside as not to the point. I then review the positions on the moral standing of patriotism: (1) extreme patriotism that trumps moral considerations that conflict with it, (2) extreme patriotism understood as the core moral virtue, (3) moderate patriotism, (4) patriotism as a morally indifferent preference, and (5) a distinctively ethical version of patriotism. I note that (1) is clearly morally unacceptable; concur with the critics of (2) that it, too, must be rejected; agree with the defenders of (3) that it is a distinctive and morally legitimate position, while also arguing that there is nothing to be said *for* it, morally speaking, and that it is therefore a morally indifferent preference (4); finally, I present (5) as a different type of patriotism which, under some fairly common circumstances, may be a moral duty.[35]

---

[34] It might be objected that this is not an argument for a certain kind of patriotism, but rather for acknowledging one's partaking in collective responsibility, entailed by one's acceptance of benefits bestowed by any group, and for showing special concern for the group's moral well-being. One could indeed argue along the same lines in relation to many groups, large or small. This type of argument becomes an argument for ethical patriotism when (i) the group in question is a country (and polity), and (ii) it is *my* country in a sense that is not purely formal. I can have 'a lively sense of collective responsibility' in relation to many groups, but can be an ethical patriot only when the collective is my country. On the other hand, I can live in a country without identifying with it in any significant sense. In such a case, I can still partake in the type of collective responsibility described here and become bound to show special concern for the country's moral record. That, too, will be an ethical stance, but it will not be ethical patriotism.

[35] In parts of this paper I draw on my 'Patriotism: A Deflationary View', *The Philosophical Forum* 33 (2002), and 'Patriotism: Mundane and Ethical', *Croatian Journal of Philosophy* 4 (2004).

An earlier version of the paper was read at the workshop 'Patriotism: Philosophical Perspectives', held at the Centre for Applied Philosophy and Public Ethics, University of Melbourne, on 21–22 August 2006. Thanks to participants in the discussion and to two referees for this journal for helpful comments.

PART III

GLOBAL POVERTY AND INTERNATIONAL DISTRIBUTIVE JUSTICE

THE DIFFERENCE PRINCIPLE, EQUALITY OF OPPORTUNITY, AND COSMOPOLITAN JUSTICE

Gillian Brock

What kinds of principles of justice should a cosmopolitan support? It would seem that because a cosmopolitan is someone who is committed to the equal moral worth of all human beings, she would need to endorse principles of justice that (somehow) are concerned with the well-being of every individual person (no matter what their group memberships), and that these principles of justice would need to have wide scope.[1] But what, more specifically, can be said about the content of these principles? Two suggestions are that a cosmopolitan should endorse a Global Difference Principle and a Principle of Global Equality of Opportunity.[2] In this paper I examine whether these two suggestions are compelling, by considering some recent arguments for these views. I argue against a Global Difference Principle, but for an alternative Needs-Based Minimum Floor Principle (where these are not co-extensive, as I explain). I develop a model of cosmopolitan justice which allows us to address not only matters of global distributive justice, but other global justice issues as well. Though I support what I refer to as a negative version of the Global Equality of Opportunity Principle, I argue that a more positive version of the ideal remains elusive.

[1] This kind of view can be found in the work of, for instance, Brian Barry, 'Statism and Nationalism: A Cosmopolitan Critique', *Nomos* XLI (1999), pp. 12–66; Charles Beitz, *Political Theory and International Relations* (Princeton: Princeton University Press, 1979); Charles Beitz, 'International Liberalism and Distributive Justice: A Survey of Recent Thought', *World Politics* 51 (1999), pp. 269–96; Charles Jones, *Global Justice* (Oxford: Oxford University Press, 1999); and Thomas Pogge, 'Cosmopolitanism and Sovereignty', *Ethics* 103 (October 1992), pp. 48–75.

[2] These suggestions are, of course, not necessarily mutually exclusive. For recent versions of both of these, see Darrel Moellendorf, *Cosmopolitan Justice* (Cambridge, MA: Westview Press, 2002). For a recent version of a Global Equality of Opportunity Principle, see Simon Caney, 'Cosmopolitan Justice and Equalizing Opportunities', *Metaphilosophy* 32 (2001), pp. 113–34.

Should Cosmopolitans Support a Global Difference Principle?

Some Reasons Offered in Support of a Global Difference Principle

I begin the analysis with the most well-developed and comprehensive recent account of cosmopolitan justice which contains in it central reasons offered in support of a Global Difference Principle, namely the work of Darrel Moellendorf as presented in *Cosmopolitan Justice*.[3] Moellendorf takes as his point of departure Rawls's early views on justice and, using Rawlsian considerations, argues that the later views on international justice must largely be rejected. Rawls's views on global justice, as outlined in *The Law of Peoples*,[4] differ markedly from his earlier views on justice, as expressed in *A Theory of Justice*.[5] In that earlier work, Rawls sets out to derive the principles of justice that should govern liberal societies and, by employing all the apparatus attached to the original position—the hypothetical choosing situation, he famously endorses two principles, namely, one protecting equal basic liberties, and the second permitting social and economic inequalities when (and only when) they are both to the greatest benefit of the least advantaged (the Difference Principle) and attached to positions which are open to all under conditions of fair equality of opportunity (the Fair Equality of Opportunity Principle). These principles should apply within liberal societies but not across them. Rather, in the international arena, Rawls thinks different principles would be chosen (in a second original position occupied by representatives of different peoples) and these would include principles acknowledging peoples' independence, their equality, that they have a right to self-defence, duties of non-intervention, to observe treaties, to honour a limited set of human rights, conduct themselves appropriately in war, and to assist other peoples living in unfavourable conditions.

Moellendorf argues that Rawls's reasoning in *The Law of Peoples* is faulty on a number of grounds, such as that the focus on peoples rather than persons means that Rawls has difficulty adequately capturing respect for persons,[6] that his focus on getting agreement means he sacrifices full justice for the sake of trying to get wider support,[7] and that

[3] Darrel Moellendorf, *Cosmopolitan Justice* (Cambridge, MA: Westview Press, 2002).
[4] John Rawls, *The Law of Peoples* (Cambridge, MA: Harvard University Press, 1999).
[5] John Rawls, *A Theory of Justice* (Cambridge, MA: Harvard University Press, 1971).
[6] Moellendorf, *Cosmopolitan Justice*, p. 14.
[7] Moellendorf, *Cosmopolitan Justice*, p. 15.

Rawls's reasons for excluding principles of socioeconomic equality and democracy are unconvincing. Moellendorf offers an alternative view which extends Rawls's picture of justice as defended in *A Theory of Justice* to the global context and notably includes: a fuller list of human rights that must be respected, requirements of constitutional democracy, global equality of opportunity, and a Global Difference Principle.

Like other cosmopolitans before him (such as Charles Beitz and Thomas Pogge),[8] Moellendorf's alternative construction is a single construction (rather than one involving two original positions) in which representatives 'are ignorant of which state the represented citizens inhabit, as well as the state's character, territory, and population size. They would also be ignorant of the various natural and social characteristics of the persons they represent'.[9] The representatives are more 'concerned with the freedom and ability of persons to pursue their own conceptions of the good life within a fair system of cooperation'[10] than they are concerned with the interests of peoples. Such representatives would thus be more concerned than Rawls is to protect democratic and egalitarian social orders, since the absence of these can importantly prevent people from pursuing their own conceptions of the good life. Why would representatives in a cosmopolitan original position choose a Global Difference Principle? If the representatives are 'ignorant of the talents and abilities of those whom they represent, they will want the collective set of talents and abilities to benefit all, not just their possessors',[11] Moellendorf reasons. So if the representatives have no knowledge of the distribution of talents, they would select principles in which inequalities of distribution that derive from differential talents and abilities are 'to the maximum benefit of the least advantaged over the course of their life'[12] and so they would choose the Difference Principle.

I agree with Moellendorf that the Rawlsian framework can provide a good way for us to think through what justice requires, because it sets up conditions for modelling impartiality well. However, I part company with Moellendorf on what this impartial choosing situation would yield. Like other cosmopolitans,[13] Moellendorf maintains that

---

[8] See, for instance, Beitz, *Political Theory and International Justice*, or Thomas Pogge, *Realizing Rawls* (Ithaca: Cornell University Press, 1989).

[9] Moellendorf, *Cosmopolitan Justice*, p. 17.

[10] Moellendorf, *Cosmopolitan Justice*, p. 17.

[11] Moellendorf, *Cosmopolitan Justice*, p. 80.

[12] Moellendorf, *Cosmopolitan Justice*, p. 80.

[13] Such as Beitz, *Political Theory and International Justice*, or Pogge, *Realizing Rawls*.

the Difference Principle would be chosen in the original position, and as I argue, this is not at all obvious; in fact there are good reasons to think it would not be chosen. I outline an alternative Rawlsian construction procedure and why it must be reasonable to choose a more minimally egalitarian principle—a particular Needs-Based Minimum Floor one. Would we not choose something that is more demanding than this Minimum Floor Principle? In order to make my case that we would not choose the more demanding Difference Principle (or a range of other more demanding principles), I introduce some compelling experimental psychology evidence. I go on to discuss why a Minimum Floor Principle is actually in the best interests of the least advantaged and so, possibly, co-extensive with what the Difference Principle would recommend, all things considered.

A Sketch of an Alternative Rawlsian-style Normative Thought Experiment

I begin by sketching a normative thought experiment that models ideal deliberating conditions. Here I focus on how it can supply us with an excellent framework for settling matters of global distributive justice (though it offers a systematic way for thinking through a number of other issues concerning global justice as well and I highlight some of these). I take my inspiration for the thought experiment from Rawls, though crucial details of my view are quite different from Rawls's account as should become quite clear soon enough. Rawlsian-style thought experiments are well suited to examining what an ideal world might require of us. These thought experiments, when properly set up, are a good way of fleshing out what we can reasonably expect of one another in a way that avoids inappropriate partiality: if people do not know what positions they might find themselves in during the lottery of life, they will pay more attention to what would constitute fair arrangements.[14]

[14] Many people raise questions of the following kinds when talk of social contracts is introduced: Is the contract supposed to be actual or hypothetical? If only hypothetical then why does a purely hypothetical contract have any binding force anyway? And if it has no binding force, then why adhere to it? I see talking in terms of social contracts as a way to specify what expectations various parties to the contract may reasonably have of each other: it is simply a way of fleshing out what those reasonable expectations might be. So, in answer to the questions listed: no, the contract developed assuming the ideal world presupposition is neither an actual contract nor a purely hypothetical one. It is a way to sift through what (actual) parties might reasonably

What should we assume about the ideal world we are asked to contemplate? In this exercise I try to make the ideal world as easy to imagine as possible so as to assist our deliberations, so I will make the assumptions about the ideal world we are to entertain such as to reflect our actual situation as much as possible. The world is divided into communities that are variously organized. Some communities may be overlapping, others may not be; some divisions may be sharp, others blurred. Some of the most obvious divisions are along political lines. Other divisions exist among some national, religious, cultural, or linguistic groups. I do not assume that all people everywhere form one community, nor do I assume homogeneity within communities.

I do not assume, further, that people are necessarily altruistic, or even mutually concerned, so as not to bias the outcome towards what one might expect will be the sorts of conclusions I will endorse. To avoid the charge of bias and so that my conclusions have maximum reach with opponents, I will assume for the purposes of the thought experiment that persons are instructed to be self-interested (understood in a fairly narrow sense). It is not that I think people are only self-interested and never other-regarding. It is more that people tend to have limited sympathies or impaired moral imagination. If we can be helped to feel the force of having to occupy another's position—of how that might be not for them, but as a real option for us—our moral imagination can be extended. The idea is to harness people's limited sympathies in ways that result in fairer solutions for everyone.[15]

An easy way to enter the thought experiment is to imagine a global conference has been organized. You have been *randomly selected* to be

expect of one another, by imagining a certain (hypothetical) choosing situation. Talking about social contracts is a way to talk about, and so uncover, the reasonable expectations people might have of one another in ongoing cooperation.

[15] The motivation of the parties in the original position is thus a mix of self-interest (as they are instructed to be self-interested) and fairness (they must arrive at a decision about what would be fair). This motivation is thus different from the typical Rawlsian story. Delegates must reach agreement on a fair basic framework, but I try to highlight how we can show what it is reasonable to expect, by leaning almost entirely on what is prudent (i.e., what rational, self-interested delegates would find of benefit). The original position helps shield them from knowledge of their identity and so helps to harness the power of self-interest.

The beauty of appealing to the experiments of Frohlich and Oppenheimer is that we need not have to make any assumptions about how the participants are motivated. We simply put them in a situation that suitably models impartiality and we see what they choose. So one of the attractions of appealing to this empirical work is we need not get into any debates about how parties are motivated: we can simply observe what they actually choose.

a decision-making delegate to this conference.[16] You are to participate in deciding what would be a fair framework for interactions and relations among the world's inhabitants. Though you have been invited to the decision-making forum, you do not know anything about what allegiances you have (or may have after the conference concludes), but you do know that whatever decisions are made at this conference will be binding ones. It may turn out that you find you belong to a developing nation, occupy a territory with poor natural resources, belong to a generation which does not yet exist, and so forth. Given these sorts of possibilities, you are provided with reasons to care about what you would be prepared to tolerate in a range of different circumstances.

You can have access to any information you like about various subjects (such as history, psychology, or economics), but so far as possible, very little (if any) information about subjects such as the demographics of world population should be made available. The idea is that you should not have access to information which could lead you to deduce odds, since (for instance) if you know that over one billion of the six billion people alive today are Indian, some might be tempted to gamble that they are going to turn out to be Indian, and so try to ensure Indians get better treatment than others. I want to eliminate scope for this sort of gambling.[17] I contend that if a rational individual does not know the odds, it is not rational to gamble (under at least certain conditions, especially the ones described). She will have to think more seriously about what 'the strains of commitment'[18] will really involve and what she will honestly be prepared to tolerate. For these reasons, delegates do not know where they live, the territory's size, how big or powerful the people are, what level of economic development is dominant in that territory, how well-endowed it is with natural resources, and so forth.

---

[16] I prefer to have my delegates randomly selected rather than being representatives for a range of reasons having to do with the problematic nature of representation, especially in this context. The notion of representation does, and can do, no real work here.

[17] I contend that if a rational individual does not know the odds, it is not rational to gamble (under at least certain conditions, especially the ones described). She will have to think more seriously about what 'the strains of commitment' will really involve and what she will honestly be prepared to tolerate.

[18] This is Rawls's term, but basically here it means that whatever decisions are made at this conference will be binding ones—you will have to live with the results knowing this imposes 'the strains of commitment'. See, for instance, John Rawls, *Justice as Fairness: A Restatement* (Cambridge, MA: Belknap, 2001), pp. 103–104.

More positively, certain information will be made available to all delegates. This information pack includes material about our urgent global collective problems and how we will have to cooperate to solve them. Delegates will have information about various threats to peace and security, including threats we face as a result of the increasing number of people who have access to weapons (especially weapons of mass destruction), and the activities of terrorists and drug traffickers. Delegates will have information about various environmental threats we face, such as the destruction of the ozone layer and the current state of knowledge about global warming. Information about threats to health such as the spread of highly infectious diseases will also be included. Some of this information will make clear that these problems have global reach and require global cooperation if they are to be resolved. Some of this material will also maintain that the people of the world are in a state of interdependence and mutual vulnerability; they rely on each other crucially if they are to achieve any reasonable level of peace, security or well-being both now and in the future.[19]

The main issue delegates must entertain concerns what *basic* framework governing the world's inhabitants we can reasonably expect to agree on as fair ones. Delegates will be aware that any entitlements selected will generate financial obligations. What is the *minimum* set of protections and entitlements we could reasonably be prepared to tolerate? What would be the minimum reasonable lot for people to agree to? Since individual contractors have no particular knowledge of how they will be positioned, who each will be once the conference adjourns, it would not be prudent to agree to any arrangements that would be unbearable, since delegates may find themselves having to occupy the position of such a person. So, the idea is that delegates would agree only to those policies that did not have unbearable effects on people, since they might end up being on the receiving end of such policies. More positively, whatever else they choose, delegates would find it prudent and reasonable for each person to be able to enjoy the prospects for a decent life and much discussion would be about the (minimum) content of such a life. I submit we would centre discussion towards the terms of agreement around at least two primary guidelines of roughly

[19] They will also have information about those who dissent from these common views. Notice how this recognition, though seemingly obvious, is decidedly lacking in Rawls's account as discussed in *Law of Peoples*.

equal importance, namely, that everyone should enjoy *some* equal basic liberties, and everyone should be protected from certain real (or high probability) opportunities for serious harms.

Reasonable people will care, at least minimally, about enjoying a *certain* level of freedom. Freedom may, of course, not be the only thing they care about and often they may not care about it very much when other issues are at stake about which they care more deeply. Nevertheless, reasonable people will care at least a little about enjoying *some* freedoms. Many kinds of freedoms will be of interest, but importantly, they would include freedom from assault or extreme coercion (such as slavery) and *some* basic freedoms governing movement, association and speech. We need to be permitted to evaluate and revise the central ideas which govern our lives should we choose to do this. Delegates should recognize that it is possible they could find themselves in a society with whose major organizing values, principles and commitments they disagree. In such situations, it would be prudent to have—and, indeed, some might reasonably insist on having—the scope to question and revise the values operative in the society, or at least a certain freedom to live their lives in accordance with values they find more congenial. Recognizing this they would, therefore, endorse a certain freedom of dissent, conscience and speech. Delegates would want certain minimum guarantees about what counts as permissible treatment. Heading the list of guarantees we would choose would be guarantees against assault, torture, imprisonment without trial or sufficient warrant, extreme coercion of various kinds (such as slavery) and so forth. But, as I have also suggested, it would be reasonable for them to add some freedoms governing dissent, conscience, speech, association and movement.[20]

---

[20] Would this idea really need further justification? Perhaps someone might press for one, especially someone concerned with the idea that those not from liberal democracies might not see this emphasis on freedom as so important or even reasonable. So let me say more about why I think the level of attention I give to freedom can be expected to be universal. If you do not know anything about what sort of position you will occupy under the new arrangements, why would you allow some people to have more freedom of a very basic kind than others? Unless you agree that everyone should have equal basic freedom, you might end up (say) giving some people more basic freedom than you have: you might deny yourself the freedom to go about your business free from assault, though others enjoy this liberty. Given their lack of knowledge about their particular interests, prudent delegates would agree to equal basic liberties. Similarly, it would not be prudent to agree to adopt (say) racist or sexist practices, since one may find oneself at the receiving end of such practices once the conference concludes. It would be better not to place constraints on one's liberties and opportunities,

In addition to caring about protecting freedom, rational decision-makers will also want protection from real opportunities for serious harms to which they would be vulnerable (and potentially powerless to resist) in certain cases. Under some kinds of arrangements there could be enormous opportunities to inflict harms. For instance, multinational corporations operating in unregulated market economies can threaten people's abilities to subsist in various ways, for instance, they can pollute so severely that they poison the soil and water such that crops are no longer able to grow properly (or perhaps more controversially, they can control labour markets so that wages are set at bare or below subsistence levels). In these kinds of cases people's abilities to subsist may be significantly undermined. Indeed, people considering what arrangements to adopt would be vigilant to ensure that meeting their needs is within their reach and so importantly protected, since being unable to meet our basic needs must be one of the greatest harms that can ensue. Reflecting on the gravity of such a harm in particular, more positively but in a similar vein, we would find it reasonable to have certain guaranteed minimal opportunities and those would be strongly influenced by a certain base-line minimum, namely, what is necessary to be enabled to meet our basic needs for ourselves.

Furthermore, adopting the perspective of self-interested persons (as the instructions to delegates require them to do), delegates should consider the possibility that they are permanently disabled and they should also consider the actual periods of extreme dependence which naturally occur in the human life-cycle. Having contemplated these issues, self-interested individuals would want adequate protections to be guaranteed should (or when) the need arises. Clearly-thinking self-interested individuals (or at least, reasonable people adopting the guise of such persons) behind an appropriate veil of ignorance should be strongly motivated to choose not only to ensure certain minimal opportunities to meet our needs for ourselves are available, but also that persons should have adequate provisions to be assisted with need-satisfaction, should they not be in a position to meet their needs themselves.

So my claim is that the minimum package it would be reasonable to agree to in the ideal choosing situation I have identified is that we

since it would be more prudent to have more rather than less freedom to pursue whatever your goals turn out to be.

should all be adequately positioned to enjoy the prospects for a decent life, as fleshed out by what is necessary to be enabled to meet our basic needs and those of our dependents (but with provisions firmly in place for the permanently or temporarily disabled to be adequately cared for) and certain guarantees about basic freedom.[21] We would use this as a base-line and endorse social and political arrangements that can ensure and underwrite at least these important goods.

The minimum package endorsed will have implications for most spheres of human activity, especially economic activity and political organization. For instance, economic activity must be sensitive to everyone's prospects for a decent life and regulations must be devised to ensure this. Extensive sets of rules would need to be outlined to make plain for all just what would constitute important threats to people's prospects for decent lives. Organizations that can monitor and enforce these rules must be established.

What sort of governance structure would we endorse? There are many kinds of arrangements we could choose but two key guiding principles would operate: we would want our vital interests (such as our ability to subsist) protected and it can be anticipated that we would want to retain as much control over affairs that directly affect us as is consistent with protection of those vital interests. Any governing authorities we endorse will have as a high priority that they are to protect our vital interests, and the legitimacy of governing bodies will rest on their ability to do an adequate job of this. Given my ideal world (strongly coloured by the actual world) assumptions include that the world is already divided into political communities, delegates might find it reasonable to use those divisions in some of their prescriptions.

---

[21] On my account, a need is basic if satisfying it is a necessary condition for human agency. This link to agency helps us derive a list of our basic needs which can circumvent concerns about how an account of such needs could be sufficiently 'objective', non-arbitrary, and enjoy widespread cross-cultural support. If basic needs are those things the satisfaction of which is necessary for human agency, by examining the prerequisites of human agency, of what being a human agent is like, we can derive a more specific list of such conditions, and so basic needs. For instance, by definition, to be an agent one must be able to deliberate and choose. In order to deliberate and choose one will need at least a certain amount of (1) physical and mental health, (2) sufficient security to be able to act, (3) a sufficient level of understanding of what one is choosing between, and (4) a certain amount of autonomy. Because of its important role in developing (and maintaining) (1)–(4), I also add a fifth basic need which underlines the importance of our social needs, namely, (5) decent social relations with at least some others. These ideas are developed in my 'Needs and Global Justice' (forthcoming in *Philosophy*).

They might agree that governments of those territories have primary authority to underwrite people's abilities to meet their needs and protect their freedoms, but when those governments are unable to do so, the duties should be distributed more effectively. Mixed forms of governance might reasonably be chosen such that in some matters local bodies have complete control; in others—where protection of vital interests can only be secured if there is widespread cooperation across states—joint sovereignty might reasonably be chosen. At any rate, whatever governing structures we endorse would (at a minimum) have as the central part of their mandate to protect people's vital interests, to ensure that people are so positioned that meeting their basic needs is within their reach and their basic liberties are protected.[22]

Delegates are aware that all entitlements chosen need to be financed and so generate financial obligations. Resources will need to be forthcoming to fund the arrangements that are chosen as minimally acceptable. We will need to address the issue of what counts as fair ownership of resources, but whatever account of fair ownership of resources we endorse, cannot be such that it effectively blocks funding reasonable arrangements necessary to underwrite the basic framework, since obligations to set up and do our part in supporting the basic framework are more fundamental.

I have suggested that a rough guiding principle we would choose is to have social and political arrangements that allow reasonable opportunities for us to be enabled to meet our basic needs. But wouldn't we want more? Would we find it reasonable to endorse something like a Global Difference Principle, or more substantive equality? As I go on to discuss in the next section, a threshold principle is the more compelling choice.

---

[22] Questions about the kind of favouritism we may show to co-members of our group can only be addressed once there is commitment to the basic framework with all its protections. Assuming this is the case and we have a suitably well-organized basic structure in which vital interests are protected, all have prospects for decent lives and control over those lives as is consistent with protection of vital interests, it may be permissible to favour other interests of compatriots and in other ways be partial to members of one's group in conferring further benefits, so long as this is not in conflict with provision of the basic agreed framework. Theoretically, at the very least, there is some permissible space for favouring our compatriots in certain matters, but the extent of the favouritism we may show must be governed by the commitment we all have to support the basic framework and does not include (for instance) favouring the non-basic interests of compatriots above more needy non-compatriots, since this would not be selected in the normative thought experiment.

Empirical Evidence for the View

A sceptic might complain that such arm-chair theorizing is all well and good, but what evidence is there really that anything like what I suggest would be chosen, would *actually* be chosen? Why, for instance, would they not choose the more demanding Difference Principle? I am happy to report that there is quite a bit of encouraging evidence to support these claims. The work of Norman Frohlich and Joe Oppenheimer is particularly instructive.[23]

Frohlich and Oppenheimer argue that the key to understanding issues of distributive justice is choosing under conditions of impartiality (that is, where one must set aside certain particular interests we actually have which might well skew our judgments about fairness). They designed some experiments to set up conditions of impartiality so that they could assess what principles would be chosen and how stable these choices prove to be over time. Imperfect information can generate ideal conditions for impartiality to operate, and so the experiments set up a situation in which subjects do not know what will be in their immediate self-interest, yet must choose, as a group, by which principle of distributive justice they will run their affairs. Frohlich and Oppenheimer (and others) repeated their experiments in different countries to ensure the results were generalizable.[24] They were particularly interested to see whether Harsanyi's principle of maximizing the average income or Rawls's idea of maximizing the income for the worst

[23] Norman Frohlich and Joe Oppenheimer, *Choosing Justice: An Experimental Approach to Ethical Theory* (Berkeley and Los Angeles, CA: University of California Press, 1992). Other experimental evidence for the salience of needs in issues in distributive justice can also be found in a host of other places, such as Maya Bar-Hillel and Menahem Yaari, 'Judgements of Distributive Justice', in Barbara Mellers and Jonathan Baron (eds.), *Psychological Perspectives on Justice: Theory and Applications* (Cambridge: Cambridge University Press, 1993), pp. 55–84; Helmut Lamm and Thomas Schwinger, 'Norms concerning Distributive Justice: Are Needs Taken into Consideration in Allocation Decisions?' *Social Psychology Quarterly* 43 (1980), pp. 425–29; and David Miller, 'Distributive Justice: What the People Think', *Ethics* 102 (1992), pp. 555–93, especially pp. 570–76.

[24] Rena de la Cruz-Dona and Alan Martina, *Diverse Groups Agreeing on a System of Justice in Distribution: Evidence from the Philippines* (Mimeo; Canberra: Australia National University, 2000); Michael Jackson and Peter Hill, 'A Fair Share', *Journal of Theoretical Politics* 7 (1995), pp. 69–179; Grzegorz Lissowkski, Tadeusz Tyszka and Wlodmierz Okrasa, 'Principles of Distributive Justice: Experiments in Poland and America', *Journal of Conflict Resolution* 35 (1991), pp. 98–119; Tatsuyoshi Saijo, Shusuke Takahashi and Stephen Turnbull, 'Justice in Income Distribution: An Experimental Approach' (Paper presented at the 1996 ISA [International Studies Association], San Diego, 18 April 1996).

off would be chosen. They offered participants four principles, but allowed them also to choose any other they could think of.[25] The four principles were:

1. Maximizing the floor income: 'The most just distribution of income is that which maximizes the floor (or lowest) income in the society.'[26]
2. Maximizing the average income: 'The most just distribution of income is that which maximizes the average income in the society.'[27]
3. Maximizing the average with a floor constraint of $_____: 'The most just distribution of income is that which maximizes the average income only after a certain specified minimum income is guaranteed to everyone.'[28]
4. Maximizing the average with a range constraint of $_____: 'The most just distribution of income is that which attempts to maximize the average income only after guaranteeing that the difference between the poorest and the richest individuals (i.e., the range of income) in the society is not greater than a specified amount.'[29]

Individual subjects then ranked which of these principles they preferred and how confident they felt about their rankings. For principles in which there is a dollar sign followed by a blank space, participants were asked to fill in the blank, if they chose that principle.

There were several stages to the experiments such as checking that participants understood all the principles, also that they understood that their selection would determine their income and that they would be randomly assigned to an income class. The participants also had to deliberate and decide as a group which principle they supported. After the group selection was made, subjects drew chits from a bag to get a distribution into an income category (low, middle or high income). Later in the experiments they were given the chance to perform tasks[30] to earn income and to have redistributive policies applied to see whether people were able to live with their choices.

Unanimous agreement was reached on a single principle in all cases in which the experiments were run properly. Interestingly, the

[25] Frohlich and Oppenheimer, *Choosing Justice*, p. 201.
[26] Frohlich and Oppenheimer, *Choosing Justice*, p. 35.
[27] Frohlich and Oppenheimer, *Choosing Justice*, p. 35.
[28] Frohlich and Oppenheimer, *Choosing Justice*, p. 35.
[29] Frohlich and Oppenheimer, *Choosing Justice*, p. 35.
[30] The tasks consisted of correcting spelling mistakes.

principles chosen in the experiment do not support either Rawls's or Harsanyi's models. Indeed, there was almost no support for the Difference Principle—it was chosen in only about 1 per cent of cases. It was certainly the least popular choice. By far the most popular choice in all countries was the principle with the guaranteed floor constraint: Around 78 per cent chose the floor constraint principle, 12 per cent chose to maximize the average income, 9 per cent chose the range constraint principle, and 1 per cent chose the Difference Principle. Overwhelmingly, groups 'wanted an income floor to be guaranteed to the worstoff individual. This floor was to act as a safety net for all individuals. But after this constraint was set, they wished to pre serve incentives so as to maximize production and hence average income.'[31]

What arguments were used for the floor constraint principle? In just about all groups there was a concern that individuals did not fall below some minimum level of income—*that they have enough to meet their basic needs.*[32] But concern was also raised about how to set the floor so that it did not undermine incentives to work.[33] There was also tension expressed between 'the desire to preserve entitlements and to ensure that people at the bottom were not too badly off'.[34] Overall, three factors dominated the discussion: balancing people's basic needs, with entitlements and incentives.

Since there was such a high level of support for a floor constraint principle, can we say the principle is a fair rule? Frohlich and Oppenheimer go on to extensively discuss whether various factors may have undermined the execution and design of the experiments, and consequently what we can say about the results. They argue that the subjects are not so homogenous in values or background that the resulting choices simply reflect that homogeneity rather than universal

[31] Frohlich and Oppenheimer, *Choosing Justice*, p. 59.

[32] Typical of such points were these two sets of comments:

1. 'I would like to see that everyone at least has the basic things. After that I don't really care. [If the floor is too low] ... a lot of people are going to be starving, and they will be without shelter and housing' (Transcripts, p. 99).
2. 'If you have people that are really poor, ... they have a tendency to just stay there because you know there isn't enough nutrition, they can't get an education, and all these kinds of things. But if you put it on a certain minimum, then they have a chance to get out of that situation. They have a chance' (Transcripts, p. 72).

[33] Frohlich and Oppenheimer, *Choosing Justice*, pp. 61–62.

[34] Frohlich and Oppenheimer, *Choosing Justice*, p. 63.

preference. They seem particularly concerned that they are not just reporting people's antecedent preferences. If that were the case the experiments would be of little value. They say: 'If the groups' choices are to have ethical validity, the answer to the following central question must be positive: Does the structure of the experiments affect the subjects' preferences and choices? ... Participating in the experiments must have a meaningful impact on the subjects if the experiments are to reveal anything about distributive justice.'[35] They go on to show how the experiments did make a difference to participants' views, since their rankings, preferences and confidence levels all change significantly during the experiments. In fact '[i]n 74 percent of the cases some individuals had a preferred principle that differed from the one chosen by the group. It is relevant to these results that Rawls indicated that a unanimous group decision need not reflect complete agreement among individuals regarding a principle. Rather, it was to reflect a workable political consensus. Our results support that interpretation: the decision is usually the result of political compromise, at least by some of the individuals.'[36] After extensive analysis of the shifts that occurred, they conclude that the changes in preferences and confidence levels constitute the kind of clear evidence needed to show the learning and decision phases made the relevant difference.[37]

As we see, then, needs matter in considering issues of justice, but even more important is the balance between needs, entitlements and incentives. We seek a balance between these three considerations. What we find when we examine the dialogue participants actually had in conditions modelling impartiality is that a balance was sought *and found* between the three central ideas: we could arrive at a reasoned view of the weight to give a commitment to meeting basic needs which does not thwart entitlement or dampen incentives. It is not the case that we care only about the worst off, nor is it the case that considerations of entitlements and incentives drown out our appropriate concern with needs. As the empirical evidence shows, concern for the needy is strong and robust, all things considered. But importantly, *it is strikingly not the case that under conditions of impartiality we want to arrange things so that we concern ourselves only with maximizing the*

35 Frohlich and Oppenheimer, *Choosing Justice*, p. 96.
36 Frohlich and Oppenheimer, *Choosing Justice*, p. 96.
37 Frohlich and Oppenheimer, *Choosing Justice*, p. 104.

position of the worst off. This tells rather dramatically against the Difference Principle.

Notice, then, what considerations actually come up in our reasoning about just principles under conditions relevantly modelling impartiality: balancing needs, (just) entitlement and incentives, rather than making things best for the worst off. Notice also that the principle chosen is a compromise principle—it is not most people's first choice, but the principle is overwhelmingly chosen as a good compromise or balancing principle between compelling considerations.

How stable are the choices when people must live with their decisions? Do the high producers feel they are not getting their due when part of what they earn is redistributed to others? What happens to productivity? Importantly, Frohlich and Oppenheimer found continued firm support for the floor constraint principle and, in fact, confidence over the principle and productivity increased when people experienced the results of having their decisions implemented.[38]

Summarizing the argument so far, I suggested that in an appropriate cosmopolitan original position, a Needs-Based Minimum Floor Principle would be chosen, rather than a Global Difference Principle. I offered two central grounds for my view here. First, I presented a theoretical argument as to why a major focus would appropriately go on being well-positioned to meet our needs, if we were in a cosmopolitan original position. Second, I presented relevant empirical evidence that supports the theoretical argument. What we would and should choose has to take account of how people actually reason under conditions of impartiality and how they are able to live with the decisions they make under such conditions. The preference for the Minimum Floor Principle shows stability over time; people become more confident rather than less when they actually have to live with the results of their choices. This all seems like pretty good evidence that in the long run this is better for the worst off, since the arrangements are likely to prove to be more stable.

Rather than forcing a choice between the two principles, though, there is a way in which we can see that the choice of a Global Difference Principle and my selection focusing on needs are actually co-extensive. If we follow the Global Difference Principle and inequalities are arranged such that they are to be maximally in the interests of the worst

[38] Frohlich and Oppenheimer, *Choosing Justice*, p. 118.

off over the long term, then the recommendations of the Difference Principle might, when cashed out, actually be the same as the recommendations of a Needs-Based Minimum Floor Principle. Why? Because, presumably, it is strongly in the interests of the worst off for people's (considered) preferences for the systems governing distribution to be extremely stable. A system that balances needs, entitlement and incentives in an appropriate way, in a way people overwhelmingly judge to be fair in conditions modelling impartiality, and in a way they grow increasingly confident rather than less confident about, strikes me as one that is very strongly in the interests of the worst off.

Can the Ideal of (Fair) Equality of Opportunity be Extended Globally?

Ideals about equality of opportunity have a powerful hold on us. Why is this? I suggest at least part of the answer has to do with the ideal's relying on a compelling negative intuition, something like this: It is unfair if some are significantly disadvantaged in life because of morally arbitrary features, so it is unfair if some have much worse prospects in life than others because of their race, ethnicity, class and so on. While the negative intuition motivating the ideal is a strong one, a problem occurs when we try to formulate the ideal more positively—when we move from the negative situation that we think must be rejected, to the positive formulation that we think can be endorsed as adequately realizing the ideal. Within one society the positive version of the ideal is often formulated along these sorts of lines: all citizens, 'regardless of class or origin, should have the same chance of attaining a favored social position, given the same talents and willingness to try'.[39] However, problems quickly emerge when we start to think about how to extend this kind of ideal globally. Two recent snapshots of how to extend the ideal have been offered and in this second part of the paper I examine them but show that each has significant problems.

Moellendorf believes a principle of equality of opportunity should apply globally and he cashes this out such that: 'a child born in rural Mozambique would be statistically as likely to become an investment banker as the child of a Swiss banker'.[40] I contend that this is an

[39] Rawls, *Law of Peoples*, p. 115.
[40] Moellendorf, *Cosmopolitan Justice*, p. 79.

inappropriate yardstick for several reasons but, most obviously and as I will go on to discuss, it is much too culturally specific. In specifying the ideal, why favour the positions of high status in one society over the positions of high status in others?

While I sympathize with the intuitions motivating the need for a principle covering equality of opportunity to be included in an adequate account of global justice, there are a number of problems with trying to articulate an adequate form of the ideal. One problem we face in trying to extend the notion of equality of opportunity from the state to the global arena is that different cultures often value different ends or goods, and positions' desirability will often vary in accordance with these different valuations. The problem with Moellendorf's formulation of the goal is his assumption that global equality of opportunity means that people equally able and motivated should have equal opportunities to achieve positions valued in one particular society. But this is not the best way to formulate the goal since it is vulnerable to criticisms of cultural insensitivity, as Bernard Boxill laments:

> The principle of fair equality can be only imperfectly carried out, at least as long as different cultures exist. Thus, if, in some societies the pinnacle is occupied by the businessman and businesswoman, this is by no means always the case; in Hindu society it was occupied by the priest, in old China, by the learned man, and in other societies, by the soldier. For which of these standards are opportunities to be equalized? To choose one over the other seems invidious and presumptuous.[41]

Simon Caney suggests that a way to express the goal that avoids this difficulty is this: 'Global Equality of Opportunity requires that persons (of equal ability and motivation) have equal opportunities to attain an equal number of positions of a commensurate standard of living.'[42] This way of expressing the goal is not vulnerable to Boxill's objections and so improves on Moellendorf's version in this respect (though as I go on to discuss, it has other weaknesses nonetheless). People should have equal opportunity to achieve 'positions of equal worth'[43] as captured by the standard of living positions enable. How do we construct a culture-neutral account of people's standard of living? The approach Caney favours follows that of Sen and Nussbaum in constructing standard of

---

[41] Bernard Boxill, 'Global Equality of Opportunity and National Integrity', *Social Philosophy and Policy* 5 (1987), pp. 143–68 (148).

[42] Simon Caney, 'Cosmopolitan Justice and Equalizing Opportunities', *Metaphilosophy* 32 (2001), pp. 113–34 (120).

[43] Caney, 'Cosmopolitan Justice', p. 120.

living in terms of people's capacity to enjoy certain functionings, and here he appeals specifically to Nussbaum's list of human goods which includes the 'capacity for (1) life, (2) health, (3) the avoidance of pain, (4) use of the five senses, (5) human relationships, (6) the deliberation about and pursuit of personal ideals, (7) relations of care for others, (8) access to the natural environment, (9) experiencing enjoyment, and (10) independence'.[44] Using this account, Caney argues that 'global equality of opportunity requires that people of equal talent have equal access to positions of an equal standard of living (where the standard of living is assessed in terms of their contribution to well-being)'.[45] In this way, Caney believes he can accommodate cultural diversity and still have the ability to judge whether opportunities are equal.

Caney's attempt to formulate the ideal is, however, still defective, since it cannot adequately block all kinds of unequal opportunities and discrimination. We can see this by looking at examples. So, consider a first example in which A's list of opportunities in one society includes: becoming a doctor with the WHO, an investigative reporter for CNN, an investment banker for the IMF and so on. Assume B's list of opportunities in a different society include: becoming a witchdoctor, a storyteller, or a circus performer and so on. Let us say that the two sets of options are judged to have equal worth within the particular societies and enable similar fulfilment of personal capabilities and, therefore, standards of living on Caney's account. Still, there might be an enormous difference in the levels and kinds of power A and B have and consequently their abilities to influence public policy, political arrangements or global institutions, which shape their lives (and those of their descendants), and this power difference alone must count as a relevant difference in their opportunities, even if they enjoy an equal standard of living, as cashed out by the relevant capabilities and their contribution to well-being.

A second example illustrates how Caney's account cannot adequately block sex discrimination. Consider B's options again: to become a witchdoctor, a storyteller, or a circus performer and so on. Now consider C's options in that same society, which we assume to be highly patriarchal: she may become a witchdoctor's wife, a storyteller's wife, a circus performer's wife and so on. Let us also assume (as is common in

[44] Caney, 'Cosmopolitan Justice', p. 121. The list is discussed more fully in Martha Nussbaum, 'Human Functioning and Social Justice: In Defense of Aristotelian Essentialism', *Political Theory* 20 (1992), pp. 202–46 (222).

[45] Caney, 'Cosmopolitan Justice', p. 121.

many parts of the world) that the wife of people of high status is similarly high. (Let us simply stipulate that in her society her role is considered to have equal worth to that of her husband.) She enjoys a commensurate standard of living as cashed out by the relevant capabilities. It is not clear to me that women truly have equal opportunities to men in this second society, but Caney's account may well not detect this.

Similarly, Caney's account is not sufficient to block societies that assign jobs on caste or ethnic lines, as long as the set enables equivalent standards of living. Consider a third example which illustrates this. In Fiji, the Fijian Indians tend to pursue and get jobs in management, business and professional occupations, and the indigenous Fijians tend to occupy more unskilled, lower-paying jobs (for instance, as cleaners). So long as they have equivalent standards of living we now have equality of opportunity, according to Caney. They may enjoy equal levels of well-being, because what the Fijian Indians may gain in material prosperity they lose in terms of political power and security, and what the indigenous Fijians lose in material prosperity they gain in terms of political power and security. We may have experienced equality of standards of living or levels of well-being, but we have not realized the ideal of equality of opportunity very well at all, I would think. This last example also illustrates how we could satisfy Caney's requirement for equality of opportunity (that is, commensurate levels of well-being are made possible) even though these levels of well-being are fairly poor. Perhaps Caney's version of the ideal is not ambitious enough, but if we get too ambitious maybe we have to get more specific?

In trying to articulate an adequate account of global equality of opportunity, we are faced, then, with a dilemma. Either we must try to articulate a version of equality of opportunity that mentions particular social positions that are favoured, and opportunities to achieve these are equalized, or we allow much cultural variation on what counts as a favoured social position, and the standards of living or levels of well-being that they enable are to be equalized. If we go with the first option, we are vulnerable to charges of being insufficiently attuned to cultural difference. If we go with the second and try to equalize standards of living, we may end up with a very weak account of equality of opportunity which permits many cases which do not look at all like a robust account of blocking disadvantage and discrimination on morally arbitrary grounds. As we have seen, Moellendorf chooses the first horn of the dilemma, Caney the second, and both paths have weaknesses. It is not clear to me which (if either) of these paths is likely, ultimately, to yield an adequate articulation of the ideal of equality of opportunity.

In the meantime, it might be best to go back to the negative version of the ideal and see what can be done to remove barriers to developing a range of skills and capacities that would be useful no matter what goals people set themselves, and here attention to enabling people to meet their needs is, once again, a useful focal point. No matter what goals people have in life, their achievement is just going to be more likely if we eliminate a range of barriers they currently face which impede human agency and these include not having secure access to clean water, food, sanitation, education, health care, and so on. This will, of course, keep us busy enough in the interim.

Let me also tentatively suggest that perhaps our focus on *equalizing* opportunities has blinded us to something more basic about the ideal that is really important, in fact providing much of the force that makes the ideal so compelling, and that concerns making sure people have a *decent* set of opportunities rather than an *equal* set strictly speaking. The decent set of opportunities is surely the primary goal rather than the equal set, because consider how we could equalize downwards, so that everyone has the same opportunities, but these be hopelessly inadequate. The real concern is surely not with equality at any cost. If faced with the option of equal, but poor, life options, or a situation in which, though there is some inequality of access, everyone has access to developing a range of skills so they can earn a living (or meet their needs) with dignity and delight, we should surely choose the second situation.[46]

---

[46] Someone might complain: if we take seriously the need for cultural sensitivity that (it is argued) rules out at least one version of the positive account of equality of opportunity, then why doesn't this rule out the negative? Won't some cultural beliefs hold that not everyone should have such barriers eliminated, for instance, the Indian caste system?

The cultural dimension gets a grip only because we are trying to examine what counts as equality of access with respect to bestowing benefits and what counts as a benefit has a cultural dimension. However, when we talk about eliminating burdens, though there is also a cultural dimension, there is also a significant non-cultural aspect, and it is the burdens that are faced in the non-cultural dimension that I have argued we should try to eliminate, e.g., removing barriers to enjoying clean water, health care, food, and so forth. It is hard to see how we could really justify how such burdens ought to be placed on others, even if we are being culturally sensitive. When we are being culturally sensitive, we need not accept all cultural claims at face value. Some cultural beliefs should be respected; other cultural beliefs or demands should rightly be rejected.

Summary and Conclusions

In this paper I considered two proposals about the sorts of principles of justice a cosmopolitan should endorse. By developing a model of cosmopolitan justice, I argued that in a reconstructed cosmopolitan original position we would choose a Needs-Based Minimum Floor Principle rather than a Global Difference Principle, if these are not co-extensive. I offered both theoretical and relevant empirical support for this view. I then examined two proposals as to how to develop a Global Equality of Opportunity Principle, but found them both to be defective. I argued that those trying to develop an ideal of global equality of opportunity thus faced a dilemma concerning how best to develop that ideal. Either we must try to articulate a version of equality of opportunity that mentions particular social positions that are favoured and opportunities to achieve these are equalized, or we allow much cultural variation on what counts as a favoured social position, and the standards of living or levels of well-being that they enable are to be equalized. If we go with the first option, we are vulnerable to charges of being insufficiently attuned to cultural difference. If we go with the second and try to equalize standards of living, we may end up with a very weak account of equality of opportunity which permits many cases which do not look at all much like a robust account of blocking disadvantage and discrimination on morally arbitrary grounds. It is not clear which (if either) of these strategies is likely to yield an adequate articulation of the ideal of equality of opportunity. In the meanwhile, I suggested that we have our work cut out for us simply attending to relevant needs and ensuring all people have a *decent* set of opportunities. Moreover, I argued that the decent set of opportunities should anyhow probably be our primary focus rather than the equal set strictly speaking.[47]

[47] I thank an anonymous reviewer for this journal for helpful comments.

POVERTY RELIEF, GLOBAL INSTITUTIONS, AND THE PROBLEM OF COMPLIANCE

Lisa L. Fuller

Among the many challenges associated with globalization, eradicating poverty stands out as both extremely urgent and ethically complex. While it is clear that what we want is a significant lessening of death and disease due to poverty, how this can be achieved and who is responsible for carrying it out are far less clear. The enormous gap between the rich and poor indicates that a redistribution of wealth from the former to the latter would make the world more just, but this fact, taken on its own, is not very illuminating. It is only when we turn to the task of hammering out a concrete solution that we can begin to see, and to work through, those issues that stand in the way of instantiating global justice. Among them are fundamental questions about the obligations of nation-states and other international actors, the nature and purpose of their interactions, and the most desirable shape of international institutions. The resolution of these background issues is by no means a simple undertaking, but the urgency of the problem demands that we take them up as they arise—keeping in mind that, ultimately, we are after practical strategies for addressing the problem. In what follows, I will explain and criticize what I call 'the institutional view' of poverty relief, and sketch out an alternative that both avoids its main defect and relies on a less ideal conception of international relations. My own view focuses on the kind of improvements that would be required for conventional international aid to acquire the legitimacy and accountability that it now lacks.

The Individual View vs. the Institutional View

In the philosophical literature, there are two standard approaches to the problem of global poverty. The first is exemplified by the work of Peter Singer, who maintains that *as individuals* we have a moral obligation to give generously to organizations such as Oxfam in order to prevent harm caused by extreme poverty. We might call this 'the individual duty view'. By contrast, philosophers such as Thomas Pogge and Andrew Kuper suggest that we should support a systemic or 'institutional' solution to global poverty. The institutional view directs our attention away from the acts of individuals and toward the institutional rules to which all individuals and states are subject. On this view, global poverty is both caused and perpetuated by political and market institutions that are badly slanted in favour of powerful nation-states. The argument for this claim goes, roughly, as follows: Historically, powerful states have used their military and economic strength to shape the way interactions take place at the global level. They have 'made the rules', so to speak. Under the current rules, many poor countries fare quite badly. Only if there were no feasible alternatives that could avoid this outcome could these rules be justified. However, there *are* feasible institutional alternatives under which poor countries would fare much better. As such, the perpetuation of the status quo amounts to the coercive imposition of an unjust order on poor countries, by affluent ones. Pogge sums this up nicely when he says:

> Citizens and governments of the affluent countries—whether intentionally or not—are imposing a global institutional order that forseeably and avoidably reproduces severe and widespread poverty. The worse-off are not merely poor and often starving, but are being impoverished and starved under our shared institutional arrangements.[1]

According to this view, institutions are at the root of the problem and so institutional reform is clearly the solution. While there are potentially very many alternative arrangements that would improve the lot of poor countries, I will restrict my focus here to the one suggested by Pogge himself. He calls his alternative scheme the 'Global Resources Dividend' (or GRD). It would work like this: those people who make extensive use of the planet's resources would compensate those who, involuntarily, are able to use very little. For instance, a $2 per barrel GRD tax on crude oil could be instituted, which would be payable to a central fund. The countries from which the oil is extracted would pay the tax, but the extra cost would ultimately be passed on to end users in the marketplace. The funds collected by the central fund could then be redistributed such that they are 'maximally effective

[1] Thomas Pogge, *World Poverty and Human Rights* (Oxford: Blackwell, 2002), p. 201.

toward ensuring that all human beings can meet their basic needs with dignity'.[2]

Pogge suggests that the disbursement of these funds should be governed by clear, straightforward rules that are cheap to administer. The disbursing body should also be maximally transparent, in order to 'exclude political favoritism and the appearance thereof'.[3] Since the allocation of funds would be exclusively geared toward meeting the basic needs of the poor (rather than toward securing other political benefits for the donors), it would be much more efficient than conventional development assistance. Moreover, the disbursement scheme should create incentives for developing countries by rewarding significant gains in eradicating poverty—the more progress a country makes in this regard, the more funds should be allocated to it.

Having outlined the institutional view, we can now ask why Pogge and Kuper might prefer this type of solution to the individual duty view. The main reason seems to be that they regard traditional methods of development aid as seriously flawed. For instance, Kuper asserts that non-governmental organizations (NGOs) 'can never be the primary agents of justice and aid in the long run', for several reasons.[4] First, their funding is too capricious, depending as it does on the inclinations of donor countries and individuals. Second, their access to particular populations depends on the whims of others (usually rulers), whose interests often diverge significantly from the aims of NGOs. Third, they are not democratically elected or sufficiently accountable for their actions and aims, and finally, they cannot produce large-scale growth or redistribution.

Pogge suggests additional reasons why we ought to reject NGO aid. He notes that it engenders donor fatigue and even contempt for the poor by requiring 'affluent citizens and governments to rally to the cause again and again while knowing full well that most others similarly situated contribute nothing or very little'.[5] Further, he thinks that NGO aid 'has an aura of handouts and dependence' which would be avoided by an institutional solution.[6]

---

[2] Pogge, *World Poverty and Human Rights*, p. 206.

[3] Pogge, *World Poverty and Human Rights*, p. 206.

[4] Andrew Kuper, 'More than Charity: Cosmopolitan Alternatives to the Singer Solution', *Ethics and International Affairs* 16 (2002), pp. 107–20 (114).

[5] Pogge, *World Poverty and Human Rights*, p. 212.

[6] Pogge, *World Poverty and Human Rights*, p. 207.

Thus, the argument for an institutional solution to global poverty actually proceeds on two fronts: by pointing out the merits of a scheme such as the GRD, and by criticizing the current system of NGO relief programmes. It is my intention here to challenge both of these lines of argument. However, far from simply suggesting that individual generosity rather than institutional reform is the answer, I would like to suggest that framing the problem in this dichotomous manner blinds us to a third possibility that does not suffer from the defects of either. So far, we have seen the defects of the NGO alternative. I'll now point out some drawbacks of the institutional approach.

Problems for the Institutional View

The central problem for institutional solutions such as Pogge's is how to generate enough goodwill among rich states that they would be willing to commit themselves to these types of reforms. Indeed, Pogge even admits that 'the GRD would cost more and return less in direct political benefits' than traditional development or humanitarian aid.[7] As a result, he recognizes that powerful states might be reluctant to comply. However, he gives two reasons for believing that the compliance of the world's two strongest powers—the United States and the European Union—could be secured. First, he notes that 'moral convictions can have real effects even in international politics ... provided the citizens of the more powerful states can be convinced of a moral conclusion that really can be soundly supported and a path can be shown that makes only modest demands on each of us'.[8] He cites the abolition of the slave trade in Britain as an example of how the moral convictions of citizens can impact international norms in a positive manner.

Secondly, Pogge argues that an enterprise such as the GRD has clear prudential value, even for powerful states, and so they might be persuaded to cooperate on this basis. He claims that we can no longer afford to ignore what is going on in the developing world. He suggests that creating greater equality between states and more prosperity in developing countries would help mitigate against the spread of terrorist attacks, epidemics, the drug trade, and pollution, all of which will

[7] Pogge, *World Poverty and Human Rights*, p. 207.
[8] Pogge, *World Poverty and Human Rights*, p. 211.

threaten rich states more in the future. Contributing to the GRD would be cheaper overall for powerful states than exposing themselves to these other threats.[9]

In addition, Pogge argues that greater prosperity in developing countries will enable governments to protect the basic rights of their citizens and provide elementary education, which will, in turn, tend toward the creation of well-ordered, democratic regimes. The emergence of democratic institutions in developing countries is in the interest of powerful states, and this aim would be promoted by entering into a scheme such as the GRD.

While I admire Pogge's optimism in this regard, I still think there are several considerations that work against the possibility of obtaining compliance from *both* very powerful and less powerful states. My first worry is about his argument from the moral consensus of citizens. Indeed, it is sometimes the case that change can be heavily influenced by the attitudes of citizens in affluent countries, but Pogge has an overly idealistic view of the dynamics of international relations. Thomas Weiss characterizes a Pogge-type view of the foundations of international politics as 'efforts to agree upon desirable international public policies within governmental, intergovernmental and nongovernmental arenas'.[10] This type of view focuses on the cooperation evident between states when they form treaties and cooperate in institutions such as the United Nations. On the other hand, it is possible to view international politics as, in Weiss's words, 'the competition among states for survival and supremacy and for maximizing national interests in an anarchical world'.[11] While I am no realist, and so would not wholly subscribe to the latter view, it does seem somewhat naïve to discount it altogether. Pogge knows this, since he admits that powerful governments and multinational corporations have historically 'negotiate[d] and re-negotiate[d] the rules of the game among themselves with each pressing vigorously for its own advantage, using war and threat of war when this seems opportune and showing no concern for the interests or even survival of the weakest "players"'.[12]

---

[9] Pogge, *World Poverty and Human Rights*, p. 213.

[10] Thomas Weiss, 'Principles, Politics and Humanitarian Action', *Ethics & International Affairs* 13 (1999), pp. 1–22 (11).

[11] Weiss, 'Principles, Politics and Humanitarian Action', p. 11.

[12] Pogge, *World Poverty and Human Rights*, p. 128.

The point here is that the power of moral consensus is always going to be tempered by considerations of national interest—and it does not seem realistic to presume that the citizens of affluent countries will be able to sustain a preference for morality over economic interest, especially when economic times are bad. In the case of slavery, its abolition affected only some of the British population for the worse, namely, slave-traders. A measure such as the GRD affects virtually everyone in affluent states, including those with not much money relative to their fellow citizens. I am skeptical that they could be convinced to cooperate, and importantly, to *lend continued support* to cooperation.

Further, history has shown that global institutions such as the UN are typically susceptible to the interests of the most powerful states, and so any 'moral mission' they adopt is going to be strongly influenced by these interests. This is the main reason such organizations have worked only imperfectly in the past, and I see no reason to suppose that this will change in the near future. While I recognize that this is exactly the type of power manoeuvering that Pogge is trying to circumvent with his proposal, the problem is how to get there from here. In any political struggle between the more powerful and the less so (or, if you prefer, the exploiters and the exploited), this is the major hurdle it must surmount. It seems to me that moral consensus is not likely to secure compliance on its own.

Likewise, Pogge's prudential argument rests on shaky foundations. It presupposes that powerful states will see the promotion of democracy as in their long-term interest. Even if we grant this assumption, there is one main problem with it—that a state's long-term interest may conflict with its shortterm interest, particularly in economic matters. Given that presidents and prime ministers need to be re-elected, it is not likely that they will support reforms which leave their people as a whole economically worse-off, even in the name of democracy. In fact, the opposite has often been the case— affluent states have been known to prop up dictators for the sake of securing economic benefits.

But these concerns pale in comparison with the final difficulty facing Pogge's proposal—the cooperation problem. Again, he is aware of this particular difficulty and has even gone so far as to give it a name. He calls it 'appealing to the sucker exemption'.[13] Rich states can refuse to unilaterally institute reforms that favor the global poor on the grounds

[13] Pogge, *World Poverty and Human Rights*, p. 128.

that this would put them at a competitive disadvantage relative to other states, who we can presume are looking out for their own interests and so would take advantage of this situation to the fullest extent. Pogge addresses this problem when he says, '[b]ut if each such society so defended itself by pointing to the others, the reasonable response would surely be to ask them all to work out a multilateral reform that affects all of them equally and thus does not alter their competitive positions, vis-à-vis one another'.[14]

In theory, this sounds good. However, in order for such a reform to work, all or most states would have to institute the GRD at roughly the same time. From a logistical point of view this seems obviously problematic, since democratic governments must be receptive to the changing attitudes of their citizens. Also, making reforms dependent upon cooperation on such a large scale sets up the real possibility of a drawn-out 'waiting game' in which each state waits for others to move towards compliance. This difficulty is made immeasurably worse by the fact that if states forgo regular aid until such time as all states can implement reform, many people will die in the meantime.[15]

Even if this logistical difficulty could be somehow worked out, continued compliance would need to be guaranteed. In order to ensure that no states renege on their obligations, there would have to be some type of global enforcement. Pogge suggests that the EU and/or the US could implement trade sanctions on those less powerful countries that fail to comply. While they may be perfectly *able* to do this, they may be reluctant to take on the role of enforcers, since sanctioned countries may then retaliate by setting up their own trade barriers which would negatively affect their 'sanctioners'. We should not discount the force of the profit motive which lies in the background here.

In addition, if the US and the EU were to be the *de facto* enforcement mechanism for the GRD, then their own compliance with the reform would always be voluntary. In international politics, there is no effective way to 'regulate the regulators', and so the US and the EU would be free to come in and out of compliance as they saw fit. *Knowing* that the US and EU need only comply when it is in their interest, it doesn't seem reasonable for any less powerful state to agree to this type of solution in the first place, because it puts them at risk of incurring sanctions for

[14] Pogge, *World Poverty and Human Rights*, p. 128.
[15] Kuper, 'More than Charity', p. 115.

non-compliance without the assurance that the powerful states will also do their part. This is, of course, one version of a classic problem associated with international cooperation.

Ideal Theory and the Best Outcome

Since they are obviously aware of the many difficulties associated with the institutional view, why do Pogge and Kuper (among others) still cling to it? What makes them want to defend something with so many flaws that must be overcome? Kuper makes his reasons explicit, and I am willing to conjecture that Pogge is similarly motivated. The institutional view is attractive because *if* it could work (and that is a big 'if—'), it would most certainly be the best solution to the problem. Kuper argues against the individual duty view precisely because he thinks it is not the best solution overall. He wants to know what policies are '*the most* beneficial to global development and poverty relief', and claims that 'an articulated philosophy is not going to recommend *sub-optimal* … courses of action'.[16]

Kuper specifically likens his view to the structural analysis of Marxism, which, famously, outright rejects piecemeal solutions to impoverishment in favour of the wholesale reorganization of societies. He notes that

> [a] theory that does not include a contextual and institutional analysis … is condemned to recommending brief symptomatic relief, or even damaging and counterproductive action. This is not a peculiarly Marxist point, and one does not need to sympathize with Marxists to think that telling the bourgeoisie to be more charitable as individual actors is unlikely to produce deep changes.[17]

No doubt there are multiple alternative structures that would be an improvement on the current rules of international interaction. However, the main issue for me is which options have some practical plausibility—not which one would create the best outcome in theory. I would be willing to settle for a 'sub-optimal' solution if it would improve the current situation of the global poor and was a realistic practical alternative. As such, I prefer to work from the type of institutions we have and ask how they might be improved and made

[16] Kuper, 'More than Charity', p. 118, my emphasis.
[17] Kuper, 'More than Charity', p. 113.

justifiable, rather than focusing on refining my conception of the optimal solution. This difference in approach ultimately comes down to conflicting background views about the relevance of ideal theory for applied ethics and political philosophy.

Kuper argues that an ideal conception of justice is a '*valuable orienteering mechanism for action*' because it allows us to see whether we are moving closer or further away from where we want to be.[18] Additionally, he notes that having such a standard in mind means that we can be proactive in working towards it. Even when tough choices need to be made along the way, since we know where we are headed, then we will not 'unwittingly make sub-optimal choices'.[19]

While I agree that ideal theory has a role to play, it is important to see that it is limited in its practical applicability. This is because, as Kai Nielsen points out, ideal theory is interested in which principles or institutions rational people would agree to '*assuming everyone will fully comply*'.[20] Moreover, Nielsen notes that even in ideal theory we must take into account 'what is humanly possible', that is, we must have an adequate conception of human nature and how societies work, before we can paint even an ideal picture of international justice.[21] Mere logical possibilities cannot do the work here. My point in bringing in the ideal/non-ideal distinction is that non-ideal theory can admit that not everyone will comply with whatever scheme is put in place. It can also admit that even if it is possible for people to comply, they often will not. Taking this fact about human nature into account, non-ideal theory can still ask what we ought to do for the worse-off.

And this seems to me to be the right question to ask, because full compliance with any cooperation scheme in a political arena that lacks effective enforcement is not a genuine possibility. Further, poverty affects peoples' well-being right now, and we do not need a picture of the ideally just world in order to take small steps in the right direction.

To be fair, Pogge argues that it is the very feasibility of the GRD which demonstrates the injustice of the current world order. As such, he is trying to appeal to what is humanly possible. Still, he does not

[18] Kuper, 'More than Charity', p. 115.

[19] Kuper, 'More than Charity', p. 116.

[20] Kai Nielsen, 'Ideal and Non-Ideal Theory: How Should We Approach Questions of Global Justice?' *International Journal of Applied Philosophy* 2 (1985), pp. 33–41 (35), emphasis added.

[21] Nielsen, 'Ideal and Non-Ideal Theory', p. 36.

treat the compliance problem as central. Instead, he addresses it after he has worked out his solution, and so in my view, takes up the issues in exactly the wrong order. Another reason to think that Pogge is working from ideal theory is that he does not consider what the implementation of the GRD would look like in the real world. One of the main problems with creating supranational institutions and organizations is that they are too large, and so are susceptible to any number of abuses by people and states behaving 'non-ideally'—that is, acting according to a sense of their interests that does not correspond with the cooperative aims of the group. One problem of this sort might be that it is hard to know in advance if the end users would really pay the GRD tax. The way new taxes affect behaviour is notoriously hard to predict, and no doubt power relations would have an influence at this level as well.

In addition, the size of the central administration required for a scheme such as the GRD is another strike against it. Large bureaucracies invite tyranny and bureaucratic waste. Pogge cannot simply stipulate that its administration should be cheap, effective and transparent. Rather, he needs to tell us how these administrative features of the scheme could be maintained on such a grand scale.

In the spirit of non-ideal theory, Onora O'Neill suggests that we ought to examine the concrete capabilities of various international actors in order to determine 'which obligations of justice they can hold and discharge'.[22] She notes that, 'the value of focusing on capabilities is that this foregrounds an explicit concern with action and the results that agents or agencies can achieve in actual circumstances, and so provides a *seriously realistic starting point for normative reasoning*'.[23] In particular, she directs our attention to the capacities of non-state actors, which she defines as 'institutions that are neither states, nor international in the sense of being either interstatal or intergovernmental, nor directly subordinate to individual states or governments, but that interact across borders with states or state institutions'.[24] NGO aid agencies are among these actors.

According to the definition just presented, we should understand NGOs as part of international civil society, and not as privately run charities that exist outside the political realm. Kuper sees them as

---

[22] Onora O'Neill, 'Agents of Justice', *Metaphilosophy* 32 (2001), pp. 180–95 (189–90).

[23] O'Neill, 'Agents of Justice', p. 189, original italics.

[24] O'Neill, 'Agents of Justice', p. 191.

distinctly private entities since he says, 'we cooperate and succeed … through social rules and institutions. Effective poverty relief will thus require above all else extensive cooperation with other agents—indeed, it will require the creation … of agencies to reduce poverty'.[25] As Singer points out, NGOs such as Oxfam and Doctors Without Borders already do this.[26] What exactly is Kuper suggesting then? He must be suggesting the creation of supranational institutions (like Pogge) because he thinks NGOs are not genuine political institutions. His problem with NGOs, then, is not that they cannot deliver the goods. Rather, it is that they are not a permanent, systematic, integrated set of agencies that are created by nation-states.

While it might be true that NGOs do not constitute a single coherent system, it is not true that they do not have either a political, or an institutional character. They are large, established, complex organizations that operate according to their own standards as well as the requirements of international law. They negotiate with both donor and recipient governments. They often represent the interests of their beneficiaries in intergovernmental forums. Some (though not all) are internally democratic. Most importantly, they *already have* the capabilities to relieve suffering due to poverty in even the most remote regions of the world. Perhaps many NGOs are not ideally structured, but it still seems gratuitous to create a whole new set of institutions to address poverty when we already have them. Moreover, it might turn out to be a good thing that NGOs are members of civil society, rather than answerable to governments.[27]

NGO Aid Reform: A Third Alternative

It should be apparent by now that I favour reform of NGO-delivered aid over the creation of new supranational institutions. However, I am not thus subscribing to the individual duty view as it is usually

[25] Kuper, 'More than Charity', p. 115.

[26] Peter Singer, 'Poverty, Facts, and Political Philosophies', *Ethics and International Affairs* 16 (2002), pp. 121–24 (123).

[27] To clarify, I am mainly thinking of large, international NGOs. I am not referring to agencies that are exclusively concerned with monitoring and reporting, such as Amnesty International, religious groups, or small-scale, local NGOs. So for the purpose of the recommendations I am about to make, I am using the term 'NGO' in this limited sense.

understood. This is because I reject the idea that the international aid community is a bunch of private organizations from which it is inappropriate to expect the type of accountability and legitimacy characteristic of political institutions. They are already an established part of the international political scene, and I will argue that certain reforms could address their weaknesses and increase their viability as a vital poverty-reduction mechanism.

My main reason for recommending NGO aid reform is that this type of solution does not suffer from the compliance problems which afflict the institutional view. However, in order for my view to be persuasive, I should also address those concerns that caused Pogge and Kuper to rule out this option in the first place. Let us recall what they were: (1) NGO funding is too capricious, (2) they are not democratically elected or accountable, (3) they are not effective on a large scale and, finally, (4) they create donor fatigue.

I will now sketch out a programme of reform intended to address these problems. My first recommendation is that donations to NGOs should be 'general' rather than directed at specific recipients. This would eliminate much of the control donor countries have over who receives aid. As a result, aid could be more efficiently directed at eradicating poverty than it is now. Indeed, Singer points out that 'three of the biggest donors—the United States, France, and Japan—direct their aid, not to those countries where it will be most effective in fostering growth and reducing poverty, but to countries where aid will further their own strategic or cultural interests'.[28] In fact, many donors already agree to make substantial general donations when they deal with certain NGOs.[29]

General donations would also eliminate the problem of competition among NGOs for funds that are too often directed exclusively at 'popular' recipients, that is, those that are currently in the news. If NGOs had greater leeway to decide where to allocate funds, they would also be better able to cooperate amongst themselves such that more populations in different areas could be helped. Also, if NGOs were to require all donations to be general in form, then they would not have to move money around according to the whims of donors and so could do more long-range projects.

---

[28] Peter Singer, *One World* (New Haven: Yale University Press, 2002), p. 191.

[29] For instance, Médecins sans Frontières (Doctors Without Borders) does not accept 'targeted' donations, but they still receive significant government aid.

One might worry that such a requirement would discourage donations, but it does not seem to do so for individuals, most of whom make their donations to a particular agency and not to a particular recipient country. Further, it seems unlikely that governments would simply stop giving to NGOs altogether, if all or most of them were to institute this requirement. After all, NGOs are the organizations that most often implement aid programmes on the ground, and it would be very costly for governments to duplicate this type of expertise for their own purposes. Finally, at least some countries already prefer their money to go to those places where it will be most efficiently used.[30]

My second recommendation would be to require all practising international NGOs to be 'accountable for reasonableness' in the sense that Norman Daniels and James Sabin have outlined.[31] This entails engaging in a process of deliberation in which the reasons for decisions are both available to all stakeholders and rationally defended. A fair and accountable process of this sort must meet several conditions—it must be publicly accessible, allow the possibility of appeals, and be effectively regulated.[32]

The first condition requires that decisions and their rationales be made publicly available. Allocation decisions, and the rationales behind them, would then begin to resemble a kind of 'case law' to which people could turn for precedents and to make objections. Daniels and Sabin argue that this would increase the fairness of decisions both substantively and procedurally—substantively because it encourages people to give justifications that are well thought out, and procedurally because like cases would be treated alike.[33] Both the transparency of public deliberations and their increased fairness would strengthen the legitimacy of international NGOs.

The 'appeals' condition requires that '[t]here must be mechanisms for challenge and dispute resolution ... and more broadly, opportunities for revision and improvement of policies in the light of new evidence or arguments'.[34] This condition would allow potential recipients of aid, current recipients of aid, governments, and the public to put

[30] Peter Singer notes that the Nordic countries in Europe already do this. See Singer, *One World*, p. 191.

[31] Norman Daniels and James Sabin, *Setting Limits Fairly* (Oxford: Oxford University Press, 2002), p. 44.

[32] Daniels and Sabin, *Setting Limits Fairly*, p. 45.

[33] Daniels and Sabin, *Setting Limits Fairly*, p. 48.

[34] Daniels and Sabin, *Setting Limits Fairly*, p. 45.

forward arguments when they disagree with certain decisions. This opportunity would likely bring much needed additional information to the table and so increase aid effectiveness. More importantly, an appeals process would greatly increase NGO accountability, because they would be forced to either justify their practices in light of objections, or change them.

What I have in mind here is *not* that donor interests and concerns would be the focus of the justification and appeals processes. Rather, I am specifically thinking about how to generate greater accountability to recipients. More transparency and public accountability would shed light on a number of key concerns, such as the nature of negotiations or agreements with local authorities, the degree of risk to which recipients are exposed as the result of unintended consequences of aid, and the reasons for changing or discontinuing projects.

Finally, Daniels and Sabin's regulation condition requires that some type of official monitoring take place to ensure that the other conditions are met. Third-party monitoring bodies could be set up, in which democratically elected members would review the practices and decisions of NGOs based in their country at set intervals. The members of these bodies could be a combination of experienced aid practitioners, representatives from developing countries and donor representatives. Decentralized monitoring would allow NGOs to retain most of their flexibility with regard to project design and location, since it would not create too much additional bureaucracy. The purpose of the monitoring would not be to standardize the activities of NGOs everywhere, but rather to increase their transparency, produce greater accountability, and check their effectiveness—recognizing that organizations may have different mandates and methods.

Unlike powerful nation-states, it would be possible to effectively regulate NGOs with relatively small, impartial monitoring bodies. NGOs could be licensed to practice by such entities, and their continued good standing could depend on being successfully reviewed. Indeed, the introduction of a license would improve aid quality in many respects, since it would weed out those organizations that do not demonstrate sufficient expertise.

These reforms would increase NGO accountability, improve their effectiveness and allow them to cooperate better in order to widen the scope of their action. As for their funding being capricious, most of the larger, more successful NGOs have solved that problem by restricting the amount any particular government can contribute in any given year, and by developing a strong base of private supporters. They also sign contracts with certain governments that extend over a period of several years to lock in their funds. By ensuring that their funding comes from many sources, they have greater control over the planning of their future projects. Moving from general to specific donations would only give them more independence in this regard, and so it seems to me that this objection is not particularly worrisome.

By contrast, the fact that NGOs create donor fatigue and exude 'an aura of dependence' may simply be something we have to live with.[35] Indeed, as we have seen, even a solution such as the GRD depends significantly on the continuing goodwill of powerful states. Certainly citizens might just as easily become 'fatigued' by a tax increase on natural resources as they are by their governments' contributions to foreign aid. Until developing countries are powerful enough to bargain on a more equal footing in the economic realm, they will always be dependent in some way on the goodwill of the stronger states. I cannot see how introducing the GRD would be more effective at rectifying this imbalance than conventional development assistance, since both depend on the goodwill of the stronger party.

These suggested reforms have one final feature to recommend them—they do not suffer from compliance problems. NGOs could institute the internal reforms and optin to the review process one at a time. Indeed, once the review systems were set up, the increased legitimacy and credibility participation would confer upon them would act as an incentive for NGOs to participate. Donors, too, could choose to contribute funds to those NGOs that comply with the reforms one at a time. They need not wait to see what other states will do because they would be using the same funds that they typically allocate to foreign aid in any given year.

Conclusion

The reforms just sketched out are not an ideal solution to poverty relief. In fact, they only apply to the roughly 36 per cent of aid that is

[35] Pogge, *World Poverty and Human Rights*, p. 207.

distributed by NGOs.[36] This means that the remaining bilateral aid would still be plagued by the problems associated with the political interests and hard-bargaining of donor states. However, these reforms would have a considerable impact on the effectiveness and accountability of aid *as it is delivered right now*. Further, these recommendations focus on those international actors that are the least affected by considerations of national interest and profit. This makes them a more realistic alternative than sweeping suggestions of new, state-centred, global institutions. We *can* have a transparent, accountable, effective system of poverty relief, which seems to be the wish of philosophers such as Pogge and Kuper. It might just look different than they thought it would.

[36] Daniel Little, *The Paradox of Wealth and Poverty* (Cambridge: Westview Press, 2003), p. 177. Here he is citing the World Bank.

THOMAS POGGE'S GLOBAL RESOURCES DIVIDEND: A CRITIQUE AND AN ALTERNATIVE

Tim Hayward*

Thomas Pogge's writings on global justice have attracted a good deal of attention in recent years. Pogge has developed powerful moral arguments in favour of global redistribution of wealth, and these are not called into question in the present article. The focus of attention here is the Global Resources Dividend (GRD) which he has proposed as a practical step towards the requisite redistribution. Pogge does not claim this is the only redistributive mechanism that could be derived from the moral argument, and certainly does not think it is the most the argument could justify—hence his characterization of it as a 'modest' proposal. But he does see it as a valuable first step, and one which also promises, as a secondary benefit, to help curb environmental pollution and the depletion of natural resources.

The problem I address in this article, after briefly describing the basic features of the GRD, is that, as others have already suggested, if implemented, the GRD's likely effects would at best be rather less predictable than Pogge supposes and at worst could actually be counterproductive to his main aim. For related reasons the GRD would also do little with respect to the secondary aim. My consideration of these criticisms in section 2 finds them, unfortunately, to be well-founded.

In section 3 I trace the problems with the GRD proposal to the insufficiently thought out conception of natural resources that underpins it. I suggest that the arbitrariness of the GRD's likely effects is due to elements of arbitrariness in Pogge's conception of natural resources. A less arbitrary conception, I argue, is one which conceives natural resources in terms of 'ecological space'. In briefly explaining this idea, I show how it can support redistributive principles that follow with a more definite logic from Pogge's own moral justification for redistribution. Moreover, as well as linking the rectification of radical inequalities

* I am most grateful to Thomas Pogge for constructive criticism of an earlier draft, as well as to my colleague Lynn Dobson and an anonymous referee.

more directly and robustly to the question of command of natural resources, the proposed alternative approach also promises a more direct contribution to Pogge's secondary aim of resource conservation and environmental protection. In section 4 I respond to an anticipated objection regarding the normative basis of my argument, and in doing so expose a new question about Pogge's justificatory argument for the GRD. I conclude that if any redistributive resource-based tax should be levied on nations, then there are at least four decisive reasons to favour levying a tax related to a nation's per capita utilization of ecological space rather than the GRD.

1. *Pogge's Proposal*

The GRD is a proposal Pogge has sketched and defended in several publications over a number of years.[1] What it envisages, in brief, is that 'states and their governments shall not have full libertarian property rights with respect to the natural resources in their territory, but can be required to share a small part of the value of any resources they decide to use or sell'.[2] Having initially called it a tax, he has come to refer to the payment they must make as a dividend

> because it is based on the idea that the global poor own an inalienable stake in all limited resources. As in the case of preferred stock, this stake confers no right to participate in decisions about whether or how natural resources are to be used and so does not interfere with national control over resources, or eminent domain. But it does entitle its holders to a share of the economic value of the resource in question, if indeed the decision is to use it.[3]

Proceeds from the GRD are to be used in the relief of the worst extremes of global poverty, with the aim of ensuring that all human beings can meet their own basic needs with dignity. Pogge does not believe that an impossibly large amount would need to be raised, and speaks of an initial maximal figure of 1 per cent of aggregate global income.[4] Such a

---

[1] An early formulation of the proposal appeared in Thomas Pogge, 'An Egalitarian Law of Peoples', *Philosophy and Public Affairs* 23.3 (1994), pp. 195–224. While I shall sometimes refer to this for the background it gives to Pogge's thinking, I shall for the most part refer to the more recent formulation to be found in chapter 8 of Thomas Pogge, *World Poverty and Human Rights* (Cambridge: Polity Press, 2002).

[2] Pogge, *World Poverty and Human Rights*, p. 196.

[3] Pogge, *World Poverty and Human Rights*, pp. 196–97.

[4] Pogge, *World Poverty and Human Rights*, p. 205.

sum could be raised, he argues, by targeting a small range of selectively chosen resources.

The GRD is thus commended by Pogge as a practical solution to a practical problem. That the problem needs to be addressed is a matter of morality. Because the solution is one that requires institutional adoption, he further insists that the morality in question is not simply that of individual conscience; moreover, because the solution would require enforcement, he also argues that it should be adopted not simply on the grounds of charity but of justice. The basic 'positive' obligation on affluent individuals and nations to assist the victims of radical inequality, he believes, would be hard to deny by anyone; but what he seeks further to establish is that radical inequality manifests 'an injustice that involves violation of a negative duty by the better-off'.[5] This involves showing that the better-off are engaged in institutionalized practices that are at least in part responsible for radical inequalities and so have a negative duty to refrain from those practices, or at least to compensate for their effects. Pogge thus posits causal connections between the wealth of the better-off and the poverty of the worse-off. These are of three main kinds:[6] the effects of a shared institutional order, which is controlled largely by the developed countries in virtue of their vastly superior military and economic strength; the continuing effects of 'a common and violent history' which has involved colonial plunder and enslavement; and the uncompensated exclusion of the poor from the use of natural resources. It is this last source of injustice that Pogge focuses on in his argument for a GRD. The other two, he notes, would support almost any reform that would improve the circumstances of the global poor. His narrowing of focus yields a more specific idea: 'those who make more extensive use of our planet's resources should compensate those who, involuntarily, use very little'.[7]

2. *Criticisms of the GRD Proposal*

In this section I consider criticisms of the GRD on the grounds that, were it implemented, its effects would be arbitrary in some significant ways, and so it would not necessarily achieve the ends which have

[5] Pogge, *World Poverty and Human Rights*, p. 198.
[6] On the question of whether each of the three sets of conditions is in fact a distinct cause of radical inequality, see section 4 below.
[7] Pogge, *World Poverty and Human Rights*, p. 204.

provided its rationale. Those ends themselves, and the moral argument that presents them as demands of justice, are not called into question here.

A major element of arbitrariness in the proposal concerns its likely distributive effects. As Joseph Heath, for instance, has argued, these could be expected to be at best random, and at worst regressive, thus actually disfavouring some of those—the poorest—whom it is intended to assist. The distributive effects would be random because even if the proceeds of the dividend go to the poor, it is levied on the extraction of primary resources whose territorial distribution includes both some rich and some poor nations. More crucially, in taxing the immediate products of primary extraction, it falls most heavily on those nations dependent on such activities rather than upon those with more capital-intensive production techniques. This means, in practice, it could tend to fall on the poorer rather than the richer nations. Recognizing this, Pogge's response is that the cost would be passed on to richer nations in the form of higher commodity prices. Heath bluntly objects that Pogge 'forgets that it will be passed right back to poorer nations, in the form of higher prices for manufactured goods, which is what those commodities are exchanged for'.[8] Although Pogge in fact does not disregard this problem, he can nonetheless only suggest considerations that will 'mitigate' the regressive effect,[9] and even these cannot be established with any certainty. For as Dirk Haubrich carefully analyses, there are many economic variables—such as demand elasticity and 'rippling through' effects—which are involved in determining where the burden of such a tax would fall.[10] Pogge does recognize that applying the GRD to certain kinds of resources would quite foreseeably harm the poor directly. He accordingly says that the GRD should apply not to the cultivation of basic commodities such as grain, beans or cotton, for instance, but rather, when it is land use at issue, to raising cattle or growing crops such as tobacco, coffee, cocoa or flowers.[11] But such ad hoc qualifications could be seen as compounding rather than

[8] Joseph Heath, 'Rawls on Global Distributive Justice: A Defence', www.chass.utoronto.ca/~jheath/rawls.pdf, p. 20. The article is forthcoming in Daniel Weinstock (ed.), *Canadian Journal of Philosophy* Supplementary Volume 29 (Lethbridge: University of Calgary Press).

[9] Pogge, 'An Egalitarian Law of Peoples', p. 200.

[10] Dirk Haubrich, 'Global Distributive Justice and the Taxation of Natural Resources: Who Should Pick Up the Tab?', *Contemporary Political Theory* 3 (2004), pp. 48–69.

[11] Pogge, 'An Egalitarian Law of Peoples', p. 203.

alleviating the arbitrariness of the proposal. If poor people are under economic pressure to switch from producing food crops to cash crops this would not be relieved simply by squeezing profit margins on the latter as well.

The arbitrariness may also extend to the quantification of the proposed tax. I do not refer simply to the open question about the rate at which it should be set, but more fundamentally to the question of identifying the relevant sum of economic value of any given resource that the tax would be applied to. There is a practical dimension to this issue, which is worth spelling out on the way to highlighting a question of more critical normative significance. In practice, even the most rudimentary forms of primary production entail a number of processes in bringing a raw material, crop, or energy source into a usable and marketable state. At which point of which process should the tax be applied? Which kinds of costs associated with the processes (from initial prospecting, through securing finance, providing capital or agricultural infrastructure, the various processes of physical extraction, the preparation for physically transferring them, and passing them through merchants for presentation on the world market) would be allowable against the tax and at what rate? Obviously such questions cannot be addressed *a priori* or in the abstract, since for any given resource in any particular context of its extraction, the range of reasonable answers will vary. Pogge's proposal aims to circumvent all such difficulties with the stipulation that the GRD should 'be based on resources and pollutants whose extraction or discharge is easy to monitor or estimate'.[12] If we grant that such monitoring and estimating may be possible for some resources, and that the national governments responsible for collecting the tax can deal with the ingenuity of tax avoiders, there remains a certain arbitrariness in taxing the resources that can easily be taxed rather than those which reasons of justice or environmental concern suggest should be taxed. The case of oil appears, in this as in other respects, to be a favourable one for Pogge's proposal, given its association with both wealth creation and environmental pollution, and it is no coincidence that most of his illustrative remarks assume the case of oil. It is also relatively clear what a GRD on oil would be proportional to: given the cartelized system of oil production, there is effectively a unitary world price that pertains to a given quantity and quality of crude oil. So the

[12] Pogge, *World Poverty and Human Rights*, p. 206.

GRD could be proportional to this price. Such standardization of production and pricing does not apply to other resources, however. And the question why the tax should be applied at the point of extraction, or even at the point of exportation, rather than elsewhere, remains to be answered.

This brings me to what I think is a crucial question whatever resource is at issue: this is the question of the justification for imposing the tax on a once-only basis at the point of extraction. (There is an arbitrariness about this that I shall further expose and diagnose in the next section.) If a tax on natural resources is to have progressive redistributive effects, there is a case for suggesting it should be levied on those who ultimately derive more economic benefit from the exploitation of raw resources rather than on those who, engaged in primary extraction, will generally yield the least added value from the resource. As Heath observes, under the GRD 'the "value-added" by the wealthy nations would be almost entirely untaxed, because their production is more capital-intensive'.[13] And I'd note that raw materials extracted have a very low economic value compared to finished products, so why levy a tax on a relatively small component of value? This leaves those most dependent on raw material exports liable to taxes while the industrialized rich are much more marginally affected, even though their command of resources (calculated fully in terms of ecological space, as I shall discuss in the next section) is much greater.

Another element of arbitrariness concerns the secondary rationale for the GRD, namely, that a tax on natural resources will generally tend to favour their conservation and that a tax on resources such as petroleum more particularly will work in favour of environmental protection. Pogge thinks the GRD will have *considerable benefits* for protection and conservation,[14] but this seems doubtful.[15] A marginal tax on the activities is more likely to have a marginal impact on them, assuming demand is not completely elastic. Moreover, since the primary aim of the tax is to generate revenues from which the poor might benefit, in order that they too can make use of the resources from which they are currently, in Pogge's own words, *involuntarily* excluded, the secondary

[13] Heath, 'Rawls on Global Distributive Justice', p. 20.

[14] Pogge, 'An Egalitarian Law of Peoples', pp. 204, 223.

[15] A fuller criticism on this point is provided by Roger Crisp and Dale Jamieson, 'Egalitarianism and a Global Resources Tax', in V. Davion and C. Wolf (eds.), *The Idea of a Political Liberalism* (Lanham: Rowman & Littlefield, 2000), pp. 99–101.

aim could in fact be annulled by it. In short, one cannot have it both ways. The only effects one can anticipate with reasonable assuredness would be that the economic costs of polluting or depleting resources would be subject to marginal redistribution, not that pollution or resource depletion would be diminished (even marginally).

It has therefore to be concluded that the GRD should not necessarily be expected efficaciously to achieve its ends,[16] either the primary one of effecting progressive economic redistribution or the incidental one of environmental protection and resource conservation. In order to try to get it to achieve at least its primary end, it is arguable that in its implementation the GRD would have to be so tweaked as to conform more to the principle 'tax the rich and redistribute to the poor' than that of compensation for the latter's exclusion from access to natural resources, which is the moral argument Pogge invokes in support of the proposal. Thus critics such as Heath maintain the further conclusion that it is profoundly arbitrary to relate global redistributive taxes to natural resources at all. In the next section I show why this further conclusion can, however, be firmly resisted.

3. *Reconceptualizing Natural Resources and the Justice of their Distribution*

In what follows I sketch a perspective from which the problems noted can be diagnosed as arising from what can be seen as a flaw in the conceptual framing of the GRD proposal. Revealing this flaw leads to the suggestion of an alternative type of proposal for achieving the ends the GRD aims at.

I would note, to begin with, that this flaw is not the one that Heath has claimed to identify. In his view, '[t]he underlying fallacy lies in thinking that wealthy nations are wealthy because they consume so many resources'.[17] Heath claims, contrariwise, that it is because they are wealthy that they consume so much. The problem with this view will become clear at the same time as I now explain the problem with Pogge.

[16] This is not to deny that the GRD could achieve the end of poverty reduction through the redistribution of the funds it raises, but the same would be true of funds raised by other methods which are not vulnerable to criticisms of their effects on the revenue-raising side.

[17] Heath, 'Rawls on Global Distributive Justice', p. 20.

The point of departure for this explanation, though, is one where I have expressed agreement with Heath. As noted, it is arbitrary to focus on primary extraction from an economic point of view, given that greater wealth is generated at subsequent stages of the productive process. The next step, though, is to recognize that wealth itself represents the command of resources, and thus to emphasize that there is further arbitrariness in supposing that only at the point of extraction does the economy have to do with natural resources. For natural resources are not straightforwardly 'used up' in their extraction; nor do they disappear at any point in the processes of production, exchange and consumption; they are certainly not destroyed, as Pogge implies.[18] What actually happens is that their form and composition change. The physical and energetic constituents of raw materials and fuels continue to be embodied in the products manufactured from them; the constituents that are not embodied in the products are also not destroyed but rather contribute to changes in the environment—changes which can also be conceived in terms of utilization of the environment itself as a resource in providing absorption services. Thus those who valorize resources, even in increasingly 'refined' forms, are all the time drawing benefits from natural resources in one state or another which are under their command. From this perspective, then, I would note that Heath's question of whether consumption causes wealth or wealth causes consumption appears misplaced: wealth and consumption are not two discrete phenomena that have some sort of serial causal linkage one way or the other. Wealth just is the command of resources, all of which in the final analysis are natural resources. The 'productive consumption' of resources produces wealth; wealth itself represents the command of resources which can be consumed, 'productively' or otherwise.

It is important also to accept that while enjoying the benefits of 'consuming' resources, productively or otherwise, one is simultaneously creating disbenefits in the form of environmental pollution. The negative environmental impacts of productive processes should not be abstracted from broader issues concerning the effective command of natural resources. Conceptually it would be artificial, and practically it would be inappropriate, to consider 'environmental bads' and 'environmental goods' as entirely separate sets of phenomena. There is just one biophysical reality to which the various categorizations of

[18] Pogge, *World Poverty and Human Rights*, p. 197.

environmental goods and bads relate. To put the point, which derives from basic principles of physics, in homespun terms: 'everything goes somewhere'.

This general perspective I am proposing is most vividly captured with the concept of 'ecological space'.[19] Systematic attempts in recent years to account for the biophysical basis and impacts of human economic activity have led to the development of converging methodologies to determine the total amount of biologically productive land and water area required to produce the resources consumed and to assimilate the wastes generated using prevailing technology. This aggregated amount is referred to as 'ecological space'; and the use or 'occupation' of an amount of it is referred to as an 'ecological footprint'.[20] Ecological footprint accounts express in 'global hectares' the amount of biologically productive space with 'world average productivity' which is necessary to maintain the current material throughput of the human economy under current management and production practices. The footprint is not made on a continuous piece of land; it corresponds to the aggregate land and water area in various ecosystem categories that is drawn on by that nation. Wherever the particular resources it utilizes may have originated, their production required amounts of ecological space. So in the total ecological space a nation's economy disposes of, its own territorial endowment may figure as a greater or smaller proportion. The ecological footprint of a nation measures its total resource consumption by adding imports to, and subtracting exports from, its domestic production.

Whatever operational difficulties and debates about value assumptions may be involved in actually supplying such accounts, the methodology of calculating ecological footprints is sufficiently refined at least to make meaningful comparisons between nations. Such accounts in fact depict a pattern of distribution which does have significant correlations with the distribution of economic wealth.[21] They thus tend to

[19] This perspective is grounded in the seminal work of ecological economist Nicholas Georgescu-Roegen, *Energy and Economic Myths* (New York: Pergamon Press, 1976). It is probably worth stressing that this perspective keeps biophysical accounts of resource throughputs quite distinct from monetary accounts and it thereby differs from those schools of *environmental* economics which seek to establish market or shadow market prices for environmental goods and services.

[20] Mathis Wackernagel and William Rees, *Our Ecological Footprint* (Philadelphia: New Society, 1996).

[21] See e.g. Jason Venetoulis, Dahlia Chazan and Christopher Gaudet, *Ecological Footprint of Nations* (Redefining Progress, 2004), www.redefiningprogress.org.

confirm, more decisively than Pogge's conceptual framework allows one to recognize, that a country's wealth indeed depends on its command of natural resources, providing that we take a *full* account of the resources at its disposal and not only of those which happen to be its natural territorial allotment.

Taking this perspective thus enables us not only to endorse, but also to help explain the basis of, Pogge's claim that the better-off enjoy significant advantages in the use of a single natural resource base from whose benefits the worse-off are largely, and without compensation, excluded. The mistake of supposing that these advantages arise in any direct way from utilizing the natural resources found on a particular territory[22] is avoided by conceiving of resources in terms of ecological space. Pogge's statement correctly refers to the benefits the rich derive from the single global natural resource base. Territorial possession of a part of that base is not necessary to yield the benefits in question.

Adopting this perspective on natural resources also allows us to forge a clearer and more robust link between redistributive proposals and their normative underpinnings than Pogge has been able to establish for the GRD. Regarding the normative foundations of his argument, Pogge has claimed that the GRD 'operates as a modern Lockean proviso'.[23] Yet he also says it 'differs from Locke's own proviso by giving up the vague and unwieldy condition of "leaving enough and as good for others"'.[24] However, the proviso need not be vague or unwieldy if applied to the appropriation of ecological space, I shall argue, and ought not to be given up, but, on the contrary, insisted upon. On Pogge's modified conception of the proviso, the difference, he says, is that one may use unlimited amounts, but one must share 'some of the economic benefit'.[25] Yet it is a material impossibility for inequalities to grow indefinitely and still yield gains for the worst off. This is because economic growth (as distinct from inflation) does in the aggregate represent increased use of natural resources. The depletion of available resources

[22] This is a mistake also found in Charles Beitz, *Political Theory and International Relations* (Princeton: Princeton University Press, 1979): see Tim Hayward, 'Global Justice and the Distribution of Natural Resources', forthcoming in *Political Studies*. That it is a mistake is widely recognized: see e.g. Heath, 'Rawls on Global Distributive Justice'; Haubrich, 'Global Distributive Justice and the Taxation of Natural Resources'; and Mathias Risse, 'What We Owe to the Global Poor', *The Journal of Ethics* 9.1–2 (2005), pp. 81–117.

[23] Pogge, 'An Egalitarian Law of Peoples', p. 201.

[24] Pogge, 'An Egalitarian Law of Peoples', p. 201.

[25] Pogge, 'An Egalitarian Law of Peoples', p. 201.

can wipe out the gains of the worst off—those who have traded away their resources—before it seriously affects the richer who are still working with the gains accruing as a result of the compound advantages they enjoy over the poor. Accordingly I want to argue that the original Lockean proviso should be preserved in a contemporary recontextualization.[26]

The utilization of ecological space can and should be conceived of as the ongoing initial appropriation of nature by humans. The idea of initial appropriation may conjure images of direct physical interaction with a parcel of territory, but there is no particularistic territorial reference for the concept of ecological space other than the planet earth as a whole; physical interaction with the natural world continues to occur not only in prospecting and cultivating, but also through the production, pollution, use and disposal of all physical products—and even as they change hands through trade. The initial appropriation of natural resources is precisely what ecological foot-print accounts track. The utilization of an amount of ecological space by any particular party would accordingly be just if, adapting the Lockean proviso, 'as much and as good' ecological space remains to be utilized by all other parties. But since any given amount of ecological space is as a point of methodological principle 'as good' as any other equal amount, then the proviso would require that *as much* ecological space remain for utilization by others.

When ecological space utilization is conceived as initial appropriation, therefore, the only inequalities that are justified are those achieved by a more efficient extraction of benefits from one's equal share of ecological space. It is worth emphasizing that there is a difference between allowing efficiency gains from an equal share of a single resource base and justifying inequalities in the share of the resource base itself. Thus the concept of efficiency, as related to the use of ecological space, has a narrowly defined meaning: it refers to the economic gains that can be achieved from the more productive use of a given amount of ecological space. Such inequalities would tend to be localized, temporary and marginal. The vast and systematic inequalities globally which Pogge depicts could not be justified at all on the revised understanding of the Lockean proviso I have sketched. At this point it therefore seems

[26] On this score, there is a similarity between my approach and that of Hillel Steiner, 'Just Taxation and International Redistribution', *Nomos* 39 (1999), pp. 171–91. But for differences between them see note 43 below.

appropriate to suggest that a global tax proportional to a nation's per capita utilization of ecological space would answer to the demands of Pogge's moral argument more thoroughly and less arbitrarily than the GRD.[27]

This brings me, finally, to remark that the potential effects of Pogge's GRD may in fact be even more modest than he supposes. In explaining why he thinks even a very modest GRD may have significant effects Pogge refers to the difference between longer-term compound inequalities and 'ordinary centrifugal tendencies of market systems'. 'Present radical inequality',[28] he observes, 'is the cumulative result of decades and centuries in which the more affluent societies and groups have used their advantages in capital and knowledge to expand these advantages further'.[29] He appears to believe, however, that if the worst effects of uneven historical accumulation could be assuaged then even quite a small GRD 'may, in the context of a fair and open global market system, be sufficient continuously to balance those ordinary centrifugal tendencies in markets enough to forestall its reemergence'.[30] Yet I believe this claim may seriously underestimate the continuing relevance of the longer-term compound advantages with which the ordinary centrifugal tendencies are contrasted. In a world of finite resources, indefinite economic growth is not possible. A 'fair and open global market system' can only facilitate the transfer of the resources that exist, not produce more, except perhaps at the margin. There is reason to think that accumulated advantages in terms of capital wealth may simply be amplified by a market system, even a 'fair' one. Cumulative historical advantages can be seen as the basis for continued systematic advantages that might more than offset the counter-vailing contribution of a GRD. Here I would refer to the account offered by Alf Hornborg of how natural resource inequalities and economic inequalities are mutually reinforcing in a cumulative and systematic fashion.

[27] Pogge has put it to me (personal communication) that his GRD would be similar in its effects to an ecological footprint charge inasmuch as it would apply differentially to different resources depending on how damaging their use is. Nonetheless, while appreciating the common spirit of the two proposals, I continue to maintain that a tax based on a nation's aggregate excess usage of ecological space does differ in significant respects from a set of taxes levied on discrete resources at the point of their extraction.

[28] 'Radical inequality' is a concept with a specific meaning for Pogge which he details in *World Poverty and Human Rights*, p. 198.

[29] Pogge, *World Poverty and Human Rights*, p. 205.

[30] Pogge, *World Poverty and Human Rights*, p. 205.

Taking the biophysical perspective which I have already commended, Hornborg argues that global patterns of trade can be viewed as revealing a prevalent occurrence of an 'unequal exchange of resources'. This is made visible 'by identifying, beneath the flows of monetary exchange value, uneven flows of real resources such as energy, labour time, and hectares of land productivity'.[31] A key point is that, from the biophysical perspective, finished products represent an increase in entropy and material disorder compared to the resources from which they were produced, even though from an economic view they have a greater value as represented by price. Accordingly, if we take a longitudinal view of the transformation of a given set of natural resources—fuels and raw materials—into an industrial product, we find a negative correlation between, on the one hand, the amount of negative entropy and usable material embodied in a product and, on the other, its price. Hornborg spells out the socio-economic consequences of this negative correlation: 'industrial centers exporting high-utility commodities will automatically gain access to ever greater amounts of available energy from their hinterlands. The more energy they have dissipated today, the more "new" energy they will be able to buy—and dissipate—tomorrow'.[32] This process has clear distributive implications inasmuch as industrialism implies a *social* transfer of negative entropy, and of usable materials. It is because of the social transfer of negative entropy and material, according to Hornborg, that world trade can be regarded as exploitative—of the poor by the rich—in relation to natural resources. As pressures on natural resources increase, so too one would expect the 'ordinary centrifugal tendencies' inherent in the global market system to intensify rather than be held in check. So to suppose that a 'fair' market system superimposed on a situation of dramatic and systematic inequalities with respect to the command of resources would prevent the further intensification of deprivation and exploitation of the world's poor is, I believe, mistaken.

My main criticisms of the GRD, though, are made not on account of its being a modest step in the right direction, but on account of doubts as to whether it is unequivocally a step in the *right* direction at all.

[31] Alf Hornborg, *The Power of the Machine: Global Inequalities of Economy, Technology, and Environment* (Walnut Creek, CA: Altamira Press, 2001), p. 33.

[32] Alf Hornborg, 'The Unequal Exchange of Time and Space: Toward a Non-Normative Ecological Theory of Exploitation', *Journal of Ecological Anthropology* 7 (2003), pp. 4–10 (6).

4. *Some Remarks on the Moral Argument*

In this article I am not attempting to present a fully-fledged alternative proposal so much as to suggest the basis for one. Nonetheless, as I am also claiming that its basis is more firmly rooted in Pogge's own moral argument than is his GRD, a comment is in order on the potential objection that the approach I commend in fact somewhat shifts its moorings away from the specific moral argument Pogge deploys in support of the GRD proposal.

Of the three possible approaches Pogge identifies as supporting a principle of global redistribution, the one he actually uses is arguably the least controversial in terms of its basic premises. This approach centres on the claim that 'the better-off enjoy significant advantages in the use of a single natural resource base from whose benefits the worse-off are largely, and without compensation, excluded'.[33] It can be said to appeal to the idea that the territorial distribution of natural resources on our globe is a consequence of brute luck and thus morally arbitrary; disadvantages arising from these morally arbitrary circumstances are therefore not 'deserved', and justice requires that they be rectified.[34] Now because my proposal does not confine attention to raw natural resources as they are found lying in, on or above the ground, it could be said to forego the basic advantage of being able to appeal to such a clear distinction between 'deserved' and 'undeserved' benefits, and thus have less compelling normative force than Pogge's does by preserving that distinction. In response,[35] I shall say first why I do not think that Pogge's position is actually so distinct on this score from the one I advocate, and then why the available normative force is anyway not diluted for my proposal.

To begin with, then, I question whether Pogge's moral argument avails itself of the pure moral force of the 'undeserved' character of

[33] Pogge, *World Poverty and Human Rights*, p. 202.

[34] This idea is explicitly drawn on by Beitz, *Political Theory and International Relations*, but for critical reservations about it see Hayward, 'Global Justice and the Distribution of Natural Resources'.

[35] I am granting *arguendo* that the un/deserved distinction carries some moral weight in an intuitive and general way, not endorsing any more specific idea of desert as a primary substantive criterion of justice—for criticisms of which see e.g. John Rawls, *A Theory of Justice* (Oxford: Oxford University Press, 1972). It would take me too far from the present topic to enter debate about the presupposition I am simply allowing here, but some challenging questions about it are raised by Elizabeth Anderson, 'What is the Point of Equality?', Ethics 109.2 (1999), pp. 287–337.

natural resources. When setting out his GRD proposal, Pogge mentions three distinct approaches to justifying global redistribution as a matter of justice. In his argument for the GRD he makes explicit appeal to just the one approach that centres on the injustice of uncompensated exclusion with regard to natural resources. The other two approaches, which he sets aside, focus respectively on the 'effects of shared institutions' and 'effects of a common and violent history'. According to the former, 'there is a shared institutional order that is shaped by the better-off and imposed on the worse-off' which 'is implicated in the reproduction of radical inequality'.[36] According to the latter, '[t]he social starting positions of the worse-off and the better-off have emerged from a single historical process that was pervaded by massive, grievous wrongs'.[37]

I draw attention to these other two approaches in order first to acknowledge the possible objection to my own proposal that it trades on these in order to account for the recurrent and historical 'ecological debt' which I claim should be repaid, and so dilutes the clear moral force of the approach Pogge actually appeals to. My other, more immediate, reason for highlighting them is that I wish to claim the three approaches are not quite so separable as Pogge suggests. In fact, I do not think the 'uncompensated exclusion' approach is simultaneously distinct and complete at all. For Pogge's purposes, it has to be sufficiently complete to add a distinct reason for redistribution over and above the positive duties of assistance that other theories might support as a matter of benevolence or humanity. This is because Pogge's aim is to show that radical inequality globally represents a violation of a stringent negative duty.[38] To establish the violation of a negative duty requires showing that the agents bound by it are doing something they ought not do, and that what they are doing materially causes the deprivation in question. The approaches that appeal to 'shared institutions' and 'common history' both incorporate explanatory hypotheses of the requisite kind. The 'uncompensated exclusion' approach, however, consists purely in description—and a description of a state of affairs which could be a result of the causes invoked by the explanatory approaches. At any rate, the description is not accompanied by any new explanatory hypothesis about how the advantages of the better-off

[36] Pogge, *World Poverty and Human Rights*, p. 199.
[37] Pogge, *World Poverty and Human Rights*, p. 203.
[38] Pogge, *World Poverty and Human Rights*, p. 198.

come about or how the exclusion of the worse-off is effected. What Pogge characterizes are the unjust *effects*: 'The global poor get to share the burdens resulting from the degradation of our natural environment while having to watch helplessly as the affluent distribute the planet's abundant natural wealth amongst themselves'.[39] The only hint of causality and agency comes at the end of his brief discussion: 'the citizens and governments of the affluent states are therefore violating a negative duty of justice when they, in collaboration with the ruling elites of the poor countries, coercively exclude the poor from a proportional resource share'.[40] He does not suggest that the causality of coercive exclusion here is other than that posited by the shared institutions approach.

So I claim that Pogge's complete moral argument for the justice of the GRD does not rest on a purer appeal to the undeserved character of natural resources than my own proposal does.

Nonetheless, perhaps Pogge's strategy in proposing the GRD is intended not to require the complete moral argument—that is, including the explanatory hypotheses—because the GRD is proposed as a modest rectificatory measure rather than an attempt to implement full distributive justice globally. The elements of arbitrariness which I have criticized it for could then be seen simply as confirmation that it is not a systematic argument for redistribution from rich to poor of the kind which needs to appeal to the explanatory approaches. The arbitrariness of territorial endowments might then just suffice. While I have doubts about this, as are explained elsewhere,[41] I shall let the matter rest here.

So meanwhile the objection may be pressed against my own approach that this achieves a closer correlation between tax levels and wealth levels only by diluting the normative force derived from the correlation of the tax to undeserved natural assets.

However, my first response to this objection is to claim that on the contrary, as a matter of principle, by conceiving of natural resources as ecological space, the latter correlation is more perfectly maintained since *all* the use of natural resources—and not merely a one-off transaction involving (some of) them—is accounted for. So if an ecological space tax is anticipated to have a generally progressive effect among economically unequal nations the reason is that levels of ecological

[39] Pogge, *World Poverty and Human Rights*, p. 203.
[40] Pogge, *World Poverty and Human Rights*, p. 203.
[41] Hayward, 'Global Justice and the Distribution of Natural Resources'.

space usage tend to correlate empirically with levels of economic wealth. The normative justification for levying the tax, however, relates not to the degree of wealth of a nation (as might indeed compromise the appeal to 'undeserved' natural assets) but to the degree of their excess use of ecological space. So the normative force at the level of basic principles is in no way diluted.

Nonetheless, it may still be objected that a tax which applies to *all* resource use, including all the various stages of production and consumption, may fail to distinguish in its impact between the value attributable to natural resource inputs ('undeserved' and thus liable for redistribution) and the value added through labour and technology ('deserved' and thus not liable for redistribution). This might be a real concern if separate products or producers were to be taxed. However, that is not envisaged. My proposal, like Pogge's, envisages that the tax would be levied on nations. Unlike the GRD, though, which targets specific resources, a tax on aggregate ecological space use would leave national governments with the discretion to decide exactly how to raise the revenue. I see no objection to nations making fiscal arrangements that support some ecologically costly enterprises, provided that they make up for the ecological deficit in other sectors, making domestic ecological subsidies across sectors or firms as they see fit.

A version of the objection, however, might still be held to apply even when nations are recognized to be the relevant units of assessment. Imagine this scenario: Nation A is richer per capita than Nation B; Nation A is more resource efficient than Nation B; Nation A also uses more resources per capita than either Nation B or its own just allowance. How, then, do we know how much of Nation A's wealth comes from resource efficiency and how much from resource overuse? My answer is that 'we' (thinking as theorists of justice) do not need to (even if a national government will have good reason to work it out in order to know how best to raise the revenue it owes). All 'we' need to know is that Nation A is in 'ecological debt'[42] due to its overuse. And how do we know how much that debt should be taken to amount to in economic terms? An illustrative, broadbrush, answer is: divide the global wealth by world population; divide global ecospace by world

[42] For more on this concept and its applicability, see the report by Erik Paredis *et al.*, 'Elaboration of the Concept of Ecological Debt' (Centre for Sustainable Development, Ghent University, 2004), http://cdonet.ugent.be/english/north-south/research/ecological_debt/index. html

population; thereby arrive at a monetary equivalent for units of ecological space.[43] But I anticipate the rejoinder: suppose Nation A is more efficient in its use of ecological space than are other nations; were it not for that efficiency, the aggregate global economic value of global ecological space would be less; therefore, as a consequence of its efficiency, Nation A has to pay more than if it had been inefficient, and this runs counter to justice. A response might be to adopt this principle: calculate total ecological space utilized by all nations except Nation A; calculate all wealth except that of Nation A; then tax Nation A according to the resultant economic value of ecological space. I would not wish to lose sight, however, of the fact that the real remedy ultimately aimed at is to let all nations which overuse ecological space reduce their usage to the permitted amount—so then they would be able to retain the benefits deriving purely from efficient use of it.

Therefore I would affirm that the requirement of sensitivity to the demands of desert can in fact be met for my proposal. The economic benefits derived from one's equal ecological space entitlement can be considered 'deserved'; gains derived from the utilization of an excess amount of ecological space cannot be considered deserved, whatever ingenuity or industriousness was applied in yielding them. Unless, that is, an entitlement to more than one's equal share can itself be shown to be deserved: but an argument showing that would rest not on an appeal to the undeserved status of natural assets but on its denial.

[43] This very general principle may be contrasted with that proposed by Steiner, 'Just Taxation and International Redistribution'. For while his proposal would similarly direct a tax at the value of natural resources calculated on the basis of their aggregate global value with the aim of redistributing it equally, his conception of natural resources differs in taking these to be 'compendiously describable as constituting a set of *territorial sites*'. As I discuss more fully in Hayward, 'Global Justice and the Distribution of Natural Resources', one of the problems with this approach is that territorial sites do not comprise all and only natural resources. Yet even aside from that problem, a further disadvantage of Steiner's approach shows in the comparison he draws with Pogge's regarding the tax base to be used: 'on Pogge's account, that base is the aggregate value of only used resources, with only some *proportion* of that value to be taxed. Whereas for the Global Fund ... that base is the aggregate value of owned resources—whether used or not—with that value to be taxed at a rate of 100%'. But imposing a 100 per cent levy—or indeed any levy at all—on the value of natural resources possessed, regardless of whether they are used or not, acts as a strong incentive to exploit rather than conserve resources. So given that I have criticized Pogge's proposal for being insufficiently systematic with regard to its secondary aim of promoting resource conservation, I would *a fortiori* criticize Steiner for advancing a proposal that systematically militates against that end.

5. *Conclusion*

In view of the criticisms of arbitrariness that can reasonably be levelled at the GRD proposal, I conclude by affirming four reasons to favour instead levying a tax proportional to a nation's ecological footprint. First, it relates to the use of all resources, not just a small selection. Secondly, it relates to the use of resources at each stage of their use, rather than just at the stage of their first extraction. In both of these respects an ecological space tax would be less arbitrary in its incidence than the GRD. Thirdly, ecological footprint accounts factor in all environmental effects of resource utilization rather than the partial and marginal environmental effects of the GRD. Fourthly, an ecological space tax, because it tracks the use of natural resources even as they are valorized in the economic process, falls proportionately on the rich rather than the poor, which is something the GRD is not certain to do.

POVERTY AND THE MORAL SIGNIFICANCE OF CONTRIBUTION

Gerhard Øverland*

Discussing our duty to fight global poverty, Thomas Pogge argues that we need to take into account the (harmful) effect of our actions and behaviour on poverty. Rather than seeing our duty to the poor as an instance of the general duty to assist people in need, we should look upon it as based on the duty not to contribute to harm. And if, indeed, it is true that we—the affluent in the West—have contributed to the poverty of the global poor, it seems plausible to concede that we have a particularly strong duty to help protect these people from dying of hunger and other poverty-related causes.[1]

Putting to one side the unresolved empirical issues at stake, I want to challenge the inference made in the last statement. More expressly, I want to challenge the necessity of bringing our putative contribution to global poverty into the assessment of our moral obligation to do something about it. I pursue this line of questioning by investigating the moral significance of contribution, and find that it does not seem to matter whether we are (partly) to blame for causing the problem we wish to assuage, when it comes to assessing our duty to provide assistance.[2]

* An earlier version of this article has been presented at a seminar held by the Ethics Programme, University of Oslo. I am grateful to all participants for their contribution. I would also like to thank Thomas Pogge, Robert Huseby, and an anonymous referee from this journal, for helpful comments.

[1] For two recent evaluations of the claim that affluent people in the West contribute global poverty see: Bashshar Haydar, 'Extreme Poverty and Global Responsibility', *Metaphilosophy* 36 (2005), pp. 240–52 (243), and Mathias Risse, 'Do We Owe the Global Poor Assistance or Rectification?', *Ethics & International Affairs* 19 (2005), pp. 9–18.

[2] Throughout the article I assume that it is possible to improve the distribution of benefits and burdens in such a way that significantly fewer people will die of poverty-related causes. This may or may not be possible through simple donations; institutional reforms could very well be required.

The Principle of Contribution

Pogge's starting point is an uncontroversial moral principle widely accepted in our society, namely that it is wrong (severely) to harm innocent people for minor gains.[3] This is a plausible principle, and it is hard to think of instances in which it does not apply. In accordance with it, one could hold that *agents have a particular responsibility to address problems when they have contributed, or are contributing, to bring them about*. We can call this 'the principle of contribution'.[4]

The intuitive force of the principle of contribution derives from the idea that it is wrong to harm others for minor gain. A pre-theoretical and conspicuous idea of harming is based on a notion of causing pain, loss, dependence and all manner of things regarded as unpleasant. To harm someone for minor gain is morally wrong because of the consequences on those affected. That we should not harm people for minor gain is in need of no further justification. On the contrary, the observation may be used to justify other moral principles. By saying this I do not intend to fight shy of philosophical controversies about what should count as harm. That there are deep philosophical problems connected to what it ultimately means to harm someone does not temper the intuitive force of the prohibition against harming others for minor gain. Here we trade on our pre-theoretical understanding of the term, as it comes into play when one person drives over or hits another person. There may therefore be good reasons for appropriating the idea that it is wrong to harm innocent people for minor gain when arguing our duty toward the global poor, namely that it is widely accepted and that it demands no further justification.

---

[3] Thomas Pogge, *World Poverty and Human Rights* (Cambridge: Blackwell, 2002), p. 25.

[4] Christian Barry used the term 'contribution principle' in a talk held at the Global Justice conference in Oslo 2003. In a recent article, Barry has given the following formulation of his contribution principle: 'agents are responsible for addressing acute deprivations when they have contributed, or are contributing, to bringing them about' (Christian Barry, 'Applying the Contribution Principle', *Metaphilosophy* 36 [2005], pp. 210–27 [211]). I do not see why a principle of contribution should include a particular concern for the acutely deprived. What is essential according to the idea of contribution is that we do not contribute to harm, not that we do not contribute to acute deprivation. In case we should show particular concern for the acutely deprived that would have to be on other grounds. Anyway, my concern here is exactly to question the idea that contributors have a particular concern for, in the sense of duty to assist, their acutely deprived victims.

To simplify matters, I only discuss cases in which it is fairly clear that the contributors in question do in fact contribute to harm.[5] I also let our pre-theoretical understanding of harming inform the examples I use. If the insignificance of contribution could be demonstrated at this level, we have no reason to assume that the kind of harm for which the affluent in the West (eventually) are responsible would impinge on their duty to assist the global poor.

The principle of contribution may be said to have two implications with regard to world poverty. The first is that we ought not to act in such a way as to add to world poverty and, if we do, we ought to stop doing so. The second implication is that we ought to help victims of poverty if we have contributed to bring it about.[6] I see no problem in accepting the first contention.[7] It is the second implication I query, namely that our contribution to world poverty will determine to a greater or lesser extent the strength of our duty to help protect people from poverty and its consequences.

I look at the general version of the principle of contribution—that by being a contributor to harm one has a particular strong duty to assist those who are victims of one's conduct. We can distinguish between two aspects of this general claim.[8] (1) A contributor to harm, rather than some bystander, has a stronger duty to assist those who are victims of his or her conduct; (2) a contributor to harm has a stronger duty to assist those who are victims of his or her conduct, rather than to assist some other needy people. The distinction here is important because while the first differentiates prospective assistors only, the second differentiates between a contributor and his or her victim.

---

[5] There is, of course, a question concerning the level of evidence that should be required in order to establish that we do so. For an interesting discussion of contribution under uncertainty, see Barry, 'Applying the Contribution Principle', pp. 210–27.

[6] This is in accordance with Haydar: 'I take the claim that an agent is responsible for some harm to mean that the agent has special obligation to alleviate that situation or prevent it from taking place' (Haydar, 'Extreme Poverty and Global Responsibility', p. 240).

[7] This first implication could be taken to imply that if we could establish that a particular society, Rich, does in fact contribute to the poverty of another society, P_1, then Rich ought to prevent this from continuing before it uses its resources to help another poor society, P_2, with whom it has no interaction. If there is an unjust interaction between Rich and P_1, and no interaction between Rich and P_2, then we could say that it is more important that Rich terminates its unjust relations to P_1 than that it assists P_2.

[8] I am grateful to Robert Huseby for helping me to be clear on these matters.

Fairness Aspect

Concerning the first aspect, I should think morality requires a contributor as well as a bystander to assist a person in need if they can do so at little cost to themselves.[9] However, *considerations of fairness* may require a contributor rather than a mere bystander to assist a person in need if both are able to do so, provided that it is enough that only one person assists the needy. A bystander may fairly require a contributor to address harm for which he or she is responsible, rather than letting others shoulder that duty.[10] This having been said, we should keep in mind that fairness considerations are something that holds between contributors and bystanders, and that the duty to assist a needy person may be left untouched by such considerations. The implication would be that the failure of a contributor to assist his or her victim is unfair towards the bystander, insofar as the duty to render assistance thereby falls on the bystander.

In *Moral Demands in Nonideal Theory*, Liam Murphy argues that the optimizing principle of beneficence imposes its demands unfairly in situations of partial compliance. If an agent is complying with the optimizing principle, but others are not, she not only has to do her own fair share, but she has to take on as much of the shares of the non-complying others as is optimal as well. This is unfair, according to Murphy, who in redress suggests a 'compliance condition', which states, 'the demands on a complying person should not exceed what they would be under full compliance with the principle'.[11] But the unfairness constraint of the compliance condition does not seem convincing.

---

[9] According to Peter Singer, a plausible principle states that if we can prevent something bad from happening without sacrificing anything of comparable significance, we ought to do it (Peter Singer, *Practical Ethics* [Cambridge: Cambridge University Press, 1993], p. 230). A less demanding reinterpretation of the principle of assistance states that if we can prevent something bad from happening at low cost to ourselves, we ought to do it.

[10] In this sense I agree with Pogge when he maintains that if having attacked a particular person, 'the attacker has more reason to ensure that his victim's injuries are treated than a bystander' (Thomas Pogge, 'Real World Justice', *The Journal of Ethics* 9 [2005], pp. 29–53 [34]).

[11] Liam Murphy, *Moral Demands in Nonideal Theory* (Oxford: Oxford University Press, 2000), p. 7. For a full discussion see Murphy, *Moral Demands in Nonideal Theory*, pp. 74–101. For a critical assessment see Richard J. Arneson, 'Moral Limits on the Demands of Beneficence', in Deen K. Chatterjee (ed.), *The Ethics of Assistance* (Cambridge: Cambridge University Press, 2004), pp. 33–58 (35–39).

If some people need assistance it seems implausible to say that a particular person's duty to assist depends on what others do; that kind of consideration concerns fairness between prospective assistors only. It would be better to say that each person's duty to render assistance depends on the costs to the agent weighed up against the needs of the unfortunate. This implies that if enough people fail to do their fair share, the cost to an agent may very well exceed what may be required of him or her. The agent would therefore have no duty to assist those in need. But unfairness between the complying and non-complying should not be conflated with what is morally required of each agent.[12]

True, when sorting out individuals' respective duty to assist people in need, we should distribute the burdens of assistance fairly.[13] In order to do that we need to know who did what to whom. And if Pogge's agenda were to determine how the burden of responsibility for helping the poor should be distributed, fairness considerations would be crucial.[14] But this, in my opinion, is not the crux of the principle of contribution, nor, indeed, do I believe it is for Pogge. The main point of the principle, I maintain, is its first aspect, namely that a contributor to harm has a stronger duty to assist those who are victims of his or her conduct rather than to assist other needy people.[15] And this is so because he or she has harmed the former and not the latter.

[12] A similar point is made by Arneson who maintains that: 'The mere fact of non-compliance by some does not automatically set an upper limit on the amount of sacrifice it is reasonable to demand of others who can provide cost-effective aid' (Arneson, 'Moral Limits on the Demands of Beneficence', p. 37).

[13] This is, as I understand it, part of what David Miller takes to be the problem of remedial responsibility. See his 'Distributing Responsibility', *Journal of Political Philosophy* 9 (2001), pp. 453–71.

[14] According to Christian Barry all participants in the debate concerning access to antiretroviral medicines for the treatment of those suffering from HIV/AIDS seem to agree that, 'were it to be shown that certain actors have substantially contributed to these deprivations, it would be their responsibility (though perhaps not *solely* their responsibility) to try to remedy them' (Barry, 'Applying the Contribution Principle', pp. 211–12). In this quote it seems as if Barry is talking about fairness considerations among prospective assistors, and not the question whether a contributor to harm has a stronger duty to assist victims of his or her conduct rather than some other people in severe need. But it is important to maintain this distinction and that though one grants the one significance, one might deny significance to the other.

[15] It might be that Pogge would say that his main focus is on what I took to be the first implication of the principle of contribution, namely that we ought not to act in such a way as to add to world poverty and, if we do, we ought to stop doing so.

Significant Features of Contribution

Before discussing whether our responsibility for generating need increases the onus on us to alleviate that need, I want to explore why we are inclined to think so in the first place. I believe we conflate the duty of assistance with other morally significant features of being a contributor (in addition to the fairness aspect already discussed). It is therefore pertinent to take a look on some such significant features.

Pogge asks us to imagine by the side of a country road,

> an injured child who must be rushed to the hospital if her leg is to be saved. As a competent bystander who ignores her plight, you are subject to moral criticism for failing to assist. But if you are the driver who injured the child in the first place, then more is morally at stake: by leaving the child's needs unattended, you would greatly increase the harm you will have done her.[16]

I think we may agree that more is morally at stake here if we are the driver of the vehicle that struck her. We do not need to assume that more is at stake because we have left our victim unattended. For example, if we were morally at fault by driving recklessly, we would have good reason to judge ourselves more harshly than if we had driven carefully. And this judgment would not depend on whether we abandoned the injured child. Leaving the child's needs unattended is a separate event from the event, which brought the child in a position of need in the first place.

In order to tease out various significant features of being a contributor to need, let me modify Pogge's example: While driving along a road you turn up the music and accelerate. Things go well for a while, but suddenly you lose control of the vehicle and hit a pedestrian on the sidewalk. You stop the car, get out and inspect the situation. The person looks as if he needs urgent medical assistance. You therefore drive him to a hospital nearby. In this case, your culpability in the accident is plain: you have harmed the person. What is not plain is the moral significance of having caused the accident in the first place.

First of all, you are to be *blamed* for not having taken appropriate steps in order to avoid harming other people by your behaviour. You ought to have driven more carefully, and since you did not you are

[16] Thomas Pogge, '"Assisting" the Global Poor', in Deen K. Chatterjee (ed.), *The Ethics of Assistance* (Cambridge: Cambridge University Press, 2004), pp. 260–88 (278).

morally responsible for a morally reprehensible deed and are therefore blameworthy. In this sense, we could say with Pogge, that 'more is morally at stake' when you have contributed to harm the injured person. Negligent or reckless behaviour is central when assessing a person's culpability.[17]

A second morally significant feature of being a contributor is that you thereby owe the person *compensation* for any material damages (and that you pay for appropriate treatment if need be). Owing him compensation is something you are responsible for, not anyone else. Indeed, if you damage another person's car, however slightly, you are still materially accountable to that owner. No one else needs to pay for the repairs, and should you fail to honour your obligation, it does not revert to anybody else. The duty to compensate applies to you only, and though it might be limited, the cost of damages for which you are liable may far exceed what would be required of others who respond to the general duty to assist people in need.[18] Moreover, many people would say that compensation is owed regardless of whether or not you were a culpable contributor.

A third implication of being a contributor of harm comes into play if the *cost* of providing assistance increases. When the costs are considerable, a contributor may seem to be obliged to render the type of assistance that mere by-standers would not. If saving the life of a stranger means one loses an arm, for instance, the cost of helping may seem too much to demand of bystanders. Yet I think we could require a contributor to assist a victim even if the cost were that acute (depending on what is at stake for the victim and the culpability of the contributor in question). Contributors to harm may have a duty to accept higher costs than mere bystanders. This is a salient feature of being a contributor.[19]

[17] Should it be pure bad luck that you were to drive down a person on the sidewalk, you would not be to blame for it (unless one believed in moral luck). Since I do not see innocent contribution to be central to the topic under discussion, I leave out innocence and assume at least recklessness or negligence.

[18] One concern that might be used to limit the duty to compensate is what it is reasonable to expect a contributor to foresee as consequences of his or her conduct. Another concern could be to what extent taking on the cost of compensation would set the compensator in a state of need.

[19] Compare Haydar, who proposes that a way 'to distinguish an agent who has special obligation to some harm from those who do not have such obligation is that less weight should be given to the former's appeal to cost in order to justify her not taking steps to alleviate the harm in question' (Haydar, 'Extreme Poverty and Global Responsibility', p. 240).

The importance of this observation with regard to our responsibility to eradicate world poverty depends on how much it would cost. If it were very costly, determining culpability would be important. But if it is true that global poverty can be eradicated at low cost, this aspect of contribution may be put to the side when considering our duty to do away with global poverty.

I would like to mention yet another morally significant feature of being a contributor, which is connected to the use of force. An individual about to be harmed may be justified in applying *defensive force*. For example, a person about to be hit by your car could permissibly take preventive action against you, causing you harm in the process. This is because you—as a likely contributor to harm—are to be regarded as an aggressor against whom it is permissible to use defensive force. However, in trying to prevent your car from hitting him or her, the prospective victim must take care not to impose equal harm on innocent third parties. You are the only permissible target of such harm, and that is because in your negligence or recklessness you are about to cause someone harm.[20] This observation may have disturbing consequences. If the claim that we contribute to the poverty and the death of many poor people can be substantiated, it would, according to the permissibility of using defensive force against contributors of harm, permit defensive force to be used on us. One could take it as being a *reductio ad absurdum* argument against Pogge's proposal. I do not think that we should, but shall say no more about it here.

The Insignificance of Contribution

In the previous section I hope I showed how being a contributor to harm matters with regard to several moral assessments. Responsibility of the people in need matters too, and significantly so. If they are responsible for the situation, the legitimacy of their claim on assistance is correspondingly weakened. If faced with a choice, we ought to save a person who, through no fault of her own, is drowning, instead of two others who are responsible for their own plight. Equally, we would be justified in attempting to save the limb of one person rather than two

[20] To the extent that the driver is innocent, it is a question of using defensive force against innocent aggressors/threats. On the permissibility of use of such force see my 'Self-defence among Innocent People', *Journal of Moral Philosophy* 2.2 (2005), pp. 127–46.

limbs of another, if the latter is responsible for her plight, and the former is not.

The contentious question concerns the extent to which responsibility for a situation should count when assessing the duty to assist people in severe need. If a person you have hit while driving suffers serious injury, you ought to provide assistance. That is not in question; what is in question is whether your obligation to assist the person in severe need depends on the extent of your *contribution* to his or her unfortunate situation.

In order to investigate that question, let us imagine that ten metres to the left from where your negligent or reckless driving came to an end there is a second person harmed by another driver who has left the scene without coming to his or her victim's assistance. It takes you little time to realize that you are unable to help both. Which of the two injured parties, then, should you assist, and what should the criterion for the selection be?

If it is true that an agent has a particular duty to address problems to which he or she has contributed, we might find it right if the agent helped the person whose injuries he or she was responsible for. But surprisingly, I think, that is not obvious.

What seems to matter more than contribution is the severity of the injuries and urgency with which they—i.e. the two injured parties—require treatment. Severity matters because it has to do with which person is most harmed; urgency because that has to do with the window of time before the risk of serious complications becomes overwhelming. Between these two parameters trade-offs must be made. Sometimes one ought to give severity priority and sometimes urgency. However, assuming that you can only help one, not both, it seems to matter very little whether you caused the one person's injury and not the other's. The proposal, therefore, is that when people need our help, we should apply the parameters of severity and urgency when deciding who to help first, and that contribution should play no, or only a very small, part in that decision.

According to the second aspect of the principle of contribution, we could expect a contributor to have a particular strong duty to come to the aid of his or her victim, and that the duty to assist therefore would be what we could call 'victim specific'. The duty to compensate, for example, is victim specific in this sense; a contributor owes compensation to his or her victim only. We saw this in the situation where we merely bumped into someone's car. If we then learn that someone else's car has been similarly damaged, we are under no obligation to compare damage and compensate the owner of the most damaged vehicle. And this is not because it might cost us more; there is no way we should give damages owed to our victim to the other person instead. But in contrast to the duty to compensate, the duty to assist should be read as *victim insensitive*. Victim insensitivity implies that we should not distinguish between people we have harmed and others in need when organizing help.

That the duty to assist is victim insensitive means that we might have to deselect a victim for whose need we are to blame and concentrate instead on helping someone else because theirs is the greater need. And similarly, one might have to compensate one's victim but have to assist someone else. Regarding blame, such a distinction should not create a problem, but with regard to compensation it could be questioned whether it is possible to distinguish between compensation and mere assistance in all relevant cases. While I do not assume it is always possible to make this distinction, I do not think it bears heavily on the arguments presented here, which mainly are about the relationship between an agent's contribution to a situation of need and his or her duty to do away with it.

Be aware that I am not taking issue with the question of the respective strength of the duty to compensate versus the duty to assist. For instance, having destroyed something belonging to a very rich person, you ought not, it seems safe to say, to compensate a second rich person whose property suffered wider damage through the actions of another agent. Yet one may be justified in asking whether you should not take the opportunity to spend the money on assisting some of the global poor instead.[21] The point is simply that, disregarding their respective strength, compensation is victim specific while the duty to assist is not.

Contractual Considerations

Inasmuch as we allow severity and urgency to play the crucial role when selecting whom to assist, would it not be unfair, one might wonder, to help people whose need we have not caused, rather than

[21] One could, of course, wonder why the duty to give away one's money should hinge on whether or not one has ruined some property belonging to another person? To the extent that we think that a contributor should give his or her sum-of-compensation to needy starving people rather than to a rich car driver, we might perhaps better say that one ought to give the money away anyway.

someone whose need was (partly) due to ourselves. According to the second aspect of the principle of contribution, a contributor to harm has a primary duty to assist victims of his or her conduct and only a secondary duty to assist other needy persons. This proposal may be said to have the following correlate: a person whose need is caused by a particular agent will have a primary claim on assistance from that agent, while all others in need would enjoy only a secondary claim. Since I deny both the initial formulation and its correlate, the challenge is to explain why it is not unfair to a particular victim if a contributor assists someone else.

We might understand this point better by looking into the reasons people have for accepting a rule, which says their duty to assist should not be constrained by contribution considerations. We might first observe that when people are in need, they have an interest in being assisted, and the importance of being assisted is determined by the severity and urgency of their situation. Second, to the needy people whether the help comes from the contributor or elsewhere appears irrelevant; what they want above all is to get help. It therefore seems rational to hold that prospective assistors ought to assist according to severity and urgency (and, of course, according to the number of people in need), and not to delegate provision of assistance according to the giver's causal role. People therefore have good reason to agree to a rule by which we ought to assist the person(s) most in need whenever there is a conflict between giving assistance to several people in need.

People obviously want to get help when they need it. But people also want a say in how their time and resources are used for the benefit of others. They therefore have grounds to restrict how far they wish to translate the duty to help people whose need they are not responsible for. A duty to assist people at low cost does not impose a very demanding burden on people, and is accordingly to a large extent compatible with the interest of maintaining control of one's time and resources. In this sense there is a trade-off between one's interest in being helped oneself, and one's interest in managing one's own time and resources. I shall not go into this discussion here; I merely want to stress that there are grounds for setting a ceiling on how far people should be expected to go in relation to helping others. It is, nevertheless, important to observe that people have a reason for accepting a duty to assist others when the cost is reasonable, disregarding their role in bringing the need about. I therefore propose that a duty to assist people in severe need at low cost, with the criteria for selecting whom to assist as being severity and urgency, would be picked in a contractual situation in which all information—except information about prospective recipients—is available to the parties to the contract. The implementation of that rule would give everyone an increased probability of being assisted when they need it most, without doing so unfairly.

The contractual argument depends on the probability of sustaining greater or lesser harm is roughly equal across all parties. There is no reason, I believe, to assume the contrary. The probability requirement should therefore be no obstacle. We should also observe that this argument could be used to justify lower claims on assistance for people responsible for their own plight, compared with other people whose needs are no fault of their own. The former, not the latter, have increased the likelihood of needing assistance by engaging in risky behaviour.

The contractual argument lends support to the view that a contributor has no victim-specific duty to assist his or her victim: whomever one ought to assist should be decided by severity and urgency. This observation could be taken to imply that our duty to assist people in need were *contribution insensitive*. Be aware, however, that although the duty to assist as a consequence of one's contribution is victim insensitive, how far the duty to assist is contribution sensitive in a victim-insensitive way remains to be settled. I shall return to this option later.

Further Considerations

One way to retort to the proposal that one ought to assist according to severity and urgency and disregard contribution is to say that urgency and severity is decisive when there is a significant difference between the respective need of two persons, but as soon as there is not much difference between them, or none at all, we should help the person whose predicament we ourselves have caused. Pogge seems at one instance to hold the view that contribution only determines whom to assist 'when what is at stake for all concerned is held constant'.[22] But then it would not be very important to establish whether we have negative duties toward the global poor. Negative duties would only come into play in situations requiring us to differentiate, for the purpose of rendering assistance, people whose needs are equal. Moreover, I am not even sure that drawing lots to decide the issue would be impermissible in a situation in which the predicament of two people were equally

[22] Pogge, 'Real World Justice', p. 34.

desperate. When faced with a decision to help one of two people in need, one better put the question of contribution to one side and concentrate on their respective urgency and severity. Should there be no difference on these grounds, one might just as well use a randomized procedure. But even though we grant that an agent should first assist his or her victim, when severity and urgency are otherwise equal, contribution cannot be said to carry much significance.

A more interesting view would be to say that there is a point—threshold—at which the duty to assist one's victim is outweighed by a duty to assist another. Imagine, for instance, a driver faced with a choice of acting to save one of the limbs of a person injured by himself, or saving two limbs of somebody he had not injured. It could then, according to the threshold view, be right for him to help the former. But if the latter were in danger of losing all four limbs, or his or her life, he or she should have precedence. This is a plausible view with regard to other moral features. Envisage, for instance, that we come to know that one of two persons, both needing urgent assistance, was responsible for his or her own predicament. This fact should influence our decision making, and it should not do so only in cases where injuries are indistinguishable. Of course, it is difficult to decide where to position the threshold, but that is not a sufficient reason for not preferring a threshold view rather than an everything-else-being-equal view. Let it be clear, however, that I am not defending any such threshold view as I deny the significance of contribution in cases of severe need. My proposal is that it is wrong to give preference to a particular person's need if more than one party requires urgent attention merely because he or she is your victim.

Another objection could be phrased as follows. Imagine two people in need. While you are to blame for the predicament of the first, you are not for that of the second. You choose to save the second individual nevertheless because their injuries are more severe or urgent. By doing this you might end up owing your victim higher compensation than if you had decided to save him or her in the first place. And this observation, one could claim, indicates that you ought to assist your victim, and not spend time and resources helping someone else. In Pogge's example, he says that by leaving the child's needs unattended, you would greatly increase the harm you will have done her. That might be true, and if so it could increase the compensation you owe her. But why should this observation be taken as meaning you ought to assist your victim rather than someone else? That would only be true if our concern were to ensure reparations due from you remained as low as possible. But why should that be our concern? Rather, I believe, our concern should be that the person most in need was assisted. The fact that you have contributed to someone's need is a separate event, and does not count as a justification for not doing your duty.[23] The need of your victim does not count as a justification as long as his or her need is less severe (or urgent) than another person's, and merely to reduce your cost of compensation should not count as justification for anything.

At this juncture it could be objected that I have not really answered Pogge's initial claim that by leaving the child's need unattended, the driver has increased the harm he has done her. Because if this increase is taken to be an instance of harming, we could be faced with the unwelcome prospect of having to let people harm certain individuals, perhaps seriously, in order for them to save others from (not so very much) greater harm. And such redistribution of harm is in general not permitted.[24] Hence, one could think, the proposal that contribution is insignificant when deciding whom to assist between the two people injured by the two different cars must be false.

One answer to this objection would simply be to acknowledge that it is permissible to impose this kind of harm on some people to save others from a greater harm. By 'this kind of harm', we should understand all instances in which one leaves one's victim's need unattended. Observe as well that to leave one's victim unattended does not seem to fall within the pre-theoretical understanding of inflicting harm, and it is therefore at least an open question if we should take it to be an instance of harming in the first place. It seems to me that we could very well take the mere fact that we think that it is permissible to leave one's victim unattended to save someone else from a slightly greater harm, to be an indication that we better not call it harming at all. And it should at least not be seen as a reason for thinking that since this kind of 'harm causing' is permissible, it is always permissible to impose serious harm on someone in order to save someone else from a greater harm. Any inference from Pogge's example will only affect instances of harming,

---

[23] Though we might think that a contributor choosing to assist his or her victim could be excused.

[24] Unless, of course, the harming is very small, like kicking a person in the leg, and the harm one saves the other person from is considerably more serious.

which is leaving one's victim's need unattended. And there should be no problem in accepting that.

'No problem' might be an exaggeration though. We should be able to say why it is the case that after injuring a particular person, we might have to let this person go unattended, causing, perhaps, the loss of a limb, in order to assist someone else whose need is greater, namely a person who is about to lose two limbs, but that it is not, by analogy, permissible to actively cause an injury leading to the loss of a limb in order to save someone else from the loss of two. One option would be to say that it is not permissible to cause harm in order to save someone else from slightly greater harm, simply because the latter does not count as a justification for doing the former. However, when the initial harm is already a fact, the allocation of assistance is a separate event needing to be assessed on its own merits. And this is the view advocated here. We should not link the question of assistance with contribution, but rather see it as requiring an assessment of its own.

Pogge uses the term 'intermediate duties' to cover situations I have been discussing.[25] Intermediate duties are supposed to stand between negative and positive duties, and are duties to protect victims of our past conduct from delayed consequences. For example, a driver who leaves a victim unattended would exacerbate the harm he had already inflicted on her. The idea behind intermediate duties is that the stringency of the negative duty not to harm people carries over to the positive duty of assisting those now in need.[26] Intermediate duties are therefore supposed to be crucial in explaining how we, the affluent in the West, have a particular duty to address world poverty because we contribute to its persistence. I have put this view into question, and proposed that the driver in the driving accident analogy, and other contributors, when faced with decisions to distribute limited aid to these and other people in need, should give precedence to severity and urgency, and not causal role.

It could be argued that Pogge's point is merely one about our duty to compensate the global poor, and not about our duty to assist. Pogge does not talk about the duty to assist because he believes such talk gives a wrong focus on our responsibilities. But ultimately, what is at stake is

---

[25] To my knowledge Pogge begins to use this term in his recent 'Real World Justice'.

[26] 'They are positive insofar as they require the agent to do something and also negative insofar as this requirement is continuous with the duty to avoid causing harm to others' (Pogge, 'Real World Justice', p. 34).

not a matter of name giving, but to clarify our duty to do away with need. My proposal is therefore that our duty to do away with need does not hinge on our relation to its cause, and I prefer to call this victim-insensitive duty to do away with need, a duty to assist.

Contribution Reconsidered

While I accept that a contributor to harm, rather than some bystander, is under a stronger duty to provide succour, I argue against the view that a contributor to harm has a stronger duty to prefer victims of his or her conduct when allocating assistance. At this point I want to investigate two further strategies that could be used to salvage the idea that a contributor to need has some special duty to assist.

The Victim-Insensitive Reading

In the first option a contributor has a stronger duty to assist a person whose predicament he has caused than what he or she would have had were it not for his or her contribution to the person's need. This counterfactual understanding of the principle of contribution may be taken to have an independent meaning. But observe that the point of comparing a contributor's duty with the duty of a bystander was exactly to evaluate the contributing aspect, which is not found among bystanders, and that the point of comparing a contributor's duty to help his or her victim rather than another needy person was to evaluate a person's duty to someone in need irrespective of causal relations. This counterfactual reading could therefore be seen as being evaluated through the two others.

All bets are not off yet, however. The appropriate understanding of the duty to assist could be taken as being victim insensitive, but sensitive nevertheless to agents' contribution to need. The correct reading of the counter-factual proposal would therefore look like this: a contributor to need is under a stronger obligation to assist persons in need than what he or she would have had were it not for his or her contribution to some need. The duty to assist is here understood to be non-directional, or victim insensitive, and hence in accordance with the previous discussion. If contributors have a stronger duty to assist people in need, due to their contribution to it, it would have to apply to all people in need without distinction.

One implication of such a victim insensitive, but contribution sensitive, duty to assist could be that a driver who had injured a person acquired a stronger duty to assist all people in need and not only his or her own victim. But is this a plausible assumption? Is it really the case that if one has contributed to a person's need then one has a stronger duty to assist other people?

Well, if someone else had to assist the contributor's victim because the contributor failed to do so, it seems fair to require that the contributor rendered assistance to a second person ending up in need, rather than letting others bear those costs as well. Fairness considerations might therefore lend support to this reading.[27] Though this seems true, we should make two observations. First, we have with this account returned to considerations that hold between contributors and bystanders only. But such fairness considerations do not explain why a contributor has a stronger duty to his or her victim for the sake of the victim; he or she has a stronger duty for the sake of bystanders. And this, I believe, is not really what we are looking for. Second, such a fairness-based duty only applies provided others had to bear the cost of assisting the contributor's victim. In situations in which no one is required to expend added resources to assist the victim—imagine, for example, that the victim is out of reach of everybody—it is not clear that the contributor's duty to assist others in need would be stronger than the bystanders'.

But if fairness cannot ground a victim-insensitive, but contribution-sensitive, duty to assist people in need, what could possibly do so? One could perhaps appeal to the moral wrongness of being a (negligent, reckless or intended) contributor in the first place. We could then say that a culpable contributor has to take on the burden of assisting people in need due to his or her moral deficit.[28] By wrongly having contributed to someone's need, one would be required to make up for it by assisting someone else. There is some appeal in this proposal, but it is difficult to see why causing need, and not other moral wrongs, necessarily generates the appropriate moral deficit. And if we accept that all wrongdoing causes a moral deficit, multiplying wrongdoers' duty to assist others in need, the principle of contribution would become inconsequential.

[27] I owe this proposal to Jakob Elster.
[28] I owe this proposal to Robert Huseby.

Moreover, it is not at all clear whether morally deficient people in fact are subject to a particular strong duty to help the needy. Is a thief, for instance, more morally bound to assist people in need than ordinary law-abiding people? Perhaps he or she is, but if so, much stretching and bending would be needed to connect this stronger duty with the principle of contribution.

The Increased Cost Reading

Another option to salvage the moral significance of contribution for our duty to assist people in need is to focus on the increased cost contributors have to shoulder when assisting their victims, and to say that this increment is their increased duty to assist. We have already seen that a contributor has a duty to expend more to help his or her victim than may reasonably be expected of bystanders. The proposal at this point is that this increment constitutes a contributor's stronger duty to assist his or her victim.[29]

It seems odd to say, though, that a contributor has a stronger duty to assist his or her victim when this alleged stronger duty has no, or at least very little, impact on whom the contributor ought to assist. If a contributor has a stronger duty to assist a particular victim because he or she caused the victim's need, but it is also the case that the contributor should apply the criteria of severity and urgency when selecting whom to assist, and not his or her causal role, the contributor might find him or herself in a situation where he or she is morally required to divert assistance from the one he or she is most morally obliged to help, to someone else. Segregating in this manner what one ought to do from one's stronger duty seems puzzling. In support of something like it, however, Frances Kamm has proposed that 'our duty' should not be thought of as what we must do.[30] One could accordingly say that although the stronger duty not to contribute to harm may have little or no implication for what we ought to do with regard to assisting needy people when we in fact contribute to a particular person's need, we do have a stronger duty to address needs which we ourselves have

[29] Is the duty to shoulder increased cost based on the mere fact of being a contributor, or is it necessary to be a culpable contributor? It seems at least plausible to assume that the duty will be affected by culpability, and not merely one's causal role.

[30] See Frances M. Kamm, 'The New Problem of Distance in Morality', in Deen K. Chatterjee (ed.), *The Ethics of Assistance* (Cambridge: Cambridge University Press, 2004), pp. 59–74 (65).

caused. I am not sure whether this proposal is very promising. If the good generated by two different acts was equal, and the burden of performing them was equal as well, one should believe that one would have to perform one's (stronger) duty. If not, we lose sight of what it means to have a duty.

Disregarding whether or not we regard contributors' duty to shoulder costs as constituting their stronger duty to assist, we could again ask whether this duty applies to their particular victims only. In other words, is the duty to bear costs victim specific? Imagine that a contributor is unable to assist his or her victim, but is in a position to help someone else in equal need. Would this contributor have a stronger duty than a bystander to shoulder added costs? Envisage, for example, a driver who gets out of his car and observes that he cannot assist his own victim but another person in need. Is the driver under a duty to expend the same resources on this second individual as he owes the victim of his own careless driving, or is he to be considered a mere bystander with regard to this duty?[31] Whatever we think about this, we should once again observe that it is difficult to see what difference contribution ultimately would have in such a victim-insensitive duty to shoulder cost. If the duty to bear costs were increased by being a contributor to need, all wrongdoers would be liable to bear costs, and being a contributor to a particular kind of need would make no difference.

As it seems difficult to find a general reason for identifying a stronger victim- insensitive duty on part of contributors to need, I conclude this section by observing that we have reasons to suspect that the duty to assist people in need is not only victim insensitive but contribution insensitive as well. That is, the duty to assist is contribution insensitive with the proviso that a contributor owes it to bystanders to assist victims of his or her own actions, and if someone else has already done so, the contributor is under an obligation to assist any subsequent person in need.[32]

31 A vexed situation arises if a contributor could save his or her victim at little cost, or another person in more severe need at considerably higher cost, and the contributor would have had a duty to assist his or her victim at such cost but not people to which harm he or she has not contributed.

32 If one wants to relate the duty to shoulder increased cost with another significant feature of being a contributor, it might seem more promising to connect it with the duty to compensate rather than with the duty to assist. I shall not pursue that option here.

Concluding Remarks

I have argued that the moral significance of having contributed to harm is not what matters when deciding whether to assist needy people. This implies that I deny the second aspect of the principle of contribution, and, accordingly, that a contributor to harm should be seen to have no stronger duty to assist those who are victims of his or her conduct, rather than to assist some other needy people. So although we should be able to make sense of the claim that we contribute to the poverty of the poor in a way that conveys some of the intuitive power of the impermissibility of not harming others, we could do just as well without this idea when arguing for our responsibilities to the very poor.

It may be permissible, Kamm suggests, to discharge one's duties by performing supererogatory acts.[33] Accordingly, we could say that assisting a person whose need has no causal relationship with ourselves would be supererogatory, but that it would be permissible to do so rather than assisting a person we had harmed as long as it promoted equal or more good. Yet, it would still be the case that the only way we could discharge our duties to the needy would be by assisting *some* people in need. This view seems to sit well with the observation made above, namely that people have a mutual interest in having a rule dictating that one save those most in need. But it fails in the sense that it sees the assisting of the more needy as supererogatory. I have argued that deciding whom to assist comes with a duty to consider severity and urgency, not simply with an opportunity to do so.

The idea is that our responsibility to render assistance obtains whether or not we have caused the problem in the first place. Though contribution is tied to compensation, the issue of assistance in cases of severe need should be evaluated on its own merit. If this is correct, contribution is not the right parameter to be singled out when arguing for our duty to assist the global poor. Although relevant for

---

[33] We might, for example, imagine someone having a duty to meet a particular person for lunch because she promised to do so. On her way, she sees someone dying of kidney failure. She is willing to give him her kidney. According to Kamm, it is wrong in this case to say that the supererogatory aiding may not take precedence over the duty. See Frances M. Kamm, 'Rescue and Harm: Discussion of Peter Unger's *Living High and Letting Die*', *Legal Theory* 5 (1999), pp. 1–44 (21).

questions of blame, compensation, the duty to bear higher costs when assisting, permissible use of defensive force, and a fair distribution of the cost of assistance, contribution carries little momentum when assessing our duty to assist people in severe need if we can do so at little cost.[34]

[34] Are there tactical reasons for alluding to contribution when arguing for our duties to help protect the global poor? Well, there might be because people could have a wrong understanding of what our duties are. But it might also be the case that people could come to be lost in arguments about whether or not we indeed contribute to world poverty, and those who are not convinced that we do could falsely conclude that we have no duties to assist its victims. Moreover, it is an open question whether it is wise to give people reason to maintain their false beliefs about the moral significance of contribution with regard to our duty to assist the severely deprived.

ASSOCIATIVE DUTIES AND GLOBAL JUSTICE*

Jonathan Seglow

Associative duties are duties we owe to people with whom we are associated in some way, family members, friends, neighbours and, according to some, even compatriots. Political philosophers are fond of elaborating grand principles of justice or human rights, but associative duties make up most of the substance of everyday morality. Associative duties supply moral reasons why parents care for their children, neighbours look in on the old person next door, and compatriots pay taxes to provide each other with hospitals, schools and universities. Associative duties are real, tangible and concrete in a way that abstract principles are not. In fact, for most people most of the time felt associative duties generally outweigh universal cosmopolitan duties to help strangers in need.[1] For anyone interested in the interests of people in the developing world, therefore, associative duties represent a severe obstacle. From a 'common sense' point of view, it is natural that we direct our energies into helping our own, but from a cosmopolitan perspective it appears an unjustifiable privilege. Cosmopolitan writers regard people's local allegiance as a parochial obstacle that stands in the way of achieving global distributive justice. This puts them at odds with most citizens' felt moral understanding. My aim here is to investigate various ways this conflict might be overcome.

I begin with some preliminary comments to clarify the nature of associative duties. The fact that we enjoy social relationships with certain people is what advocates of associative duties turn to for their moral justification.[2] Relationships supply a justifiable distinction

* This paper has had a rather long gestation. For comments on previous versions I am grateful to John Horton, Peter Jones, Graham Long, Andrew Mason, Cillian McBride, Dorota Mokrosinska, Peter Seglow, Saul Smilansky, David Stevens, two anonymous referees for this Journal, and Thom Brooks.

[1] R. Goodin, *Protecting the Vulnerable* (Chicago: Chicago University Press, 1985), pp. 23–24.

[2] S. Scheffler, *Boundaries and Allegiances: Problems of Justice and Responsibility in Liberal Thought* (Oxford: Oxford University Press, 2001); M. Hardimon, 'Role Obligations', *The Journal of Philosophy* 91 (1994), pp. 333–63; I. Honohan, 'Friends, Strangers or Countrymen? The Ties between Citizens as Colleagues', *Political Studies*

between the worth of all persons to whom we owe (universal) duties and the worth of certain people—such as fellow citizens—to whom we owe associative duties. There are, however, other ways of making that distinction. In particular, associative duties are not the same as other kinds of special duties. All special duties only obtain between certain groups of people, but only associative duties are justified by the relationship those people share. That is the first clarificatory point. Other kinds of special duties are grounded in moral principles such as contribution, compensation or contract. The holders of these sorts of special non-associative duties may also share a prior social relationship, but that does not explain the moral force of their duty. For example, some writers have sought to justify national partiality on the grounds that compatriots have contributed to a cooperative enterprise and thus incur special rights against each other.[3] The fact that the compatriots enjoyed a prior social relationship does not add to this argument. Special associative duties, by contrast, are grounded in the relationship which duty-holders and duty-bearers share.

Second, I shall assume (a) that the relationships which ground associative duties are themselves valuable and (b) it is that moral value which serves to justify the duty. (a) need not imply (b).[4] One could argue, for example, that the moral value of X and Y's relationship is a necessary condition of their owing duties to one another, but deny that it is that value which grounds their duties. But I shall stipulate that associative duties are justified by the moral value of the relationship which participants share. I distinguish this from what Wellman calls 'associativism', where 'the fact you are my sister, my colleague, or my compatriot is of moral moment independent of any more fundamental morally significant features of our relationship'.[5] *Pace* Wellman, I believe that many relationships themselves are morally valuable just because they are constitutive of human flourishing.

49.1 (2001), pp. 51–69; D. Jeske, 'Associative Obligations, Voluntarism and Equality', *Pacific Philosophical Quarterly* 77 (1996), pp. 289–309; A. Mason, 'Special Obligations to Compatriots', *Ethics* 107 (1997), pp. 427–47; S. Reader, 'Distance, Relationship and Moral Obligation', *The Monist* 86.3 (2003), pp. 367–81.

[3] See, for example, R. Dagger, *Civic Virtues: Rights, Citizenship and Republican Liberalism* (Oxford: Oxford University Press, 1997), pp. 46–48; cf. R. Goodin, 'What's So Special about our Fellow Countrymen?' *Ethics* 98 (1988), pp. 663–86 at pp. 675–78.

[4] Cf. S. Caney, 'Individuals, Nations and Obligations', in S. Caney *et al.* (eds.), *National Rights, International Obligations* (Boulder, CO: Westview, 1996).

[5] C.H. Wellman, 'Relational Facts in Liberal Political Theory: Is There Magic in the Pronoun "My"?' *Ethics* 110 (2000), pp. 537–62, at p. 539.

Third, while associative duties may be both positive and negative, it is positive associative duties which seem the more important. This is consistent with maintaining that associates' negative duties towards one another may take precedence over their negative duties towards non-associates. In discussing negative associative duties, Goodin and Scheffler both cite as an example the fact that it would be less acceptable to harm one's child, in the course of rescuing a stranger, than it would be to harm another stranger.[6] That may be true, but parents' central duties to their children are surely positive in nature; to nurture, care for them, and so on. As far as compatriots are concerned, Goodin has pointed out elsewhere that there are many ways that we are less obliged to avoid harming our fellow citizens than we are strangers, suggesting that negative duties can be weaker when they are of the associative sort.[7] By contrast, in meeting their positive associative duties, people serve their important social relationships.

Finally, I assume that while associative duties may be perfect or imperfect, they are not supererogatory. Supererogatory acts are morally praiseworthy, but not morally required. Generosity is an example. Imperfect duties are those we have some scope in fulfilling (unlike perfect duties where we do not). We are required to meet them, but we can do so in our own way. One reason for this assumption is that the main associative duties (neighbourliness perhaps excluded) do not appear supererogatory to their bearers. We believe we ought to attend to the basic interests of our children, compatriots and so on. On the contrary, it is wider non-associative acts such as giving to overseas aid charities which seem supererogatory to many people. Another reason for resisting the supererogatory classification is that if associative duties were supererogatory, it might be hard to distinguish them from mere permissions. Common sense morality may over-inflate the scope and stringency of our associative duties, but I think it is right to assume that social relationships direct us to act in various ways.

Civic Associative Duties

Some writers have concluded from the conflict between civic associative duties and global justice that the former do not exist at all:

[6] Goodin, *Protecting the Vulnerable*, pp. 23–24; Scheffler, *Boundaries and Allegiances*, p. 53.

[7] Goodin, *Protecting the Vulnerable*, pp. 671–74.

associative duties, if they do exist, obtain only between friends, family members and other small groups. Let me briefly defend, therefore, the very idea of civic associative duties.

Friendship and family life are often thought to exemplify duties between associates because of the immediacy and concreteness they exhibit as relationships. However, it is the moral value of social relationships, not the relationships per se, which ground associative duties. We participate in many social relationships besides our families and friendship networks and if these also foster human flourishing it is natural to believe that associative duties can obtain in these relationships too. We participate in clubs, communities, associations, neighbourhoods, cities, armies, firms, churches, schools, universities, trade unions and other social forms. Most of these are median groups; we typically know some of our fellow members but not all of them. The associative duties which obtain there, however (assuming they do obtain), extend to all members qua members, not just those we know. Social relationships of these larger kinds are embedded in institutions which through the interconnected roles they give members enable them to enjoy mutual relations which are real and tangible though nonetheless not immediate. Institutional rules and roles enable members to do things together, engaging in common activities, without necessarily sharing personal relationships. Thus colleagues engage in work projects together, associations work towards common goals, neighbourhoods campaign on issues and so on. Engagement in common activities means that those brought together in a certain social relation are not arbitrarily set apart from outsiders; they do things together, and through this cooperative activity realize certain goods—community for example—as well as reproducing their institution over time. Indeed, it is worth pointing out that families are institutions too. They give their members definite roles which have a certain independence from their purely personal relationships, and the existence of the family—like many other institutions—continues beyond the lives of any of its members.[8]

In political society we engage with other citizens through institutionally defined common activities. Citizens debate issues, scrutinize their government, vote, run for office, work in public service, pay taxes, claim benefits, have civil marriages, apply for passports and permits

[8] Hardimon, 'Role Obligations'.

and licences, give information to public authorities, recycle their rubbish, call on the police, serve on juries, serve in the armed forces, and so on. In doing so, citizens enact their roles as citizens and maintain them over time. The institutional embeddedness of roles and the duties attached to them publicize our activities; in this case our activities as citizens. Thus even a fairly private act, like a civil marriage ceremony, is one that can be communicated to and understood by one's fellow citizens; and there would be some point in communicating it since they too might have a civil marriage. Institutional embeddedness enables us to participate in more proximate social relationships with larger numbers of people, not simply those with whom we have direct contact. Institutions are the medium for larger, more complex forms of common activity.

There is not the space here properly to defend the moral value of median social relationships. That would require an extended discussion of modes of human flourishing and the values constitutive of and in conflict with them. What we can say is that if *ex hypothesi* more proximate relationships can embody moral value, then it seems somewhat arbitrary to rule out citizenship as a relationship too large to do so too. (Opponents of civic associative duties sometimes point to Benedict Anderson's study *Imagined Communities* to make the point that nations are fictitious entities in contrast to the dense reality of families and friendship networks. But Anderson stressed that all communities besides face-to-face ones are imagined and his point was that an imagined community is one *manufactured* by its members, not a community which is not real).[9]

To be sure, civic relationships are more slender than the close connections we enjoy among friends and in families. But that does not mean their allied associative duties do not exist at all. It may only mean that these associative duties can be outweighed by other more compelling duties. My suspicion is that much of the hostility associative duties attract from more cosmopolitan-minded philosophers stems from the fact that felt associative duties can easily be used as a cloak to disguise the self-interest of richer states. But associative duties are duties, not self-interest, and if we have them that means only that they have some weight when we decide what, on balance, citizens have most reason to do. It does not mean that we do not have other duties

[9] Benedict Anderson, *Imagined Communities* (London: Verso 1983), p. 14.

besides these, duties which in certain circumstances may be more powerful.

The Distributive Objection to Associative Duties

I shall now say a little more about global justice, and how precisely its achievement comes into conflict with citizens' associative duties. Suppose, then, that the rationale for distributive justice is to provide every person with a decent life, some of which requires a fair measure of wealth, resources, opportunities, freedom and so on. Plainly, many millions of citizens across the globe lack the amounts of these goods necessary to lead decent lives.[10] The idea of living a decent life, however, the basic metric by which we compare people for purposes of distributive justice, may be glossed in a number of ways. A strong egalitarian view would have it that A and B cannot both live decent lives unless there is a roughly equal division of the constituents of decency between them. Even if that view were rejected, almost all proponents of social justice would maintain that if A has less than B we should give priority to A's basic interests. At the very least A's life should contain sufficient constituents of decency (where sufficiency is defined by reference to an ideal standard and not what B holds). Such abstract thoughts animate theorists of global justice. Some maintain that the current distribution of global wealth is arbitrary from a moral point of view, and hence justice demands a large measure of redistribution.[11] Others argue that richer states' wealth is the result of theft from what was once owned in common by all humankind, and hence richer states owe reparative duties to poorer ones.[12] Another suggestion is that citizens in rich states are complicit in maintaining a global institutional order which harms the interests of the global poor, preventing them from living decent lives.[13]

[10] For the sake of simplicity, I assume throughout that rich states consist of fairly rich (i.e. not poor) people and that poor states are home to poor (i.e. not rich) people. Though false, I do not believe this assumption affects the central argument.

[11] C. Beitz, *Political Theory and International Relations* (Princeton: Princeton University Press, 2nd edn, 1999).

[12] T. Pogge, *World Poverty and Human Rights* (Cambridge: Polity, 2002), pp. 203–204.

[13] Pogge, *World Poverty and Human Rights*, pp. 112–16, 198–205.

It is also worth bearing in mind that associative duties grounded in social relationships are not the only means by which sceptics of global distributive justice have sought to draw a justifiable distinction between duties owed universally and duties owed to one's fellow citizens alone. Some argue that only citizens experience the degree of economic interdependence which brings principles of distributive justice into play. For example, it could be argued that citizens are vulnerable to one another's actions in a way that strangers are not, or that the state is a scheme for the mutual advantage of its members. I am sceptical of such arguments because it seems to me that economic interdependence, whether conceived of as vulnerability, advantage or whatever, is a matter of degree, and if that is so it's not clear that the scope of justice can be so sharply limited to the state. Along related lines, Nagel and Blake have separately argued that it is citizens' shared subjection to coercive laws—laws of which they are nonetheless co-authors—which makes justice applicable at the state level alone.[14] Again, while there is not the space to consider it in full here, this argument too is problematic. It is plausible that the poor overseas are subject to coercive measures—indeed that is the thrust of the global institutional order argument mentioned above. If, on the other hand, it is citizens' authorship of the laws which govern them which is important, the argument is in danger of being circular unless some way is found of identifying authorship independent of the citizenship of a state. In any case, as I said in the first clarificatory point at the start of this paper, it is duties grounded in the moral value of social relationships which are my focus here.

Nagel and Blake both distinguish between global justice, and measures to alleviate the absolute deprivation to which so many of the world's people remain subject, and both stress the important of alleviating the latter.[15] This highlights the important distinction between comparative and non-comparative global distributive justice.[16] On a comparative interpretation, person A's life is less decent in part because person B enjoys more resources, opportunities and freedom. The strong

[14] T. Nagel, 'The Problem of Global Justice', *Philosophy and Public Affairs* 33 (2005), pp. 113–47; M. Blake, 'Distributive Justice, State Coercion and Autonomy', *Philosophy and Public Affairs* 30 (2001), pp. 257–96.

[15] Nagel, 'The Problem of Global Justice', pp. 118–19; Blake, 'Distributive Justice, State Coercion and Autonomy'.

[16] J. Feinberg, 'Non-Comparative Justice', *Philosophical Review* 83.3 (1974), pp. 297–358.

egalitarian view mentioned above is one comparative account. On a non-comparative interpretation we don't make direct comparisons between the parties to justice: those goods necessary for a decent life are defined by reference to an abstract standard of decency. (I leave aside the problem of how that abstract standard is arrived at.) This distinction has crucial implications for how we understand global justice. On a non-comparative interpretation, the point of justice is simply to secure citizens' basic needs. Usually this is interpreted as alleviating global poverty. Laudable though this is, it falls short of the ideal of comparative global justice where citizens' interests in living a decent life are defined by reference to one another. Here the aim is to narrow the gap between rich and poor since the size of that gap is relevant for justice. (We shall return to this distinction later.)

Several writers have explored the way that civic associative duties stand in the way of achieving global distributive justice. However, in the essays in his book *Boundaries and Allegiances*, Samuel Scheffler has explored the conflict in an especially clear and perspicuous way. For that reason, and because the essays have attracted interesting critical comment, I draw on his discussion here.[17] Scheffler imagines two individuals, A and B, who on entering a relationship of some kind, come to owe associative duties to one another as a consequence.[18] This works to the detriment of a third party C who is outside the relationship and is not the beneficiary of any associative duties. The priority which A and B, by virtue of their social relationship, give to each other's interests, works systematically to C's disadvantage. What Scheffler calls the distributive objection sees C's omission from A and B's duty-generating relationship as a morally arbitrary exclusion. The proper grounds of distributive justice are the interests of the affected parties, and by virtue of the relationship they share A and B do not give C's interests the moral weight they deserve. The distributive objection thus appeals to the value of impartiality.[19]

---

[17] Scheffler, *Boundaries and Allegiances*; and see E. Ashford, 'Individual Responsibility and Global Consequences', *Philosophical Books* 44.2 (2003), pp. 100–110; Jeske, 'Associative Obligations, Voluntarism and Equality'; J. Kane, 'Who is my Neighbor? A Response to Scheffler', in I. Shapiro and L. Brilmayer (eds.), *Global Justice* (New York: New York University Press, 1999); N. Kolodny, 'Do Associative Duties Matter?' *Journal of Political Philosophy* 10.3 (2002), pp. 250–66; D. Miller, 'Liberalism, Desert and Special Responsibilities', *Philosophical Books* 44.2 (2003), pp. 111–17.

[18] Scheffler, *Boundaries and Allegiances*, pp. 56–58.

[19] Jeske, 'Associative Obligations, Voluntarism and Equality', p. 299.

The problem is that associative duties are constitutive of social relationships (though at the same time justified by them), and hence we cannot claim that A and B share a relationship, as compatriots for example, without at the same time conceding that they owe duties to one another on that account.[20] Of course, a poorer citizen such as C will also have a compatriot, D, on whom she too can make claims. But the distributive objection points not to the lesser stringency of C's claim on D compared to A's claim on B but to the more limited wealth to which C and D have access, compared with that which A and B can command.

While associative duties obtain in different kinds of social relationships, Scheffler suggests (correctly, I believe) that the distributive objection is most acute at the global level.[21] His view is that the moral claims arising from associative duties can never finally be reconciled with the impartial concern required by global distributive justice. The plausibility of this conclusion depends in part on whether global justice is conceived of in comparative or non-comparative terms. While the distributive objection could be directed at non-comparative justice, it is credible to claim that poorer people's basic needs could be met while at the same time richer citizens fulfilled their associative duties to one another. Only if the latter were relatively weighty and/or if the normative threshold of a decent life was set fairly high would the distributive objection become apposite. But if global justice is conceived of in comparative terms, it is not obvious how the distributive objection could be avoided. Comparative global justice grounded in impartial concern for all the world's people means that citizens' universal duties to strangers overseas are demanding indeed, and it is difficult to see how they could owe further associative duties to one another without jeopardizing the former. This seems to be Scheffler's main concern too because of his interest in how C loses out just because A and B are fellow citizens.

Achieving Global Justice

How might we best respond to the distributive objection to civic associative duties in the face of global injustice? The first response I shall

[20] Scheffler, *Boundaries and Allegiances*, pp. 59, 92–93, 100.
[21] Scheffler, *Boundaries and Allegiances*, p. 58.

consider questions how far that objection affects the reality of how global justice would be achieved. Scheffler's spare illustrative methodology may encourage us to think that the only way for rich states A and B to avoid liability to the distributive objection is to transfer resources to poor state C, their mutual associative duties notwithstanding.[22] But two considerations complicate this simple view of how poor states such as B could become better off. The first is that states engage in significant economic interchange and by implication individuals in rich states A and B will very often have an economic (though not an associative) relationship with individuals in poor state C. Second and relatedly, the most effective way for individuals in C to become richer is through their own economic efforts, including economic trade with other states such as A and B.

What makes some states rich and others poor is a difficult question, much discussed in the global justice literature. Some combination of resource-holdings, economic growth, the functioning of global markets, climate, geographical location, education and productivity of the workforce, stable property rights, the rule of law, bureaucratic capacity, good governance and social cohesiveness and trust all seem to play a part, and different factors may well be predominant in different states.[23] For global wealth inequalities to be a distributive injustice we need only assume that some salient causes of those inequalities are to some degree beyond the control of poorer states and to some degree within the control of richer ones.[24] But how that injustice is, morally and practically speaking, best addressed is not an easy question. (For one thing, what is morally desirable may at times conflict with what is practically most efficacious.) Writers and activists call for a variety of concrete measures to alleviate global injustice. For example, they urge the abolition of export subsidies, tariffs and import quotas to promote fair trade. They want to see debt cancellation, and the democratic reform of the international financial institutions which impose them. They call for good governance for its own sake and as a vital pre-requisite for economic prosperity (it would also increase foreign direct investment).

---

[22] This assumption is also made by some cosmopolitan writers. See, for example, Beitz, *Political Theory and International Relations*; Kolodny, 'Do Associative Duties Matter?'; H. Shue, *Basic Rights: Subsistence, Affluence and U.S. Foreign Policy* (Princeton: Princeton University Press, 2nd edn, 1996).

[23] M. Risse, 'How Does the Global Order Harm the Poor?', *Philosophy and Public Affairs* 33.4 (2005), pp. 349–76 at pp. 355–56.

[24] Here I leave aside the problem of democracy: how far the actions of—especially poorer—states' leaders reflect their citizens' choices.

Universal free education, it is argued, would better enable future generations to compete in world markets. Besides ending a human tragedy, human capital would also be improved through the eradication of diseases such as AIDS and malaria. Challenging social norms such as those that prefer male children or restrict women to a child-bearing role would likely have a positive impact on developing states' prosperity. So too would development and increased private charitable donations.

There are naturally complex interdependencies between these different factors, varying local situations across developing countries, and debates among academics, activists and politicians about how precisely to achieve global justice. All this serves to establish an important general point: we will not achieve global distributive justice in a non-comparative or, in the long term, a comparative sense simply through richer states channelling an ever greater proportion of their public spending overseas. Poor countries are not made richer by rich countries getting poorer. We will achieve it through some combination of fair trade, debt cancellation, global democracy, good governance in developing states, improved education, eradication of serious diseases and so on, together with some measure of tax-financed official development aid. This empirical conclusion shows that, insofar as the distributive objection assumes that the way to make poorer people richer is through wealth redistribution from rich to poor the objection is misplaced. In consequence, it may not be unjust for developed states to spend more per capita on their own citizens than people overseas provided they undertake the other sorts of measures outlined above to help developing states help themselves. They will likely still need to augment their foreign aid budgets, but that is only one part of achieving global justice. For all the factors above are concerned with strengthening the ability of members of poorer states to generate their own wealth and opportunity. This may seem to erode some of the moral force of the distributive objection.

These considerations do not, however, show that the distributive objection is merely a theoretical problem. On one interpretation of it, the objection does assume that wealth redistribution is the main way to achieve global justice. But it also can be recast to include some of the factors canvassed above. To begin with, there are still financial implications involved in better-off states abolishing subsidies, tariffs and import quotas, cancelling debts, promoting health and education overseas, and so on. Further, since the wealth held by individuals and institutions is finite, there are also financial implications in any transfers made overseas by them: loans, investment or charitable donations may mean less is available for domestic goals. Importantly, many of the measures listed above, while not primarily redistributive in nature, still demand substantial effort on the part of richer states' citizens to achieve. Reforming supranational institutions, negotiating fairer global trade, encouraging good governance overseas, promoting a liberal culture in illiberal states and so on, all require time, energy, effort and attention, not least because of the coordination necessary among the actors involved. We do not need to have to hand a common metric to measure the comparative burdensomeness of different sorts of positive duties, to realize that these non-distributive duties too may threaten the fulfilment of compatriots' associative duties. Reversing the point, if political leaders devote most of their time and energy to their own citizens' interests, they will have little left to attend to the interests of the global poor. Provided we assume that poorer states cannot develop their own economies without substantial external assistance, comparative global justice will remain a far-off aspiration. In sum, the practicalities of achieving global justice reveal that a conflict remains between fulfilling associative and universal duties. The distributive objection thus remains largely intact.

The Additional Duties Defence of Associative Duties

The second reply to the distributive objection is more philosophical. It says that associative duties do not compete with the duties we owe to strangers, but rather supplement them. Pogge, for example, contends that associative duties that arise from particular relationships are permissible provided that we do not, on their account, owe less to non-associates than we would have owed them in the absence of the relationship. '[S]pecial relationships can increase what we owe to our associates', he writes, 'but they cannot decrease what we owe to everyone else'.[25] Similarly, Jeske, imagining a situation in which I must attend to the interests of Henry (a stranger) and Emma (to whom I owe special obligations), argues that 'I must continue to give Henry's needs the same weight in deliberations as I would have given to those needs if

[25] T. Pogge, 'Cosmopolitanism: A Defence', *Critical Review of Social and Political Philosophy* 5.3 (2002), pp. 86–91 at 90–91; cf. Pogge, *World Poverty and Human Rights*, pp. 78–79; cf. K.-C. Tan, *Justice Without Borders: Cosmopolitanism, Nationalism and Patriotism* (Cambridge: Cambridge University Press, 2004), pp. 163–79.

I did not have special obligations to Emma'.[26] On this view, then, we first arrive at a notion of those positive duties we justifiably owe to others, and then augment what we owe to associates on the grounds that we share relationships only with them. I shall call this the additional duties defence of associative duties.

Scheffler himself sees a problem with the additional duties defence.[27] According to him, the defence concedes that the moral claims of associates are greater than those of strangers which is just what the distributive objection takes issue with. The distributive objection attacks the idea that we have greater responsibilities to associates than non-associates. Hence, he argues, if the additional duties defence were correct, it would rebut the distributive objection, but in doing so 'it would nevertheless grant the conclusion that objection seeks to establish'.[28] On this view, the additional duties defence is self-defeating because it concedes our duty to give greater weight to associates' interests than non-associates' interests, and that is unjust. But how convincing is Scheffler's reply? If we deliver to strangers the substantial duties that justice requires need there be a wrong involved in giving greater weight still to the interests of associates? The distributive objection to associative duties is triggered if A and B, by virtue of their associative relationship, do not give stranger C's interests the moral weight they deserve. But provided that A and B take care to give C's interests the same substantial weight in their moral deliberations about what each of them owes C that they would absent their own duty-generating relationship, there is no obvious distributive objection if A and B can make an extra claim on each other in addition. Further, this reply seems consistent with the empirical reply to the distributive objection discussed above. Suppose state A devoted the time, effort, money and so on which is its proper moral share of the work needed to achieve global justice. Is any injustice *necessarily* involved if A's citizens owed associative duties to one another in addition?

This returns us to Pogge's and Jeske's view that associative duties are legitimate if and only if they are additional to those we have towards non-associates. There is another objection to this view, however, which can be presented via a dilemma. On the one hand, if we first discharge

---

26 Jeske, 'Associative Obligations, Voluntarism and Equality', p. 300.

27 Scheffler, *Boundaries and Allegiances*, pp. 86–87; cf. S. Scheffler, 'Replies to Ashford, Miller and Rosen', *Philosophical Books* 44.2 (2003), pp. 125–34 at pp. 128–29.

28 Scheffler, *Boundaries and Allegiances*, p. 86.

the duties to strangers which global justice requires, it is not clear that we really do owe associates substantial duties in addition. On the other hand, if we do owe associates significant duties, then, as Scheffler recognizes, there seems good reason to think we will fall short of what our global justice duties morally require. Take the first horn of the dilemma first. We noted the fairly obvious point that achieving global justice is a colossal task that requires substantial time, effort, energy and (not least) money on the part of rich states and their citizens. It requires continual work, over a substantial period, until such time as citizens in what are now poorer states have increased their wealth and opportunity to such a degree that the demands of some global comparative principle are satisfied. Plainly, since the world is marked by such huge wealth disparities, citizens in better-off states would need to increase the moral weight they accord to strangers' interests by several orders of magnitude in order to diminish the current comparative gap. If this is the case, however, it is not certain whether there are significant extra associative duties that citizens in rich states would owe one another in addition. I stipulated earlier that (consistent with common usage) associative duties are not merely permissions: they are positive actions that citizens ought to perform for one another. But under comparative justice the duties owed to strangers are weighty indeed, for they are grounded in some notion of impartiality across borders. Thus while, as I have maintained, it is not in principle unjust for a rich state's citizens to owe one another additional associative duties if they meet their global justice duties, the demands of justice towards the global poor may not leave very much to be owed. There would be a strong argument that any substantial associative duties that richer citizens owed each other, any surplus, as it were, at their command, ought first to be redirected towards worse-off strangers.

On the second horn of the dilemma, global justice is defined in non-comparative terms, for example by reference to people's basic needs. The corresponding duties of citizens in richer states are consequently less demanding. They involve ensuring that all the world's people enjoy lives above a certain threshold of decency. Consistent with this, richer states' citizens might owe each other something extra: the value of their citizenship could plausibly involve civic associative duties denied to those outside the relevant duty-generating relationships. The additional duties defence could, on this interpretation, succeed. In the grossly unjust world in which we live we should not under-estimate how much of an achievement it would be if every person could live a decent life.

But such measures would still fall foul of the distributive objection which questions whether citizens in the rich world can enjoy so much more than the poor for morally arbitrary reasons. Global justice, as most of its advocates understand it, would not have been achieved. Either for this reason, therefore, or because, as maintained above, more impartially-minded citizens could not owe one another significant duties if they owed substantial duties to strangers, the additional duties defence does not seem likely to succeed.

Defending Associative Duties

In this section I outline a third—and, I believe, more promising—strategy to defend associative duties and defuse the distributive objection. To begin with, consider briefly what civic associative duties might consist in and why that might be thought valuable. Thus many people believe that citizens have duties to their fellow citizens to maintain an effective welfare state on the grounds that through the domestic social justice the welfare state helps secure, better-off citizens foster the citizenship they share with their poorer compatriots. Associative duties, in other words, are grounded in their common membership of a civic community.[29] Specifically, citizens have duties to maintain institutions such as a properly functioning health service, an education system which prepares young people for their society's labour market and for citizenship, and to underwrite reasonable state-financed provision for the poor, the old, the disabled and other vulnerable groups. Performing these sorts of duties strengthens the bonds that exist between citizens and helps each citizen feel, with justification, that she is a member in full standing of a larger civic community. Citizenship, on this view, is a collective political project, and it is made so, in large part, because of the positive duties of justice that citizens deliver to one another. Moreover, in a liberal democratic state, citizens have also an input into determining the nature of their socio-economic provision. Besides helping realize civic community, citizenship is also valuable because through it citizens have an input in co-determining the conditions of their collective life with each other.[30] Most valuable relationships are valuable in

[29] Cf. D. Harris, *Justifying State Welfare* (Oxford: Blackwell, 1987); Miller, 'Liberalism, Desert and Special Responsibilities', pp. 115–17.

[30] Mason, 'Special Obligations to Compatriots', p. 442.

part because participants in them are able to negotiate their terms, and the claims and demands they can make on one another, and the goods they co-produce. Citizenship is no exception. Thus through their more political civic associative duties—duties to take an interest in public affairs, to scrutinize their government, to vote—they also realize the value of democracy.[31]

Certainly, this sketch could be contested. It may seem, for example, to assume a rather republican understanding of citizenship. But it is not, I hope, implausible. My aim here is not to spell out precisely what civic associative duties involve but to show, in general terms, how they might survive the distributive objection.

One feature of this account is that it does not at base involve the notion of priority. Citizens have no duty to put each other's interests ahead of non-citizens; their basic duties are simply to realize the values of civic community and democracy.[32] Those basic duties are realized by more specific duties such as paying taxes and debating issues, and through meeting these duties they help achieve these values. But, as a group of individuals who engage in (duty-generating) common activities, citizens have no duty to rank each other's interests ahead of outsiders. Their duties simply involve meeting each other's interests. The grounds of their duties—civic community and democracy—are values in and of themselves; they do not direct participants to rank each other's interests before those of strangers. After all, citizens in poorer states also have associative duties, and they too may be able to realize the values of civic community and democracy without putting each other's interests ahead of rich outsiders. This may seem, however, disingenuous. While the root justification of these civic associative duties may not be prioritarian, their practical effect certainly is. Welfarist associative duties involve money, and in a world where wealth is so hugely unevenly

---

[31] Cf. Honohan, 'Friends, Strangers or Countrymen?', pp. 59–64.

[32] A more apposite problem might appear to be that civic associative duties, while grounded in the values of civic community and democracy, also serve those values: it is by meeting their associative duties that community and democracy are promoted. This seems circular since the grounds of duties are also the effects of meeting them. However, citizenship involves more than simply the duties that citizens owe one another (Mason, Special Obligations to Compatriots', pp. 439–47; cf. J. Raz, 'Liberating Duties', *Law and Philosophy* 8 [1999], pp. 3–21 at p. 21). Citizenship is a value, a shared sentiment, a legal status, a symbol of belonging and part of the meaning of a state: these things also are fostered by civic associative duties, but they are not directly the object of them. We thus avoid the problem of citizenship being justified by just what it is that citizens qua citizens have a duty to do.

distributed the effect of rich states meeting these duties will be that the interests of poorer peoples in living a decent life are not adequately met. Even realizing the democratic values in better-off states, insofar as they involve citizens' time and energy, may well prejudice the interests of the global poor. In practice if not in theory, then, meeting our global justice duties will slip down the political agenda if associative duties are sufficiently strong.

There are two replies to this practical objection. The first points out that just because associative duties are outweighed by other duties does not mean they are not duties. The second is to outline circumstances in which they are not outweighed.

Civic community and democracy in richer states would not collapse if politicians and citizens in those states spent the time, energy and money necessary to deliver their global justice duties. What is true is they may not be realized as much as they might if the latter kinds of duties were adequately fulfilled. A more basic welfarist system might foster less of a civic communitarian ethos than a more comprehensive one. If, counterfactually, richer states' citizens devoted more time, effort and energy to the needs of the global poor then by implication they would devote less to democracy and civic life in their own society. The latter values would then not be realized to the degree that they might. Short of spelling out in more detail what our civic associative and global justice duties involve, we do not know precisely what the comparative gains and losses would be. We do, however, know that constructing a world which is just (in comparative terms) is a hugely demanding task. It involves increased development aid; creating conditions in which poorer states can enjoy economic growth: fair international trade and effective supra-international institutions to regulate it, as well as measures to promote democracy and social capital in developing states, and so on. The likelihood is that this would have a negative impact on the fulfilment of our civic associative duties, and hence on the achievement of their constitutive values.

However, claiming that a duty is eroded, or even over-ridden, by the performance of another duty is quite different from claiming that it disappears, even if in practice the two situations look the same from the outside. The values which associative duties serve—civic community and democracy—are universal ones and remain significant whatever the situation in other states and the world as a whole. Civic community and democracy do not suddenly lose their importance just because there are other duties that are more urgent and compelling. We quite often face conflicts of duties, but when we decide that meeting one duty is more morally urgent than another, we still feel the pull of the less compelling duty. Saving ten people from drowning does not mean the duty to save one person elsewhere from drowning suddenly goes away. In fact, situations in which attending to an important harm or wrong get in the way of meeting our associative duties are not uncommon in everyday life. You might be called upon to give first aid to victims of a road accident on your way home, for example, or you might take up Oxfam's invitation and buy a goat for an African village instead of giving your friend a birthday present. Duties do not magically disappear when other more powerful duties intrude. What is true is that very few, if any, duties, are of such moral power that they take priority across the board, in every situation. Civic associative duties give citizens a strong *prima facie* reason to engage in certain activities. I have claimed that that reason can be articulated through the values that associative duties serve.

Having said that, civic associative duties would be an odd kind of duty if they were *always* outweighed. To make credible the claim that they exist, it will therefore help to outline the circumstances in which they may be substantially fulfilled. Again, it is difficult to do this without a full specification of what associative (and non-associative) duties involve, but the following sketch, I hope, gives an idea.

My suggestion is that associative duties can be performed alongside universal duties in ideal circumstances.[33] I use the phrase ideal circumstances rather than ideal theory partly because ideal theory is defined in different ways by different writers—sometimes as full compliance with our moral duties,[34] sometimes as the claim that normative truths are independent of empirical ones[35] and sometimes as moral theory that does not offer guidance on real world problems[36]—but also because my concern is not so much with the nature of normative theory as in a

[33] For a similar idea, though not developed, see Jocelyne Couture and Kai Nielsen, 'Cosmopolitanism and the Compatriot Priority Principle', in Gillian Brock and Harry Brighouse (eds), *The Political Philosophy of Cosmopolitanism* (Cambridge: Cambridge University Press, 2005).

[34] Liam Murphy, *Moral Demands in Non-Ideal Theory* (New York: Oxford University Press, 2000).

[35] G.A. Cohen, 'Facts and Principles', *Philosophy and Public Affairs* 31 (2003), pp. 211–45; Andrew Mason, 'Just Constraints', *British Journal of Political Science* 34 (2004), pp. 251–68.

[36] Colin Farrelly, 'Justice in Ideal Theory: A Refutation', *Political Studies* 55.4 (2007), pp. 844–64.

situation in which global justice, defined in comparative terms, finally obtains. We have to imagine a world in which the distribution of wealth and opportunities satisfied some recognized principle of social justice, however far removed that is from our present reality. To simplify matters, we might imagine a world of two states, A and B, neither of which is much wealthier than the other. A and B trade with each other. A sells B goods in which it specializes, and B does the same. Suppose there is perfect free trade with no tariffs or quotas, and goods are bought and sold at the market rate. Such a situation should be advantageous to both states so that their economies grow. Now both A's and B's citizens are concerned with civic community and democracy in their own societies. Each therefore finances an effective welfare state and each ensures that their citizens' public standing—in part a function of their material well-being—is such that they can have a genuine input into public deliberation on the direction of their society. The two states' citizens have duties to realize the values of civic community and democracy, and this sees them devoting more time, energy and money to each other's interests, than to the interests of citizens in the other state. That is the practical sense in which associative duties involve the idea of priority. It is also the only sense. As explained above, the grounds of associative duties are just to realize certain values where one lives; this does not involve winning a race, as it were, against the other state. We can make sense of associative duties through the claim that A's and B's citizens, through their common civic activities, can enjoy a certain sort of collective flourishing. There is no need to stipulate that associative duties are only satisfied if A is better off than B, or vice versa.

Now this happy situation may not obtain forever. Perhaps B's government make less than wise economic decisions, and its economy stalls, or A's citizens work harder and its economy grows at a faster rate. A's citizens' global justice duties might therefore for a time become more substantial, as it seeks to assist B, and this would likely have a negative impact on welfarist spending in A, as well as limiting its democratic freedom to determine its future. But this would not cause its civic associative duties to disappear. They would simply be trumped for a time until global justice once again obtained.

For an example closer to home and to current realities, consider the distribution of wealth and income in contemporary liberal democracies, and the duties between family members. The latter (it is plausible to think) are justified by the values of love, care and intimate association. Familial associative duties need not direct family members to make themselves better off than strangers. They do naturally involve family members being more committed to fulfilling each other's needs than strangers': through such commitment the distinctive familial modes of flourishing—constituted by values such as love, care and intimate association—are realized. I don't think it's unrealistic to believe that such flourishing may be consistent with achieving a just distribution of wealth and income in society.

What would Scheffler make of the defence of associative duties outlined above? He might interpret it through the claim that the scope and stringency of associative duties may seem, on this account, to be limited by what global justice duties require. A counter-argument would then be that this gives global justice priority over associative duties in which case the distinctive nature, as well as appeal, of the latter is eroded. Now this is a convincing objection to what I called the additional duties defence of associative duties. For on that defence we do first determine what non-associative duties of justice we owe strangers, and I suggested that if these were demanding enough they would not leave citizens with significant duties to one another (though they would be permitted to act within just bounds). But the defence above does not understand priority in this way. It distinguishes between the grounds of duties—the values which justify them and which they serve—and their concrete practical demands. Civic community and democracy are instances of the former. They have intrinsic value for the citizens of a particular state independent of the position of citizens of other states. The practical demands they make as duties, by contrast, do vary with context. In our present context the demands of global justice do take priority but that need not always be the case. Which duty gives us the strongest reason to do something depends upon the situation we face. If associative duties *always* took priority over non-associative duties they would be a strange sort of duty because duties are justified by values and one normally compelling value can be over-ridden by considerations of greater moral importance in certain circumstances. I have suggested by contrast that associative duties behave much like other kinds of duties. They are more than simply permissions; they give us reasons to do things, they serve important values and they are not absolute.

Conclusion

Associative duties owed to compatriots are firmly embedded in the common moral consciousness. That does not mean they are correct, but it seems to me a more fruitful strategy to see if we can re-interpret the intuitions of common sense morality, channelling them in a more progressive direction so as to reconcile them with our considered moral principles, rather than abandoning them altogether just because they do conflict. Proponents of associative duties tend to defend them by claiming that the interests they serve are of such value that they outweigh the performance of our global justice duties, at least if the latter are interpreted in a more demanding comparative sense.[37] The problem with this sort of defence is that given the grievous wrong that global inequality represents, we would have to attach inordinate value to those interests and it seems unlikely that citizens' interests can have that extraordinary importance. Cosmopolitan critics of associative duties tend to claim that because they come into conflict with global justice duties, they probably don't exist at all, especially as states seem just too large for their members to owe one another associative duties compared to groups of friends and families. The first plank of a defence of civic associative duties consists in showing how political institutions enable relatively stable and enduring mediated relationships where, by virtue of their collective institutional membership, citizens can engage in common activities. The second plank is the claim that such common activities realized certain values, and I suggested civic community and democracy were one plausible interpretation of those values. The third plank maintained that those values did not go away if citizens' activities were redirected (in large part) towards outsiders' interests. Finally, we can at least imagine a situation where people's interests as citizens are met largely by their own compatriots, enabling civic community and democracy to flourish in the world more than they currently do. In the end, most people's intuition that they owe their compatriots a peculiar form of duty is correct; where ordinary thinking goes wrong is simply in over estimating that duty's potency and power.

[37] See Wellman, 'Relational Facts in Liberal Political Theory'; and David Miller, 'Reasonable Partiality towards Compatriots', *Ethical Theory in Moral Practice* 8.1 (2005), pp. 63–81.

PART IV

WAR AND TERRORISM

PARTIALITY AND WEIGHING HARM TO NON-COMBATANTS

David Lefkowitz

Suppose that under certain conditions, combatants waging a just war are morally permitted to engage in acts that cause collateral damage; that is, harm done to non-combatants as a side effect of an attack on a morally permissible target.[1] Does it matter morally whether those non-combatants who will be harmed are citizens of the same state as the combatants who carry out the attack, or are instead citizens of the state against whom these combatants are waging war? Frances Myrna Kamm and Thomas Hurka each claim that it does.[2] They argue that combatants ought to be partial to their compatriot non-combatants, assigning greater weight to harm done to them than they assign to harm done to enemy non-combatants. This entails that in some cases whether a collateral damage causing act of war satisfies the *jus in bello* criterion of proportionality depends on the citizenship of the non-combatants harmed by it.[3] Moreover, Kamm suggests that combatants ought to assign even greater weight to harm done to neutral non-combatants

---

[1] For purposes of this article, I will assume that no non-combatant is morally liable to attack as part of the conduct of a just war; combatants are not morally permitted to deliberately or negligently harm them. Both Kamm and Hurka note (rightly, in my view) that degree of moral culpability for an unjust war may provide a superior criterion for distinguishing those who are morally liable to attack from those who are not than does the combatant/non-combatant distinction. But since they carry out their discussion in terms of the latter distinction, I do so here as well.

For discussion of various attempts to provide a moral justification of acts of war that cause collateral damage, see D. Lefkowitz, 'Collateral Damage', in D. Lefkowitz, 'Collateral Damage', in L. May (ed.), *War: Essays in Political Philosophy* (Cambridge: Cambridge University Press, 2008), pp. 145–64.

[2] F.M. Kamm, 'Terror and Collateral Damage: Are They Permissible?' *Journal of Ethics* 9 (2005): 381–401; F.M. Kamm, 'Failures of Just War Theory: Terror, Harm, and Justice', *Ethics* 114 (July 2004): 650–92; Thomas Hurka, 'Proportionality in the Morality of War', *Philosophy and Public Affairs* 33.1 (2005): 34–66.

[3] Throughout this article, I write as if harm to non-combatants is the sole factor to be taken into account when assessing whether a given act of war meets the *jus in bello* criterion of proportionality. In fact, other factors, such as the destruction of infrastructure or harm to the natural environment, may also be relevant. But whether there are other relevant factors, and whether their relevance is simply a matter of the effect that harm to them will have on people's well-being, makes no difference to the issues under examination here.

than they assign to their own compatriot non-combatants. In some cases, and holding all else equal, a combatant ought to carry out an attack that will cause a greater number of compatriot non-combatant deaths as collateral damage, rather than one that will collaterally kill a lesser number of neutral non-combatants. As Kamm puts it, 'non-combatants in one country have a higher degree of inviolability than those in another country'.[4] In what follows, however, I will demonstrate that neither Kamm nor Hurka provide a plausible justification for their conclusions. Absent further argument, combatants ought to treat all non-combatants impartially, weighing harm to them equally regardless of their citizenship.

I begin by describing several ways in which partiality to compatriot non-combatants affects the moral permissibility of acts that cause collateral damage. I then refute Kamm's attempt to defend partiality to compatriot non-combatants by appeal to an alleged asymmetry between the sacrifice one must make to save others, and the sacrifice one may impose on a third party in order to save those same people. Next I focus on both Kamm's and Hurka's efforts to defend partiality to compatriot non-combatants by appeal to an analogy with parents' justifiable partiality toward their children. I contend that Kamm and Hurka employ the wrong analogies, and that the proper ones generate less or no intuitive support for the conclusion they seek to defend. Finally, I argue that Kamm fails to provide a compelling reason to believe that neutral non-combatants enjoy a higher degree of inviolability than do compatriot or enemy non-combatants. Nevertheless, I suggest that given a certain understanding of the nature and moral value of state sovereignty, it is possible to provide a non-instrumental justification for Kamm's claim that given a choice between causing a greater number of compatriot non-combatant deaths and a lesser number of neutral deaths, a combatant ought to choose the former over the latter.

1. *Partiality and* Jus in Bello *Proportionality*

Practically all contributors to the just war tradition argue that only those acts of war that meet the criteria of discrimination and

[4] Kamm, 'Failures of Just War Theory', p. 673.

proportionality are morally permissible. Discrimination requires those who carry out military operations to distinguish between combatants, whom they are morally permitted to target, and non-combatants, whom they may not target, and whom they should make reasonable efforts to avoid harming. Discrimination does not absolutely prohibit engaging in acts of war that cause harm to non-combatants, however. Many just war theorists contend that attacks on legitimate targets that also involve or result in unintended harm to non-combatants may still be morally permissible if the harm done is proportional to the good achieved by that act.[5]

Though proportionality has applications in just war theory other than to acts that inflict collateral damage, it is with these cases that I am concerned here, for it is the moral permissibility of such acts that is affected if partiality to compatriot non-combatants is morally justifiable. Hurka argues that such partiality warrants engaging in acts of war (and so, ultimately, an entire war) even if it is foreseen that the number of enemy non-combatants killed as collateral damage will exceed the number of compatriot non-combatants whose deaths the war prevents. Thus with respect to military attacks undertaken by the United States and Israel to prevent terrorist attacks against them (or their citizens), Hurka contends that US and Israeli combatants ought to assign less weight to the harm done to Pakistani, Afghan, or Palestinian non-combatants killed as a side effect than we should assign to the harm prevented to Israeli or American non-combatants.[6] If Hurka is right about this, then the claim that Israel's 2006 attacks on Hizbullah forces in Lebanon caused a disproportionate amount of collateral damage may

[5] Two additional criteria must also be met. First, the act the agent does intentionally, and which causes the unintended harm, must be one he is morally permitted to do, and second, the unintentional harm must be no more than is necessary to achieve the good end. Together with the requirements that the harm to non-combatants be unintended and proportional, these criteria constitute the doctrine of double effect. Only the proportionality criterion will be at issue here; I will assume that all of the examples under discussion satisfy the other conditions for the doctrine of double effect's applicability—or whatever alternative principle justifies collateral damage.

With respect to justifying collateral damage, Kamm rejects the doctrine of double effect in favor of what she labels the principle of permissible harm. See F. M. Kamm, *Morality, Mortality Volume II* (New York: Oxford University Press, 1996), pp. 143–204. Exactly what justifies acts of war that cause collateral damage is unimportant for the issue under discussion in this article, since Kamm, Hurka, and I all argue under the assumption that some principle does. See Kamm, 'Failures of Just War Theory', p. 673; Hurka, 'Proportionality', p. 61.

[6] Hurka, 'Proportionality', pp. 59–60.

not be as obvious as numerous commentators around the world have thought.[7]

Kamm claims that in a case where a combatant waging a just war can achieve the same good by conducting one of two aerial bombardments, both of which qualify as permissible, but where bombardment A will result in the death of 100 compatriot non-combatants, while bombardment B will result in the death of 200 enemy non-combatants, the combatant ought to choose B over A.[8] Though Kamm's example may seem artificial, it is not difficult to conceive of an actual scenario with the same essential features. For example, members of the Free French Air Force during World War II might have faced a choice between bombing a German munitions factory located in occupied France, or one in Germany proper, with the expectation that attacking the latter would result in twice as many non-combatant casualties as attacking the former. According to Kamm, the Free French would not only have been permitted to bomb the factory located in Germany, they would have acted incorrectly had they bombed the French plant instead, even though doing so likely would have produced fewer non-combatant casualties.

Partiality to compatriot non-combatants also permits warriors to bear less risk of harm to themselves at the expense of greater risk of harm to non-combatants if those non-combatants are enemy ones rather than compatriots. As Michael Walzer writes,

> if saving [non-combatant's] lives means risking soldier's lives, the risk must be accepted. But there is a limit to the risks that we require. These are, after all, unintended deaths and legitimate military operations, and the absolute rule against attacking [harming?] civilians does not apply. War necessarily places civilians in danger; that is another aspect of its hellishness. We can only ask soldiers to minimize the dangers they impose.[9]

---

[7] See, for example, 'Too High a Price', *The Nation*, 14 July 2006; Larry Derfner, 'Flirting with State Terrorism', *The Jerusalem Post*, 17 August 2006. Hurka does not believe Israel's 2006 invasion of Lebanon met the *jus in bello* proportionality condition (personal communication).

[8] Kamm, 'Failures of Just War Theory', p. 672; 'Terror and Collateral Damage', p. 397. It would beg the question against Kamm to assert that, given the possibility of carrying out bombardment A, bombardment B violates the no more harm than necessary condition on the applicability of the doctrine of double effect.

[9] Michael Walzer, *Just and Unjust Wars* (New York: Basic Books, 3rd edn, 2000 [1977]), p. 156. Walzer claims that 'the degree of risk that is permissible is going to vary with the nature of the target, the urgency of the moment, the available technology, and so on' (ibid., 156). As will become clear below, however, Walzer does not believe that

The idea that soldiers ought to seek to minimize the risk of harm to non-combatants, even at the cost of increasing their own chances of suffering harm, suggests that combatants' lives and/or well-being have value proportionate to that of non-combatants' lives and/or well-being.[10] If combatants ought to assign greater importance to the lives of compatriot non-combatants than they do to enemy ones, it follows that the number of enemy non-combatant lives 'equal' to the life of a combatant will be less than the number of compatriot non-combatant lives 'equal' to the life of a combatant. Assuming that risk to the combatant varies inversely with the likelihood of harm to non-combatants, it follows that combatants may bear less risk of harm to themselves when carrying out an attack that will cause collateral damage to enemy non-combatants than when carrying out one that will collaterally harm compatriot non-combatants. Thus were the French pilots to attack the munitions factory in Germany, they would be morally permitted to fly higher, and so likely inflict more harm on non-combatants, than they would be permitted to fly were they to attack the plant in occupied France.[11]

As these examples indicate, if partiality to compatriot non-combatants were morally justifiable, it would significantly shape the form that the morally permissible conduct of war may, or must, take. As I will demonstrate, however, neither Kamm nor Hurka provides a plausible defense of such partiality.[12]

2. *Self/Other Asymmetry and Partiality to Compatriot Non-Combatants*

One argument Kamm offers to buttress her claim that combatants ought to be partial to compatriot non-combatants rests on the alleged

the nationality or citizenship of the at-risk non-combatants affects the degree of risk combatants may permissibly impose upon them. See n. 27.

[10] See also Kamm, 'Failures of Just War Theory' and Kamm, 'Terror and Collateral Damage'.

[11] As Pierre Mendes-France, a Free French pilot, writes: 'It was … this persistent question of bombing France itself which led us to specialize more and more in precision bombing—that is, flying at a very low altitude. It was more risky, but it also permitted greater precision …' (quoted in Walzer, *Just and Unjust Wars*, p. 157).

[12] Note that I will not be arguing that partiality to compatriots is never morally justifiable, but only that neither Kamm nor Hurka demonstrate that combatants ought to be partial to their compatriot non-combatants when choosing between various collateral damage causing acts of war.

permissibility of imposing on a third party the cost of saving others where one is not morally required to bear the same cost in order to achieve the same end. Call this permissible self-other asymmetry. Kamm contends that an agent who confronts a scenario in which she can prevent a trolley from killing five people only by directing it down either a second track, on which she stands, or a third track, on which one (or two) strangers stand, may choose to direct it down the third track, rather than the second one (or flipping a coin). Individuals enjoy 'a prerogative not to make big sacrifices in order to aid others'.[13] Kamm then draws an analogy between this case, and the permissible self-other asymmetry she claims applies in it, and the example of a state (or state official, such as a bomber pilot) faced with a choice between carrying out bombardment A, which will kill 100 compatriot non-combatants, and bombardment B, which will kill 200 enemy non-combatants. She writes,

> one may conceive of the situation as one in which country A must decide whether to harm itself or harm someone else, both options involving (assumed) permissible ways to harm non-combatants. It may simply be supererogatory … to direct a threat to oneself rather than send it to someone else to whom it is also permissible to send it.[14]

Unfortunately for Kamm, several disanalogies between the two cases she considers undermine her attempt to extend the application of permissible self/other asymmetry from the above variation on the trolley problem to the bombing example.[15]

First, Kamm's argument ignores the difference between the threat facing the agent on the second track, and the threat facing the state if it opts to carry out bombardment A. Choosing to direct the trolley down the second track will result in an enormous loss to the agent who stands on it, namely her death; it is the 'ultimate' nature of the sacrifice that likely leads many people to form the intuition that the agent is permitted to direct the trolley down track three rather than track two. The potential loss to the state in the bombardment example, however, is of nowhere near the same magnitude. In practically every scenario, the state will continue to exist even if the bomber pilot chooses bombardment A over bombardment B. Nor is it clear that harm to some of the

---

[13] Kamm, 'Failures of Just War Theory', p. 674.

[14] Ibid.

[15] For the sake of argument, I accept permissible self/other asymmetry in the trolley problem, though in fact I am skeptical of it even in this case.

state's subjects will necessarily harm the state. It is conceivable, at least, that the individuals the bombing will kill are engaged in acts that interfere with the proper functioning of the state, such that their deaths actually benefit the state, rather than harming it.[16]

Second, Kamm describes the trolley problem as an instance of deciding whom to save from harm. But that is not the question the bomber faces; his choice is a matter of deciding whom to harm, not whom to save from an independently originating harm. Even if we assume that either bombardment is morally permissible, it could be that partiality to compatriots is morally justifiable in the case of preventing harm, but never in the case of causing it. Given that many moral theorists think there is an important moral distinction between causing harm and giving aid, this discrepancy between the two cases Kamm considers should raise a red flag regarding her extension of a moral principle from one to the other.[17]

A third disanalogy between Kamm's two examples involves the moral conclusions she draws in them. In the trolley problem, Kamm defends *permissible* self/other asymmetry; agents are permitted, but not required, to forgo making big sacrifices in order to aid others. In the bombing example, however, Kamm claims that it would be *incorrect* to carry out bombardment A rather than bombardment B, and also speaks of a '*duty* not to harm one's own non-combatants rather than non-citizens, if someone must be harmed in a permissible manner'.[18] Permissible self/other asymmetry cannot give rise to a duty to be partial, nor can it entail that an agent who elects not to be partial acts incorrectly. Thus even if the two cases Kamm considers are sufficiently analogous to warrant the extension of the principle of permissible self/other asymmetry to the bombing example, that principle does not justify the conclusion Kamm draws.

---

[16] The reader might take this objection to Kamm's argument, together with some of the criticisms set out later in this article, as reasons to reject the use of domestic analogies as a method for defending particular moral principles for the just conduct of war. I do not believe the wholesale rejection of this method is necessary, though as the text indicates, careful attention must be paid to specific disanalogies between domestic and war scenarios that may have morally important implications.

[17] It should be noted, however, that Kamm is unlikely to find in this disanalogy a compelling objection to her argument, since she does not think the distinction between causing harm and giving aid a morally relevant one. See her principle of permissible harm, which she defends as the true governing principle for cases like the trolley problem, the munitions factory, and so on (and on). Kamm, *Morality, Mortality Volume II.*

[18] Kamm, 'Failures of Just War Theory', p. 674, italics mine.

3. *Parental Partiality and Partiality to Compatriot Non-Combatants*

Kamm's second argument in defense of partiality to compatriot non-combatants also takes the form of an argument by analogy. She begins with the assumption that it is generally permissible for an agent to direct a runaway trolley away from a track with five people on it and toward a track occupied by only one person. However, Kamm contends that if the one person is the agent's child, then the agent has a special duty to the child not to direct the trolley down the track he occupies. Similarly in the bombing example, both bombardment A and bombardment B are of a type assumed to be morally permissible. But just as the parent owes a special duty to his child, so too the bomber pilot owes a special duty to his compatriot non-combatants, one that requires him to give their lives and well-being greater weight than he assigns to the lives of enemy non-combatants. Thus it is the existence of a special duty to compatriots that requires the pilot to choose bombardment B, and the resulting death of 200 enemy non-combatants as collateral damage, over bombardment A, and the 100 compatriot non-combatant collateral deaths it will cause.

Hurka also rests his case for partiality to compatriot non-combatants on an analogy to special duties parents owe their children. He describes a scenario in which the only way for an agent to save an innocent victim from a fatal attack by an aggressor involves the use of a grenade that will kill the aggressor, but also kill an innocent bystander. Hurka concedes that it is arguable whether the agent may throw the grenade in this scenario, sacrificing one innocent person's life (albeit unintentionally) for another's. He draws a different conclusion, however, if the innocent victim threatened by the aggressor is the child of the agent in position to carry out the rescue.

> It seems to me that he [the father] may throw the grenade, and may do so even if this will kill some number of bystanders greater than one. If he is not aiming at the bystanders but killing them collaterally, he may show some preference for his daughter.[19]

Hurka suggests that a combatant may display an analogous partiality by unintentionally killing a greater number of innocent enemy

[19] Hurka, 'Proportionality', p. 61.

non-combatants in order to prevent the killing of a lesser number of his compatriot non-combatants.[20]

Both Kamm's and Hurka's arguments depend on the extension of an intuition from a non-war scenario to a war one.[21] I suggest, however, that they employ the wrong non-war scenarios. Take Kamm's argument: if the question concerns the extent of the partiality compatriots may justifiably display to one another, then a more closely analogous non-war scenario involves the following variation on the trolley problem. Suppose that a runaway trolley will run over and kill either one person who is a compatriot, or five people who are foreigners, but who are alike in all other morally relevant respects. Are you permitted, or even required, to direct the trolley toward the five people, rather than the one? The intuition that you may, or must, do so would provide the kind of intuition in a non-war scenario that would best support partiality in a case like the bombing example, since it more closely mirrors the choice the bomber pilot confronts than does Kamm's parent/child variation. For what it is worth, my intuition is that the compatriot relationship does not justify directing the trolley so that it kills the five foreigners rather than the one compatriot. Interestingly, David Miller, one of the most prominent defenders of partiality to compatriots, agrees. He writes:

> If we think about cases modeled on the trolley problem made famous by Judith Thomson, I don't think it would be justifiable to switch the trolley from a track on which it was hurtling towards a compatriot on to a track on which it would hurtle towards a foreigner. Nor do I think, if one takes the view that when the difference between the numbers on the two tracks becomes large enough, one ought to switch the trolley, that there should be any additional weighting in favor of compatriots. If one should switch the trolley to kill one in order to save ten, then the identity of the ten and

[20] Hurka's use of the term 'may' implies a *permission* to give greater weight to the lives of compatriot non-combatants over enemy non-combatants, but in an earlier article where he develops a general account of partiality to compatriots, he talks of *duties* of partiality (Thomas Hurka, 'The Justification of National Partiality', in Robert McKim and Jeff McMahan (eds), *The Morality of Nationalism* [New York: Oxford University Press, 1997], p. 152).

[21] They also depend, of course, on the transfer of an intuition regarding parents' obligations to their children to compatriots' obligations to one another. This transfer may also be challenged, though I will not do so here. See Christopher Heath Wellman, 'Associative Allegiances and Political Obligations', *Social Theory and Practice* 23 (1997): 181–204.

> the one is irrelevant. At this level, morality appears to me to require strict impartiality at least as far as nationality is concerned.[22]

At a minimum, then, employing the more closely analogous variation on the trolley problem weakens the argument for partiality to compatriot non-combatants, and it may well undermine it altogether.[23]

As for Hurka's non-war scenario, a variation on it more closely analogous to choosing between harm to compatriot or to enemy non-combatants would involve throwing a grenade that will kill one or even several foreigners in order to save one compatriot. I contend that such an act is not morally justifiable. The moral duty not to kill an innocent person is commonly thought to be stronger than the moral duty to save an innocent person from being killed. It follows, then, that holding all else equal, the duty a combatant has to her compatriots not to kill them is stronger than the duty she has to save them from being killed by a third party. Supposing that to be the case, if it is not justifiable to kill a greater number of enemy non-combatants in order to avoid killing a lesser number of compatriot non-combatants, as I maintain against Kamm, then surely it is not justifiable to kill a greater number of enemy non-combatants in order to save a lesser number of compatriot non-combatants from being killed by a third party.

Note, too, that Hurka's original grenade throwing example seems closely akin to (if not an example of) cases of duress that practically all theorists agree provide an excuse, but not a justification, for an agent's conduct. I am slightly more sympathetic to the claim that agents may point to the fact of common membership in a political community as a partial excuse, rather than justification, for giving greater weight to the lives of compatriot non-combatants in comparison to enemy ones. I suspect, however, that whatever it is about being a parent, or the parent–child relationship, that provides the basis for an excuse will be realized to a significantly weaker degree in the case of compatriots, and so the degree of exculpation it provides will be far less.

---

[22] David Miller, 'Reasonable Partiality Towards Compatriots', *Ethical Theory and Moral Practice* 8 (2005): 75.

[23] Exactly when, and with what detail, to pose this variation on the trolley problem raises some difficult questions regarding the weight we ought to assign to people's intuitions, and what counts as a genuinely considered judgment. For example, asking current citizens of the United States whether it would be permissible or required to direct the trolley at five Iraqis rather than one American might elicit a different response than if 'Irishmen' or 'Canadians' were substituted for 'Iraqis'. It may also make a difference if the question is posed while a state is at war, since feelings of nationalism (compatriotism) tend to be highest at such times.

It may be that the compatriot/foreigner variation on the trolley problem, while better than the one Kamm employs, still contains an important disanalogy to the kind of wartime scenarios that are of concern in this article. The actors on whom we focus in the latter scenarios are state officials. Therefore, in order to maintain the analogy, we ought to consider whether a state official is permitted, or even required, to turn the trolley toward five foreigners rather than one subject of her state, or whether in the above variation on Hurka's example, the addition of the fact that the agent in position to affect a rescue is a state official makes any difference to the intuition we form. I suggest that the answer is no in both cases. Surely we do not think a New York City policeman would be justified in killing three innocent German tourists, even unintentionally, in order to save one innocent American. Suppose, however, that I am wrong about this, and that some of those who consider this last variation on Hurka's example act reasonably when they conclude that the official should save the American, though in doing so he will unintentionally kill the Germans. Their intuition may follow not from the belief that partiality to compatriots is morally justifiable in this case, but rather from certain views about what follows from the agent's status as a state official. It is at least conceivable that an agent might occupy a state office without himself being a citizen of that state; indeed, in countries where military service is a path to citizenship, a significant number of combatants may not bear the relationship of compatriot to non-combatant citizens of that state.[24] The question would then be why occupying the role of state official permits or requires that, when he engages in a permissible act that will cause collateral damage, the agent should give greater weight to avoiding harm to citizens of the state he serves than he gives to avoiding harm to foreigners. One reason to think that being a state official makes no difference in this case is Thomas Pogge's observation that it would be bizarre if agents could circumvent moral prohibitions on certain types of acts simply by having officials do those acts for them.[25] If I am right to think

[24] As this example illustrates, the relationship between legal citizenship and the relationship of the compatriot is somewhat unclear. Suppose that in Kamm's bombing example, the 100 people who would be killed by bombardment A lived in the territory of the combatant's state, but were not citizens of it. Should the combatant still be partial to them? Does it matter whether they arrived in the territory legally or illegally, or whether they are guest workers or resident aliens?

[25] Thomas Pogge, *World Poverty and Human Rights* (Oxford: Blackwell, 2002), p. 126. Note that Pogge's claim is compatible with officials enjoying moral entitlements to do certain things that private individuals are forbidden from doing.

that an individual may not appeal to the compatriot relationship to justify throwing a grenade that kills three innocent foreigners as a side effect of saving one compatriot, then it should not be permissible to circumvent this prohibition by having a state official carry out the same act.

Both Kamm and Hurka recognize that all non-combatants have a (possibly defeasible) claim not to be targeted by combatants as part of the latter's conduct of a war. Given that none of the non-combatants have done anything to make themselves liable to attack, they enjoy an equal claim against all combatants that they not be intentionally harmed, as well as a claim that all combatants exercise due care to avoid harming them unintentionally.[26] However, Kamm and Hurka both go on to claim that combatants have an additional reason to avoid harming their compatriot non-combatants, one that they do not have vis-à-vis enemy non-combatants. This reason is the compatriot relationship, which in the paradigm case consists of being full members, or citizens, of the same political community. In virtue of this reason, combatants may, or must, assign a greater weight to harm done to a compatriot non-combatant than they assign to harm done to an enemy non-combatant. As I have tried to show, however, neither Kamm nor Hurka provides a plausible case for the claim that merely because they are members of the same political community combatants ought to be partial to their compatriot non-combatants. If my arguments succeed, then it follows that Kamm and Hurka should accept that combatants ought to be impartial with respect to the morally permissible collateral damage they cause. This is so because the prohibition on targeting non-combatants follows from a property had by all non-combatants, namely their not having done anything to make themselves liable to attack.[27] Therefore, holding all else equal, when deciding between two munitions factories a pilot ought to choose to bomb whichever factory's destruction will result in less collateral harm to non-combatants. And when engaging in a war justified at least in part as necessary to prevent

---

[26] But see n. 1.

[27] Walzer agrees, though with his typical lack of clarity: 'the structure of rights stands independently of political allegiance; it establishes obligations that are owed, so to speak, to humanity itself and to particular human beings and not merely to one's fellow citizens. The right of German civilians [during WWII]—who did no fighting and were not engaged in supplying the armed forces with the means of fighting—were no different from those of their French counterparts ...' (Walzer, *Just and Unjust Wars*, p. 158).

future attacks on their state and its citizens, as in the case of Israel's 2006 war against Hizbullah, combatants must at the very least refrain from causing more harm to enemy (and neutral) non-combatants than they prevent their enemy from inflicting on their compatriot non-combatants.

All else may not be equal, however. Suppose, for instance, that the enemy combatants are responsible for placing the enemy non-combatants at risk. That is, had the enemy combatants not chosen to take cover in the middle of a village, it would have been possible for our combatant to attack them without posing a risk of harm to either compatriot or enemy non-combatants. In this case, the enemy combatants' responsibility for placing their compatriot non-combatants at risk, when, let us assume, it was not morally permissible to do so, may provide a consideration sufficient to justify our combatant choosing the act that will collaterally harm a greater number of enemy non-combatants, rather than a lesser number of compatriot non-combatants.[28] I am not sure that the enemy combatants' (share of?) responsibility for putting the enemy non-combatants at risk does provide such a consideration.[29] All I wish to claim here, though, is that *if* it does, then the rejection of partiality to compatriot non-combatants does not entail that combatants are never morally permitted to collaterally kill a greater number of enemy non-combatants, rather than a lesser number of compatriot non-combatants.

Another possibility is that all (adult? voting?) members of an aggressor state share collective responsibility for their state's aggression, and that therefore non-combatant members of that state are either (a) liable to attack by just combatants (though perhaps less liable than unjust combatants, who may bear a greater degree of responsibility for the unjust war), or (b) not liable to attack, but left with a weaker claim not to be collaterally harmed than is had by those who do not share in the collective responsibility for launching or perpetuating an unjust war. The former implication of collective responsibility for an unjust war threatens to undermine the distinction between legitimate and illegitimate target of war that is essential to the very notion of collateral

[28] As this example illustrates, combatants' duty to reduce the risk of harm to non-combatants, even at the cost of increasing the risk to themselves, affects not only the permissibility of various modes of attack, but also various modes of defense.

[29] For discussion of this point, see Hurka, 'Proportionality', pp. 46–50, and Walzer, *Just and Unjust Wars*, pp. 158–96.

damage, and so I set it aside here. If it can be successfully defended, the latter implication of collective responsibility for an unjust war may warrant a just combatant's collaterally killing a greater number of enemy non-combatants, rather than a lesser number of compatriot non-combatants. The justification in this case, however, does not involve appeal to the compatriot relationship as a reason to give greater weight to the harm that will likely be suffered by compatriot non-combatants than to the harm that will likely be suffered by enemy non-combatants. Instead, it involves an appeal to the enemy non-combatants' collective responsibility for an unjust war as a reason to give less weight to the harm that will likely be done to them than they would merit had they not acted wrongly. As with the foregoing discussion of responsibility for placing non-combatants at risk of being collaterally killed, I take no stand here on the correctness of the argument from (alleged) collective responsibility for an unjust war to a lesser claim against being collaterally harmed.[30] Once again, I aim only to make clear that rejecting Kamm's and Hurka's defense of partiality to compatriot non-combatants does not necessarily entail that combatants are never morally justified in collaterally killing a greater number of enemy non-combatants, rather than a lesser number of compatriot non-combatants.[31]

In the remainder of this article, I consider another reason (in addition to the two just mentioned) that may morally permit, or even require, a combatant to carry out an attack that will result in collateral harm to a greater number of non-combatants than would have been harmed by an alternative, equally effective, attack. I do so by way of a critical discussion of Kamm's claim that given a choice between two courses of action, equally desirable from a military standpoint, a combatant ought to choose the one that will inflict collateral harm on a

[30] For a defense of non-combatant liability in virtue of collective responsibility for an unjust war, see Erin Kelly, 'The Burdens of Collective Liability', in Deen K. Chatterjee and Don E. Scheid (eds.), *Ethics and Foreign Intervention* (New York: Cambridge University Press, 2003), pp. 177–92. For a critique of this argument, see Larry May, *Aggression and Crimes Against Peace* (New York: Cambridge University Press, 2008), chapter 13.

[31] Yet another possible justification for collaterally killing more enemy non-combatants, instead of fewer compatriot non-combatants, is if each of the former bear a degree or type of *individual* culpability for an unjust war that warrants giving less weight to harm done to them than would be the case had they not acted wrongly (or wrongly enough). How often such cases would arise depends on what type or degree of individual responsibility for an unjust war renders a non-combatant liable to attack. For discussion of this issue, see Jeff McMahan, 'The Ethics of Killing in War', *Ethics* 114.4 (2004): 693–733.

greater number of compatriot non-combatants, rather than the one that will collaterally harm a lesser number of neutral non-combatants.

4. *Weighing Harm to Neutrals*

While Kamm claims that compatriot non-combatants have a greater inviolability than do enemy non-combatants, she also suggests that their inviolability is less than that enjoyed by neutral non-combatants.[32] Kamm briefly notes two arguments that might be given in support of this claim. The first is an argument by analogy:

> War by its nature involves engagement between designated parties who are expected to absorb all costs. The appropriate analogy for war is a prize fight; people in the audience are not liable at all to being punched.[33]

As stated, there is one obvious disanalogy between a war and a prize fight, namely that audience members at a prize fight are said not to be liable *at all* to being harmed by the fighters, while Kamm claims only that neutrals enjoy a high degree of, but not absolute, inviolability. This disanalogy can be addressed easily enough, however, by weakening the claim regarding the inviolability of the audience members at a prize fight. If a prize fighter can save himself from death at the hands of his opponent only by causing a relatively minor harm to one of the audience members, doing so seems permissible. If so, then audience members enjoy a (very) high degree of inviolability vis-à-vis the prize fighters, but not total inviolability.

A more significant difficulty with Kamm's suggested argument by analogy is that many non-combatants in the warring states are also like audience members at a prize fight, in that they are not involved in the fight itself, but simply bystanders caught up in it.[34] Moreover, unlike the typical audience member at a prize fight, many non-combatants in

[32] It may be that the claim should be stronger—neutral combatants may enjoy a greater degree of inviolability than do compatriot non-combatants.

[33] Kamm, 'Failures of Just War Theory', p. 675. The first sentence in this quote suggests an analytic argument for the claim that neutrals enjoy a greater degree of inviolability (indeed, total inviolability) than do members of the states or groups at war with one another. Such an argument seems implausible, since many paradigm examples of war have been fought by parties who had no expectation that they would absorb all of the costs. Perhaps the parties to a war *should* expect to absorb all of the costs, but this is a moral claim, not an analytic one regarding what it means (or is) to wage war.

[34] Or at least this is so if the collective responsibility argument mentioned earlier proves to be false.

warring states (as well as most neutrals) have not voluntarily chosen to 'attend' the fight; indeed, some of them may have actively opposed it (and continue to do so). Non-combatant members of a warring state may be *designated* as participants in the war (as the first sentence in the above quote suggests), but that they have the legal status of citizen in a state that happens to be at war does not ipso facto entail that they are participants in the fight itself. Were it to do so, then it would be impossible to distinguish between combatants and non-combatants, a distinction that Kamm wishes to retain.

The defense of the greater inviolability of neutrals by appeal to an analogy with audience members at a prize fight may seem more compelling if we focus on states rather than individuals. But even states may not be voluntary participants in a war. As Walzer points out, 'the wrong the aggressor [state] commits is to force men and women to risk their lives for the sake of their rights.'[35] States (or their members) may choose to sacrifice the enjoyment of their rights or to risk their lives to defend them, but in either case their choice is not a free one. If what accounts for the fact that the prize fighters are liable to be harmed, while audience members are not so liable, is that the former but not the latter have voluntarily chosen to participate in the fight, then members of a state that has not voluntarily chosen to wage war should enjoy the same level of inviolability as neutrals. Such a conclusion conflicts, however, with Kamm's claim that compatriot non-combatants enjoy a lesser degree of inviolability than do neutrals, at least on the assumption that the former are citizens of a state that declares and wages war justly.

Moreover, as I noted earlier in this article, harm to some members of the state is not the same thing as harm to the state itself. One can imagine, for instance, that the neutrals who will be killed are members of a minority political or ethnic group that is complicating the governance of the neutral state, so that their deaths actually strengthen the state, rather than harming it. This is not to say that these neutrals ought to be killed, of course, but only to point out that harm done to some of the state's subjects need not equate to harm done to the state itself. If so, then the argument that neutral states ought not to be harmed by the participants in the war does not necessarily rule out an attack that collaterally kills some members of the neutral state.

Kamm briefly notes a second, instrumental, argument for the claim that neutrals enjoy a higher degree of inviolability than do compatriot

[35] Walzer, *Just and Unjust Wars*, p. 51.

non-combatants. According to this line of argument, the weightier prohibition on causing harm to neutrals is justified because it reduces the likelihood that the neutral state will be drawn into the conflict, with the likely consequence that even greater harm and/or wrong will occur. It seems that such an argument will often provide a sufficient moral justification for not carrying out an attack that will harm neutrals, even when the only other permissible option is an attack that will harm a greater number of compatriot non-combatants. However, Kamm does not think this argument identifies a necessary condition for the assignment of greater inviolability to neutrals in comparison to compatriot non-combatants. She writes that 'even if C [the neutral state] were weak and posed no threat to A [the state whose combatants carry out the attack], it seems to have greater inviolability'.[36] For Kamm, then, the greater inviolability enjoyed by neutrals is not simply a matter of the consequences that may follow from an attack that causes harm to them.

Once again, the description of states as if they were individuals misleads. Even if the neutral state enjoys greater inviolability than the warring states, it does not follow that the latter states' non-combatants enjoy a lesser degree of inviolability than do the members of the neutral state. It might mean only that the combatants of the neutral state enjoy greater inviolability than that enjoyed by combatants of the warring states (or at least those of the warring state without a just cause for war). Alternatively, or in addition, it might mean (only) that the neutral state enjoys a greater degree of inviolability with respect to the use of its territory by the warring states than does either of those states vis-à-vis their opponent. For example, it could mean that state A's seizure of some of its enemy's public assets—e.g. bridges and highways—would not violate the moral constraints on war, but A's seizure of a neutral state's public assets would. Whatever the details, the general point should be clear enough: there is no obvious inference from the claim that a neutral state enjoys a greater degree of inviolability than do warring states to the claim that the non-combatant members of a neutral state enjoy a greater degree of inviolability than do non-combatant members of warring states.

Is it the case, then, that when faced with a choice between permissible collateral damage causing acts of war, a combatant ought to select whichever one will result in the fewest number of non-combatant

[36] Kamm, 'Failures of Just War Theory', p. 675.

deaths, regardless of the citizenship of those non-combatants? In particular, is Kamm mistaken when she claims that a combatant ought to collaterally kill a greater number of compatriot non-combatants rather than collaterally kill a lesser number of neutrals, at least up to a point? Perhaps not. Given a certain understanding of the value and nature of state sovereignty, Kamm's claim may still be correct, though not on the basis of the reasoning she employs. Space does not permit a thorough defense of this understanding of state sovereignty, nor am I at all certain that a satisfactory defense of it can be offered. Therefore my argument is conditional: if a certain understanding of the value and nature of state sovereignty can be defended, then in some cases combatants ought to choose a course of action that will result in the death of a larger number of compatriot non-combatants, rather than one that will result in the death of a lesser number of neutrals, and the violation of the neutral state's sovereignty.

Suppose that the neutral state enjoys a morally justified claim to sovereignty, understood to consist in a particular status I will characterize vaguely as a right to self-government, or self-determination. A self-governing state is the final arbiter of its affairs, in principle and (usually) in fact, and it exercises this normative and de facto authority within a given territory.[37] Perhaps this notion of state sovereignty should be understood reductively, in terms of the individual rights of the state's members, or perhaps it must be understood non-reductively, in terms of moral entitlements held collectively by the state's members or by the group as a whole. However it is understood, though, any act that violates the neutral state's sovereignty wrongs it because it fails to respect the states' status as self-governing. In wronging the neutral state, the warring state either wrongs the individual members of the neutral state, or wrongs the members of that state as a group. But just as in the case of a violation of individual self-determination, it is not essential to the wrong at issue that the state whose sovereignty is violated be harmed by that violation. The complaint is not 'we are worse off because of what you did', but rather 'you are not entitled to do what you did; you have encroached upon our moral dominion'. Thus, in the case of an attack that impacts the territory and/or citizens of a neutral

[37] This characterization of sovereignty is consistent with both the voluntary transfer of authority, so that the final arbiter over some of a state's affairs may be a body created by an international treaty with other states, and with the scope of a state's moral claim to sovereignty being limited by, and conditional upon respect for, principles of justice.

state, even if the ability of the neutral state to govern itself is not reduced at all, and even if no one in the neutral state is harmed, the warring state still wrongs it.

Suppose that something like this account of state sovereignty as a moral status can be fleshed out and defended. If it can, then we have a possible explanation for why state A ought to choose a course of action that collaterally kills more of its own subjects rather than one that will result in collateral harm to a lesser number of neutrals. Every non-combatant (and perhaps neutral combatant) enjoys the same level of inviolability, since none have done anything to make themselves liable to being targeted as part of the conduct of war. However, an attack that causes harm to neutrals also violates the neutral state's sovereignty; the latter is a particular kind of wrong that does not occur if the combatant elects the course of action that involves collaterally killing some of his compatriot non-combatants. It may be, then, that the moral prohibition on violating a state's sovereignty provides a justification for Kamm's intuition that the combatant has a non-instrumental moral reason to choose the act that will result in a greater number of compatriot non-combatant deaths, instead of the one that will result in a lesser number of neutral deaths and the violation of the neutral state's sovereignty. Of course, the neutral state surely does not enjoy an absolute right not to have its sovereignty infringed; for example, a combatant with the choice between killing a far greater number of compatriot non-combatants or a very few neutrals, but violating the neutral state's sovereignty, may still be morally permitted (or even required) to choose the latter course.

What about a choice between killing a larger group of enemy non-combatants or a lesser number of neutrals? The correct answer to this question depends on whether the enemy state has a just cause for war. If it does (e.g. it is fighting in self-defense), then regardless of which act the combatant chooses, he violates the sovereignty of the state whose citizens he harms. More importantly, it is extremely unlikely that the combatant will have a just cause for war if the enemy state has one (indeed, this may even be conceptually impossible), in which case I believe the combatant is not morally permitted to kill anyone, collaterally or not.[38] Suppose, however, that the just conduct of war does not

[38] For a defense of the claim that in order for an agent to wage war in conformity with the criteria of *jus in bello*, he or she must have a just cause for going to war (or be part of a political organization that has a just cause for going to war), see McMahan, 'The Ethics of Killing in War'.

depend on the justice of one's cause (or on having met all six of the *jus ad bellum* criteria). Then holding all else equal, the deciding factor is the number of people harmed who are not morally liable to being harmed by an act of war.[39] However, if the enemy state does not have a just cause for war, then it is unlikely that the harm done to enemy non-combatants will also constitute the violation of the enemy state's sovereignty.[40] In that case, the same reasoning that applies in the case of a choice between killing a larger number of compatriot non-combatants or a lesser number of neutrals holds in the case of a choice between killing a larger number of enemy non-combatants or a lesser number of neutrals.

In sum, Kamm is wrong to think that combatants ought to be partial to their compatriot non-combatants, assigning greater weight to harm done to them than they assign to harm done to enemy non-combatants. All non-combatants enjoy the same degree of inviolability, and so holding all else equal, a combatant ought to choose whichever course of action will result in the fewest number of non-combatant deaths. Kamm may well be correct, however, when she asserts that a combatant ought to kill a greater number of compatriot non-combatants rather than a lesser number of neutrals. But the reason for this is not that the lives and well-being of compatriot non-combatants count for less than those of neutrals. Rather, it is because an attack that causes harm to neutrals involves a distinct moral wrong absent from an attack that harms only compatriot non-combatants, namely a violation of the neutral state's sovereignty. The disvalue of this wrong is great enough that, at least up to a point, it requires choosing an act that will result in more non-combatant deaths than would result from committing the alternative act under consideration.[41]

---

[39] All else may not be equal, of course. If the violation of the neutral state's sovereignty would bring it into the war, and thereby increase the amount of harm and/or number of wrongs done, then this would count in favor of an attack that harmed a greater number of enemy non-combatants over an attack that harmed a lesser number of neutrals (at least up to a point).

[40] Without a fully fleshed-out account of the moral justification for state sovereignty, it is not possible to be certain of this. But, for example, if a state enjoys a moral claim to sovereignty only if it does not wage unjust wars, then harm done to its non-combatants will not count as a violation of the state's sovereignty.

[41] I wish to thank Craig Derksen, Tom Hurka, and Scott James for their comments on an earlier version of this paper.

CONDITIONAL THREATS

Gerhard Øverland

A person might want your money and be willing to kill you for it. But instead of just shooting you and making off with the dough, she might offer the infamous choice, your money or your life! Situations like this land us with difficult choices. Not, of course, whether you should hand over the money and live, or decline and die. Yet, if you were presented with the option of killing the threat to save both money and life, whether it would be permissible to proceed is not clear.

David Rodin uses the notion of 'conditional threat' to describe people who, instead of trying to kill you outright, threaten to kill you unless you give them what they want.[1] The problem of conditional threats comes about when the threat posed by an aggressing party is an immediate threat only to something of a lesser value, and merely conditionally a threat to life. The term may also be applicable to invading forces.[2] Invading forces will often not kill anybody unless people put up a show of resistance. Since one might believe that responding to conditional threats with lethal force is impermissible unless what is extorted is of sufficient merit to justify so doing, one might conclude that it would be impermissible for an invaded country to mobilize its armed forces to protect something of only a lesser value.[3]

In this paper I ponder the moral status of conditional threats, in particular the extent to which a threatened party would be permitted to use (lethal) defensive force. I first investigate the mugger case before turning briefly to the more complicated issue of national defence in the face of an invading army. One should not, I argue, exaggerate the level of protection people under threat owe their conditioned killers simply

---

[1] See David Rodin, *War and Self-Defense* (Oxford: Oxford University Press, 2002), pp. 133–38.

[2] Richard Norman has, for instance, argued that the Falklands War was a classic example of a situation where defensive force should not have been applied (see Richard Norman, *Ethics, Killing and War* [Cambridge: Cambridge University Press, 1995], pp. 156–58).

[3] Norman holds that 'the fact that unjust demands are backed up by lethal threats does not by itself justify killing in response; it depends on the importance of what is defended' (*Ethics, Killing and War*, p. 133).

because what is extorted is of little value. After all, either the conditional threat is willing to kill for something she has no claim on at all, or, if she has a just claim on it – or good reason to believe that she has – she is willing to kill to (re)acquire something of not much worth. In both cases the moral culpability of the conditional threat could be seen as reducing her claim on protection from harm.

Risk

Jeff McMahan has little sympathy with conditional threats, and holds that if a thief threatens to kill you if you resist, then 'one is permitted to create the conditions of one's own lethal defense. For the thief's threat does not nullify one's right to resist'.[4] McMahan's idea is that if someone is trying to steal money from you, you are permitted to use proportional means to avert the crime, for example, by pushing the assailant away. He then maintains that this option cannot become impermissible by being presented with a conditional threat.[5] And then, the argument goes, since trying to push someone who's waving a gun at you is not always the most advisable formula, the defendant may bypass that step and activate the lethal force alternative forthwith.

But this move merely seems to imply that a person is killed for an unjustified cause, namely an individual's right to resist a mugging. We therefore need to know *why* it is permissible to set in motion events that will lead to the death of the aggressor when what is being protected is of little value. What is it about the conditional threat that makes lethal force permissible despite the fact that the value at stake does not make it so?

Initially Rodin's view is that 'it is never legitimate to respond to conditional threats with lethal force unless what is extorted is itself of sufficient value to justify the use of lethal force'.[6] That sounds counterintuitive. It neither takes into account the culpability of the agent, nor the danger to which the person under threat has been exposed. After having discussed the views of John Locke, Rodin agrees to let the risk

---

[4] Jeff McMahan, 'Innocence, Self-Defence and Killing in War', *Journal of Political Philosophy* 2 (1994): 193–221, at p. 196.

[5] Observe nevertheless that if the conditional threat affects a third party, and pushing the aggressor out of the way exposes the third party to a higher risk, it could be impermissible to take that course of action.

[6] Rodin, *War and Self-Defense*, p. 134.

imposed on the victim play a role. Whether there is a right to kill in response to conditional threats, he now maintains, turns on 'the nature and value of what the aggressor demands and the level of risk assumed'.[7]

But if there is a significant risk one might question the importance of being a conditional threat, as the risk itself might justify lethal defensive force. If a person for no good reason poses a significant risk to another, the latter should be morally free to forcibly defend himself. Take Russian roulette with an unwilling player as a case in point. Although there is only a one in six risk of death, shooting and killing the player would seem entirely permissible if that were the least intrusive way of preventing the player from pulling the trigger.

Anyway, the risk factor itself may not change things very much with regard to a *trustworthy* conditional threat, i.e. a person who will only cause harm if she doesn't get what she wants. In those cases, it could be argued, the level of risk depends mainly on the response of the victim. The victim will only be killed if he defends himself forcibly – provided we assume with Rodin that it is wrong to use defensive force in a situation in which one is not exposed to significant risk, and that trustworthy conditional threats do not expose us to a significant risk. But the latter assumption is not true; a victim is exposed to risk whether or not he responds by acting 'wrongly' such as trying to kill the conditional threat. For example, the victim may falsely believe that he will be able to run for cover, which means that he will be shot dead if he tries. And clearly, trying to escape is not morally wrong, no matter how stupid. Hence, not even a trustworthy conditional threat is in overall control of the risk she poses. Risk caused by the unwise behaviour of the victim, for instance, is something the conditional threat is willing to impose upon other people. That counts against her.

Moral Responsibility

The mere fact that what is at stake is of minor value speaks against permitting killing conditional threats. If you are sitting in a café, and an unarmed pickpocket tries to relieve you of a few dollars, you would not be permitted to resist if killing the thief was your only recourse. Yet, this simple observation does not take us very far. There is a big difference between ordinary thieves and conditional threats.

[7] Rodin, *War and Self-Defense*, p. 137.

To illustrate the difference, imagine an escalated situation between a petty thief and a victim. The victim resorts to lethal defensive force to protect his money. The thief, on her side, happens to have access to a weapon and can use it to protect herself against the victim's use of lethal force. However, she neither intended to use any weapon to obtain the money nor was it reasonable to construe her behaviour as threatening. We have to take immediate and possibly lethal action to save either the victim, who is trying to protect a few dollars, or the petty thief, who out of the blue has procured a gun from somewhere. It would at this point seem permissible to save the thief who was not a threat to anyone and rather kill the person who knowingly resorted to lethal force to defend something of as little value as a few dollars (assuming here that the owner of the money is not poor or in any particular urgent need). If that is true, it must be because the wrong committed by resorting to lethal force to deter a petty thief is a significantly greater moral wrong than the thief's unsuccessful unarmed attempt to purloin the few dollars.

The same does not seem to be true when the thief is a trustworthy conditional threat. If a person not only wants the victim's money but also is willing to kill for it, as revealed by holding him at gunpoint while offering the choice between money and life, things take on a different hue. If the victim now resorted to defensive force, and we had to select whom to help, it would be wrong to save the conditional threat at the cost of the other. We may want to say that responding with lethal force was wrong, given that what was at stake was something of minor value. Yet, we nevertheless seem obliged to give priority to the person defending himself against the conditional threat.

This observation cannot be explained by the fact that victims of conditional threats are exposed to risk, and that we therefore can see that they have a reason for using lethal force, although what is at stake is not of much worth. At the time of the intervention there is no difference in risk between the escalated situation involving the petty thief and the one with the conditional threat. It must therefore be explained by the serious moral wrong it is to be a conditional threat in the first place. It is the threat's moral responsibility for waiving a loaded gun that would require third parties to assist the defendant whenever there is a question of saving either of them. The aggressor's willingness to use deadly force to obtain something of lesser value makes him morally culpable, and this culpability affects the amount of force that it would be proportional for the victim and others to use. Hence, the means we permissibly may invoke to frustrate conditional threats is neither a simple question about whether what is extorted is itself of sufficient value to justify the use of lethal force, nor a conjoined evaluation of the risk to the defending party and the value at stake, but a conjoined evaluation of the two former *and* the moral culpability of the agent.

Generally, moral culpability matters in self- and other-defence. For instance, if an innocent aggressor is about to cut off somebody's limb there are strict proportionality considerations that would limit the means that could be used to prevent it. It would, for instance, not be permissible to kill the innocent aggressor to save the limb. By contrast, if the agent is a culpable contributor, who enjoys splitting people from their limbs, it seems uncontroversial to assume that significantly more may be done toward the wrongdoer if that is necessary to save a limb of the victim.[8] Even killing a culpable aggressor seems permissible when need be to save a limb. Proportionality considerations still apply, but are more relaxed compared to situations where force is used against an innocent contributor, and the degree to which they are more relaxed depends on the degree to which the agent is morally responsible for his or her actions.[9] It is therefore not surprising that the moral responsibility on the part of a conditional threat should likewise impinge on the permissibility of using force against her.

Asymmetry

Having seen that moral culpability matters, there is a certain peculiarity to a conditional threat that might lead one to suggest that she would be more culpable when less is at stake. The rationale would be the following. First, if what is at stake is something of minor value that will reduce the permissibility of killing in its defence. But if so, we should also expect that the moral culpability of the person who is willing to take life in order to obtain something of minor value would be

[8] Judith Jarvis Thomson observes this in 'Self-Defence', *Philosophy and Public Affairs* 20 (1991): 283–310, at p. 289. See also Yitzhak Benbaji, 'Culpable Bystanders, Innocent Threats and the Ethics of Self-Defense', *Canadian Journal of Philosophy* 35 (2005): 585–622, at pp. 597–99.

[9] This proposal does not imply that I am committed to a punitive account of defensive force. A punitive account seems to imply that the person deserves that something bad happens to her; my proposal is compatible with the weaker claim that she deserves less protection in a conflict between persons.

increased. This will then reduce her claim on protection from harm. Granted the threat is trustworthy, she is now willing to kill for almost nothing. That is a serious wrong on her part. It is therefore not obvious that a reduction in the value at stake will narrow the permissible range of defence options. One might even be tempted to say that it is the other way around, as a willingness to kill for very little may look worse than killing for something of significant value.

But as it stands, that proposal cannot be correct. It doesn't seem to apply to the acquisition of values you have no claim on in the first place. Whether or not the conditional threat attempts to get hold of a few dollars or millions doesn't seem to alter our judgments about her moral culpability. It is not OK to be a conditional threat as soon as the value at stake is 'worth' killing for.

A plausible option is to say that when an agent is willing to kill for something she has no just claim on, her moral culpability is immune to changes in its value. It is equally wrong to be a conditional threat for the sake of a few dollars, as it is for the sake of a million. And then the interest at stake will work as an independent factor making use of lethal force increasingly proportional. For instance, if the person threatens to kill you unless you sign off a significant part of your wealth, killing the threat could be justified.

This proposal implies that it might be morally permissible to use lethal force in order to protect a particular interest from a conditional threat and impermissible in order to protect it from a simple thief. For instance, you may have to let a thief take off with your car, but be permitted to defend it with lethal force if you are threatened with deadly consequences. Moreover, the significance of the moral culpability for being a trustworthy conditional threat ensures that we should always side with the victim and never the conditional threat, as the moral culpability associated with the latter trumps the moral wrong of resorting to lethal force to defend something of minor value.[10]

---

[10] Clearly, part of the explanation why it seems wrong to shoot a conditional threat when only a few dollars are at stake might in the ordinary case be that we do not really believe the person is actually prepared to kill us if we refuse to submit to her demand. I am therefore alluding to trustworthy conditional threats, that is, people who will not kill unless they are met with resistance, but they will if need be. If we alter the second part of this clause, things take on a different hue. If the agent will not kill for money, and is merely putting up a show to increase her chances of success, she would not be exposing anyone to risk – except herself, as she may be taken to be trustworthy and therefore killed – and her moral culpability would be considerably smaller.

Things look different when the conditional threat attempts to extort things to which she has a just claim. In this case, her moral culpability will be determined by its value, but in inverse proportion. Even though a person correctly believes that her neighbour has stolen something from her, a hundred dollars say, she better know that killing to obtain it is disproportional. Hence, trustworthy threatening her neighbour with lethal consequences if he doesn't hand back the money would be morally wrong. By contrast, if the neighbour had stolen something significant, being a conditional threat may very well be a permissible option.

The value at stake bears differently on the culpability of conditional threats. For a conditional threat with no just claim, it simply has no impact; she is fully culpable no matter the value of what she is after. For a conditional threat with a just claim, the interest at stake will impact inversely on her moral culpability; she becomes fully culpable as the value at stake approaches zero. This implies that a conditional threat with a just claim on something of insignificant value is (almost) as culpable for waiving a gun as any conditional threat with no claim. A difference between them is nevertheless observable in that the fully culpable conditional threat without a just claim may in addition try to extort something of value, making defensive force easier to justify.

It may at this point pay to observe how the value at stake and the moral culpability of the conditional threat with a just claim interact. If the value is significant – perhaps almost worth killing for – it is not very wrong to be willing to kill for it. Moreover, the conditional threat has now a just claim on something valuable, and since the neighbour's initial theft was of this item, it was a significant wrong on his part. Third parties would therefore have to side with the conditional threat. By contrast, if it is something of little value, it is indeed very wrong to be willing to kill for it. And now the interest of the conditional threat would not carry much weight either. This leaves her with very little to support her case. And although the neighbour's initial theft was wrong, it would not be significant enough to outweigh the wrong on her part. Hence, third parties should side with the neighbour (the simple thief) in this case.[11]

[11] If we vary the neighbour's moral culpability by assuming that he has an excuse in the sense that he had good reason to believe that the object at stake was his to take in the first place, things become more difficult. In that case you defend something of significant value, but yet not worth killing for, leaving some culpability on your part, while your neighbour is innocent in the relevant sense.

War

A surprising event during Germany's invasion of Norway, early on 9 April 1940, was the sinking of the German Navy's newest ship, the heavy cruiser *Blücher*, by the 47-year-old 28cm guns of Oscarsborg fortress. A total of 830 German soldiers died that morning either from the blast or by drowning in the cold water. As it turned out, the Germans persecuted the Jewish community in Norway as well, which, had one known at the time, would have justified lethal resistance against the invading forces.[12] But when sailing up the Oslo fjord, the Germans had no intention of killing anybody; they only wanted to take over a country.

The asymmetry between the permissibility to use defensive force against simple thieves and conditional threats has gone mostly unnoticed, and that is particularly unfortunate with regard to the question of defensive wars. In such cases, the aggressor typically claims to have some kind of just cause, but fails to note that the value they are about to fight for is something of a lesser value not worth killing for. They may even have a just claim on it, but they ought to know that killing to obtain it is disproportional. Their culpability will therefore be set inversely to the value at stake, securing permissibility to defend with lethal means that which it otherwise would not have been permissible to kill for.

Invading soldiers may, of course, have a just claim – or a just cause – and they may therefore be permitted to kill the defending soldiers. Certain instances of humanitarian interventions would be examples. I will not discuss such cases here. My interest is primarily with situations where the invading soldiers have no just claim, but have good reason to believe that they have, and therefore perhaps are fully excused for their mistake in this regard. It is at least possible that the soldiers on the deck of *Blücher* fell within this category.

There are important differences between self- and other-defence in civil life and war. Let me here point to two considerations that seem to pull in different directions, the question of soldiers' innocence and the likelihood of collateral damages. Many think that soldiers' participation in unjust aggression can often be morally excused. The fact that soldiers tend to be young, uneducated, and are strongly loyal to their country are some reasons for this. And if indeed the belligerent soldiers

[12] It might also arguably have helped the Norwegian royal family, parliament and cabinet to escape to London.

are innocent, the defending party appears to have a duty to endure higher risk and expose their own forces to greater harm so as to reduce the harm done to the aggressing soldiers. I cannot here discuss whether soldiers normally have a moral excuse for participating in their country's unjust war, but let me say a few words about the claim that defending soldiers ought to endure higher risks in order to avoid harming excused soldiers.

One might perhaps wonder why innocent defending soldiers, who are not acting wrongly, should bear greater costs to avoid harming innocent aggressing soldiers engaged in wrongdoing. Note, however, that the claim is only that they should bear greater cost in this case than if the aggressors were morally culpable. I have already indicated that if an innocent aggressor is about to cut off somebody's limb the proportionality considerations limiting the means that could be used to prevent it would be stricter than if the aggressor were morally culpable. It is easy to envisage situations involving numerous aggressors where similar considerations apply. Moreover, I am not suggesting that the innocence of the aggressors would make defensive force impermissible. Simply being an innocent contributor to harm has severe implications for the amount of defensive force that may be used. Yet, moral culpability expands the range of permissible defensive means. Innocent aggressors are not on par with innocent bystanders as has been suggested by quite a few philosophers recently,[13] but they are not on par with culpable aggressors either, as I discuss elsewhere.[14]

As for a conditional threat, the idea is that the risk one is required to take in order to avoid harming this person decreases as a function of her moral culpability. But then observe that it is not clear whether invading soldiers who pose only a conditional threat to life should be regarded as innocent, even though they may be excused for reasons of

---

[13] See N. Zohar, 'Collective War and Individualistic Ethics: Against the Conscription of "Self-Defense"', *Political Theory* 21 (1993): 606–622; Michael Otsuka, 'Killing the Innocent in Self-Defence', *Philosophy and Public Affairs* 23 (1994): 74–94; Jeff McMahan, 'Self-Defense and the Problem of the Innocent Attacker', *Ethics* 104 (1994): 252–290; David Rodin, *War and Self-Defense* (Oxford: Clarendon Press, 2002), pp. 70–99; Jeff McMahan, 'The Basis of Moral Liability to Defensive Killing', *Philosophical Issues* 15 (2005): 386–405; and Kimberley Kessler Ferzan, 'Justifying Self-Defense', *Law and Philosophy* 24 (2005): 711–49.

[14] A first attempt is found in 'Forced Assistance', *Law and Philosophy* 28 (2009): 203–232, where I propose an asymmetrical fair share procedure, according to which innocent contributors have a duty to take on a fair share of the harm if dividing it is possible, and a fair share of the risk of being harmed if redistribution is impossible. I develop the account further in 'Dividing Harm', a work in progress.

loyalty etc. After all, soldiers are typically geared up to kill if ordered to do so. We can therefore assume that an invading army is trustworthy, and that its soldiers are ready to kill to advance their objective. But making a conditional threat to life in order to obtain something of a lesser value reveals a moral fault on part of the threat. Hence, although soldiers may (falsely) believe their country is fighting in order to reclaim something they have a just claim on, they ought to know it is wrong to kill in the service of the objective for which they are invading the other country. Compare with the mugger. While she might have good reason to believe that the few dollars belong to her, she should know that she ought not to kill in order to obtain them – provided she is not starving or finds herself in a particularly desperate situation. Similarly, we may partly excuse the forces of a belligerent state engaged in unjust aggression, as they may, for instance, have good reason to believe that the land they are about to occupy was unjustly stolen from them some years back. What cannot be excused is their willingness to resort to lethal means to secure their prize. Hence, though they are excused for having wrong beliefs about who are entitled to what, there is no excuse for their decision to take up arms, and they are morally culpable in that respect.

Now, these lines of thought might seem to entail that whilst soldiers who are killing in the name of an unjust war should be afforded protection by those they aim to kill, soldiers who pose only a conditional threat in the name of an unjust war are not innocent, and thus are fair game for the defending forces. That is not the proposal, of course. First of all, if it is morally wrong to be a conditional threat because the value at stake is of minor importance, it is wrong to carry out the killing as well. Moreover, merely being an innocent contributor is significant, but so is moral culpability. I take no stand here as to what is most significant, and, needless to say, that would very much depend on the degree of moral culpability. It might be worth observing, though, that in a choice between harming a conditional threat and an innocent aggressor, it is not at all obvious that you ought to harm the latter. Suppose that you can survive by way of killing a person on your left or on your right. On the left there is an innocent aggressor coming against you; on the right there is a conditional threat that will kill you unless you hand her some money. Your morally preferred option in this case seems to me that you kill the conditional threat.

Of course, the aggressing soldiers may have been deluded about the true cause of the war as well. They might, for example, believe they are on a liberating mission, when they are really engaged in an attempt to gain control over some natural resources. That being the case they should be considered innocent and the defending party should accept a higher risk of harm to avoid killing them. It is, however, not clear what one could have told the soldiers on *Blücher*'s deck early that morning which gave them reason to believe they were justified in killing people in a democratic state like Norway in order to gain control over their country.[15]

While there clearly may be instances in which what is at stake is something of a lesser value and not worth killing for, it seems that Rodin and others overstate the instances in which that should have implications for conditional threats. They seem to think that a state that launches a defensive war against an invading army that's only seeking to take away things like collective self-determination, land and valuable resources, or a people's 'common way of life', fails to meet the requirement of proportionality because the value of such factors is not high enough to warrant the taking of life.[16] I think it is perfectly permissible to kill if protecting such values requires it, provided the conditional threats are trustworthy and are aware of their mission's real aims. By knowingly engaging in such threats, one demonstrates serious disrespect of others. They may have reason to believe that they have a just claim on what they are ready to fight for, but they have seriously misjudged the extent to which it is permissible to take up arms to claim it. Hence, resorting to lethal defensive force might not be permissible simply because one wants to protect something of a lesser value, nor perhaps simply because one is exposed to a particular risk – though that may be the case if the risk is significant – but because the aggressors are willing to kill for these objectives.

Turning now to the obverse case, namely the likelihood of death of non-threatening innocent people, or collateral damage. While it often

[15] One might perhaps also like to argue that the value at stake should be evaluated differently from the two viewpoints. To gain control over others may have some value, but to maintain control over oneself seems to have higher value. Hence, the Germans' case looks even worse. Their allegedly just claim would clearly not be worth killing for, making their culpability quite severe, while the Norwegians' interest in maintaining self-control strengthen their case of taking up arms.

[16] Rodin, *War and Self-Defense*, p. 134. See also David Rodin, 'Beyond National Defense', *Ethics and International Affairs* 18.1 (2004): 95. Richard Norman holds essentially the same view; see his *Ethics, Killing and War* (Cambridge: Cambridge University Press, 1995), pp. 120–56.

is permissible to kill well-informed trustworthy conditional threats to protect something that in itself does not merit lethal defence, this observation does not imply that waging a defensive war in order to protect such objectives always is permissible. The reason is simply that more than well-informed trustworthy conditional threats might be killed in the war.[17] Since an essential justification of resorting to lethal means against conditional threats is based on the moral culpability of the threat, this type of justification will not suffice for actions that cause the death of people outside the ranks of the belligerent soldiers.[18]

[17] McMahan argues that defensive war waged by a victim state can be proportionate given that other nations will be dissuaded from committing aggression as a result of waging the defensive war. Jeff McMahan, 'War as Self Defense', *Ethics and International Affairs* 18.1 (2004): 79. While this looks like a plausible consideration when it is talk of merely killing trustworthy well-informed conditional threats, it seems much less weighty in order to justify killing innocent non-threatening people, collaterally or otherwise.

[18] I would like to thank an anonymous referee of this journal for helpful and challenging comments.

DEFINING TERRORISM FOR PUBLIC POLICY PURPOSES: THE GROUP-TARGET DEFINITION

Eric Reitan

Introduction

Any public policy response to terrorism achieves coherence only to the extent that there is a clear understanding of *what* is being targeted. Put another way, in order to fashion and assess public policy responses to the kind of threat exemplified by paradigms of 'terrorism', we need to agree on what 'terrorism' will mean for public policy purposes. Stated simply, we need a clear *public definition.*

Unfortunately, ordinary usage does not provide the needed clarity. At the same time, a public definition must strive to avoid being so divorced from ordinary usage that it amounts to a *technical* definition—one that frames a discourse of specialists disconnected from the pervasive public discourse and largely inaccessible to the general public. In a democratic society, active public engagement in the discourse culminating in policy decisions should be encouraged and facilitated. A public definition ought therefore to be *true* to ordinary usage in some sense, even if such usage is too messy to immediately provide us with an adequate public definition.

In this essay, I do four things: first, I discuss the prospects for a public definition of terrorism that will minimally comport with ordinary usage while still providing the kind of precision that ordinary usage does not offer; second, I argue that such a definition will encompass dominant paradigms of terrorism while having essentially pragmatic goals in view, and then construct criteria for an adequate definition with these ideas in mind; third, I develop what I call the 'group-target' definition of terrorism, which identifies a feature of terrorism that may be especially helpful for public policy purposes; and finally, I argue that this definition fits the criteria for a good public definition especially well. In doing the last, I hope also to demonstrate the useful role that a public definition can play in evaluating public policy.

The Problem with Defining 'Terrorism'

Whenever we develop public policies to fight terrorism, we are supposing that 'terrorism' picks out a distinctive class of actions whose members are sufficiently alike that one can devise a coherent terrorism policy that effectively addresses the actions within the class. But given what 'terrorism' means in ordinary usage, this is simply not true. 'Terrorism', in its ordinary use, simply does not pick out a class of actions sufficiently unified to guide public policy.

There are two reasons why this is so. First, there is the diversity of phenomena falling within the scope of ordinary use. As Jenny Teichman puts it, 'if we list all the different phenomena which are at one time or another described as terrorism in ordinary conversation, or in ordinary newspapers, or by ordinary politicians, we will end up with a huge rag-bag of not very similar items'.[1] Second, there is the polemical use of the term. As Virginia Held notes, '[u]sage characteristically applies the term to violent acts performed by those of whose positions and goals the speaker disapproves and fails to apply it to similar acts by those with whose positions and goals the speaker identifies'.[2] This is true because 'terrorism' serves as a label of condemnation. 'To identify someone as a terrorist', Claudia Card observes, 'is to render a judgment on them, not simply to make a discovery'.[3]

Both of these features of ordinary usage can be made sense of if terrorism is construed as an essentially contested concept in W.B. Gallie's sense—that is, as a concept characterized by competing definitions unified by a common appraisive meaning and a shared set of paradigms.[4] Gallie argues that essentially contested concepts regulate moral discourse in which the issue at stake is which phenomena deserve the appraisal we attach to the paradigms. An essentially contested concept

---

[1] Jenny Teichman, 'How to Define Terrorism', *Philosophy* 64 (1989), pp. 505–517 (506).

[2] Virginia Held, 'Terrorism, Rights, and Political Goals', in James. B. Brady and Newton Garver (eds.), *Justice, Law, and Violence* (Philadelphia: Temple University Press, 1991), pp. 223–40 (223).

[3] Claudia Card, 'Making War on Terrorism in Response to 9/11', in James P. Sterba (ed.), *Terrorism and International Justice* (Oxford: Oxford University Press, 2003), p. 166.

[4] W.B. Gallie, 'Essentially Contested Concepts', *Proceedings of the Aristotelian Society* 56 (1956), pp. 167–98. For a development of Gallie's understanding of essentially contested concepts and an application of the idea to negative appraisive terms, see Eric Reitan, 'Rape as an Essentially Contested Concept', *Hypatia* 16 (2001): 43–66.

is therefore not merely descriptive, but evaluative. To attach the concept to a phenomenon is to pass judgment on it. The paradigms provide a kind of point of unification in ordinary usage, insofar as there is general agreement that each paradigm deserves to be judged or evaluated in the relevant way. But the paradigms are complex, and so there is disagreement concerning which features *of* these paradigms justify the distinctive appraisal that the concept carries. Competing uses therefore arise, and these are expressed in competing definitions that aim to pick out those features of the paradigms most salient for the purposes of assigning the relevant appraisal. Ordinary usage is not captured by any one of these definitions, but by the set of overlapping contenders. A proposed definition is *consonant* with ordinary usage so long as it extends to the paradigms, excludes what no one would classify under the concept, and preserves the concept's distinctive appraisive meaning.

For Gallie, essentially contested concepts perform the valuable function of preventing some voices from being cut out of public debate by a kind of *definitional fiat*. If the 'true' meaning of the concept is identified with one particular competing definition—that is, by *one* perspectival assessment of what it is about the paradigms that justifies the relevant appraisal—the danger is that other perspectives that deserve a hearing will be silenced.

But even if this is right, essentially contested concepts are perilous when it comes to making public policy. For the public to participate democratically in the development and assessment of terrorism policies, we must be able to examine how proposed and actual policies contribute, if at all, to the prevention or reduction of the threat that 'terrorism' designates. And to do *that*, we need a precise, shared understanding of what 'terrorism' is taken to mean, *at least for the sake of these policies*.

Since ordinary usage cannot provide such an understanding, a public definition must therefore be stipulative. But a stipulative public definition may do the very thing that the recognition of essential contestability is supposed to prevent—namely, trammel public discourse by silencing significant moral perspectives by definitional fiat. Consider those who observe that domestic battery has much in common with terrorism paradigms. Their claim that domestic violence is a form of terrorism, and that comprehensive efforts to combat the distinctive evil of terrorism ought therefore to include it, may be unfairly dismissed if the reigning public definition has latched onto features of the paradigms *other* than those which justify the comparison with domestic abuse.

I suspect the only way to avoid this danger while acknowledging the need for a coherent public definition is to regard any such definition as *provisional* and *situational*. A public definition is introduced *in a particular sociopolitical and historical context, in order to formulate policies to address a particular salient problem*. Outside this context, it has no special authority. Furthermore, as I will argue in the next section, the criteria for choosing a public definition should seek to avoid any *favoritism* in the definitional debate that essential contestability is supposed to regulate. Insofar as that definitional debate turns on the question of which features of the paradigms justify our moral condemnation of them, it follows that a public definition should answer a *different* question. But what question?

Criteria for an Adequate Public Definition

A clear understanding of the kind of problem terrorism poses will require us to say both *what* terrorism is and *why* it is problematic. Ordinarily, the *first* task would seem to be the definitional one, and the latter a normative question that we address only once we have our definition in place. David Rodin, however, has argued that we should define terrorism in terms of what makes the paradigm cases morally problematic. As he sees it, we need 'a clear and coherent understanding of what the *morally relevant features* of terrorism are'.[5] To this end, we should seek a 'moral definition' of terrorism by beginning with the question of why the 'core instances of terrorism' (what I am calling the paradigms) are morally problematic, and then defining as terrorism those things that share the identified wrong-making properties.[6]

It should be clear from what I have said, however, that this definitional strategy—while valuable in a number of ways—will not serve for arriving at a public definition of terrorism. What drives the essential contestability of a concept such as terrorism is precisely the fact that different constituencies disagree about which features of the paradigms justify the negative appraisal that accompanies the term's use. That is,

[5] David Rodin, 'Terrorism without Intention', *Ethics* 114 (2004), pp. 752–71 (752); italics are mine.

[6] Ibid., p. 753.

contested definitions arise precisely because the strategy favored by Rodin is invoked. Acknowledging essential contestability is supposed to allow for *competing* moral definitions so as to prevent one account of terrorism's chief wrong-making property from silencing, by definitional fiat, those who would locate the central moral problem elsewhere.

While offering moral definitions as Rodin does is thus *constitutive* of what we might call the 'language game' of terrorism, employing this definitional strategy in order to arrive at a *public* definition is dangerous. A precise, stipulative public definition may well be required for public policy purposes, but it ought not to stifle the ongoing moral discourse facilitated by the concept's essential contestability. To privilege *one* of the competing moral definitions in that discourse over others by making it *the* definition for public policy purposes cannot help but stifle the discourse that essential contestability is supposed to protect.[7]

How, then, should we arrive at a public definition? My proposal is that, insofar as a public definition is required for formulating coherent public policy responses to a class of problems or threats to society, *pragmatic usefulness for developing such responses* may be the most salient basis for forming such a definition. What a public definition ought to do, on my view, is to identify a class of problematic phenomena which is such that (A) the relevant paradigms belong to the class; (B) phenomena in this class can be addressed under a reasonably unified public policy rubric; and (C) phenomena in this class are not adequately addressed under existing policies targeting other established classes of phenomena.

Criterion (A) serves to ensure minimal fidelity to ordinary usage. Even if ordinary usage cannot provide us with an adequate definition, any definition that is to guide public policy must at least be *consonant* with ordinary usage in the *minimal sense* that it cannot include things within its scope that no one would call terrorism (such as nonviolent acts), nor exclude *paradigms* of terrorism.[8] With respect to the latter, it is particularly important to keep in mind the context within which

[7] It should be clear that this is not intended as a criticism of Rodin, since Rodin nowhere recommends that his proposed definition serve as *the* public definition of terrorism.

[8] Walter Sinnot-Armstrong makes fruitful use of essentially this criterion in his critique of Primoratz's definition of terrorism. See his 'On Primoratz's Definition of Terrorism', *Journal of Applied Philosophy* 8 (1991), pp. 115–20.

anti-terrorism policies are introduced. In post-9/11 America, there is little doubt that when 'terrorism' is uttered, what come to mind first are the coordinated attacks on the World Trade Center and the Pentagon (even if other paradigms, such as the bombing of the Murrah Building in Oklahoma City, remain vivid in the American consciousness). And when the Bush administration launched its 'war on terrorism', it presented itself to the American public as initiating a concerted public policy effort to bring to an end the *kind* of phenomenon exemplified in the 9/11 attacks. Thus, for the sake of guiding public policy in post-9/11 America (and for evaluating the efficacy of the Bush administration's policies), we need a definition of terrorism that is especially suited *to these attacks*.

But the 9/11 attacks are not the only terrorism paradigms. And even if we cannot include within our definition everything that is called terrorism in ordinary use, a public definition would be improved to the extent that it can at least encompass all the *paradigms*. Achieving this aim is complicated by the fact that there are a diversity of paradigms, ranging from the lone pipe-bombing campaign of the reclusive Unabomber, to the coordinated efforts of Al Qaeda in the 9/11 attacks, to the French 'Reign of Terror'. The aim of preserving minimal fidelity to ordinary usage may therefore come into some tension with criterion (B). A public policy initiative that may be effective in response to one paradigm may not be effective in response to another.

Hence, to define 'terrorism' in a way that is helpful in shaping public policies *while* respecting ordinary usage enough to encompass all the paradigms, we may need to specify subtypes, or *kinds* of terrorism. And a public policy response to *one* kind of terrorism should not be represented as targeting terrorism in *every* sense. For example, the current 'war on terrorism' is represented as a concerted public policy effort to reduce or eliminate *the kind of thing exemplified in the 9/11 attacks*. To treat public support for such a policy as *carte blanche* permission to target terrorism of every kind would be a mistake, as would supposing that policies suited to reducing terrorism of the given kind are equally suited to eliminating terrorism of other kinds.

Turning to (C), this criterion reminds us that if public policy is going to be shaped by the imperative to fight terrorism, then 'terrorism' must denote a *particular kind* of violent threat to public welfare *distinct from other species of violence* for which there already exist established and effective public policy programs and institutions. Specifically, terrorism must be distinguished from criminal violence and acts of war.

'Terrorism' as a public category makes sense only if there is a distinctive class of violence not adequately addressed through conventional criminal justice and military institutions.[9] In the absence of such a distinctive class of violence, the use of 'terrorism' in public discourse becomes *merely* polemical. It ceases to be a useful concept for public policy purposes (which would be better served by reclassifying the things we call terrorism into the categories of 'crime' and 'acts of war'). And so, even if a public account recognizes distinct kinds of terrorism, these kinds should ideally fall under an overarching definition that identifies how terrorism of every kind is distinct (in a pragmatically salient way) from both ordinary criminal violence and acts of war.

In what follows, I construct a public definition of terrorism with these criteria in mind. By treating terrorism as a species of violence, I avoid including within the scope of the concept things that no one, in ordinary usage, would call terrorism.[10] In terms of including all of the agreed paradigms, my task is more challenging for reasons noted above. Given the current sociopolitical and historical context, a public definition should aim to be especially suited for framing public policy responses to the class of phenomena exemplified in the 9/11 attacks. Hence, I am most interested in offering a definition for the 'kind' of terrorism at issue in the ongoing 'war on terrorism'. But I will locate this kind under a broader definition which, as I will argue, specifies a distinct class of threats not adequately addressed by standard criminal justice and military institutions.

The Inadequacy of Traditional Defining Characteristics

Philosophical definitions of terrorism have tended to emphasize one or more of the following characteristics:[11] (1) It directly targets civilians/

---

[9] I believe that there is such a class (and it is partly for this reason that I view the very literal way in which the current administration is pursuing its 'war' on terrorism to be gravely misguided).

[10] Carl Wellman's contention that terrorism may be nonviolent *defies* ordinary use, and is problematic for precisely this reason. His is a technical philosophical definition that might have some value as a stipulative definition in some contexts, but will only be confusing if offered up as a public definition. See C. Wellman, 'On Terrorism Itself', *Journal of Value Inquiry* 13 (1979), pp. 250–58 (251).

[11] I leave out two characteristics that have sometimes appeared in official definitions of terrorism, namely that the violence is perpetrated by subnational groups and that the violence is illegal or illegitimate. I exclude these from consideration because they have both been subjected to compelling philosophical criticism in the literature.

noncombatants;[12] (2) It seeks to achieve some goal by creating terror in a population;[13] (3) It directly targets one victim in order to coerce another;[14] (4) It aims to achieve some political goal—especially that of 'destabilizing (or maintaining) an existing political or social order';[15] (5) It aims to call public attention to the perpetrator's cause.[16] Are any of these suitable candidates for constructing a public definition of terrorism?

Brief reflection should reveal that none of (1)–(5) is *singly* sufficient to distinguish terrorism from both criminal violence and acts of war.[17] While some *combination* might be sufficient, the deeper problem is

---

[12] Coady offers a good example of a definition of terrorism that emphasizes this characteristic. He defines terrorism as 'A political act, ordinarily committed by an organized group, which involves the intentional killing or other severe harming of non-combatants or the threat of the same or intentional severe damage to the property of non-combatants or the threat of the same'. See his essay, 'The Morality of Terrorism', *Philosophy* 60 (1985), pp. 47–69 (52). Primoratz's definition of terrorism emphasizes innocence, rather than noncombatant status, but it seems that by 'innocence' he intends roughly the same as Coady intends by 'concombatant' (see esp. Igor Primoratz, 'What is Terrorism?', *Journal of Applied Philosophy* 7 (1990), pp. 129–138 (p. 131). The difficulty with defining terrorism in terms of innocence is that, as J. Angelo Corlett has recently pointed out, most terrorists perceive their targets to be wrongdoers (even if they are not combatants). See Corlett, *Terrorism: A Philosophical Analysis* (Dordrecht, Netherlands: Kluwer Academic, 2003), p. 117.

[13] The creation of terror features prominently in both Carl Wellman's definition and Martin Hughes's understanding. See Wellman, 'On Terrorism Itself', *Journal of Value Inquiry* 13 (1979), pp. 250–58, and Hughes, 'Terrorism and National Security', *Philosophy* 57 (1982), pp. 5–26. Primoratz agrees that the creation of terror is an important characteristic of terrorism, but does not treat it as a defining characteristic. See Primoratz, 'What is Terrorism?' p. 134.

[14] In line with both Wellman and Primoratz, Claudia Mills distinguishes terrorist coercion from other forms of coercion by characterizing terrorism as 'third-party' coercion: A attacks C in order to coerce B. See Mills, 'The Distinctive Wrong of Terrorism', *International Journal of Applied Philosophy* 10 (1995), pp. 57–60.

[15] Corlett emphasizes this feature in his definition of terrorism. See Corlett, *Terrorism*, p. 119. He is here following Burleigh Taylor Wilkins, *Terrorism and Collective Responsibility* (London: Routledge, 1992), p. 6.

[16] Again, see Corlett, *Terrorism*, p. 119.

[17] (1) is typical of criminal violence. (2) is typical of many military tactics that seek to demoralize the enemy forces and the civilian population through displays of terrifying force (consider the 'shock and awe' strategy that launched the US invasion of Iraq in 2003). (3) is not uncommon in ordinary criminal violence (for example, kidnapping for ransom, or threatening a spouse or child in order to get a victim to unlock a safe). (4) is characteristic of many if not most wars (consider the goal of 'regime change' that motivated the Iraq war). (5) is probably not uncommon of military acts in the early stages of a revolutionary war, and can also be observed in certain acts of criminal violence. Consider a man who, outraged because his son is being denied medical coverage for a potentially life-saving experimental treatment, publicly murders an executive at his HMO while shouting, 'This is what you are doing to my son!'

that none seems *necessary*—that is, none would extend to all the things that we would like to include within a public definition. (1) would exclude the attack on the U.S.S. Cole and the 1983 suicide bombing of the Marine barracks in Lebanon.[18] More significantly, insofar as the Pentagon is arguably not a civilian target, we have the problematic result of treating the 2001 attack on the World Trade Center as an act of terrorism, but not similarly treating the tandem attack on the Pentagon. In general, two violent acts, one targeting civilians and the other targeting the military, may be sufficiently similar that they should be treated under the same policy guidelines. To make the targeting of civilians the chief defining characteristic of terrorism would therefore compromise the pragmatic usefulness of a public definition.

(2)–(5) all identify objectives (intermediate or final) that perpetrators of terrorist violence intend to achieve (creating fear, coercing a third party, destabilizing or maintaining some political order, or publicizing a cause). With respect to each, we can apply C.A. Coady's objection to defining terrorism in terms of the intent to cause terror. As Coady puts it, when we do so 'we are prejudging an empirical investigation into the specific motives' of terrorists.[19] Suppose that when Timothy McVeigh blew up the Murrah building in Oklahoma City, his intent was not to inspire fear in a population but to *punish* the federal government for infringing on civil liberties. Would we be willing to say, on learning these motives, that the Oklahoma City bombing was, after all, not an act of terrorism? Clearly not. Hence, (2) is not necessary.

We can argue along similar lines with respect to (3)–(5). With respect to (3), it is helpful to consider Claudia Card's recent discussion of the 9/11 attacks in terms of Carl Wellman's definition of terrorism—according to which an act is terrorist if it directly harms one target in order to coerce another. Card, noting the ambiguity of the motives behind the 9/11 attacks, argues that 'if the attacks' intent was not coercive but was, say, punitive, or if it was simply to show the world that the United States is not invulnerable, then the deed was not basically terrorist, in Wellman's sense'.[20] But surely the proper conclusion to reach here is that Wellman's definition is defective, not that the 9/11 attacks

[18] Held thinks the attack on the Marine barracks in Lebanon is 'among the leading candidates for inclusion' within the scope of the concept, and that its exclusion would be 'arbitrary'. Held, 'Terrorism, Rights, and Political Goals', p. 225.

[19] Coady, 'The Morality of Terrorism', p. 53.

[20] Card, 'Making War on Terrorism', p. 173.

wouldn't be terrorism if these proposed motives proved correct. To be minimally consonant with ordinary usage (at least ordinary usage post-9/11), the 9/11 attacks *must* count as terrorism regardless of what the motives of the terrorists might turn out to be. And for the purposes of shaping contemporary public policy responses to terrorism, the 9/11 attacks must be included within the scope of a public definition for the simple reason that these public policy responses to terrorism are fundamentally conceived as responses to the kind of thing exemplified in the 9/11 attacks.

But if all of this is right, then terrorism needs to be defined without reference to the specific motives of terrorists. And if that is so, then neither (4) nor (5) will be a necessary characteristic of terrorism either.

The reason why none of (1)–(5) appear to be necessary *might* be because the extension of 'terrorism' is determined by Wittgensteinian family resemblances, such that no common feature is to be found *even among paradigm cases*. In fact, however, I think the paradigms of terrorism widely share a common characteristic that can also serve to distinguish terrorism from both criminal violence and acts of war. In the next section, I discuss this characteristic and, on the basis of it, propose a definition that is broadly inclusive of terrorism paradigms.

The Terrorist Principle of Discrimination

Those who define terrorism in terms of the targeting of civilians are, I think, on the right track. But for reasons already mentioned, their definition does not quite work. My alternative proposal is this: what makes an act terrorist is not the *fact* that civilians are targeted, but rather the fact that targets of terrorist violence are selected according to a distinctive principle of discrimination, one which bears a superficial similarity to that endorsed in just war theory but differs crucially in that it includes civilians within the class of legitimate targets.

A review of the just war principle of discrimination may be helpful here. In so-called 'just' wars, *three* principles actually operate in selecting targets. The first is that acts of war are directed against some opposing *group* as a whole. Thus, in order to be a legitimate target, you must be a member or agent of the group (usually a nation) against which war is waged. But in just war, mere membership in the targeted group is insufficient. The second principle for selecting targets, which is what is typically referred to as the principle of discrimination, distinguishes between legitimate targets and illegitimate targets according to combatant status. Only if you are a combatant may you be directly targeted (although it might be permissible to kill noncombatants as a side-effect of attacking military targets). The third principle, what might be called a principle of efficacy, chooses which of the legitimate targets to actually attack based on the extent to which doing so furthers the goals of the war.

There is a sense in which the targeting of enemy combatants in war is *morally* indiscriminate: there need not be anything special about *this* combatant (who is attacked) that distinguishes him or her in any morally relevant way from another combatant (who is not attacked). Combatant targets are typically selected for strategic or tactical reasons, not by virtue of any special moral desert that distinguishes them from other legitimate targets. Along these same lines, one is not in the class of legitimate targets because one is an *actual* threat. One is a member of that class because one has a designated role in the prosecution of the war, a role whose faithful execution *would* pose a threat. Thus, a soldier who consistently shoots to miss is still a legitimate target.

Terrorism, like war, is directed against an enemy group as a whole. But what distinguishes terrorism from war waged according to just war conventions is that membership in the enemy group is treated as sufficient to render one a legitimate target. In other words, legitimate targets are distinguished, not by virtue of whether they occupy a combatant role, but by virtue of their membership in an enemy group *that admits of a diversity of roles, including noncombatant roles that do not pose any direct threat to the lives of terrorists or those on whose behalf the terrorists perceive themselves as acting.*

The targeted group might be a nation or a group defined by such properties as ethnicity, nationality, race, gender, sexual orientation, religion, or even participation in a given economic system. What is crucial is that the criterion of group membership is *not* that one occupies a role whose function is to cause harm to the terrorists (or those close to them). One isn't a member of the enemy group because one is a combatant whose role poses a direct threat to terrorists (or those on whose behalf they see themselves as acting). Rather, one is a member of the enemy group because one is Jewish, or American, or a citizen of a capitalist nation—some group marker that encompasses a variety of roles, many of which pose no direct threat to anyone.[21]

As in war, it is the group taken as a collective that is the main or primary target of terrorism, not the individuals who are directly attacked. This distinguishes terrorism from ordinary criminal violence. But unlike in war (at least 'just' war), relevant group membership is taken as sufficient to render one a legitimate target. Specific targets are chosen for attack, not by virtue of some special moral property that distinguishes them from other members of the group, but by virtue of accessibility, symbolic value, or other strategic considerations. Membership in the targeted group, like combatant status in just war theory, is thus treated as decisive grounds for forfeiture of the ordinary moral right not to be harmed. Subsequent selection of targets is morally (but not strategically) indiscriminate.

Since the *group* is the ultimate target of terrorism, the effect on the immediate targets is not the primary effect sought. The real goal is some effect on the group conceived as a whole. In this respect, immediate victims are mere instruments, and the violence directed against them is instrumental. But it is instrumental only in the minimal sense that it aims to produce some effect on the broader group to which the immediate victims belong. The effect might be to coerce the group's leaders into making decisions favored by the terrorists, or to disrupt the group's political structure, or to perpetuate the group's subordinated status—but it might also be something as abstract as humiliating the group or exacting vengeance. In fact, the violence might not be construed as instrumental *by the terrorists*, insofar as there may be *a metaphysical reification of the group* such that its members are viewed as parts of a whole, and an attack on one part is instrumentally directed towards harming the whole only because one cannot strike every part of the whole at once. If I take harming you to be valuable in itself, but I can only reach your little finger, when I break your little finger I will not conceive of the act as merely instrumental. Nevertheless, it is instrumental in the sense that my aim or goal is not to injure your little finger (I have nothing special against *it*). I injure your little finger in order to harm *you*.

[21] Interestingly, if I despise soldiers and seek to terrorize soldiers everywhere through selective executions, I am a terrorist even though my targets are all combatants. The reason is that, unless all soldiers everywhere have been formally mobilized to seek me out and destroy me, it is not the case that all members of the group I have targeted occupy a role whose explicit function involves directly threatening me.

Even when the violence is conceived of as instrumental by the terrorists, this does not mean that the *immediate targets* are seen as instruments for influencing some other target. I might twist back your left little finger in the hope of coercing you to stop hitting me with your right fist. In this case the violence is clearly instrumental, but I conceive of the act as attacking *you* in order to get *you* to change your behavior—even though your little finger is not striking me, and even though it is not your little finger that is responsible for choosing whether to continue hitting me. Analogously, even though a terrorist attack on civilians may aim to coerce the group's leaders, the attack is still an attack *on the group* to achieve an effect *on the group*. The common idea that one immediate but secondary target is directly attacked in order to affect an indirect but primary target[22] fails to appreciate that terrorism is directed against a group *as a whole*, even if the part attacked is not the same as the part in which a practical effect is sought. Metaphysical reification of the group may be what ultimately justifies the terrorist principle of discrimination, as well as explaining the motivational connection between the choice of target and the effect sought.

With these considerations in mind, we can define terrorism as follows:

> 'Terrorism' is any act or pattern of violence such that (a) the primary or ultimate target is a group *conceived of as a whole*; (b) the immediate targets are members of the targeted group; (c) membership in the targeted group is regarded as sufficient to render one a legitimate target; (d) the violence against targeted group members is instrumental to producing some effect on the group conceived of as a whole (which *may* mean influencing the group's perceived leadership).

I will call this the 'group-target' definition of terrorism. Defined in this way, terrorism turns out to be closely related to the concept of collective violence as developed by John Ladd in 'The Idea of Collective Violence'.[23] In fact, I would like to suggest that terrorism can be construed as a *species* of collective violence in Ladd's sense. Exploring this possibility will both shed light on the group-target definition and introduce some ideas that will be useful, in a later section, for addressing its pragmatic value.

---

[22] This idea is endorsed by Wellman, Primoratz, Mills and Card. A particularly concise formulation of it is offered by Primoratz, 'What is Terrorism?', p. 131.

[23] John Ladd, 'The Idea of Collective Violence', in Brady and Garver, *Justice, Law, and Violence*, pp. 19–47.

Terrorism as Ideological Violence

Ladd defines collective violence as 'violence that is practiced by one group on another and that pertains to individuals, as agents or as victims, only by virtue of their (perceived) association with a particular group'.[24] Perpetrators of collective violence act as agents of a group, and their targets are chosen, not for any individual characteristics they possess, but by virtue of their perceived membership in the targeted group.

As Ladd sees it, perpetrators of collective violence typically rationalize their acts according to a distinctive ideological framework, which he sketches out in terms of five key 'premises' or 'doctrines': (i) the Doctrine of Bifurcation, according to which the world is divided into two groups—a 'Chosen Group' and an 'Other Group'—that are 'irretrievably separated and divided';[25] (ii) the Doctrine of Moral Disqualification, according to which members of the Other Group are perceived as 'moral outcasts' who 'lack the minimum attributes necessary for being members of the moral community, or even for being human';[26] (iii) the Doctrine of the Double Standard, which establishes two distinct moralities, one for interactions with those who belong to the Chosen Group and hence to the moral community (a standard that demands respect and concern), and a different one for interactions with Others, who fall outside the moral community and may thus be treated in ways that would never be permitted in relation to the Chosen;[27] (iv) the Doctrine of Group Mission, 'which assigns a plenary mission, often divinely commanded, to the members of the Chosen Group to protect the Chosen Group and its values from perceived threats to it by the Other Group';[28] and (v) the Doctrine of Zero-Sum Struggle, according to which the two groups are 'locked in a conflict for which compromise or reconciliation are absolutely inconceivable', and which is such that the flourishing of one group can only be achieved by the defeat or destruction of the other.[29]

Ladd stresses that agents of collective violence do not see themselves as private individuals acting for private reasons, but as agents of the

[24] Ibid., p. 19.
[25] Ibid., p. 40.
[26] Ibid.
[27] Ibid., pp. 40–41.
[28] Ibid., p. 41.
[29] Ibid. Ladd does not name this fifth premise. I do so here to preserve parallel structure.

Chosen Group acting on behalf of that group and ready to sacrifice themselves for the sake of the group mission. This feature of collective violence may at first seem to offer a point of contrast with terrorism as I'm defining it here. On the group-target definition, there is at least no *explicit* requirement that the perpetrators see themselves as agents of a group. Given the group-target definition, terrorism requires the existence of an 'Other Group' that is the target of terrorist violence, but it does not clearly demand a 'Chosen Group' on whose behalf the terrorist acts. A terrorist might be a loner such as Theodore Kaczynski.

But there may be a sense in which even the lone terrorist is acting as an agent: the terrorist is acting for a cause that is perceived to be greater than personal welfare, a cause that *at least in principle* could serve as a rallying point for others. While this cause might not be the welfare of some group (it might be, say, the glory of God), it nevertheless seems to be true that those who share the terrorist's cause (and do not fall into the targeted group) constitute a kind of chosen group on whose behalf the terrorist acts. This idea is supported by the fact that Kaczynski, even though he was a hermit who acted entirely alone, *represented* himself to the world as an agent of a group called 'F.C.' (probably short for 'Freedom Club' or 'Freedom Collective') in his famous manifesto, 'Industrial Society and its Future'.[30]

The Unabomber example raises an interesting possibility: In order to act on the group-target principle of discrimination, it may be psychologically if not theoretically necessary to absorb, in a general way, the identity of individuals into their group affiliations.[31] In order to target individuals simply by virtue of their group memberships, terrorists may need to see the world in terms of groups, and see individuals as nothing more than agents of those groups—a perception that extends not only to their targets, but inevitably to themselves. Something like the ideology sketched by Ladd may offer the *Weltanschauung* necessary for acting on a group-target principle of discrimination.

But another basis for acting on a group-target principle of discrimination may also be possible—specifically, Michael Walzer's doctrine of *supreme emergency*. For Walzer, when a political community faces a dire threat to its existence from an enemy group, it may—when the

[30] See Kirkpatrick Sale, 'The Unabomber's Secret Treatise: Is There Method in his Madness?' *The Nation* 261 (25 September 1995), pp. 305–311.

[31] Some may wonder whether Theodore Kaczynski actually followed the group-target principle of discrimination. On this, see my discussion in the next section.

threat is imminent and there is no other way to overcome it—set aside the ordinary injunction against targeting noncombatants.[32] Thus, Walzer offers a restricted justification for engaging in terrorism in the group-target sense.

What is interesting about Walzer's doctrine is that, while it makes no explicit commitment to premises (i)–(iii) of Ladd's ideological framework, it endorses premises (iv) and (v). A 'supreme emergency' exists when the political community has a solemn duty to preserve itself from a dire and imminent threat posed by an enemy group, and the nature of the threat is so extreme and intractable that nothing short of inflicting dire harms on the enemy, without regard for traditional distinctions, has any hope of saving the community. Stated inversely, premises (iv) and (v) of Ladd's framework essentially amount to the claim that a supreme emergency in Walzer's sense obtains. Premises (i)–(iii) serve the preparatory role of rendering indiscriminate attacks *permissible* by virtue of the subhuman status of the enemy.

Walzer, by contrast, makes no attempt to dehumanize the enemy so as to justify violence under conditions of supreme emergency. For him, what serves this role is 'the rule of necessity (and necessity knows no rules)'.[33] It is worth noting, however, that Walzer's chief example of a supreme emergency is the threat posed by the Nazis during the Second World War. And, according to Walzer, the Nazis were an enemy group organized in terms of and committed to 'an ideology and a practice of domination so murderous, so degrading even to those who might survive, that the consequences of its final victory were literally beyond calculation, immeasurably awful'.[34] Thus, while the enemy group may not be morally disqualified in the way Ladd envisions, the enemy group distinguishes itself in a morally relevant way from other groups—namely, by its collective commitment to evil so profound as to be *incalculable*.

Perhaps, then, what is most essential to the ideological framework that Ladd sketches out is that it establishes both that (a) the Other Group poses a threat to the Chosen Group that amounts to a supreme emergency and (b) traditional moral constraints against harming the innocent are waived in relation to the Other Group. As Walzer's

[32] See Michael Walzer, *Just and Unjust Wars* (New York: Basic Books, 2nd edn, 1992), especially pp. 251–54.
[33] Ibid., p. 254.
[34] Ibid., p. 253.

thinking demonstrates, (b) might well be thought to follow from (a) *without* additional ideological premises. However, it may be *psychologically* necessary for those engaged in indiscriminate violence against a group to embrace something like premises (i)–(iii).

Even if this is *not* the case, what this review of Walzer suggests is that collective violence in general, and group-target terrorism in particular, requires its practitioners to embrace something substantially similar to Ladd's premises—at least (iv) and (v) and probably some premises that do the work that (i)–(iii) do for Ladd. We might say that, for Walzer, the *truth* of an ideology of this sort is what gives rise to the condition of supreme emergency.[35]

I say that terrorism on the group-target definition can be construed as a *species* of collective violence, rather than a synonym for it, because collective violence seems to be a broader category. First, those who adhere to an ideology of collective violence, while their ultimate target will be the enemy group as a whole, *may* nevertheless restrict themselves to targeting only enemy combatants. Imagine a warring nation whose dominant ideology in relation to the enemy nation fits with the ideology outlined by Ladd. But imagine that its soldiers are strictly trained to target only enemy combatants—purely out of allegiance to international treaties that bar targeting civilians. In such a case, what rules out the legitimacy of civilian targets has nothing to do with the moral qualities of enemy civilians. The commitment to the principle of noncombatant immunity is, in this case, purely formal. Given their substantive beliefs about the vitiated moral status of all members of the enemy nation, their war effort is collective violence in Ladd's sense. But it is not terrorism.

Furthermore, it is part of my definition that a *part* of the group is targeted in order to affect the whole. In this respect terrorism differs from a campaign of extermination in which the objective is to directly target *every* part in order to *eliminate* the whole. The Nazi 'final solution' was *worse* than terrorism. Sometimes, the only reason terrorism does not rise to the level of genocide may be because the terrorists lack the power to pursue the latter; but it might also be because the

35 Although I doubt Walzer would be happy with labeling as 'ideology' a set of beliefs entailing the existence of a supreme emergency, the fact that many such belief sets *are* merely ideological seems clear enough. Hence, I will follow Ladd's lead in calling the beliefs that justify the group-target principle of discrimination ideological, but with the understanding that these beliefs being true is not thereby strictly ruled out.

terrorists' goals are less extreme than extermination (for example, territorial expulsion).

Respect for Ordinary Usage

My claim is that the group-target definition of terrorism is particularly suitable as a public definition for the following reasons: (a) It respects ordinary usage by encompassing the dominant contemporary paradigms of terrorism, including the Unabomber attacks, the Oklahoma City bombing, the 1998 Omagh car bombing in Northern Ireland, the 9/11 attacks, ongoing suicide bombings in Israel (such as the August 2004 suicide bombings of two buses in Beersheba), the 2002 nightclub bombings in Bali, the public transit bombings in Madrid (in March 2004) and London (July 2005), etc.; (b) It identifies a common feature of these paradigms that distinguishes them in important ways from ordinary criminal acts and acts of war, thereby facilitating the development of public policy responses uniquely suited to a class of violence not adequately addressed by existing policies aimed at criminal violence and acts of war.

I begin with a consideration of (a). To comprehensively demonstrate (a)—that is, to show that the group-target definition encompasses most or all of the paradigmatic terrorism cases—I would need to examine each such case, in part by contextualizing the individual attacks within the broader practices and ideologies of those responsible. Such an examination falls outside the scope of this essentially philosophical essay, but I suspect that (a) is sufficiently plausible, given what is generally known and suspected about these attacks and their perpetrators, that a somewhat less comprehensive review is sufficient here.

Specifically, I want to highlight the fact that the paradigms of terrorism most vivid in our public consciousness typically fit a common model characterized by two criteria: First, they are perpetrated by subnational groups engaged in ongoing ideological conflicts with other groups (the 'Real' IRA, the various militant groups such as Hamas organized to oppose Israel, the radical Islamist groups such as al-Qaeda and Jemaah Islamiah, etc.). Second, these groups routinely ignore the combatant/noncombatant distinction (even though they sometimes target combatants) in the pursuit of their goals. We might call this the 'extremist group model' of terrorism. The group-target definition of terrorism obviously extends to exemplars of terrorism corresponding to this model, and thus extends readily to the most prominent paradigms of terrorism today, including the 9/11 attacks.

But some paradigms of terrorism deviate from the extremist group model, including such exemplars as the Oklahoma City bombing and the Unabomber attacks. Does the group-target definition encompass them? I think so, which is one reason I favor it over a definition in terms of characteristics unique to the extremist group model. While the groups targeted in the Oklahoma City bombing and the Unabomber attacks were not ones that are usually recognized as distinctive social groups, they nevertheless functioned in the attackers' psychologies in the same way that more conventionally recognized social groups function in the psychologies of, say, Palestinian terrorists. Timothy McVeigh clearly conceived of himself as targeting *the federal government*, construed as encompassing not only elected officials but employees in a federal building. For McVeigh, 'the federal government' took on the stature of an enemy group, so fully reified that an attack on a fairly remote federal building could be conceived of as a way to attack the group as such, to punish the federal government for its perceived wrongs.[36]

The case of Theodore Kaczynski, the so-called 'Unabomber', is more complicated. In his manifesto, Kaczynski sees his mission as the revolutionary dismantling of modern technological society. At stake, for Kaczynski, is the capacity of humans to live and flourish according to their nature, which Kaczynski claims is stifled by technological society. Thus, his self-conceived mission sets him up as a kind of liberator of *humanity*, and his enemy is an oppressive *system*.[37]

It might therefore seem as if Kaczynski's bombing campaign did not operate in terms of the group-target principle of discrimination. He was an agent of humanity attacking, not a group, but a *system*. But the fact is that even though Kaczynski styled himself a savior of humanity against a system that had taken on a life of its own, as he understood it

[36] There are a number of book-length examinations of Timothy McVeigh's psychological evolution into the person who carried out the Oklahoma City bombing. See especially Mark S. Hamm, *Apocalypse in Oklahoma: Waco and Ruby Ridge Revenged* (Boston: Northeastern University Press, 1997); and Lou Michel and Dan Herbeck, *American Terrorist: Timothy McVeigh and the Oklahoma City Bombing* (New York: HarperCollins, 2001). Both works dramatically reveal how the federal government came to be perceived, in McVeigh's eyes, as a monolithic evil force that needed to be violently opposed.

[37] Kaczynski's manifesto is widely available over the internet, and is available in monograph from Filiquarian Publishing.

the system is maintained and expanded by the activities of human beings. Human beings have, for Kaczinsky, been reduced to *components* of a vast machine. To destroy the machine, the key components—which include human beings—have to be targeted.[38] What we see, then, is a sophisticated variant of the group-targeting characteristic of terrorism. Kaczynski's ideology treats a system, constituted by human beings in connection with technological infrastructure, as a reified whole. It is this whole that he thinks must be destroyed, and the way to destroy it is to attack its parts, choosing targets based on strategic efficacy. Insofar as the targeted parts include human beings, and the whole is a system largely constituted by human beings organized in a certain way, the Unabomber case may actually highlight the value of the group-target definition as a tool for recognizing the motivations and convictions shaping a terrorist campaign.

A critic may worry, however, that the group-target definition fails to adequately capture ordinary usage, because it falls prey to the very same Coady-style challenge I used to reject the adequacy of definitions that rely on characteristics (2)–(5). Earlier, I argued that numerous attempts to define terrorism are inadequate because they prejudge terrorist motives. Insofar as the 9/11 attacks are the dominant paradigm of terrorism in the US, a definition of terrorism must extend reliably to these attacks, *whatever the motives of the perpetrators should turn out to be*. But wouldn't this also apply to the *principle of discrimination* employed by these terrorists? Whatever their principle of discrimination, or lack thereof, shouldn't the 9/11 attacks still qualify as terrorism?

Of course, these attacks would not have been perpetrated by anyone adhering to the principle of noncombatant immunity. Thus, that this principle was ignored can be known just by looking at the acts. But on

---

[38] In paragraphs 190 and 191 of his manifesto, 'Industrial Society and its Future' (available online at http://www.gseis.ucla.edu/~howard/Anarchism/Unabon/manifesto.html, accessed 13 November 2009), Kaczynski represents the fundamental human conflict as existing between 'the power-holding elite (which wields technology) and the general public (over which technology exerts its power)' (paragraph 191). Included within the 'power-holding elite' are 'politicians, scientists, upper-level business executives, government officials, etc.' (paragraph 190). The power-holding elite, while not only beneficiaries of the system but also victims of it, are nevertheless such integral components of the 'system' that needs to be destroyed that Kaczynski conceived them to be legitimate targets of violent attack. But their appropriateness as targets was not based on any personal fault of theirs, but rather their status as components of the system that needed to be destroyed.

the group-target view, terrorism is characterized not merely by the failure to apply the just war principle of discrimination, but also by the presence of an alternative principle that takes group membership as sufficient to render one a legitimate target. Does *this* requirement fall prey to the Coady-style challenge?

There is good reason to think that it does not. Consider the following examples. Suppose a plane is piloted into the World Trade Center by an enraged former employee of a company housed in the building, in a maddened attempt to kill his boss. Consider, alternatively, a case in which the plane is piloted by a schizophrenic driven by voices urging her to kill herself and take as many random people as possible with her, in order to feed the God of Death. The former has more in common with the case of the outraged former employee who goes on a killing spree in his former office than it does with the paradigms of terrorism. And the latter is an example of insanity culminating in a single act of inexplicable violence. In both of these cases, we are more inclined to call the acts 'mass murder' than we are to call them 'terrorism'.

These examples highlight an important relationship between terrorism and the creation of terror. On my definition, the creation of fear in a larger population needn't be an explicit part of the terrorist's intent. But insofar as terrorists consider anyone who belongs to a certain group to be a legitimate target, everyone in the targeted group has *reason* to fear (so long as the terrorists remain capable of inflicting harm). Terrorism tells all the members of a targeted group that *they could be next*. It does so because it treats membership in the targeted group as sufficient to render one a legitimate target. It is because the two examples above don't embody this feature that we're not inclined to call them terrorism, but rather cases of horrific criminal violence (or criminal insanity).

When America awoke to reports and images of the attacks on September 11, 2001, it soon became clear that *America* was under attack, and that *being an American* was sufficient to render one a legitimate target.[39] This fact was enough to justify calling the attacks terrorism, whatever their motives. Of course, we might have jumped to the same conclusion had it turned out that, by some strange coincidence, all in one morning two angry former World Trade Center employees had

[39] Although living in the middle of nowhere in Oklahoma meant that I was not a strategic target, and was probably safe.

independently hijacked planes, a schizophrenic had hijacked another plane and steered it towards the Pentagon, and a passenger enraged about delays had attacked the cockpit crew of a fourth plane, causing it to crash in Pennsylvania. But in that case, learning the truth would have led us to change our conclusion. Learning these facts, we'd say it wasn't terrorism after all.

In short, the group-target definition extends to what are arguably the most important contemporary paradigms of terrorism, and thus meets the condition of being minimally consonant with ordinary usage. What remains to be seen, then, is how pragmatically useful such a definition can be.

Reshuffling Categories: Terrorist Crimes and Wartime Terrorism

One concern regarding the pragmatic usefulness of the group-target definition is that, while it distinguishes terrorism from *most* criminal violence and acts of war, there is overlap in both categories—specifically, it encompasses hate crimes and such war-time military attacks as the fire-bombing of Dresden. A critic may worry that this overlap undermines the value of the definition for the purposes of framing a unified public policy response to a *distinctive* class of violence.

However, the fact that a stipulative public definition of terrorism requires some reshuffling with respect to other categories does not undermine the usefulness of the definition, but may actually contribute to producing more useful public definitions in the other categories. It has long been recognized that hate crimes differ importantly from more ordinary criminal violence, and cannot be satisfactorily addressed in the same ways.[40] Moving hate crimes out of the category of criminal violence committed for private reasons, and into a category that focuses on violence that targets groups, may be an improvement for the sake of formulating coherent public policy. Likewise, when armies stop attending to the principle of discrimination and begin attacking *any* member of the opposing nation, something fundamental has changed. Reflecting that change in our categories may be helpful: Warriors have become terrorists.

[40] As Ladd notes, to confuse the categories of private violence and collective violence, and to treat the latter as the former, 'is to dangerously miss the point and foolhardily lock oneself into a misdirected and inappropriate mode of response'. Ladd, 'The Idea of Collective Violence', p. 22.

But saying that a reshuffling of our categories *may* be helpful is not the same as showing that it is. A pragmatic defense of the group-target definition of terrorism calls for something more: a *reason* to think that such a reshuffling of categories *would* be helpful. I think there is such a reason. Specifically, public policy responses to violence, both criminal violence and international military threats, typically have two interrelated goals: the forceful incapacitation of the perpetrators and the concomitant deterrent effect on other potential or actual perpetrators. I will argue that the group-target definition picks out a class of violence which is such that primary reliance on these goals is likely to be counterproductive.

More precisely, the likelihood that pursuing these goals will be counterproductive is sufficiently high with respect to terrorism (as defined here) that there is *presumptive reason* to be suspicious of policies that adopt them as primary goals. While no one can deny that *some* cases of terrorism can be effectively addressed through standard incapacitation/deterrence strategies, there are uniquely powerful reasons to *suspect* the efficacy of such strategies in response to group-target terrorism. The group-target definition of terrorism thus picks out a class of violence about which we should be *uniquely cautious* when it comes to public policies that *rely* on these strategies.

To make this case, it will be useful first to consider why someone might reject the group-target definition on pragmatic grounds. Specifically, someone might argue that the most useful categorizing principle for developing public policy responses to violence is not the means whereby targets of violence are selected, but rather what I will call the *organizational character* of the perpetrators—that is, how the perpetrators organize themselves in relation to one another and to external constituencies.

Clearly, the organizational character of perpetrators matters for the sake of public policy. Violent perpetrators who act alone or in temporary collaboration with a few others pose a different kind of threat to society than do well-organized sub-national groups, let alone nation-states. How a society must respond to these distinctive threats is inevitably going to vary. But to treat this fact as reason to shape our most basic public categories of violence in terms of the organizational character of perpetrators betrays an implicit prejudice. It assumes that public policy responses to violence should rely primarily on the incapacitation of perpetrators through the use of force and on the deterrent effect that such forceful responses generate. When the main objective is incapacitation—capturing or killing perpetrators, disrupting their chains of command or communication, cutting off resources, etc.—knowing the organizational character of the perpetrators seems more important than knowing the principle of discrimination they use to select targets.[41] But if public policy focuses at least as much on preventing violent threats by *mitigating the underlying causal forces that generate them*, then understanding what motivates the selection of targets, and why these targets are seen as legitimate, may well prove to be the most important thing to know.

Before developing this latter point fully, we should recall that the group-target definition *can* accommodate the pragmatic need to pursue different methods of incapacitation depending on the organizational character of terrorists, by specifying distinct *species* of terrorism: independent-agent terrorism (exemplified by the Unabomber attacks and the Oklahoma City Bombing), sub-national group terrorism (exemplified by Hamas and Al Qaeda and the Real IRA), and state terrorism. Within state terrorism, one can identify two further subspecies: *external* state terrorism, which targets groups outside the state's established territories or sphere of influence (exemplified by civilian bombings during World War II); and *internal* state terrorism, which targets groups that reside within the state or its sphere of influence (exemplified by the attacks of Saddam Hussein's regime against the Kurds and Shiite majority in Iraq, and also by the 'Reign of Terror' that prevailed in post-revolutionary France, which gave us the term 'terrorism').

In other words, the group-target definition does not *preclude* making distinctions in terms of organizational character, distinctions that are useful for public policy purposes. The chief question, then, is whether it *offers* anything of particular value.

Here, it may help to note the dubiousness of assuming that the organizational character of violent perpetrators can be understood *apart* from the principles of discrimination they use to select targets. As noted above, what justifies the terrorist principle of discrimination will typically be either an ideology of the sort described by Ladd or a belief structure which shares many of its features (e.g., the view that a 'supreme emergency' in Walzer's sense obtains). Allegiance to such an

[41] Which is not to say that the latter is not relevant—for example, for the detectives seeking to anticipate a killer's next move.

ideology will play an important role in determining the organizational character of the terrorist group—not in terms of *formal* structures (which are more likely to be shaped by strategic concerns), but in terms of informal relationship networks with a broader community, networks that are crucial to both terrorist operations and recruitment efforts.

For example, if a terrorist group is *formally* organized into independent cells, with members of each cell having limited knowledge of other cells, this will likely be explained by the effort to preserve operations in the face of opponents with a capacity to infiltrate the group or apprehend and interrogate its members. But if these terrorist cells remain well hidden in part because a regional population sympathizes with and abets their cause, this fact may be better explained by common allegiance to the ideologies that justify the group-target principle of discrimination. The terrorists are protected and concealed by members of the broader community because they are viewed as *heroes*—and they are viewed as heroes rather than as criminals, despite their targeting of innocent civilians, because the broader community shares the ideological commitments which imply that these civilian targets are legitimate (because they are members of the enemy group and so deserve what they get).

And if membership in the terrorist group tends to increase as their 'enemy' becomes more aggressive in its interdiction efforts, this may be explained by recruitment practices that depend on sympathy with the terrorists' ideology. Terrorists may deliberately organize themselves such that aggressive efforts to incapacitate them will inevitably have 'collateral damage', injuring or killing members of the very group that the terrorists have identified as the chosen group caught in a zero-sum struggle with the enemy group. The anguish caused by such collateral damage may be exploited to inspire more widespread sympathy with the terrorists' ideology, thereby expanding the numbers of those who agree that the normal prohibition against targeting innocents in the enemy group can be waived. Even when terrorists do not deliberately *court* collateral damage in this way, the effect of mounting collateral damage will likely be the same. Ongoing conflicts between Palestinian terrorists and the state of Israel are instructive here.

These considerations lead directly to the most important reason why the group-target definition has pragmatic value: the policy of group-targeting offers *a presumptive reason to suspect the adequacy of responses that rely on standard incapacitation/deterrence strategies.* The scope of terrorist violence depends on how many potential and actual perpetrators accept its permissive principle of discrimination. And belief systems of the sort outlined by Ladd may be the primary tools for legitimating the group-target principle. But, as Ladd argues, these ideologies do not only legitimate violence against any member of the targeted group; they inculcate in the perpetrators a sense of purpose that transcends self-interest. These ideologies pit group against group in a manner that subordinates individual identity to group identity. And this subordination not only affects how terrorists think of their targets, but how they think of themselves. It follows that such violence often involves self-sacrifice for the sake of the group's mission. Terrorists can therefore be expected to act *selflessly* for the sake of the group and its goals.

And this means that standard public policies that rely on the deterrent power of forceful incapacitation are likely to backfire. Those who operate on a group-target principle of discrimination are so routinely willing to act against self-interest for the sake of their cause that they are hard to deter. Hence, policies reliant on forceful incapacitation cannot presuppose that deterrence will fill the gap of prevention where incapacitation efforts fall short. Primary reliance on such policies will therefore require an escalation in the scope of incapacitation: since the enemy group won't be deterred, the enemy must be *wiped out*. But such escalation is precisely what is most likely to make the ideological picture of a zero-sum struggle between enemy groups (or belief in the existence of a supreme emergency) more plausible to the broader population with whom the terrorists identify, especially when such escalation increases the severity of collateral damage. Such escalation can thus be expected to *increase* the number of prospective terrorists.

In sum, insofar as adherence to the group-target principle of discrimination indicates allegiance to ideologies of collective violence, it also indicates cases of violence in which perpetrators are unlikely to be deterred by forceful responses, in which reliance on force to prevent future attacks may thus require an escalated scope of incapacitation, and in which such an escalated scope of incapacitation can reasonably be expected to facilitate the creation of new prospective perpetrators. If all of this is right, public policy responses to terrorism may need to emphasize strategies aimed at *eliminating the conditions that inculcate allegiance to ideologies of collective violence*, rather than strategies aimed at incapacitating and deterring terrorists. This is not to say that incapacitation and deterrence will play *no* role in responses to terrorism, but rather that it will not play the primary role that it plays in response to other forms of violence.

The extent to which all of this is true may depend, in any given case, on the number of terrorists and the nascent support, in the broader population, for the ideology motivating them. If one or two terrorists act on an ideology for which there is little wider sympathy—as was arguably the case with respect both to Ted Kaczynski and to Timothy McVeigh and Terry Nichols—forceful interdiction may have few of the suggested counterproductive implications. A handful of terrorists with few public supporters conspiring to protect them might be effectively tracked down through standard detective and police work. Forceful interdiction will most likely take the form of criminal apprehension and prosecution, and so will be a *measured* response, with little collateral damage. But had either Kaczynski or McVeigh enjoyed significantly broader public sympathy (had there been a substantially wider audience of disaffected Luddites or Federal Government conspiracy theorists), responding to the threat they posed by *relying* on interdiction might well have taken a more dangerous turn.

Here, it is worth remembering that McVeigh's decision to bomb the Murrah Building was prompted by the siege and federal assault on the Branch Davidian complex in Waco, Texas (and to a lesser extent by the FBI raid on Ruby Ridge). McVeigh's ideology—according to which he was part of a noble struggle against an oppressive government, one that viewed the citizens' right to bear arms as the gravest threat to its totalitarian power—inspired him to identify with the Branch Davidians, who were targeted largely because of their weapons stockpile. Thus, even though the apprehension and execution of McVeigh did not apparently inspire others to take up his mission (presumably because the response was measured, had no collateral damage, and was strongly overshadowed by the horror of the bombing itself), there is a real sense in which the Federal Government's reliance on forceful incapacitation in the *Waco case* created the conditions that consolidated McVeigh and his co-conspirators in *their* ideology.[42]

Of course, the Branch Davidians were not terrorists, and the Waco assault was thus not a case of force-dependent antiterrorist policies

[42] Mark Hamm is especially useful in tracing out the development and entrenchment of McVeigh's terrorist ideology in response to the Bureau of Alcohol, Tobacco, and Firearm's assault on the Branch Davidian complex. See especially chapters 7–10 of *Apocalypse in Oklahoma*.

exacerbating terrorism. But insofar as the ideological affinity of the Branch Davidians to those with the potential for terrorist violence *played an instrumental role in turning these potential terrorists into real ones*, this example highlights the risks of blind reliance on forceful incapacitation, even in a society where we do not typically think that terrorism-prone ideologies are widespread.

In short, the effort to minimize violence that operates according to the group-target principle of discrimination requires a special awareness of the ideological affinities and sympathies that exist within society (or between and among societies), and a sensitivity to the ways that public policies affect those affinities and sympathies. Even though McVeigh was apprehended through standard police procedures, and even though his apprehension and execution did not (as far as we know) make of him an inspiring martyr or a brother to be avenged in the eyes of like-minded ideologues, the fact remains that in cases such as McVeigh's there is a special need to be sensitive to ideological affinities and sympathies. And this is true even if such sensitivity might culminate in the judgment that, in the particular case, conventional criminal justice policies will be appropriate to defuse the threat. My point is that such a judgment needs *defense* in the case of violence that fits the group-target definition. It cannot be assumed (as it is so routinely assumed with respect to other kinds of violence). For this reason more than any other, making a special category for this species of violence has particular pragmatic value.

BIBLIOGRAPHY

The *Journal of Moral Philosophy* originally published the essays in this collection. This bibliography lists the full contents of all articles published since the *JMP* was launched in April 2004. The *JMP* acceptance rate is about 7%.

Allen, Robert Francis, 'Robust Alternatives and Responsibility', *Journal of Moral Philosophy* 1(1) (2004), pp. 21–29.

Alm, David, 'Deontological Restrictions and the Good/Bad Asymmetry', *Journal of Moral Philosophy* 6(4) (2009), pp. 464–81.

Anderson, Scott A., 'Of Theories of Coercion, Two Axes, and the Importance of the Coercer', *Journal of Moral Philosophy* 5(3) (2008), pp. 394–422.

Andreou, Chrisoula, 'Standards, Advice, and Practical Reason', *Journal of Moral Philosophy* 3(1) (2006), pp. 57–67.

Bedi, Sonu, 'Expressive Exclusion: A Defense', *Journal of Moral Philosophy* 7(4) (2010), pp. 427–40.

Bennett, Christopher, 'Forgiveness and the Claims of Retribution', *Journal of Moral Philosophy* 1(1) (2004), pp. 89–101.

Bennett, Christopher, 'State Denunciation of Crime', *Journal of Moral Philosophy* 3(3) (2006), pp. 288–304.

Besser-Jones, Lorraine, 'Personal Integrity, Morality and Psychological Well-Being: Justifying the Demands of Morality', *Journal of Moral Philosophy* 5(3) (2008), pp. 361–83.

Besson, Samantha, 'Democracy, Law, and Authority', *Journal of Moral Philosophy* 2(1) (2005), pp. 89–99.

Bittner, Rüdiger, 'A Horse in the Basement: Nietzschean Reflections on Political Philosophy', *Journal of Moral Philosophy* 7(2) (2010), pp. 321–33.

Brake, Elizabeth, 'Rawls and Feminism: What Should Feminists Make of Liberal Neutrality?' *Journal of Moral Philosophy* 1(3) (2004), pp. 293–309.

- Reprinted in Thom Brooks and Fabian Freyenhagen (eds), *The Legacy of John Rawls*. New York: Continuum, 2005.

Brock, Gillian, 'The Difference Principle, Equality of Opportunity, and Cosmopolitan Justice', *Journal of Moral Philosophy* 2(3) (2005), pp. 333–51.

Broome, John, 'Does Rationality Consist in Responding Correctly to Reasons?' *Journal of Moral Philosophy* 4(3) (2007), pp. 349–74.

Brown, Stephen, 'Naturalized Virtue Ethics and the Epistemological Gap', *Journal of Moral Philosophy* 1(2) (2004), pp. 197–209.

Butler, Brian E., 'Rorty, the First Amendment and Antirealism: Is Reliance upon Truth Viewpoint-Based Speech Regulation?' *Journal of Moral Philosophy* 1(1) (2004), pp. 69–88.

Carens, Joseph, 'The Integration of Immigrants', *Journal of Moral Philosophy* 2(1) (2005), pp. 29–46.

Carter, Alan, 'The Evolution of Rawls's Justification of Political Compliance: Part 1 of The Problem of Political Compliance in Rawls's Theories of Justice', *Journal of Moral Philosophy* 3(1) (2006), pp. 7–21.

Carter, Alan, 'Political Liberalism and Political Compliance: Part 2 of The Problem of Political Compliance in Rawls's Theories of Justice', *Journal of Moral Philosophy* 3(2) (2006), pp. 135–57.

Clark, Michael, 'Retribution and Organic Unities', *Journal of Moral Philosophy* 3(3) (2006), pp. 351–58.

Choi, Yoon, 'Revisiting Kant's Ethics: Two Challenges to the Status Quo', *Journal of Moral Philosophy* 5(1) (2008), pp. 137–49.

Cholbi, Michael, 'A Kantian Defense of Prudential Suicide', *Journal of Moral Philosophy* 7(4) (2010), pp. 489–515.

Christie, Tim W., 'Natural Separateness: Why Parfit's Reductionist Account of Persons Fails to Support Consequentialism', *Journal of Moral Philosophy* 6(2) (2009), pp. 178–95.

Coyle, Sean, 'The Ideality of Law', *Journal of Moral Philosophy* 6(4) (2009), pp. 521–34.

Crisp, Roger, 'Ethics Without Reasons?' *Journal of Moral Philosophy* 4(1) (2007), pp. 40–49.

Cruft, Rowan, 'On the Non-instrumental Value of Basic Rights', *Journal of Moral Philosophy* 7(4) (2010), pp. 441–61.

D'Agostino, Fred, 'The Legacies of John Rawls', *Journal of Moral Philosophy* 1(3) (2004), pp. 349–65.

- Reprinted in Thom Brooks and Fabian Freyenhagen (eds), *The Legacy of John Rawls*. New York: Continuum, 2005.

Dancy, Jonathan, 'Defending the Right', *Journal of Moral Philosophy* 4(1) (2007), pp. 85–98.

DeGrazia, David, 'Moral Vegetarianism from a Very Broad Basis', *Journal of Moral Philosophy* 6(2) (2009), pp. 143–65.

de Muijnk, Wim, 'Thinking about Normativity: Ralph Wedgwood on "Ought"', *Journal of Moral Philosophy* 7(1) (2009), pp. 133–44.

Deonna, Julien A., 'The Structure of Empathy', *Journal of Moral Philosophy* 4(1) (2007), pp. 99–116.

Dietsch, Peter, 'Distributive Lessons from Division of Labour', *Journal of Moral Philosophy* 5(1) (2008), pp. 96–117.

Enoch, David and Ehud Guttel, 'Cognitive Biases and Moral Luck', *Journal of Moral Philosophy* 7(2) (2010), pp. 372–86.

Eylon, Yuval, 'Just Threats', *Journal of Moral Philosophy* 6(1) (2009), pp. 94–108.

Flikschuh, Katrin, 'Duty, Nature, Right: Kant's Response to Mendelssohn in *Theory and Practice III*', *Journal of Moral Philosophy* 4(2) (2007), pp. 223–41.

Friedman, Alex, 'Intransitive Ethics', *Journal of Moral Philosophy* 6(3) (2009), pp. 277–97.

Fuller, Lisa F., 'Poverty Relief, Global Institutions, and the Problem of Compliance', *Journal of Moral Philosophy* 2(3) (2005), pp. 285–97.

- Reprinted in Thom Brooks (ed.), *The Global Justice Reader*. Oxford: Blackwell, 2008.

Goddu, G. C., 'More on Blameworthiness and Alternative Possibilities', *Journal of Moral Philosophy* 3(1) (2006), pp. 69–75.

Grau, Christopher, 'Moral Status, Speciesism, and Liao's Genetic Account', *Journal of Moral Philosophy* 7(2) (2009), pp. 387–96.

Green, Michael, 'Social Justice, Voluntarism, and Liberal Nationalism', *Journal of Moral Philosophy* 2(3) (2005), pp. 265–83.

Hall, Timothy, 'Doing Harm, Allowing Harm, and Denying Resources', *Journal of Moral Philosophy* 5(1) (2008), pp. 50–76.

Harcourt, Edward, 'Crisp's "Ethics Without Reasons?": A Note on Invariance', *Journal of Moral Philosophy* 4(1) (2007), pp. 50–54.

Hayward, Tim, 'Thomas Pogge's Global Resources Dividend: A Critique and an Alternative', *Journal of Moral Philosophy* 2(3) (2005), pp. 317–32.

Hendrix, Burke A., 'Authenticity and Cultural Rights', *Journal of Moral Philosophy* 5(2) (2008), pp. 181–203.

Hills, Alison, 'Practical Reason, Value and Action', *Journal of Moral Philosophy* 4(3) (2007), pp. 375–92.

Hirose, Iwao, 'Aggregation and Non-Utilitarian Moral Theories', *Journal of Moral Philosophy* 4(2) (2007), pp. 273–84.

Hofmeyr, Benda, 'The Power Not to Be (What We Are): The Politics and Ethics of Self-creation in Foucault', *Journal of Moral Philosophy* 3(2) (2006), pp. 215–30.

Holroyd, Jules, 'Substantively Constrained Choice and Deference', *Journal of Moral Philosophy* 7(2) (2010), pp. 180–99.

Hookway, Christopher, 'Ethics and the Pragmatist Enlightenment', *Journal of Moral Philosophy* 3(2) (2006), pp. 231–36.

Hutton, Eric, 'Han Feizi's Criticism of Confucianism and Its Implications for Virtue Ethics', *Journal of Moral Philosophy* 5(3) (2008), pp. 423–53.

James, Aaron, 'Rights and Circularity in Scanlon's Contractualism', *Journal of Moral Philosophy* 1(3) (2004), pp. 367–74.

- Reprinted in Thom Brooks and Fabian Freyenhagen (eds), *The Legacy of John Rawls*. New York: Continuum, 2005.

Kaufman, Alexander, 'Rawls's Practical Conception of Justice: Opinion, Tradition and Objectivity in Political Liberalism', *Journal of Moral Philosophy* 3(1) (2006), pp. 23–43.

Kirchin, Simon, 'Moral Particularism: An Introduction', *Journal of Moral Philosophy* 4(1) (2007), pp. 8–15.

Kirchin, Simon, 'Particularism and Default Valency', *Journal of Moral Philosophy* 4(1) (2007), pp. 16–32.

Knight, Carl, 'Egalitarian Justice and Valuational Judgment', *Journal of Moral Philosophy* 6(4) (2009), pp. 482–98.

Knight, Kelvin, 'MacIntyre's Progress', *Journal of Moral Philosophy* 6(1) (2009), pp. 115–26.

Kristjánsson, Kristján, 'A Utilitarian Justification of Desert in Distributive Justice', *Journal of Moral Philosophy* 2(2) (2005), pp. 147–70.

Laden, Anthony Simon, 'Taking the Distinction between Persons Seriously', *Journal of Moral Philosophy* 1(3) (2004), pp. 277–92.

- Reprinted in Thom Brooks and Fabian Freyenhagen (eds), *The Legacy of John Rawls*. New York: Continuum, 2005.

Landemore, Hélène, 'Politics and the Economist-King: Is Rational Choice Theory the Science of Choice?' *Journal of Moral Philosophy* 1(2) (2004), pp. 177–96.

Landrum, Ty, 'Persons as Objects of Love', *Journal of Moral Philosophy* 6(4) (2009), pp. 417–39.

Lang, Gerald, 'Luck Egalitarianism, Permissible Inequalities, and Moral Hazard', *Journal of Moral Philosophy* 6(3) (2009), pp. 317–38.

Lefkowitz, David, 'Partiality and Weighing Harm to Non-Combatants', *Journal of Moral Philosophy* 6(3) (2009), pp. 298–316.

Lenard, Patti Tamara, 'Motivating Cosmopolitanism? A Skeptical View', *Journal of Moral Philosophy* 7(2) (2010), pp. 346–71.

Lenman, James, 'How to Live, What to Do: A Critical Study of Allan Gibbard, *Thinking How to Live*', *Journal of Moral Philosophy* 3(3) (2006), pp. 359–69.

Liao, S. Matthew, 'Time-Relative Interests and Abortion', *Journal of Moral Philosophy* 4(2) (2007), pp. 242–56.

Liao, S. Matthew, 'The Basis of Human Moral Status', *Journal of Moral Philosophy* 7(2) (2010), pp. 159–79.

Lippert-Rasmussen, Kasper, 'Publicity and Egalitarian Justice', *Journal of Moral Philosophy* 5(1) (2008), pp. 30–49.

Lippke, Richard L., 'Imprisonable Offenses', *Journal of Moral Philosophy* 3(3) (2006), pp. 265–87.

Lippke, Richard L., 'Punishing the Guilty, Not Punishing the Innocent', *Journal of Moral Philosophy* 7(4) (2010), pp. 462–88.

Ludwig, Bernd, 'Kant, Garve, and the Motives of Moral Action', *Journal of Moral Philosophy* 4(2) (2007), pp. 183–93.

Lynch, Sterling, 'The Fact of Diversity and Reasonable Pluralism', *Journal of Moral Philosophy* 6(1) (2009), pp. 70–93.

Mahoney, Jon, 'Public Reason and the Moral Foundation of Liberalism', *Journal of Moral Philosophy* 1(3) (2004), pp. 311–31.

- Reprinted in Thom Brooks and Fabian Freyenhagen (eds), *The Legacy of John Rawls*. New York: Continuum, 2005.

Marino, Patricia, 'Expressivism, Deflationism and Correspondence', *Journal of Moral Philosophy* 2(2) (2005), pp. 171–91.

Marino, Patricia, 'Moral Rationalism and the Normative Status of Desiderative Coherence', *Journal of Moral Philosophy* 7(2) (2010), pp. 227–52.

Martin, Rex, 'Twp Concepts of Rule Utilitarianism', *Journal of Moral Philosophy* 5(2) (2008), pp. 227–55.

Martin, Wayne, 'Hegel and the Philosophy of Food', *Journal of Moral Philosophy* 7(2) (2009), pp. 279–90.

Matravers, Matt, '"Who's Still Standing?" A Comment on Antony Duff's Preconditions of Criminal Liability', *Journal of Moral Philosophy* 3(3) (2006), pp. 320–30.

McKeever, Sean and Michael Ridge, 'Turning on Default Reasons', *Journal of Moral Philosophy* 4(1) (2007), pp. 55–76.

Merritt, Maria W., 'Aristotelian Virtue and the Interpersonal Aspect of Ethical Character', *Journal of Moral Philosophy* 6(1) (2009), pp. 23–49.

Mookherjee, Monica, 'Feminism and Multiculturalism—Putting Okin and Shachar in Question', *Journal of Moral Philosophy* 2(2) (2005), pp. 237–41.

Moyar, Dean, 'Unstable Autonomy: Conscience and Judgment in Kant's Moral Philosophy', *Journal of Moral Philosophy* 5(3) (2008), pp. 327–60.

Mulnix, M. J., 'Harm, Rights, and Liberty: Towards a Non-Normative Reading of Mill's Liberty Principle', *Journal of Moral Philosophy* 6(2) (2009), pp. 196–217.

Naticchia, Chris, 'The Law of Peoples: The Old and the New', *Journal of Moral Philosophy* 2(3) (2005), pp. 353–69.

- Reprinted in Thom Brooks and Fabian Freyenhagen (eds), *The Legacy of John Rawls*. New York: Continuum, 2005.

Nolan, Daniel, 'Consequentialism and Side Constraints', *Journal of Moral Philosophy* 6(1) (2009), pp. 5–22.

Norman, Richard, 'Particularism and Reasons: A Reply to Kirchin', *Journal of Moral Philosophy* 4(1) (2007), pp. 33–39.

Nussbaum, Martha C., 'Radical Evil in the Lockean State: The Neglect of the Political Emotions', *Journal of Moral Philosophy* 3(2) (2006), pp. 159–78.

O'Neill, Martin, 'The Facts of Inequality', *Journal of Moral Philosophy* 7(2) (2009), pp. 397–409.

O'Neill, Onora, 'Experts, Practitioners, and Practical Judgement', *Journal of Moral Philosophy* 4(2) (2007), pp. 154–66.

O'Neill, Onora, 'Normativity and Practical Judgement', *Journal of Moral Philosophy* 4(3) (2007), pp. 393–405.

Øverland, Gerhard, 'Self-defence among Innocent People', *Journal of Moral Philosophy* 2(2) (2005), pp. 127–46.

Øverland, Gerhard, 'Poverty and the Moral Significance of Contribution', *Journal of Moral Philosophy* 2(3) (2005), pp. 299–315.

Øverland, Gerhard, 'Conditional Threats', *Journal of Moral Philosophy* 7(2) (2010), pp. 334–45.

Papdaki, Lina, 'What is Objectification?' *Journal of Moral Philosophy* 7(1) (2010), pp. 16–36.

Peterson, Martin, 'The Mixed Solution to the Number Problem', *Journal of Moral Philosophy* 6(2) (2009), pp. 166–77.

Pink, Thomas, 'Normativity and Reason', *Journal of Moral Philosophy* 4(3) (2007), pp. 406–31.

Primoratz, Igor, 'Patriotism and Morality: Mapping the Terrain', *Journal of Moral Philosophy* 5(2) (2008), pp. 204–26.

Redondo, María Cristina, 'Legal Reasons: Between Universalism and Particularism', *Journal of Moral Philosophy* 2(1) (2005), pp. 47–68.
Reitan, Eric, 'Defining Terrorism for Public Policy Purposes: The Group-Target Definition', *Journal of Moral Philosophy* 7(2) (2010), pp. 253–78.
Richardson, Henry S., 'Our Call: The Constitutive Importance of the People's Judgment', *Journal of Moral Philosophy* 5(1) (2008), pp. 3–29.
Ridge, Michael, 'Anti-Reductionism and Supervenience', *Journal of Moral Philosophy* 4(3) (2007), pp. 330–48.
Riley, Evan, 'Libertarian Self-Defeat', *Journal of Moral Philosophy* 7(2) (2010), pp. 200–26.
Riley, Patrick, 'Kant against Hobbes in *Theory and Practice*', *Journal of Moral Philosophy* 4(2) (2007), pp. 194–206.
Riley, Jonathan, 'Ethical Pluralism and Common Decency', *Journal of Moral Philosophy* 1(2) (2004), pp. 211–21.
Ronzoni, Miriam, 'Constructivism and Practical Reason: On Intersubjectivity, Abstraction, and Judgment', *Journal of Moral Philosophy* 7(1) (2010), pp. 74–104.
Rosebury, Brian, 'Reply to Silcox on Moral Luck', *Journal of Moral Philosophy* 6(1) (2009), pp. 109–13.
Sable, Andrew, 'Virtue for Pluralists', *Journal of Moral Philosophy* 2(2) (2005), pp. 207–35.
Scarre, Geoffrey, 'Corrective Justice and Reputation', *Journal of Moral Philosophy* 3(3) (2006), pp. 305–19.
Scarre, Geoffrey, 'The "Banality of Good"?' *Journal of Moral Philosophy* 6(4) (2009), pp. 499–519.
Segall, Shlomi, 'How Devolution Upsets Distributive Justice', *Journal of Moral Philosophy* 4(2) (2007), pp. 257–72.
Seglow, Jonathan, 'Associative Duties and Global Justice', *Journal of Moral Philosophy* 7(1) (2010), pp. 54–73.
Shafer-Landau, Russ, 'Moral and Theological Realism: The Explanatory Argument', *Journal of Moral Philosophy* 4(3) (2007), pp. 311–29.
Sheinman, Hanoch, 'Raz on the Social Dependence of Values', *Journal of Moral Philosophy* 3(1) (2006), pp. 77–87.
Silcox, Mark, 'Virtue Epistemology and Moral Luck', *Journal of Moral Philosophy* 3(2) (2006), pp. 179–92.
Silcox, Mark, 'Reply to Rosebury', *Journal of Moral Philosophy* 6(2) (2009), pp. 245–48.
Simpson, Matthew, 'A Paradox of Sovereignty in Rousseau's *Social Contract*', *Journal of Moral Philosophy* 3(1) (2006), pp. 45–56.
Sin, William, 'Trivial Sacrifices, Great Demands', *Journal of Moral Philosophy* 7(1) (2010), pp. 3–15.
Singleton, Jane, 'Neither Generalism nor Particularism: Ethical Correctness is Located in General Ethical Theories', *Journal of Moral Philosophy* 1(2) (2004), pp. 155–75.
Slomp, Gabriella, 'Kant against Hobbes: Reasoning and Rhetoric', *Journal of Moral Philosophy* 4(2) (2007), pp. 207–22.
Smith, M. B. E., 'Does Humanity Share a Common Moral Faculty?' *Journal of Moral Philosophy* 7(1) (2010), pp. 37–53.
Smith, Stephen R., 'Keeping Our Distance in Compassion-Based Social Relations', *Journal of Moral Philosophy* 2(1) (2005), pp. 69–87.
Sobel, David, 'The Limits of the Explanatory Power of Developmentalism', *Journal of Moral Philosophy* 7(4) (2010), pp. 517–27.
Spector, Jessica, 'The Grounds of Moral Agency: Locke's Account of Personal Identity', *Journal of Moral Philosophy* 5(2) (2008), pp. 256–81.
Stark, Susan, 'A Change of Heart: Moral Emotions, Transformation, and Moral Virtue', *Journal of Moral Philosophy* 1(1) (2004), pp. 31–50.

Stern, Robert, 'The Autonomy of Morality and the Morality of Autonomy', *Journal of Moral Philosophy* 6(3) (2009), pp. 395–415.
Stone, Alison, 'Essentialism and Anti-Essentialism in Feminist Philosophy', *Journal of Moral Philosophy* 1(2) (2004), pp. 135–53.
Talisse, Robert B., 'Does Value Pluralism Entail Liberalism?' *Journal of Moral Philosophy* 7(2) (2010), pp. 303–20.
Taylor, Robert S., 'Self-Realization and the Priority of Fair Equality of Opportunity', *Journal of Moral Philosophy* 1(3) (2004), pp. 333–47.
- Reprinted in Thom Brooks and Fabian Freyenhagen (eds), *The Legacy of John Rawls*. New York: Continuum, 2005.

Telfer, Elizabeth, '"Animals Do It Too!": The Franklin Defence of Meat-Eating', *Journal of Moral Philosophy* 1(1) (2004), pp. 51–67.
Thomas, Alan, 'Practical Reasoning and Normative Relevance: A Reply to McKeever and Ridge', *Journal of Moral Philosophy* 4(1) (2007), pp. 77–84.
Tideman, Nicolaus, 'Secession as a Human Right', *Journal of Moral Philosophy* 1(1) (2004), pp. 9–19.
Timmermann, Jens, 'Good but Not Required?–Assessing the Demands of Kantian Ethics', *Journal of Moral Philosophy* 2(1) (2005), pp. 9–27.
Timmermann, Jens, 'Simplicity and Authority: Reflections on Theory and Practice in Kant's Moral Philosophy', *Journal of Moral Philosophy* 4(2) (2007), pp. 167–82.
Tropman, Elizabeth, 'Renewing Moral Intuitionism', *Journal of Moral Philosophy* 6(4) (2009), pp. 440–63.
Tyler, Colin, 'Brian Barry and Writings on Social Justice from the Left', *Journal of Moral Philosophy* 5(2) (2008), pp. 301–12.
Upton, Candace, 'Virtue Ethics, Character, and Normative Receptivity', *Journal of Moral Philosophy* 8(1) (2008), pp. 77–95.
van Zyl, Liezl, 'Agent-based Virtue Ethics and the Problem of Action Guidance', *Journal of Moral Philosophy* 6(1) (2009), pp. 50–69.
Vargas, Manuel, 'Taking the Highway on Skepticism, Luck, and the Value of Responsibility', *Journal of Moral Philosophy* 6(2) (2009), pp. 249–65.
Ward, Lee, 'Locke on Punishment, Property and Moral Knowledge', *Journal of Moral Philosophy* 6(2) (2009), pp. 218–44.
Webber, Jonathan, 'Virtue, Character and Situation', *Journal of Moral Philosophy* 3(2) (2006), pp. 193–213.
Weirich, Paul, 'Utility Maximization Generalized', *Journal of Moral Philosophy* 5(2) (2008), pp. 282–99.
Wenar, Leif, 'The Unity of Rawls's Work', *Journal of Moral Philosophy* 1(3) (2004), pp. 265–75.
- Reprinted in Thom Brooks and Fabian Freyenhagen (eds), *The Legacy of John Rawls*. New York: Continuum, 2005.

Westphal, Kenneth R., 'From "Convention" to "Ethical Life": Hume's Theory of Justice in Post-Kantian Perspective', *Journal of Moral Philosophy* 7(1) (2010), pp. 105–32.
White, Heath, 'Fitting Attitudes, Wrong Kinds of Reasons, and Mind-Independent Goodness', *Journal of Moral Philosophy* 6(3) (2009), pp. 339–64.
Wiland, Eric, 'On Indirectly Self-defeating Moral Theories', *Journal of Moral Philosophy* 5(3) (2008), pp. 384–93.
Williams, Reginald, 'Morality and Privilege', *Journal of Moral Philosophy* 5(1) (2008), pp. 118–35.
Wolff, Jonathan, 'Equality: The Recent History of an Idea', *Journal of Moral Philosophy* 4(1) (2007), pp. 125–36.
Zaibert, Leo, 'The Fitting, the Deserving, and the Beautiful', *Journal of Moral Philosophy* 3(3) (2006), pp. 331–50.
Zaibert, Leo, 'The Paradox of Forgiveness', *Journal of Moral Philosophy* 6(3) (2009), pp. 365–93.
Ziegler, Rafael, 'Tracing Global Inequality in Eco-space: A Comment on Tim Hayward's Proposal', *Journal of Moral Philosophy* 4(1) (2007), pp. 117–24.

INDEX

www.ingramcontent.com/pod-product-compliance
Lightning Source LLC
LaVergne TN
LVHW081514300926
849161LV00006B/1176